HANDBOOK OF
MICROBIOLOGY

HANDBOOK OF
MICROBIOLOGY

by

MORRIS B. JACOBS, Ph.D.

Associate Professor of Occupational Medicine,
School of Public Health and Administrative Medicine,
Columbia University

AND

MAURICE J. GERSTEIN, B.S., M.S.

Department of Biology
William H. Maxwell Vocational High School
Brooklyn, New York

D. VAN NOSTRAND COMPANY, INC.

PRINCETON, NEW JERSEY

TORONTO LONDON

NEW YORK

D. VAN NOSTRAND COMPANY, INC.
120 Alexander St., Princeton, New Jersey (*Principal office*)
24 West 40 Street, New York 18, New York

D. VAN NOSTRAND COMPANY, LTD.
358, Kensington High Street, London, W.14, England

D. VAN NOSTRAND COMPANY (Canada), LTD.
25 Hollinger Road, Toronto 16, Canada

Published simultaneously in Canada by
D. VAN NOSTRAND COMPANY (Canada), LTD.

Library of Congress Catalogue Card No. 60-15811

PRINTED IN THE UNITED STATES OF AMERICA

PREFACE

Ready access to the data of microbiology is provided in this Handbook. It organizes, in convenient tabular form, the facts and figures which the authors have compiled by a thorough search of the literature covering the information most needed in practical work.

The major classes of data include, first, the characteristics of microorganisms, on which the information is tabulated by the use of key words in key positions. The preparation of culture media, stains and microbiological reagents is detailed and arranged alphabetically so as to be readily available. The methods of culturing and staining microorganisms; the tests by means of which they can be differentiated; and the biochemical methods for testing biologics are fully described. Methods for the testing of antiseptics and disinfectants are included and are accompanied by a comprehensive table on phenol coefficients. In addition, information concerning antibiotics is detailed, and data relating to toxoids, antitoxins, vaccines, and bacterial, rickettsial, and viral diseases are presented.

A number of methods have been devised to arrange for convenient reference those tables to which most frequent reference is made. They include temperature conversion values, saturated steam temperatures, pH indicators, buffer solutions, most probable numbers, and test dilutions. Tables of classification of bacteria, rickettsia, viruses, and fungi have been made especially comprehensive.

The authors acknowledge with thanks the valuable suggestions of Miss Rebecca Shapiro, President, Hudson Laboratories, New York, New York and the assistance of Mrs. Anna C. Gelman, Assistant Professor of Epidemiology, School of Public Health and Administrative Medicine, Columbia University, New York, New York for reviewing Table 1.

It is the hope of the authors that this Handbook will prove to be of wide value. They will welcome comments from the reader on the scope and organization of this book, leading to broadened coverage and greater usefulness in future editions.

MORRIS B. JACOBS
MAURICE J. GERSTEIN

EXPLANATORY NOTES

1. The information in the tables of *Handbook of Microbiology* is arranged in an alphabetical order, numbers, Greek letters, spaces, hyphens, and the prefixes *m*-, *o*-, and *p*- being ignored in the arrangement. Thus *o*-cresolphthalein, cresol red, cresolsulfonphthalein are arranged in that order.

2. Cross references are given in the text in bold font and should be sought in the appropriate table. Thus a cross reference to a medium in Table 9 on microbiological reagents and tests should be looked up in Table 7 on culture and media methods.

3. The term *water,* particularly when used in a method, means distilled water.

4. The terms *alcohol* and *ether* refer, respectively, to 95% ethyl alcohol and ethyl ether.

5. When species of a given genus are mentioned in a section, the initial letter abbreviation refers to the same genus, for example: "Active against enterobacteria, *Vibrio comma, Shigella paradysenteriae, S. sonnei, S. dysenteriae, Salmonella enteritidis,*" means "Active against enterobacteria, *Vibrio comma, Shigella paradysenteriae, Shigella sonnei, Shigella dysenteriae, Salmonella enteritidis.*"

6. The following abbreviations are used and have the indicated meaning:

g	gram	ml	milliliters
C	centigrade degrees	F	Fahrenheit degrees
mm	millimeters	mg	milligrams
μ	microns	mμ	millimicrons
sp	species	*N*	normal, with reference to solutions

7. The terms used in this book as, for instance, "thermal death point" and "thermal death time" are defined in the *Dictionary of Microbiology* by M. B. Jacobs, M. J. Gerstein and W. G. Walter, Van Nostrand, Princeton, 1957.

CONTENTS

TABLE 1. CHARACTERISTICS OF MICROORGANISMS

TABLE 1. CHARACTERISTICS OF MICROORGANISMS

Acetobacter aceti

Taxonomy
- Order — *Pseudomonadales*
- Suborder — *Pseudomonadineae*
- Family — *Pseudomonadaceae*
- Genus — *Acetobacter*
- Species — *aceti*

Cellular Characteristics
- Morphology—Rods, some large, clavate cells.
- Motility—Some cells are motile.
- Flagella—Single polar flagellum on motile cells.
- Staining—Gram negative.
- Occurring—Singly and in long chains.
- Size—0.4 to 0.8 by 1.0 to 2.0 μ.
- Habitat—Vinegar and beverages, fruits and vegetables turning sour.

Cultural Characteristics
- Beer-gelatin, containing 10 per cent glucose—Large, shiny colonies.
- Liquid media—Slimy pellicle; ring or turbidity, at times, without pellicle.

Physiological Characteristics
- Biochemical action
  - Acetic acid—Oxidized to carbon dioxide and water.
  - Ammonia and other inorganic nitrogen—Utilized as sole source of nitrogen.
  - Ethyl alcohol—Rapid and complete oxidation.
  - Glucose—Rapid and complete oxidation.
  - Catalase reaction—Positive.
- Fermentation reactions
  - Monosaccharides
    - Arabinose—No acid.
    - Glucose—Acid.
    - Fructose—No acid.
    - Galactose—No acid.
    - Sorbose—No acid.
  - Disaccharides
    - Lactose—No acid.
    - Sucrose—No acid.
    - Maltose—No acid.
  - Polysaccharides
    - Raffinose—No acid.
    - Starch—No acid.
    - Inulin—No acid.
    - Dextrin—No acid.
    - Glycogen—No acid.
  - Alcohols and polyalcohols
    - Methyl alcohol—No acid.
    - Ethyl alcohol—Acid.
    - Propyl alcohol—Acid.
    - Isopropyl alcohol—No acid.
    - Butyl alcohol—No acid.
    - Isobutyl alcohol—No acid.
    - Amyl alcohol—No acid.
    - Ethylene glycol—No acid.
    - Glycerol—No acid.
    - Erythritol—No acid.
    - Mannitol—No acid.
    - Dulcitol—No acid.
  - Aldehydes
    - Acetaldehyde—No acid.
- Growth factors
  - Temperature
    - Optimum—30 C.
    - Growth range—10 to 42 C.
  - Nutrition—Can utilize inorganic nitrogen salts as sole source of nitrogen; can oxidize ethyl alcohol and glucose rapidly and completely.
  - pH—Tolerant to acid reaction.

Industrial Utilization
- Products—Acetic acid.
- Processes—Vinegar manufacture; sorbose from sorbitol; dihydroxyacetone from glycerol; gluconic acid from glucose.

Spoilage
- Beer—Causes sourness.

Addenda. Quick Vinegar Process. In this process developed in Germany, alcohol or beer is continuously put through vats or barrels packed with beech shavings and is converted into vinegar. The organisms grow on an almost invisible film. *A. aceti* is thought to be the organism involved. Pasteur described the organism as *Mycoderma aceti.*

Acetobacter pasteurianus

Taxonomy
- Order — *Pseudomonadales*
- Suborder — *Pseudomonadineae*
- Family — *Pseudomonadaceae*
- Genus — *Acetobacter*
- Species — *pasteurianus*
- Synonym — *Mycoderma pasteurianum*

Cellular Characteristics
- Morphology—Rods, may show clubbed forms.
- Motility—Variable.
- Flagella—When motile possess a single polar flagellum.
- Zoogloeal membrane—Not formed.
- Staining—Blue with iodine; gram positive.
- Occurring—Singly and in chains.
- Size—0.4 to 0.8 by 1.0 μ.
- Habitat—Vinegar, beer, and beer wort.

Cultural Characteristics
- Wort gelatin colonies—Small, entire, gray, slimy.
- Meat gelatin infusion—Widespread, toothed, rosette form.
- Double beer with 1 per cent alcohol medium—Wrinkled, folded pellicle.

Physiological Characteristics
- Biochemical action
  - Cytochrome oxidase activity—Minute in the extract of the organism as compared to yeast.
  - Respiratory activity—Appears to be different from that of yeast.
  - Ammonium salts—Not utilized as sole source of nitrogen.
- Fermentation reactions
  - Monosaccharides
    - Arabinose—No acid.
    - Glucose—Acid.
    - Fructose—No acid.
    - Galactose—No acid.
  - Disaccharides
    - Lactose—No acid.
    - Sucrose—No acid.
    - Maltose—No acid.
  - Polysaccharides
    - Starch—No acid.
    - Inulin—No acid.
    - Glycogen—No acid.
  - Alcohols and polyalcohols
    - Glycerol—No acid.
    - Erythritol—No acid.
    - Mannitol—No acid.
    - Ethyl alcohol—Acid.
    - Propyl alcohol—Acid.
- Growth factors
  - Temperature
    - Optimum—30 C.
    - Range—5 to 42 C.

Biochemical Characteristics
- Enzyme production—Catalase produced.
- Chemical end products—Can dismutate acetaldehyde to acetic acid and ethyl alcohol.

Industrial Utilization
- Products—Produces acetic acid.

Acetobacter suboxydans

Taxonomy
- Order — *Pseudomonadales*
- Suborder — *Pseudomonadineae*
- Family — *Pseudomonadaceae*
- Genus — *Acetobacter*
- Species — *suboxydans*

Cellular Characteristics
- Morphology—Short rods.

Motility—Nonmotile.
Staining—Gram negative.
Occurring—Singly or in chains.
Habitat—Beer.

Cultural Characteristics
Wort agar colonies—Small, circular, slightly yellow.
Fluid media—Thin, hardly visible pellicle.

Physiological Characteristics
Biochemical action
Acetic acid—Not oxidized.
Fermentation reactions
Monosaccharides
Glucose—Acid.
Alcohols and polyalcohols
Glycerol—Acid.
Sorbitol—Acid; oxygen and extracts of rice bran will help the organism yield more sorbose from sorbitol.
Propyl alcohol—Acid.
Ethyl alcohol—Acid.
Ethylene glycol—Acid.
Growth factors
Temperature
Optimum—30 C.
Nutrition
Vitamins—Pantothenic acid, nicotinic acid, and *p*-aminobenzoic acid required.
Amino acids—Alanine, cystine, histidine, isoleucine, and valine required.
Mineral salts—Required.
Alcohol or glucose—Required or adequate substitute.

Biochemical Characteristics
Enzyme production—Catalase produced.
Oxidation—Partial oxidation of substrates. Formation of 5-ketogluconate crystals on surface of agar slants containing glucose and calcium carbonate.
Chemical end products—Substrates oxidized by *A. suboxydans* and the end products produced:

Substrate	*Products Formed*
D-Glucose	D-Gluconic acid
D-Glucose acid	D-5-Ketogluconic acid
	D-2-Ketogluconic acid
D-Sorbitol	L-Sorbose
Glycerol	Dihydroxyacetone
2, 3-Butylene glycol	Acetylmethylcarbinal
α-Propylene glycol	Acetol

Industrial Utilization
Products—Forms acetic acid. Associated with dihydroxyacetone, sorbose, and gluconic acid fermentation. Can form D-tartaric acid from glucose. Ethyl alcohol produced.

Spoilage
Beer—Causes sourness.

Addenda. Extracts of the organism contain material which can catalyze (a dehydrogenase) the oxidation of polyols at pH 5 without the addition of diphosphopyridine nucleotide (DPN). Other extracts contain a soluble DPN-linked polyol dehydrogenase which is best activated at pH 8. *A. suboxydans* can oxidize D-arabitol to D-xylose but does not attack L-arabitol. This organism can ferment glucose to vinegar in which case hexodiphosphate is converted to triose $\longrightarrow$ pyruvate $\xrightarrow{\text{decarboxylase}}$ acetaldehyde $\xrightarrow{\text{oxydase}}$ $\longrightarrow$ acetate. Glucose to alcohol and carbon dioxide can also be accomplished. The organism is also active in oxidizing some of the aromatic and hydroaromatic compounds, such as mesoinositol to ketoinositol, in which instance a hydrogen atom is removed.

Acetobacter xylinum

Taxonomy
Order *Pseudomonadales*
Suborder *Pseudomonadineae*
Family *Pseudomonadaceae*

Genus *Acetobacter*
Species *xylinum*

Cellular Characteristics
Morphology—Rods.
Capsules—Cells have a slimy envelope.
Staining—Gram negative.
Zoogloeal membrane—Formed; contains cellulose.
Occurring—Singly and in chains.
Size—About 2 μ long.
Habitat—Vinegar, souring fruits, vegetables.

Cultural Characteristics—Film forms on the surface of liquids, film will fall to the bottom after becoming cartilagenous. This thick zoogloeal membrane forms on all liquids.

Physiological Characteristics
Fermentation reactions
Monosaccharides
Arabinose—No acid.
Glucose—Acid.
Fructose—No acid.
Galactose—No acid.
Disaccharides
Lactose—No acid.
Maltose—No acid.
Polysaccharides
Starch—No acid.
Dextrin—No acid.
Alcohols and polyalcohols
Sorbitol—The use of oxygen and extracts of rice bran will yield a better amount of sorbose from sorbitol.
Ethyl alcohol—Acid.
Propyl alcohol—Acid.

Growth factors
Temperature
Optimum—28 C.
Inhibition—Chlorides, such as calcium chloride (0.8 per cent) and sodium chloride (1 per cent), will inhibit the organism from growing.

Biochemical Characteristics
Enzyme production—Catalase produced.

Industrial Utilization
Products—Acetic acid production. Associated with the fermentation of sorbose from sorbitol. Used in the production of dihydroxyacetone from glycerol.

Academic or Research Utilization
Physiological mechanisms—Cellulose C-14 can be biosynthesized by the organism using D-mannitol 1-C^{14}. Ethyl alcohol in the medium increased the yield.

Spoilage
Beer—Found as a specific agent in beer sourness.

Addenda. This organism is one of the three species that can form cellulose in the cell wall. It has the capability of converting 19 per cent of the sugar in the medium to cellulose. The cellulose is excreted in the medium as fine fibrils along with a gummy substance (polysaccharide) to form a network. X-ray diffraction shows the network to be similiar to cotton.

The organism can possibly yield 80 per cent sorbose from sorbitol and many reducing sugars, such as mannitol, arabitol, and erythritol from other alcohols.

Achromobacter delicatulus

Taxonomy
Order *Eubacteriales*
Family *Achromobacteraceae*
Genus *Achromobacter*
Species *delicatulus*

Cellular Characteristics
Morphology—Rods.
Motility—Motile.
Flagella—Peritrichous.
Staining—Gram negative.

Occurring—Singly.
Size—1.0 by 2.0 μ.
Habitat—Widely distributed.

Cultural Characteristics
Agar stroke—Whitish, glistening.
Gelatin colonies—Whitish with radiate margin and homogeneous.
Gelatin stab—Infundibuliform liquefaction.
Nutrient broth—Turbid; gray pellicle with sediment.
Potato—Gray growth in streaks.

Physiological Characteristics
Biochemical action
Indole production—Negative.
Hydrogen sulfide production—Negative.
Starch hydrolysis—Negative.
Nitrite—Produced from nitrate.
Trimethylamine—Produced from trimethylamine oxide, acetylcholine, and choline; not produced from betaine.

Protein liquefaction
Gelatin—Liquefied.

Fermentation reactions
Monosaccharides
Glucose—Acid.
Disaccharides
Lactose—Acid, slowly.
Sucrose—Acid.
Maltose—Acid.

Growth factors
Oxygen—Aerobic.
Temperature
Optimum—30 to 35 C.
Nutrition—Utilizes hydrocarbons as nutrients; sulfur requirements may be satisfied by inorganic sulfur; amino acids may serve as source of nitrogen and carbon; ammonium chloride may serve as source of nitrogen.

Addenda. The organism is usually found in petroleum sources; it is probably able to utilize the oil.

Achromobacter superficialis

Taxonomy

Order	*Eubacteriales*
Family	*Achromobacteraceae*
Genus	*Achromobacter*
Species	*superficialis*

Cellular Characteristics
Morphology—Rods.
Motility—Motile.
Flagella—Peritrichous.
Staining—Gram negative.
Occurring—Singly.
Size—1.0 by 2.2 μ.
Habitat—Distributed widely in nature.

Cultural Characteristics
Agar stroke—Growth gray, filiform.
Gelatin colonies—Gray, small, circular, translucent.
Nutrient broth—Slightly turbid.
Potato—Both growth and no growth reported.

Physiological Characteristics
Biochemical action
Indole—Not formed.
Nitrite—Not formed from nitrate.
Trimethylamine—Not formed from trimethylamine oxide, acetylcholine, choline, or betaine.

Protein liquefaction
Gelatin—Slow liquefaction.

Indicator reactions
Litmus milk—No change.

Growth factors
Oxygen—Aerobic, facultative.
Temperature
Optimum—25 to 30 C.
Nutrition—Sulfur requirements may be satisfied by inorganic sulfur; many amino acids, but not alanine or aspartic acid, may serve as source of nitrogen and car-

bon; ammonium chloride can be used as source of nitrogen; can utilize hydrocarbons.

Addenda. Possibly associated with the organism, *Urographis fasciata.* It is usually found where petroleum is found and is probably able to use the oil.

Actinobacillus mallei

Taxonomy
- Order — *Eubacteriales*
- Family — *Brucellaceae*
- Genus — *Actinobacillus*
- Species — *mallei*
- Synonym — *Malleomyces mallei*
- Common name — Glanders bacillus

Cellular Characteristics
- Morphology—Slender rods with rounded ends.
- Staining—Gram-negative bipolar or irregular staining; good staining with Löffler's alkaline methylene blue.
- Occurring—Singly, in pairs or sometimes in groups or filaments.
- Size—0.5 to 1.0 by 2.0 to 5.0 μ.
- Source—Infected horses.

Cultural Characteristics
- Agar colonies—Grayish-white, ropy, translucent, colonies with irregular borders.
- Agar stroke—Grayish-white, moist and glistening.
- Gelatin stab—Poor growth; liquefaction debatable.
- Nutrient broth—Surface pellicle, slimy, ropy, and sediment.
- Potato—Yellow drop-like colonies after one to two days; various other colors may be apparent.
- Löffler's serum—Yellowish, moist, viscid growth.

Physiological Characteristics
- Biochemical action
  - Indole production—Negative.
  - Nitrite—Reaction negative.
- Protein liquefaction or digestion
  - Gelatin—Usually not liquefied.
- Indicator reactions
  - Litmus milk—Slow coagulation and slight acid production after a week.
- Fermentation reactions—Carbohydrates usually not attacked.
  - Monosaccharides
    - Glucose—Some strains may produce slight acid.

Serology—Complement fixing antibodies are used for diagnostic purposes. Normal and immune sera will agglutinate the organism. Diagnostic test is obtaining a titer of 1:500. No lasting immunity is conferred.

Biochemical Characteristics
- Toxin production—An endotoxin called mallein is produced. It is thermostable at 120 C, and can stand long periods in storage and yet retains its potency.

Pathogenicity
- Animals—The organism causes a disease known as glanders in horses. The disease comes in two forms: *acute* form, limited to the nasal mucosa and upper respiratory tract; and *chronic* form, in which ulcers and lesions of the joints and muscles appear. The Straus test can be used as a diagnostic test. Can be transmitted to cats, dogs, guinea pigs, rabbits, and field mice but not to white mice.
- Human beings—May develop either chronic or acute form of glanders.

Actinomyces bovis

Taxonomy
- Order — *Actinomycetales*
- Family — *Actinomycetaceae*
- Genus — *Actinomyces*
- Species — *bovis*

Cellular Characteristics
- Morphology—Short diphtheroid or coccoid elements may be found; filamentous fungus form; rough colonies become smooth in repeated transfer.
- Mycelium—Undergoes fragmentation, branching is rare; nonseptate.
- Hyphae—No aerial hyphae; hyphae present are less than 1 μ in diameter; club-shaped hyphae in diseased tissue.
- Staining—Gram positive, nonacid fast; in a hematoxylin and eosin stain the filaments take the hematoxylin stain and the clubs take the eosin stain.
- Habitat—Mouth of cattle.

Cultural Characteristics
- Semisolid media—With a paraffin seal, excellent growth; radiate sulfur-color granules seen in pus; colonies adhere to medium; club-shaped forms at the margin of a colony.
- Gelatin colonies—Scant, flaky growth, no liquefaction.
- Broth—At times some turbidity with slight flocculation.
- Sabouraud's media—No growth.
- Thioglycollate broth—Good growth.
- Deep stroke cultures of infusion glucose agar—Pinpoint colonies in 4 to 5 days.
- Hormone agar—Can be cultivated in a Brewer anaerobic jar.

Physiological Characteristics
- Biochemical action
  - Indole production—Positive.
  - Hydrogen sulfide production—Positive in some strains.
  - Hemolysis—Washed human blood cells positive in some strains.
  - Nitrate—Reduced.
- Protein liquefaction or digestion
  - Gelatin—Not liquefied.
  - Blood serum—No hemolysis.
  - Egg albumin—No proteolytic action.
- Indicator reactions
  - Litmus milk—Acid, no peptonization or coagulation; at times no growth at all.
- Fermentation reactions
  - Monosaccharides
    - Glucose—Acid.
  - Disaccharides
    - Sucrose—Acid.
    - Maltose—Acid.
  - Glucosides
    - Salicin—No acid.
- Growth factors
  - Oxygen—Anaerobic to microaerophilic. Bovine strains tolerate oxygen on egg or serum media better than *A. israelii* human strains.
  - Temperature
    - Optimum—37 C; saprophytic organisms usually grow best at 25 C.
    - Thermal death time—Killed at 60 C for 1 hour.
  - Nutrition—10 per cent carbon dioxide good for growth.
  - pH
    - Optimum—7.4 to 7.6.
  - Dehydration—Resists drying.
  - Tolerance—Sensitive to penicillin, chloroamphenicol; streptomycin has some effect; not sensitive to neomycin.
- Color and light characteristics
  - Chromogenesis—No pigments on protein media.

Serology

Antigenic grouping—No cross-agglutination between bovine strains and *A. israelii.*

Agglutination—Agglutinins have been demonstrated in patients with severe disease.

Pathogenicity

Human beings—The cause of actinomycosis; infection in man may be in the face, neck, lungs (pulmonary actinomycosis) abdomen (abdominal actinomycosis).

Animals—Cause of "lumpy jaw" in cattle; infectious disease characterized by tissue destruction; lesions resemble tuberculosis. Guinea pigs can be infected experimentally.

Addenda. Similar disease is caused by *Nocardia asteroides.*

Actinomyces israelii

Taxonomy

Order	*Actinomycetales*
Family	*Actinomycetaceae*
Genus	*Actinomyces*
Species	*israelii*

Cellular Characteristics

Morphology—Forms, larger than 5 μ, club-shaped, found in infected tissues.

Mycelium—At first unicellular, then forms long branching filaments which fragment.

Hyphae—Erect aerial type formed with low oxygen pressure, 1 μ in diameter; sometimes septate.

Spores—None formed in hyphae.

Motility—Nonmotile.

Staining—Gram positive, nonacid-fast.

Habitat—Human mouth and tonsils.

Cultural Characteristics—Polymorphic colonies, having a tougher texture than *A. bovis;* old colonies become warty.

Gelatin—Sometimes small amount of flaky growth.

Liquid media—Generally clear.

Physiological Characteristics

Biochemical action

Hemolysis—Negative.

Protein Liquefaction or digestion

Gelatin—Not liquefied.

Blood serum—No hemolysis; no proteolytic action.

Egg albumin—No proteolytic action.

Indicator reactions

Litmus milk—Acid, generally no clotting; frequently no growth; no peptonization.

Fermentation reactions

Monosaccharides

Xylose—Acid.

Glucose—Acid.

Galactose—Acid.

Fructose—Acid.

Disaccharides

Sucrose—Acid.

Lactose—Acid.

Maltose—Acid.

Polysaccharides

Raffinose—Acid.

Polyalcohols

Mannitol—Acid.

Growth factors

Oxygen—Anaerobic-microaerophilic.

Temperature

Optimum—37 C.

Serology

Agglutination—No cross agglutination between human strains and bovine strains of *Actinomyces.*

Pathogenicity

Human beings—Cause of human actinomycosis.

Aerobacter aerogenes

Taxonomy
- Order — *Eubacteriales*
- Family — *Enterobacteriaceae*
- Tribe — *Escherichieae*
- Genus — *Aerobacter*
- Species — *aerogenes*

Cellular Characteristics
- Morphology—Rods.
- Motility—Usually nonmotile.
- Capsules—Frequently present.
- Staining—Gram negative.
- Occurring—Singly.
- Size—0.5 to 0.8 by 1.0 to 2.0 μ.
- Habitat—Grains and plants and to some degree in the intestinal canal of human beings and animals.

Cultural Characteristics
- Agar colonies—Thick, white, raised, smooth, and entire.
- Agar slant—Moist, glistening, spreading growth.
- Gelatin colonies—Thick, white, moist, entire.
- Gelatin stab—Spreading, white, no liquefaction.
- Nutrient broth—Turbid, pellicle and large amount of sediment.

Physiological Characteristics
- Biochemical Action
  - Indole production—May or may not occur.
  - Methyl red reaction—Negative.
  - Acetylmethyl carbinol—Produced.
  - Citrate utilization—Positive; may be used as sole source of carbon.
  - Uric acid utilization—Positive; may be used as sole source of nitrogen.
  - Hydrogen sulfide production—Negative.
  - Nitrite—Formed from nitrate.
  - Catalase—Positive.
  - Sodium hippurate—Hydrolyzed.
  - Gas ratio—Two or more volumes of carbon dioxide to one of hydrogen from glucose.
- Protein liquefaction
  - Gelatin—Not liquefied.
- Indicator reactions
  - Litmus milk—Acid, coagulation, but no peptonization.
- Fermentation reactions
  - Monosaccharides
    - Arabinose—Acid and gas.
    - Glucose—Acid and gas (see **gas ratio**).
    - Fructose—Acid and gas.
    - Galactose—Acid and gas.
  - Disaccharides
    - Lactose—Acid and gas.
    - Sucrose—May or may not be fermented.
    - Maltose—Acid and gas.
    - Cellobiose—Acid and gas.
  - Polysaccharides
    - Raffinose—Acid and gas.
    - Inulin—May or may not be fermented.
    - Protopectin—Not fermented.
  - Polyalcohols
    - Glycerol—Acid and gas; trimethylene glycol not produced.
    - Mannitol—Acid and gas.
    - Sorbitol—Acid and gas.
    - Dulcitol—May or may not be fermented.
    - Adonitol—May or may not be fermented.
  - Glycosides
    - alpha-Methyl glucoside—Acid and gas.
    - Salicin—Acid and gas.
    - Esculin—Acid and gas.
- Growth factors
  - Oxygen—Aerobic, facultatively anaerobic.
  - Temperature
    - Optimum—30 C.

Thermal death time—60 C for 30 minutes, except for heat-resistant strains.

Eijkman test—Negative.

Nutrition—Laboratory media are suitable for good growth; sensitive to salt in butter; inhibited by fluoride; activated by cysteine.

Industrial Utilization

Products—Production of 2,3-butanediol from glucose and wood hydrolyzates; acetylmethylcarbinol from 2,3-butanediol.

Research Utilization

Genetics—Organism used to study the possibility of recombination characteristics.

Spoilage

Cheese—Cause of pinholes in cheese resulting from the growth of the organism while the cheese is in press.

Addenda. Forms glucose-1-phosphate from glucose diphosphate; attacks adenylic acid to yield ammonia, phosphoric acid, and ribose; yields trimethylene glycol; yields per gram of bacteria (in micrograms) biotin 1.1, riboflavin 41, thiamine 43, nicotinic acid 89. The formation of acetone appears to follow two different paths:

(a) Pyruvic acid $\xrightarrow{\text{cocarboxylase, Mg or Mn}}$ acetaldehyde or acetyl-coenzyme A.

(b) Utilization of phosphate suggesting formation of acetylphosphate.

Converts radioactive glucose and acetate to tryptophane; ferments L-erythrulose anaerobically to yield acetic acid, succinic acid, formic acid, glycolic acid, hydrogen, carbon dioxide, and ethyl alcohol; different strains attack glycerol by two pathways: (a) direct dehydrogenation to dihydroxyacetone, and (b) phosphorylation to L-alpha-glycerophosphate.

Various enzyme systems are elaborated: in the cytochrome system, *A. aerogenes* has the A_2 component band which is strong at 645 mμ; the enzyme which caused decarboxylation of diaminopimelic acid is inhibited by copper and cyanide which can be removed by dialysis; pyridoxal phosphate is required for maximum activity; yields an enzyme which can catalyze the amination of xanthine-5-phosphate by ammonia to give guanine-5-phosphate.

Citrate-grown cells seem to utilize the citric acid as the source of carbon, whereas acetate-grown cells use acetate carbon incorporation by the tricarboxylic acid cycle.

Strains trained to resist crystal violet have a surface structure which is lipid in nature; nonresistant strains have a polysaccharide surface structure.

Reduces methylene blue and resazurin and therefore can be used in the reductase test for tomato contamination.

Agrobacterium tumefaciens

Taxonomy

Order	*Eubacteriales*
Family	*Rhizobiaceae*
Genus	*Agrobacterium*
Species	*tumefaciens*

Cellular Characteristics

Morphology—Rods.

Motility—Motile 1-4 flagella.

Capsules—Capsules present.

Staining—Gram negative.

Occurring—Singly or in pairs.

Size—0.7 to 0.8 by 2.5 to 3.0 μ.

Habitat—Found in certain diseased plants.

Cultural Characteristics

Agar colonies—Circular, smooth, small, white, glistening, translucent, entire.

Nutrient broth—Thin pellicle and slight turbidity.

Sodium selenite agar—With mannitol, abundant growth.

Physiological Characteristics
Biochemical action
Indole production—Slight.
Starch—Not hydrolyzed.
Nitrites—Produced from nitrates to a low degree.
Indicator reactions
Litmus milk—Slowly coagulated; reduced, neutral to alkaline.
Fermentation reactions
Monosaccharides
Arabinose—Slight acid formation.
Glucose—Slight acid formation.
Fructose—Slight acid formation.
Galactose—Slight acid formation.
Alcohols and polyalcohols
Mannitol—Slight acid formation.
Glucosides
Salicin—Slight acid formation.
Growth factors
Oxygen—Facultatively anaerobic.
Temperature
Optimum—25 to 28 C.
Biochemical Characteristics
Composition—Lipids of the organism contain palmitic acid, *cis*-vaccenic acid—lactobacillic acid.
Nutritional activities—Mitogenic radiations are given off by the organism that can influence the growth of yeast; the radiation can pass through quartz but not glass.
Differentiation
Genetics—Absorbs congo red and aniline blue in large amounts; distinction from *A. rhizogenes*.
Pathogenicity
Plants—Causes gall formation in plants. Cause of disease in peach trees; infection can be reduced by removing low branches and thinning stands in orchards.

Alcaligenes faecalis

Taxonomy
Order *Eubacteriales*
Family *Achromobacteraceae*
Genus *Alcaligenes*
Species *faecalis*
Synonym *Bacillus faecalis alcaligenes*
Cellular Characteristics
Morphology—Rods.
Motility—Positive.
Flagella—Peritrichous, some strains show only a single flagellum.
Staining—Gram negative.
Occurring—Singly, in pairs, and in chains.
Size—0.5 by 1.0 to 2.0 μ.
Habitat—Intestinal tract; decomposing organic materials.
Cultural Characteristics
Agar colonies—Transparent, center being opaque, undulate margin.
Agar stroke—White growth, glistening, undulate margin as in colonies.
Gelatin colonies—Circular, gray-translucent.
Gelatin stab—No liquefaction, surface growth, gray.
Broth—Turbidity, pellicle, viscid sediment.
Potato—Yellow to brown color when growth occurs.
Physiological Characteristics
Biochemical action
Indole production—Negative.
Ammonia—Produced in broth.
Nitrite—Production from nitrate variable.
Odor—Not characteristic.
Urea hydrolysis—Negative.
Protein liquefaction or digestion
Gelatin—Not liquefied.
Indicator reactions
Litmus milk—Alkaline.
Fermentation reactions

Carbohydrates—No acid or gas.
Growth factors
Oxygen—Aerobic.
Temperature
Optimum—25-37 C.
Nutrition—Aspartic acid, asparagine, glutathione, and histidine support growth in broth; aliphatic amines generally toxic.

Serology
Agglutination—Not agglutinated by polyvalent *Salmonella* serums.

Academic or Research Utilization—*Escherichia coli* seems to have an inhibitory effect upon *A. faecalis*. *A. faecalis* can easily be confused with *Vibrio alcaligenes*, the latter has lophotrichous flagella. A medium labeled SMG can destroy *A. faecalis* 24 hours after plating. Used to differentiate *A. faecalis* from intestinal organisms.

Pathogenicity
Human beings—Was found in abscesses related to intestinal canal; considered nonpathogenic.

Spoilage
Food—Capable of forming slime on cottage cheese.

Alcaligenes viscolactis

Taxonomy

Order	*Eubacteriales*
Family	*Achromobacteraceae*
Genus	*Alcaligenes*
Species	*viscolactis*
Synonym	*Alcaligenes viscosus*

Cellular Characteristics
Morphology—Rods, almost spherical.
Motility—Nonmotile.
Capsules—Produced in milk cultures.
Staining—Gram negative.
Occurring—Singly, in pairs, and in chains.
Size—0.6 to 1.0 by 0.8 to 2.6 μ.
Habitat—Found in water near dairy farms and in manure.

Cultural Characteristics—Viscid consistency.
Agar colonies—After 72 hours, circular, white viscid growth with entire edge.
Agar stroke—White, abundant, spreading, viscid shiny growth.
Gelatin colonies—Gray, becoming yellowish; small.
Gelatin stab—No liquefaction, surface growth, villous growth in stab.
Nutrient broth—Turbid, thin pellicle, some sediment; ropiness produced.
Potato—Dirty white, spreading growth.

Physiological Characteristics
Biochemical action
Indole production—Negative.
Methyl red reaction—Negative.
Voges-Proskauer test—Negative.
Hydrogen sulfide production—Negative.
Fat hydrolysis—Positive.
Nitrites—Not ordinarily produced.
Protein liquefaction or digestion
Gelatin—Not liquefied.
Indicator reactions
Litmus milk—Ropiness, pellicle, alkaline, no coagulation.
Growth factors
Oxygen—Aerobic.
Temperature—Growth at 10 to 20 C, variable at 37 C.

Biochemical Characteristics
Enzyme production—Lipases produced.

Academic or Research Utilization—Ropiness may be lost with subculturing the organism.

Spoilage
Food—Produces ropiness in milk; stringy, mucilaginous type; some species do not produce ropiness.

Aspergillus flavus

Taxonomy
- Class — *Fungi Imperfecti*
- Subclass — *Hyphomycetes*
- Order — *Moniliales*
- Family — *Moniliaceae* (*Mucidinaceae*)
- Genus — *Aspergillus*
- Species — *flavus*

Mycological Characteristics
Mycelium
Vegetative—Submerged.
Aerial—Fruiting hyphae.
Sterigmata—Single, 3 to 5 by 10 to 15 μ; when double, primary 3 to 4 by 7 to 10 μ and secondary 2.5 to 3 by 7 to 10 μ.
Conidia—Colorless to yellow-green, rough and pitted pyriform to globose, 3 to 5 μ; heads range from few chains to large columnar masses.
Conidiophores—Arise from submerged mycelium, 5 to 15 μ in diameter, 400 to 1000 μ long; end in vesicles 10 to 40 μ in diameter.
Sclerotia—If present, white to brown, hard, sterile.
Perithecia—Not present.

Cultural Characteristics
Czapek's solution agar colonies—Spread rapidly with aerial felt; conidial areas range in color from light yellow-green to dark green.

Physiological Characteristics
Biochemical action
Starch—Hydrolyzed to dextrins and sugars.
Growth factors
Temperature
Optimum—37 C.

Biochemical Characteristics
Enzyme production—Amylases and proteinases produced.
Antibiotic production—Kojic acid, aspergillic acid, and flavicidin produced.
Chemical end products—Kojic acid; malic acid produced in small amounts.
Composition—The organism contains more than 15 per cent crude fat.

Industrial Utilization
Products—The organism can produce kojic acid from sucrose. Highest yields of carbon-producing substances for the production of kojic acid were obtained with *A. flavus.* A 20 per cent concentration of glucose was used. The pH range for good yields of kojic acid when using xylose was 2 to 3.5. The ideal temperature for yields is 30 to 35 C.
Processes—Manufacture of different types of koji: salt koji for rice wine, shochu koji for shochu (a distilled alcoholic beverage), shoyu koji for soybean sauce, miso koji for soybean paste. Proteolytic processes like chill-proofing beer, dehairing hides, degumming silk, manufacture of glue.

Pathogenicity
Human beings—Found in infections of the ear.

Aspergillus niger

Taxonomy
- Class — *Fungi Imperfecti*
- Subclass — *Hyphomycetes*
- Order — *Moniliales*

Family *Moniliaceae* (*Mucidinaceae*)
Genus *Aspergillus*
Species *niger*

Mycological Characteristics—Mycelium submerged. Mostly colorless strains but few have some yellow color in the hyphae. Color may be pronounced with age. Conidia are colored black, purple, or brown, globose or radiate. Conidiophores arising from substrate, smooth, thick walls, nonseptate or occasionally thin septa. Sterigmata in one series in young cultures.

Spores

Asexual—Spore formation is inhibited by the presence of 0.01 *M* sodium arsenite.

Habitat—Found in the soil, dried vegetable matter.

Cultural Characteristics—Rapidly growing colonies with submerged mycelium. Usually when different high acid strains are mixed in a medium, the acid production is curtailed. When either strain is grown alone, acid production is high. Two low-strain acid producing organisms, when grown together, produce more acid than when grown separately. *p*-Chlorophenol used in conjunction with an alkyl, cycloalkyl, or aryl group increases the fungistatic activity of *p*-chlorophenol. Organisms obtained from castor oil seeds demonstrate great lipolytic activity at a pH of maximum 6.2.

Physiological Characteristics

Biochemical action—The succinoxidase system is sensitive to malonate, cyanide, and azide and is therefore similar to other systems like that of mammalian tissues. Arsenite does not inhibit system up to 0.01 *M*.

A substance given off by the spores can inhibit the regular growth of the organism on Currie's synthetic medium. Material can be removed by working.

A strain of the organism demonstrated pectin-decomposing properties. For retting, submerged cultures were better than surface cultures. Inorganic nitrogen proved to be favorable for pectin decomposition.

Growth factors—Organism can tolerate high osmotic concentration. It can also extract water from substances that are almost dry. Can also tolerate higher temperatures than *Penicillium*.

Zinc used in a medium affects the glucose metabolism of the organism. Iron, copper, phosphorus, potassium, and manganese are required.

Arsenite can reduce the carbon dioxide output. Arsenite has a stimulatory effect on mycelial concentration, produces more acids (citric, oxalic) and utilizes more sugar.

Biochemical Characteristics

Enzyme production—An enzyme amyloglucosidase produced by the organism can hydrolyze starch to glucose. A dextrinogenic activity can also be obtained from the enzyme. When the enzyme is used, hydrolyzates of maltose and starch exhibit beta-mutarotation.

The following enzymes were extracted by freezing, thawing, and use of 0.04 *M* ammonium hydroxide and centrifugation: aldolase, carboxylase, phosphohexoisomerase, hexokinase, phosphofructokinase, and enolase.

Antibiotic activity—An antibiotic isolated from *Houttuynia cordata* inhibited the organism. When the *n*-alkylide chain is substituted, reduction in antimicrobial activity results.

The organism produces a substance to inhibit *Xanthomonas pruni.* It is thermostable.

Industrial Utilization—Can be used in the citric and gluconic acid production. Can also be used to assay phosphorus and potassium in the soil. Controlled aeration in slow concentration of carbon dioxide passed over the culture slightly increases the metabolic rate. Production is not influenced by this method.

Addenda. Aspergillin antibiotic substance is produced by the organism. The activity of the substance may be tied up with gliotoxin, aspergillic acid, and flavacin. The organism causes spoilage in cheese. Black spores are very resistant to ultraviolet light. Spores are on sterigmata. The organism has an enzyme which can convert maltose into glucose. The enzyme tannase is found in this organism. Tannase can convert gallotannin into gallic acid and sugar. It can hydrolyze chebulinic acid into ellogic and quercetic acid. Cause of black mold onion rot.

Aspergillus oryzae

Taxonomy
- Class — *Fungi Imperfecti*
- Subclass — *Hyphomycetes*
- Order — *Moniliales*
- Family — *Moniliaceae* (*Mucidinaceae*)
- Genus — *Aspergillus*
- Species — *oryzae*

Mycological Characteristics

Mycelium

Vegetative—Principally submerged.

Sterigmata—Single, 3 to 5 by 15 to 20 μ; when double, primary 5 by 12 μ, secondary 3.5 by 12 μ.

Conidia—Pyriform, rough 3 to 5 by 4 to 10 μ; heads, profuse, globose with radial separate chains.

Conidiophores—Rough, colorless, 20 to 25 μ wide by 2000 μ long; end in globose to clavate vesicles up to 70 μ in diameter.

Sclerotia—Scarce, no clumps formed.

Cultural Characteristics

Czapek's solution agar colonies—Spread rapidly; tough felt-like mass; greenish-yellow conidial areas.

Physiological Characteristics

Biochemical action

Starch—Hydrolyzed to dextrins and sugars.

Growth factors

Temperature

Optimum—30 C.

Biochemical Characteristics

Enzyme production—Amylases, poteinases produced; specifically, the enzymes formed by the organism are amylase, catalase, cutase, alpha-glucosidase, beta-glucosidase inulase, invertase, lactase, lipase, maltase, protease, rennet. Adenosine deaminase can be prepared by culture of *A. oryzae.* Takadiastase which hydrolyzes sucrose contains the enzyme glucosaccharase.

Industrial Utilization

Processes—Manufacture of different types of koji (see *A. flavus*); proteolytic processes like chill-proofing beer, dehairing hides, degumming silk, manufacture of glue, and the like; manufacture of malt.

Products—This organism produces kojic acid with a carbon source in the medium; for best yields glucose and xylose are used in the medium with a carbon percentage of 3 to 5 per cent; the optimum pH range is 2 to 5; addition of calcium carbonate will diminish the yield of kojic acid; the temperature range is 29 to 35 C; complete fermentation takes about 9 to 20 days.

Azotobacter agilis

Taxonomy

- Order — *Eubacteriales*
- Family — *Azotobacteraceae*
- Genus — *Azotobacter*
- Species — *agilis*
- Synonym — *Azotobacter vinelandii*

Cellular Characteristics

Morphology—Rods, nearly spherical.

Motility—Motile; some strains may be nonmotile.

Flagella—Peritrichous.

Staining—Gram negative.

Size—4-6 μ in length.

Habitat—Water and soil.

Cultural Characteristics

Mannitol agar colonies—Gray-white, translucent, circular.

Agar stroke—Yellow to white, glistening, smooth, opaque center.

Nutrient broth—Turbidity and sediment.

Peptone glucose broth—Growth.

Potato—Yellow to white, slimy, may become brown.

Physiological Characteristics

Biochemical action

Nitrogen utilization—Can fix atmospheric nitrogen giving off carbon dioxide; nitrous oxide can inhibit nitrogen fixation, although the reaction is reversible.

Protein liquefaction or digestion

Gelatin—Not liquefied.

Indicator reactions

Litmus milk—Becomes clear in 2 weeks

Growth factors

Oxygen—Aerobic.

Temperature

Optimum—25 to 28 C.

Nutrition—Does not need organic nitrogen.

Color and light characteristics

Chromogenesis—No brown pigment.

Fluorescence — Occasionally fluorescent.

Biochemical Characteristics—Two submicroscopic particle types were separated by sonic extraction. One was ribonucleoprotein. Purified hulls of the organism contain hydrogenase. Extracts examined for enzyme activity showed hexokinase, phosphoglucomutase, phosphohexoisomerase. The organism can split 6-phosphogluconate to glyceraldehyde-3-phosphate and pyruvate. Some of the G-3-P formed appears to go back into the cycle, through aldolase, fructose diphosphate, and phosphohexoisomerase to G-6-P. Extracts are able to convert ribose-5-phosphase to sedoheptulose-7-phosphate and triose phosphate. The two are further broken down to hexose phosphate.

Composition—Nitrogen fraction:

1 per cent + amide N_2
1 per cent + humin N_2
2 per cent basic N_2

4-day culture on mannitol agar:
4 per cent hemicellulose
45 per cent crude protein
4 per cent lignin-like material
7 per cent ash

Azotobacter chroococcum

Taxonomy
- Order — *Eubacteriales*
- Family — *Azotobacteraceae*
- Genus — *Azotobacter*
- Species — *chroococcum*

Cellular Characteristics
- Morphology—Rods; refractile granules may be seen
- Motility—Motile.
- Flagella—Peritrichous.
- Capsules—Organisms surrounded by a slimy membrane; in older cultures membrane usually becomes brown.
- Staining—Gram negative.
- Occurring—In pairs, packets, and occasionally chains.
- Size—2.0 to 3.0 by 3.0 to 6.0 μ.
- Habitat—Isolated from soil; found in alkaline fields.

Cultural Characteristics—Cannot grow in peptone media
- Mannitol agar stab—Gray becoming brown.
- Gelatin colonies—Circular, small, granular, yellow becoming yellowish to brown.
- Gelatin stab—No liquefaction; slight growth.
- Nutrient broth—No growth.
- Potato—Slight growth; glossy, slimy to wrinkled; may turn color from yellowish to brown.

Physiological Characteristics
- Respiration reactions
  - Monosaccharides
    - Arabinose—Utilized by the organism in its fixing of atmospheric nitrogen; carbon dioxide produced.
    - Fructose—Utilized by the organism in its fixing of atmospheric nitrogen; carbon dioxide produced.
    - Galactose—Utilized by the organism in its fixing of atmospheric nitrogen; carbon dioxide produced.
  - Disaccharides
    - Maltose—Utilized by the organism in its fixing of atmospheric nitrogen; carbon dioxide produced.
  - Polysaccharides
    - Inulin—Utilized by the organism in its fixing of atmospheric nitrogen; carbon dioxide produced.
    - Dextrin—Utilized by the organism in its fixing of atmospheric nitrogen; carbon dioxide produced.
  - Alcohols and polyalcohols
    - Mannitol—Utilized by the organism in its fixing of atmospheric nitrogen; carbon dioxide produced.
- Growth factors
  - Oxygen—Aerobic.
  - Temperature
    - Optimum—25 to 28 C.
  - Nutrition—Less than 1 g of nitrate per liter improves growth; more is deleterious.
- Color and light characteristics
  - Chromogenesis—Coloring matter in slime that surrounds the bacterium; insoluble in water, alcohol, ether, and chloroform.

Biochemical Characteristics
- Enzyme production—Very little cytochrome C oxidase activity. Age of the organism and substrate adaption are related to each other. Experiments revealed

that oxidation of two substances in the substrate could be possible if the cell was partially adapted. The formation of new enzyme systems is also possible.

Nitrogen fixation—Fixation of atmospheric nitrogen. Glucose and sucrose utilized. Carbon dioxide given off.

Composition—Chemical analysis: dried 4-day cultures grown on mannitol agar contained:
- hemicelluloses 0.5 per cent
- crude protein 20 per cent
- ash 5 per cent
- lignin-like material > 30 per cent

Nitrogen part contained:
- amide nitrogen < 1 per cent
- humin nitrogen < 1 per cent
- basic nitrogen about 1 per cent

Addenda. Possess an absorption band of 505, 589 to 590 mμ.

Certain chemicals can be used for enriching the medium to isolate the organism from the soil: calcium citrate, potassium acetate, potassium lactate. *A. agilis* was isolated by using cinnamic acid, calcium butyrate, calcium benzoate.

Azotomonas insolita

Taxonomy

Order	*Pseudomonadales*
Suborder	*Pseudomonadineae*
Family	*Pseudomonadaceae*
Genus	*Azotomonas*
Species	*insolita*

Cellular Characteristics
- Morphology—Rods nearly coccoid.
- Motility—Motile.
- Flagella—One to three polar.
- Staining—Gram negative.
- Size—0.6 to 1.2 by 0.6 to 1.8 μ.
- Habit—Soil.

Cultural Characteristics
- Agar colonies—Flat; edge is entire and white.
- Agar stroke—Glistening, white.
- Broth—Turbid, sediment, pellicle.
- Potato—Dry, gray, spreading growth.

Physiological Characteristics

Biochemical action
- Hydrogen sulfide production—Positive.
- Starch hydrolysis—Positive.
- Nitrogen fixation—Positive.
- Ammonium salts—Utilized.
- Nitrite—Produced from nitrate.
- Milk—No action.

Fermentation reactions

Monosaccharides
- Arabinose—Acid and gas.
- Rhamnose—Acid and gas.
- Xylose—Acid and gas.
- Glucose—Acid and gas.
- Fructose—Acid and gas.
- Galactose—Acid and gas.
- Mannose—Acid and gas.

Disaccharides
- Lactose—Acid and gas.
- Sucrose—Acid and gas.
- Maltose—Acid and gas.

Polysaccharides
- Raffinose—Acid and gas.
- Starch—Acid and gas.
- Dextrin—Acid and gas.

Alcohols and polyalcohols
- Glycerol—Acid and gas.
- Mannitol—Acid and gas.
- Sorbitol—Acid and gas.
- Dulcitol—Acid and gas.
- Arabitol—Acid and gas.
- Adonitol—Acid and gas.
- Inositol—Acid and gas.

Glucosides
- Salicin—Acid and gas.

Growth factors

Oxygen—Aerobic.
Temperature
Optimum—25 to 63 C.
Maximum—48 C.
Minimum—7 to 9.5 C.
Thermal death point—60 C.
pH
Range—3.3 to 9.5 C.
Color and light characteristics
Fluorescence—Slight.

Bacillus anthracis

Taxonomy

Order	*Eubacteriales*
Family	*Bacillaceae*
Genus	*Bacillus*
Species	*anthracis*
Synonom	anthrax bacillus

Cellular Characteristics
Morphology—Rods, ends are square or concave; cells grown on certain media may be granular; fat globules are present.
Motility—Nonmotile.
Capsules—Encapsulated.
Staining—Gram positive, nonacid fast; stains with aniline dyes, carbol fuchsin, and methylene blue.
Occurring—In chains and in diplobacillary forms.
Size—1.0 to 1.3 by 3 to 10 μ.
Spores—Nonbulging ellipsoidal; central and off center spores are also found; in polar germination no spores produced *in vivo;* some reports show the anthrax spores to be viable after 10 years in the dry state.
Size—0.8 to 1.0 by 1.3 to 1.5 μ.
Sporangia—Ellipsoidal to cylindrical, not swollen; chains are often seen.
Habitat—Found in the soil; parasitic in cattle, sheep, man, and other animals and isolated from blood of infected animals.

Cultural Characteristics—Cultivation of the organism is easy.
Agar colonies—Large, irregular, curly growth in which the colony looks like chains in parallel; the colony is irregular and dense.
Agar stroke—Grayish, abundant, dense growth, spreading with fimbriate growth.
Gelatin stab—Crateriform to stratiform liquefaction; arborescent growth.
Nutrient broth—Thick pellicle, little turbidity.
Potato—Creamy spreading growth.

Physiological Characteristics
Biochemical action
Indole production—Negative.
Voges-Proskauer test—Acetylmethylcarbinol produced.
Starch hydrolysis—Positive.
Ammonia—Production is slight.
Nitrites—Formed from nitrates.
Milk—Coagulation is positive with peptonization and slight acidity.
Protein liquefaction or digestion
Blood serum—Creamy-yellow abundant growth; slight liquefaction.
Gelatin—Liquefied.
Fermentation reactions
Monosaccharides
Arabinose—Inconclusive evidence.
Rhamnose—Inconclusive evidence.
Glucose—Acid.
Fructose—Acid.
Galactose—Inconclusive evidence.
Disaccharides
Sucrose—Acid.
Maltose—Acid.
Trehalose—Acid.
Polysaccharides
Raffinose—Inconclusive evidence.
Dextrin—Acid.

Alcohols and polyalcohols
Glycerol—Possible acidity.
Growth factors
Temperature
Optimum—35 C.
Range—Growth at 42 C; growth of the organism above its optimum temperature results in loss of virulence.
Nutrition—Certain constituents of an artificial medium must be present for growth such as the vitamin thiamine; sodium bicarbonate, calcium ion, leucine, isoleucine, proline, histidine, phenylalanine; threonine and glutamic acid stimulate growth.
Color and light characteristics
Pigment—Some strains produce a brown-yellow pigment.
Serology
Antigenic grouping—There are cross reactions to other members of the spore-bearing groups. The Ascoli precipitin test is used in diagnosis (post-mortem) of the disease. It is also used to detect contamination of hides.
Immunization—The Pasteur method is used to immunize animals actively; serum therapy confers only temporary immunity.
Antigen—The antigen of the organism can be precipitated by using 0.1 *M* potassium aluminum sulfate solution and pH of 5.9.
Pathogenicity
Human beings—Man may be infected with anthrax in several ways: (1) cutaneous anthrax, in which case the organism infects the skin; the lesion is vesicular and undergoes necrosis; (2) pulmonary anthrax, called woolsorter's disease, is caught by inhaling spores of the organism; the disease resembles pneumonia, (3) intestinal anthrax is acquired by swallowing uncooked meat of infected animals.
Animals—The cause of anthrax in cattle, sheep, and swine. The disease can be diagnosed by collection of material, smears, cultures, and animal inoculation. Anthrax bacillus is more virulent in the rough form than in the smooth form.

Addenda. Colony growth forms a medusa head which is a result of large spores. The division of the organism starts with the separation of the cytoplasm, and the formation of a septum which may be continuous and doubled with the outer wall. In young cells the organism appears to be divided into four cells, and this extends into the polypeptide capsule.

The Feulgen reaction was confirmed on the organism; streaks of definite purple color were observed.

The capsule is composed principally of a polypeptide of D-glutamic acid. Capsule formation takes place only in the presence of carbon dioxide. Virulence of the organism is helped by the polyglutamate capsule. Polysaccharides are also found in the capsule.

Spores of the organism, after being put into broth at 37 C, begin to consume oxygen after 5 minutes and are heat sensitive after 10 minutes.

Some useful criteria have been put forth for the identification of the organism: The positive staining of intracellular fat by Sudan black B-safranin and fermentation tests in tryptophane agar slant butts.

The organism can be differentiated from *B. cereus* by phage typing.

Benzathine penicillin can be used effectively against the organism and its spores.

Naked protoplasts were observed to unite into a spherical body when the regular cells were put into decreasing sucrose solutions.

The organism can remain viable for 2 years at 4 C.

Bacillus cereus

Taxonomy
- Order — *Eubacteriales*
- Family — *Bacillaceae*
- Genus — *Bacillus*
- Species — *cereus*

Cellular Characteristics

Morphology—Rods, ends square; variations: filaments, rounded ends.

Motility—Smooth strains motile; rough strains may be motile; variations: nonmotile.

Flagella—Peritrichous.

Capsules—None; variations: encapsulated.

Staining—Gram positive; light staining shows a granular or foamy protoplasm; variations: uniformly stained protoplasm; atypical staining if grown on glucose or glycerol agar; unstained inclusions observed after 24 hours, lipid in nature; may interfere with nuclear study.

Occurring—Tangled chains, both short and long.

Size—1.0 to 1.2 by 3.0 to 5.0 μ; variations: 0.8 to 1.3 by 2.0 to 6.0 μ.

Spores—Ellipsoidal.

Position—Central or paracentral.

Wall—Thin.

Size—1.0 to 1.5 μ; variations: 0.5 to 1.2 by 1.3 to 2.5 μ.

Sporangia—Ellipsodal to cylindrical, chains, not swollen.

Habitat—Soil, dust, milk, plant surfaces.

Cultural Characteristics

Agar colonies—Large, flat, may be entire or irregular; characteristic growth occurs as spreading, rough, and arborescent white.

Agar stroke—Abundant, nonsticking, spreading white to yellow.

Gelatin stab—Liquefaction usually fast.

Nutrient broth—Thick turbidity.

Potato—Thick, creamy-white to pinkish growth.

Physiological Characteristics

Biochemical action

Voges-Proskauer test—Positive.

Citrate—Usually used as sole source of carbon.

Starch hydrolysis—Positive.

Ammonia—Ammoniacal nitrogen from sugar media.

Nitrite—Usually produced from nitrate.

Milk—Peptonization; coagulation may occur.

Protein liquefaction or digestion

Hemolyzed blood serum agar—Liquefaction may occur in degrees.

Gelatin—Liquefied.

Fermentation reactions—(with ammonium salts)

Monosaccharides

Arabinose—No acid.

Ramnose—No acid.

Xylose—No acid.

Glucose—Acid, no gas.

Fructose—Acid, no gas.

Disaccharides

Lactose—Usually no acid.

Sucrose—Acid, no gas.

Maltose—Acid, no gas.

Polysaccharides

Raffinose—No acid.

Inulin—No acid.
Dextrin—Acid, no gas.
Alcohols and polyalcohols
Glycerol—Acid, no gas.
Glucosides
Salicin—Usually acid.
Growth factors
Oxygen—Aerobic, facultatively anaerobic.
Temperature
Optimum—30 C.
Maximum—Up to 48 C.
Nutrition—Amino acids required for growth.
pH—Usually below 5.2.
Inhibition—Growth of vegetative cells was stopped by 500 ppm of 2,4-dichlorophenoxyacetic acid. 300 to 475 ppm of 2,4-D caused an initial lag of gelatin decomposition; ammonia production was inhibited at 900 ppm.
Color and light characteristics
Fluorescence—Some strains give a greenish fluorescence.
Biochemical Characteristics
Enzyme production—Lecithinase produced; ultraviolet radiation inhibits synthesis of penicillinase.
Chemical end products—Two types of condensations; first from acetaldehyde and pyruvate which yield acetoin; an aldol second type of condensation of acetaldehyde and glyceraldehyde-3-phosphate yields 2-desoxyribosephosphate.
Academic or Research Utilization—Strain of the organism was active against *Candida albicans.*
Pathogenicity
Insects—The organism can multiply in the gut and blood of the larch sawfly because of the optimum pH value; also a good environment for lecithinase activity. The organism was used to destroy the larval stage of the cabbage butterfly. The 3rd stage was totally destroyed at temperatures of 16 and 32 C.
Spoilage
Food—Agent causing spoilage of canned pimentos.

Addenda. Spores produced endotrophically seem to contain less dipicolinic acid than spores produced in synthetic or organic media.

Protein and a labile phosphorus appear to be constituents of the spore chromatin.

Old cultures may show whiplike growth.

Spore studies made by phase contrast and interference microscopy indicate that spores contain little water.

Bacillus macerans

Taxonomy
Order *Eubacteriales*
Family *Bacillaceae*
Genus *Bacillus*
Species *macerans*
Cellular Characteristics
Morphology—Rods.
Motility—Motile.
Staining—Gram variable.
Occurring—Singly or in pairs.
Size—0.6 to 1.0 by 2.5 to 6.0 μ.
Habitat—Soil, water, decomposing starchy materials, retting flax.
Spores—Ellipsoidal.
Position—Subterminal or terminal.
Wall—Thick, readily stained.
Size—1.0 to 1.5 by 1.2 to 2.5 μ.
Sporangia—Swollen terminally, clublike.
Cultural Characteristics
Agar colonies—Transparent to whitish, small, thin, usually smooth.

Agar stroke—Moderate, spreading growth.
Gelatin stab—Hydrolyzed, liquefaction variable.
Nutrient broth—Sediment, turbid; slime may be formed in sugar broth.
Potato—Digested, gas formed.
Milk agar plate—Casein not hydrolyzed in 96 hours.

Physiological Characteristics
Biochemical action
Voges-Proskauer test—Negative.
Citrate utilization—Cannot be utilized as sole source of carbon.
Starch hydrolysis—Positive.
Nitrogen utilization—Ammonium salts can be used as sole source of nitrogen.
Nitrite—Formed from nitrate.
Milk—Acid and gas.
Protein liquefaction or digestion
Gelatin—Variable liquefaction.
Casein—Not hydrolyzed in 1 week.
Indicator reactions
Methylene blue—Reduced, then reoxidized.
Fermentation reactions (with ammonium salts)
Monosaccharides
Arabinose—Acid and gas.
Rhamnose—Acid and gas.
Xylose—Acid and gas.
Glucose—Acid and gas.
Fructose—Acid and gas.
Galactose—Acid and gas.
Disaccharides
Lactose—Acid and gas.
Sucrose—Acid and gas.
Maltose—Acid and gas.
Polysaccharides
Raffinose—Acid and gas.
Melezitose—Acid and gas.
Alcohols and polyalcohols
Glycerol—Acid and gas.
Erythritol—Not fermented.
Mannitol—Acid and gas.
Dulcitol—Not fermented.
Growth factors
Oxygen—Aerobic; facultatively aerobic.
Temperature
Optimum—37 C; good growth, 42 to 45 C.
Maximum—45 to 50 C.
Vitamins required—Thiamine and biotin.

Serology
Agglutination—Positive by homologous sera. *B. polymyxa* serum cannot agglutinate.

Biochemical Characteristics
Enzyme production—Amylases produced.

Differentiation from *B. polymyxa*—By production of crystalline dextrins from starch.

Addenda. Starch can be converted into dextrans due to the enzymic action of *B. macerans* amylase. The organism is grown on a potato medium. pH is about 6.

Bacillus megaterium

Taxonomy
Order *Eubacteriales*
Family *Bacillaceae*
Genus *Bacillus*
Species *megaterium*
Synonym *Bacillus megatherium*

Cellular Characteristics
Morphology—Rods, in some media, irregular shapes; fat stored in cells grown on glucose or glycerol agar; ghost forms; many variations.
Motility—Motile.
Flagella—Peritrichous.
Spores—Ellipsoidal, almost round.
Sporangia—Ellipsoidal to cylindrical.

Staining—Gram positive.
Occurring—Singly or in short chains.
Size—1.2 to 1.5 by 2.0 to 4.0 μ.
Habitat—Found in soil, water, and decomposing materials.

Cultural Characteristics
Agar colonies—Creamy-white to yellow, smooth, soft, convex, entire, opaque; ridged edges may be indicative of rough stage.
Soybean agar slants—Abundant growth, good sporulation, few shadow forms.
Glucose agar—Heavy, raised growth.
Gelatin stab—Slow liquefaction.

Physiological Characteristics
Biochemical action
Voges-Proskauer test—Acetylmethylcarbinol not formed.
Citrate utilized—As sole source of carbon.
Starch hydrolysis—Positive.
Nitrite—Usually not produced from nitrate.
Milk—Peptonized.
Protein liquefaction or digestion
Gelatin—Liqufied.
Fermentation reactions (with ammoniacal nitrogen)
Monosaccharides
Arabinose—Acid.
Rhamnose—No acid.
Glucose—Acid.
Fructose—Acid.
Disaccharides
Lactose—Variable.
Sucrose—Acid.
Maltose—Acid.
Polysaccharides
Inulin—Acid.
Dextrin—Acid.
Alcohols and polyalcohols
Glycerol—Acid.
Mannitol—Acid.
Growth factors
Oxygen—Aerobic.
Temperature
Optimum—28 to 35 C.
Maximum—About 40 to 45 C.
Color and light characteristics
Chromogenesis—A few strains produce a black pigment on tyrosine agar slants.

Biochemical Characteristics
Enzyme production—Lecithinase not produced.

Addenda. The organism is resistant to 44 antibiotic drugs. It also shows cross resistance to the drugs. Some of the drugs are neomycin, catenulin, pliacin, streptothricin, viomycin.

Synergism—double enzyme systems consisting of lysozyme with papain or trypsin accompanied by heat cause lysis of the cell. The lytic action and its extent is greater than an additive action alone.

Spore position, which is usually centrally located, is influenced by the substrate or the medium. On 0.1 per cent casein hydrolyzate there is little displacement.

Molecular weight is about 15,000.

Bacillus polymyxa

Taxonomy
Order *Eubacteriales*
Family *Bacillaceae*
Genus *Bacillus*
Species *polymyxa*

Cellular Characteristics
Morphology—Rods.
Motility—Motile.
Flagella—Peritrichous.
Staining—Gram variable.
Occurring—Singly or in short chains.
Size—0.6 to 1.0 by 2.5 to 6.0 μ.
Spores—Ellipsoidal.
Position—Central to subterminal.

Wall—Usually thick.
Size—1.0 to 1.5 by 1.5 to 2.5 μ.
Sporangia—Swollen, spindle or club-shaped.
Habitat—Found in water, soil, milk, feces, decaying vegetables.

Cultural Characteristics
Agar colonies—Thin spreading over entire plate; rough forms round, whitish.
Glucose agar—Raised, gummy growth; gas formed.
Gelatin stab—Hydrolysis positive when Frazier technique is used.
Nutrient broth—Turbidity uniform to granular; sometimes flocculent, slimy sediment.
Glucose broth—pH 5.2 to 6.8.
Potato—White to light tan, moderate to abundant growth; gas formed.

Physiological Characteristics
Biochemical action
Indole production—Negative.
Voges-Proskauer test—Production of acetylmethylcarbinol positive.
Citrate—Usually not utilized as sole source of carbon.
Starch hydrolysis—Negative; crystalline dextrins not formed.
Nitrites—Produced from nitrates; no gas under anaerobic conditions.
Hemicellulose—Attacked.
Pectin—Attacked.
Protein liquefaction or digestion
Gelatin—Slowly liquefied.
Indicator reactions
Methylene blue—Reduced.
Fermentation reactions (with ammoniacal nitrogen)
Monosaccharides
Arabinose—Acid, gas, and gum.
Rhamnose—Acid, gas, and gum or variable.
Xylose—Acid, gas, and gum.
Glucose—Acid, gas, and gum.
Fructose—Acid, gas, and gum.
Galactose—Acid, gas, and gum.
Mannose—Acid, gas, and gum.
Disaccharides
Lactose—Acid, gas, and gum.
Sucrose—Acid, gas, and gum.
Maltose—Acid, gas, and gum.
Cellobiose—Acid, gas, and gum.
Trehalose—Acid, gas, and gum.
Polysaccharides
Raffinose—Acid, gas, and gum.
Melezitose—Acid, gas, and gum.
Inulin—Acid, gas, and gum.
Dextrin—Acid, gas, and gum.
Pectin—Attacked.
Hemicellulose—Attacked.
Alcohols and polyalcohols
Glycerol—Acid, gas, and gum.
Erythritol—Not fermented.
Mannitol—Acid, gas, and gum.
Sorbitol—Acid, gas, and gum variable.
Dulcitol—Not fermented.
Adonitol—Not fermented.
Inositol—Not fermented.
Glucosides
Salicin—Acid, gas, and gum.
Growth factors
Oxygen—Aerobic; facultatively anaerobic.
Temperature
Optimum—28 to 35 C.
Maximum—40 C (most strains).
No growth—45 C.
Nutrition
Vitamins—Biotin necessary.
pH—4.8 to 7.2 in glucose broth.

Biochemical Characteristics
Enzyme production—Lecithinase variable; amylase can be developed on a peptone-starch medium at room temperature.
Antibiotic production—Polymyxin produced by some strains.
Chemical end products—Ethyl alcohol, butylene glycol, and small amounts of acetone are produced in glucose broth.

Bacillus subtilis

Taxonomy
- Order — *Eubacteriales*
- Family — *Bacillaceae*
- Genus — *Bacillus*
- Species — *subtilis*

Cellular Characteristics
- Morphology—Rods with rounded ends.
- Motility—Motile.
- Capsules—Generally no capsules; some strains encapsulated.
- Staining—Gram positive.
- Occurring—Singly or in short chains.
- Size—0.7 to 0.8 by 2.0 to 3.0 μ.
- Habitat—Soil and decomposing organic matter.
- Spores—Ellipsoidal to cylindrical.
  - Position—Central to paracentral.
  - Size—0.6 to 0.9 by 1.0 to 1.5 μ.
- Sporangia—Ovoid to cylindrical.
- Variants—Rods or filaments.
  - Motility—Nonmotile.
  - Capsules—Present.
  - Staining—Very seldom; gram variable.
  - Occurring—Long chains.
  - Size—0.6 to 1.0 by 1.3 to 6 μ.

Cultural Characteristics
- Agar colonies—Slightly spreading, finely wrinkled, dull, opaque, adherent.
- Agar stroke—Abundant, flat spreading growth; wrinkled and adherent; variations may occur.
- Nutrient broth—Turbid, becoming clear; wrinkled pellicle.
- Potato—Growth luxuriant, warty or wrinkled, whitish to pink or yellow.

Physiological Characteristics
- Biochemical action
  - Acetylmethylcarbinol—Produced.
  - Citrate utilization—Positive.
  - Starch hydrolysis—Positive.
  - Ammonia—Utilized.
  - Nitrite—Formed from nitrate.
  - Nitrate—No gas under anaerobic conditions.
- Protein liquefaction
  - Gelatin—Liquefied.
  - Casein (milk agar plate)—Hydrolyzed.
- Indicator reactions
  - Methylene blue—Reduced.
  - Resazurin—Reduced.
- Fermentation reactions (in presence of amoniacal nitrogen)
  - Monosaccharides
    - Xylose—Acid.
    - Glucose—Acid.
    - Fructose—Acid.
    - Galactose—Acid.
    - Mannose—Acid.
  - Disaccharides
    - Lactose—Usually no acid.
    - Sucrose—Acid.
    - Maltose—Acid.
  - Polyalcohols
    - Glycerol—Acid.
- Growth factors
  - Oxygen—Aerobic; facultatively anaerobic (some strains).
  - Temperature
    - Optimum—30 to 37 C.
    - Range—May grow at 50 to 56 C.
  - Nutrition—Poor growth in glucose broth under anaerobic conditions.
  - pH—Higher than 5.2.
- Color characteristics
  - Fluorescence—Some strains show green fluorescence at 45 C on nutrient agar.

Biochemical Characteristics
- Enzyme production
  - Amylases—Produced.
  - Lecithinase—Not produced.
- Antibiotics—Subtilin, bacitracin, bacillin,

bacillomycin, subtenolin, subtilysin, endosubtilysin, and eumycin.

Industrial Utilization

Products—Antibiotics (as above).

Processes—Commercial bacterial amylases from wheat bran.

Research Utilization

Genetics—Cells grown in the presence of D-fructose and L-arabinose show two consecutive growth cycles separated by a lag phase; this is due to inhibition by the first compound of adaptive enzymes attacking the second.

Spoilage

Dry milk and dry-milk products—Cause of defects.

Tomato—Contamination can be detected by methylene blue or resazurin reduction.

Addenda. It has been suggested that the spores of *B. subtilis* may be uninucleated and the nucleus haploid. The following tabulation shows the percentage of biochemical mutants after exposure to several mutagenic factors.

More manganese than is required for full vegetative growth is essential for the sporulation of the organism.

A large scale method for the production of proteinase includes submerging the organism in air for 30 hours, removal of the organism by centrifugation and precipitation of the solutes using sodium sulfate and then drying the precipitate.

Beta-propiolactone is able to kill the spores of *B. subtilis*. Spores, once exposed to the chemical become sensitive to 100 C. At room temperature, beta-propiolactone is converted to a substance that does not have sporicidal activity.

During sporulation there is an increase in the calcium content of the cell which appears to be in conjunction with the synthesis of dipicolinic acid.

Spores can germinate in nutrient media even though the temperature is too low to permit vegetative growth.

Some of the amino acid constituents of *B. subtilis* protein and their percentages are glycine 5.64, alanine 6.02, valine 5.55, leucine 6.42, proline 4.4, tryptophane 6.19.

(*a*) *Incubated Before Plating*			(*b*) *Immediate Plating*
Spores	*Veg. cells*		*Spores*
——	6%	(x ray)	6%
3%	3%	(ultraviolet)	——

A comparison should be made between side (a) and side (b).

Some investigators claim there may be some kind of a recombination factor operating in the organism. This is based upon morphological explorations.

Mutant strains of the organism need threonine or threonine plus methionine.

The reductase test can be used to detect contamination of tomato products by *B. subtilis*.

Bacillus thuringiensis

Taxonomy

Order	*Eubacteriales*
Family	*Bacillaceae*
Genus	*Bacillus*
Species	*thuringiensis*

Cellular Characteristics

Morphology—Rods, same as *B. cereus*.

Spores—Same size and shape as *B. cereus;* lie obliquely in sporangia.

Sporangia—Not always swollen; knobs of

protoplasm, called inclusion bodies, remain in each end.
Habitat—Diseased insects.
Cultural Characteristics—Same as *B. cereus.*
Physiological Characteristics
Biochemical action—Same as *B. cereus.*
Industrial Utilization
Products—Approved by Food and Drug Administration in 1958 as microbial insecticide.
Pathogenicity
Insects—Pathogenic to insects.

Bacteroides fragilis

Taxonomy

Order	*Eubacteriales*
Family	*Bacteroidaceae*
Genus	*Bacteroides*
Species	*fragilis*

Cellular Characteristics
Morphology—Rods with rounded ends.
Motility—Nonmotile.
Staining—Gram negative; staining at poles is deeper.
Occurring—Singly or in pairs.
Source—Alimentary and urogenital tract of man and other animals.
Cultural Characteristics
Agar colonies—Small, irregular gray.
Nutrient broth—Turbid.
Physiological Characteristics
Biochemical action
Indole production—Negative.
Hydrogen sulfide production—Negative.
Nitrite—Not produced from nitrate.
Protein liquefaction or digestion
Gelatin—Not liquefied; slight amount of gas.
Indicator reactions
Litmus milk—No coagulation; some gas.
Fermentation reactions
Monosaccharides
Arabinose—Acid.
Glucose—Acid.
Fructose—Acid.
Galactose—Acid.
Disaccharides
Lactose—Acid produced by some strains.
Sucrose—Acid.
Maltose—Acid.
Growth factors
Oxygen—Anaerobic.
Temperature
Optimum—37 C.
Pathogenicity
Human beings—May produce septicemia, urinary tract abscesses, acute appendicitis.
Animals—May produce abscesses in rabbits, mice, and guinea pigs.

Bordetella pertussis

Taxonomy

Order	*Eubacteriales*
Family	*Brucellaceae*
Genus	*Bordetella*
Species	*pertussis*
Synonym	*Hemophilus pertussis*

Cellular Characteristics
Morphology—Ovoid, pleomorphic, coccobacilli.
Motility—Nonmotile.
Capsules—Positive.
Staining—Gram negative; toluidine blue staining reveals metachromatic granules; Lawson's modification of Smith's stain is used to reveal capsules. Tendency for bipolar staining.

Occurring—Singly, in pairs, and sometimes in short chains.
Size—0.2 to 0.3 by 1 μ.
Source—Respiratory tract of cases of whooping cough.
Reservoir—Human beings.

Cultural Characteristics
Agar colonies—Best growth; agar colonies are pearly, glistening, smooth, raised, and entire; they are surrounded by a hemolytic zone of indefinite periphery; 3 to 4 days required.
Bordet-Gengou medium—Used for fluids.
Cohen and Wheeler medium—Used for fluids.
Liquid media—Mucoid mass develops.

Physiological Characteristics
Biochemical action
Indole production—Negative.
Citrate—Does not serve as sole source of carbon.
Urea—Not hydrolyzed.
Nitrate—Not reduced.
Indicator reactions
Litmus milk—Alkaline in 10 to 12 days.
Fermentation reactions—Carbohydrates generally not fermented.
Monosaccharides
Glucose—Acid.
Galactose—No action.
Disaccharides
Lactose—Acid.
Sucrose—No action.
Maltose—No action.
Polysaccharides
Inulin—No action.
Growth factors
Oxygen—Aerobic.
Temperature
Optimum—35-37 C.
Nutrition—Smooth phase, does not grow on plain agar.

Serology
Agglutination—Cross agglutination with *B. parapertussis* and *B. bronchiseptica.*
Antitoxin—Antitoxin of *B. pertussis* neutralizes toxins produced by *B. parapertussis* and *B. bronchiseptica.*

Biochemical Characteristics
Enzyme production—Catalase produced.

Academic or Research Utilization—Variant forms appear on artificial media. Attempts to isolate endotoxin by distruction of organism by sonic vibration and by grinding.

Pathogenicity
Human beings—Cause of whooping cough.

Borrelia duttonii

Taxonomy

Order	*Spirochaetales*
Family	*Treponemataceae*
Genus	*Borrelia*
Species	*duttonii*

Cellular Characteristics—See *B. recurrentis.*

Cultural Characteristics—See *B. recurrentis.*

Serology
Antigens—Different from those of *B. recurrentis* and from other organisms causing relapsing fever.

Pathogenicity
Human beings—Cause of Central and South African relapsing fever. Transmitted through bite of *Ornithodorus moubata,* a tick, in which the organism goes through a fragmentation step.
Animals—Pathogenic, particularly to new born, white rats and white mice; nonpathogenic to guinea pigs.

Borrelia recurrentis

Taxonomy
- Order *Spirochaetales*
- Family *Treponemataceae*
- Genus *Borrelia*
- Species *recurrentis*

Cellular Characteristics
- Morphology—Spiral having from 3 to 20 waves but usually 5; cylindrical tapered at both ends, slightly flattened.
- Motility—Motile by active corkscrew action; lashing movement in fresh blood.
- Staining—Best observation can be made by use of dark-field illumination. Can be stained with aniline dyes; gram negative and violet with Giemsa's stain.
- Occurring—Singly.
- Size—8 to 15 μ in length and 0.5 μ in breadth.
- Source and reservoir—Blood of infected human beings and animals and infected lice.

Cultural Characteristics—Can be cultivated in ascitic fluid or hydrocoele fluid.

Physiological Characteristics
- Biochemical action
  - Bile salts—Disintegration of the organism can be accomplished in 10 per cent solution.
  - Saponin—Immobilized in 30 minutes in 10 per cent solution.

Serology—Some immunity is developed. This may be due to the chronic infection of the disease.

Pathogenicity—The organism is a blood parasite and causes epidemic relapsing fever. The spirochetes can be demonstrated in the blood during the fever which is characteristic of the disease. The spirochete may infect man by a louse vector. The organism may survive in lice for long periods of time.

Brevibacterium linens

Taxonomy
- Order *Eubacteriales*
- Family *Brevibacteriaceae*
- Genus *Brevibacterium*
- Species *linens*
- Synonym *Bacterium linens*

Cellular Characteristics
- Morphology—Rods.
- Motility—Nonmotile.
- Staining—Gram positive.
- Size—0.62 by 2.5 μ.
- Habitat—Found in dairy products and in water, soil, air, hay, straw.

Cultural Characteristics
- Tryptone glucose agar colonies—After 48 hours, convex, glistening, entire, cream colored; on cheese agar good growth, orange to red-brown in a few days.
- Agar stab—Good surface growth on tryptone glucose extract agar at 21 C.
- Agar slant—On tryptone glucose extract agar abundant, glistening, filiform nonviscid growth; color changing to brown.
- Potato—Scanty smooth, glistening, after 5 days of growth; grayish to brownish-orange.
- Broth—Turbidity and sediment.
- Gelatin stab—Crateriform liquefaction, becoming infundibuliform on incubation; varied liquefaction.
- Nutrient broth—Turbidity and sediment.

Physiological Characteristics
Biochemical action
Indole production—Negative.
Methyl red reaction—Negative.
Voges-Proskauer test—Negative.
Hydrogen sulfide production—Positive in broth, variable in agar.
Nitrite—Produced from nitrate.
Natural fats—Not hydrolyzed.
Indicator reactions
Litmus milk—At 21 C changes are slow, after 6 or 7 days becomes alkaline; yellow sediment. After 10 days some digestion, no coagulation. Ropiness may be produced.
Fermentation reactions
Monosaccharides
Arabinose—No acid or gas.
Glucose—No acid or gas.
Galactose—No acid or gas.
Disaccharides
Sucrose—No acid or gas.
Polysaccharides
Inulin—No acid or gas.
Dextrin—No acid or gas.
Alcohols and polyacohols
Ethyl alcohol—Oxidized to acetic acid.
Propyl alcohol—Oxidized to propionic acid.
Butyl alcohol—Oxidized to butyric acid.
Amyl alcohol—Oxidized to valeric acid.
Hexyl alcohol—Oxidized slowly.
Heptyl alcohol—Oxidized slowly.
Dulcitol—No acid or gas.
Growth factors
Oxygen—Aerobic.
Temperature—Growth at 8 C and 37 C; no growth at 45 C.
Tolerance
Salt—Tolerates 15 per cent salt.
pH—Growth at 6.0 to 9.8; no growth at pH 5.0 or below.
Other—Low heat resistance. Sensitive to acid conditions.
Color and light characteristics
Chromogenesis—Red or rose; absence of abundant oxygen may decrease chromogenesis.

Biochemical Characteristics
Enzyme production—Catalase produced in media; produces proteolytic enzymes; proteinase produced with casein as substrate at pH 7.0.

Industrial Utilization
Products—Makes up the normal surface of limburger cheese; yeast contributes to the growth of the acid-sensitive strains by decreasing the curd acidity and secreting growth factors. Responsible for stronger limburger-like flavor and aroma. Appears to replace yeast in the curing of blue cheese.

Brucella abortus

Taxonomy

Order	*Eubacteriales*
Family	*Brucellaceae*
Genus	*Brucella*
Species	*abortus*

Cellular Characteristics
Morphology—Morphological characteristics the same as *B. melitensis.*
Staining—Ordinary aniline dyes will stain organism.
Size—0.4 by 1 μ.
Habitat—Cow.

Cultural Characteristics—The same as *B. melitensis.*

Physiological Characteristics
Biochemical action

Lysis—The rate of phagocytosis depends upon the media used; tryptose agar seems to help in the lysis of the cell.

Urease activity—Variable.

Hydrogen sulfide production—Positive.

Catalase activity—Less than that of *B. melitensis* or *B. suis.*

Fermentation reactions

Monosaccharides

Rhamnose—Fermented by type I; types II and III variable.

Glucose—Fermented.

Mannose—Fermented by type I.

Disaccharides

Maltose—Not fermented.

Trehalose—Not fermented.

Polyalcohols

Inositol—Fermented.

Growth factors

Oxygen—Rough types of cultures grow more rapidly in reduced oxygen environment.

Temperature—Resists cold and drying. The organism can survive for long periods of time in bovine semen and at freezing temperatures. A lecithin compound found in cells of the organism acts as a protective mechanism for the enhanced viability of surviving cells during freezing and drying.

Inhibition

In thionine media—Inhibited.

In basic fuchsin media—Not inhibited.

Other—Changes in smooth and non-smooth types of cells can be inhibited by adding to the medium nitrate ion, methylene blue, or resazurin.

Nutrition

Carbon dioxide—Requires 5 per cent carbon dioxide for isolation; may require 25 per cent carbon dioxide in primary isolation.

Serology—Agglutinins and complement-fixation antibodies are produced. A titer of 1:80 or 1:100 is considered diagnostic. Bacteremia may be present, but if cultures are negative a 1:500 titer is diagnostic. Lasting immunity results from the initial infection.

Biochemical Characteristics

Enzyme production—An enzyme found in the organism can combine pentoyl lactone and beta-alanine to produce pantothenic acid. When pentoyl lactone is not available, no pantothenic acid is produced.

Pathogenicity

Animals—The cause of contagious abortion in cattle and undulant fever in man. The disease may be transmitted by milk contaminated with the organism. Antibiotics, such aureomycin and chloromycetin, have helped in cases of undulant fever.

Addenda. The principal symptom is abortion in females of cattle. This one symptom is not sufficient to diagnose a case of Bangs disease or contagious abortion. Other manifestations are sterility, enlarged joints, lameness, and inflammation of the testes in males. The incidence in the U.S. is about 5 per cent. *B. abortus* strains are inhibited when placed in Petragnani's medium. Some strains of *B. melitensis* and *B. suis* grow well on this medium. In some species of *Brucella,* glutamic acid and alanine synthesized from ammonia and carbon dioxide accumulate in the cell due to the action of urease upon the urea. One function of the ornithine cycle in bacterial cells may be the detoxification of ammonia by synthesis of urea.

A type II strain of the organism was isolated from milk of infected dairy cows. Differential dyes on agar inhibit growth as well as low concentrations of penicillin G.

D-Alanine has the power to change many organisms growing in media, affecting particularly the smooth and nonsmooth varieties. L-Alanine has the same action. L-Alanyl-L-valine can reverse the action of D-alanine whose activity is to suppress the growth of smooth types.

Ripening temperature and the increased acidity in milk do not influence the death rate of the *Brucella* organisms. Some organisms were still viable. A 60-day holding period used as an alternative to pasteurization was found to reduce pathogens.

The cytochrome oxidase activity in strains of the organism that were thionine-sensitive was 22.5 to 33.0, with an average of 27.0. Strains that were resistant showed a cytochrome activity between 9.0 and 12.0. Cytochrome activity differentiated between this organism and *B. suis,* but not from *B. melitensis.*

Tryptophane and cystine, when put into the medium as the only sources of amino acids, were toxic to the organism.

A vaccine was prepared using a strain of ether-killed organisms that were carbon dioxide dependent. The vaccine protected guinea pigs against affects of virulent strains. An experiment was set up to determine if antibody protection, virulency, and carbon dioxide dependability had any relationship. Controls and various strains were used. Results showed that the degree of resistance varied.

Brucella melitensis

Taxonomy
- Order *Eubacteriales*
- Family *Brucellaceae*
- Genus *Brucella*
- Species *melitensis*

Cellular Characteristics
- Morphology—Ellipsoidal rods, short, coccoid.
- Motility—Nonmotile.
- Staining—Gram negative; nonacid fast.
- Occurring—Singly and in pairs.
- Size—0.3 to 0.4 μ.
- Habitat—Goats.

Cultural Characteristics
- Agar colonies—Bluish-green, possibly grayish, small circular, convex, entire, smooth, and glistening.
- Agar stroke—Slow, moist, entire growth; agar may turn brown and crystals may appear.
- Gelatin colonies—Small, clear, entire.
- Gelatin stab—No liquefaction, slow growth.
- Nutrient broth—Moderate grayish sediment after 10 days.
- Beef liver—Growth enhanced.
- Tryptose agar 6.8 pH—Growth enhanced.
- Potato—Gray to brown scanty growth.

Physiological Characteristics
- Biochemical action
  - Indole production—Negative.
  - Urease activity, 4 hours—Variable.
  - Ammonia—Produced from urea.
  - Nitrite—Sometimes reduced.
  - Nitrate—Reduced to nitrite.
  - Catalase activity, 30 minutes—Positive.
- Indicator reactions
  - Litmus milk—Unchanged in 24 hours; then becomes alkaline.
- Fermentation reactions
  - Carbohydrate media—No acid or gas.
  - Monosaccharides
    - Rhamnose—Not fermented.
    - Glucose—Fermented.
    - Mannose—Not fermented.
  - Disaccharides
    - Maltose—Not fermented.
    - Trehalose—Not fermented.
  - Polyalcohols
    - Inositol—Not fermented.

Growth factors
Oxygen—Aerobic.
Temperature
Optimum—37 C.
No growth—< 6 C, > 45 C.
Thermal death point—59 C.
pH
Optimum—7.4.
Nutrition—Does not require increased carbon dioxide pressure.
Inhibition
In thionine media—Not inhibited.
In basic fuchsin media—Not inhibited.
Antibiotics—Thiocymetin inhibits *B. melitensis;* when used with streptomycin, there is no inhibition.
Pathogenicity
Animals and human beings—The cause of brucellosis, a disease attacking farm animals. The primary host of *B. melitensis* is the goat. In goats the disease is called Malta fever. Can also affect man.

Addenda. Strains of this organism had a cytochrome activity of 7.5 to 24.5.

The organism is easily killed by common disinfectants and it is also killed by pasteurization. It may live in dairy products and in soil and dust for a long time.

In addition to other distinctions among the *Brucella* group, one of the basic differences between *B. melitensis* and the other members of the group is the nature of the oxidative and synthetic ability of the organism. *B. suis* differs from *B. abortus* and *B. melitensis* for it can utilize L-glutamic acid and D-alanine as the sole source of nitrogen and carbon.

Brucella suis

Taxonomy
Order *Eubacteriales*
Family *Brucellaceae*
Genus *Brucella*
Species *suis*
Cellular Characteristics
Morphology—Morphological characteristics same as *B. melitensis.*
Habitat—Swine.
Cultural Characteristics—Same as *B. melitensis.*
Physiological Characteristics
Biochemical action
Urease activity—Positive, more strongly than *B. melitensis* or *B. abortus;* positive for type I; types II and III variable.
Catalase activity—Positive, stronger than *B. abortus.*
Fermentation reactions
Monosaccharides
Rhamnose—Not fermented.
Glucose—Fermented.
Mannose—Fermented.
Disaccharides
Maltose—Fermented.
Trehalose—Fermented.
Alcohols and polyalcohols
Inositol—Not fermented.
Growth factors
Nutrition
Carbon dioxide—Not required for growth.
Inhibition
In thionine media—Not inhibited.
In basic fuchsin media—Inhibited.
Serology—Smooth cultures of *B. suis* can be differentiated from smooth cultures of *B. melitensis* but not from *B. abortus.*
Pathogenicity
Human beings—The most severe form of brucellosis affecting man. The disease is characterized by fever (intermittent), sweating, lassitude, rheumatic joint pains. In-

fection lasts about 3 months. The disease may become chronic.

Animals—It has been observed that the organism is transported to lymph node by blood phagocytes in guinea pig infections of the respiratory tract. The increase in serum glycoprotein is part of the antibody response due to infection of the organism in guinea pigs. The organism infects geese. May infect cattle where swine and cattle are not separated.

Addenda. Strains of this organism showed a cytochrome activity of 5.0 to 14.5. This permits differentiation between this organism and *B. abortus* but not with *B. melitensis.*

Tetracyclines are used for drug therapy. Serological reaction may disappear in treatment.

Brucellin P.S. administered may counteract a brucellosis attack.

Cellvibrio ochraceus

Taxonomy
- Order — *Pseudomonadales*
- Suborder — *Pseudomonadineae*
- Family — *Spirillaceae*
- Genus — *Cellvibrio*
- Species — *ochraceus*

Cellular Characteristics
- Morphology—Rods that are curved, with rounded ends, stocky; in rare instances may be spirals.
- Motility—Positive.
- Flagella—Single flagellum.
- Staining—Gram negative; chromatic granule generally present in center.
- Size—2.0 to 4.0 μ in length.
- Habitat—Soil.

Cultural Characteristics—Quick yellowish growth.
- Agar—No growth unless enriched.
- Hydrocellulose agar—Growth without clearing.
- Cellulose silica gel medium—Mucilaginous colonies.

Physiological Characteristics
- Starch hydrolysis—Negative.
- Cellulose—Oxidized but no gas or reducing substances formed.
- Gum tragacanth—Not hydrolyzed.
- Fermentation reactions
  - Monosaccharides
    - Glucose—No action.
- Growth factors
  - Oxygen—Facultatively aerobic.
  - Temperature
    - Optimum—20 C.
  - Nutrition—Experimental results indicate that sodium chloride and phosphates or sulfate are required for propagation.
- Color and light characteristics—Produces diffuse yellowish light.
  - Chromogenesis—Yellowish color on filter paper streaks in 36 to 48 hours.

Biochemical Characteristics
- Enzyme production—Elaborates enzyme which can disintegrate vegetable fibers.

Chromobacterium janthinum

Taxonomy
- Order — *Eubacteriales*
- Family — *Rhizobiaceae*
- Genus — *Chromobacterium*
- Species — *janthinum*

Cellular Characteristics
- Morphology—Rods.
- Motility—Motile.
- Flagella—Peritrichous.
- Staining—Gram negative.

Size—0.5 to 0.8 by 1.5 to 5.0 μ.
Habitat—Water and soil.

Cultural Characteristics
Agar colonies—Center is creamy; edge is violet.
Agar stroke—Yellow, glistening, moist, turning deep violet.
Gelatin colonies—Circular; yellow turning violet.
Gelatin stab—Infundibuliform liquefaction; surface is white to violet.
Broth—Pellicle, turbid.
Potato—Spreading growth, violet to black.

Physiological Characteristics
Biochemical action
Indole production—Negative.
Nitrite—Usually formed from nitrate.
Indicator reactions
Litmus milk—Coagulation in time, producing a violet color decolorized beneath surface.
Fermentation reactions
Monosaccharides
Glucose—Acid.
Disaccharides
Lactose—No acid.
Sucrose—No acid.
Maltose—No acid.
Growth factors
Oxygen—Facultatively aerobic.
Temperature
Optimum—30 C.
Good growth—37 C.
No growth—2 to 4 C.
Color and light characteristics
Chromogenesis—Violet color in culture media.

Pathogenicity
Human beings and animals—Cause of a fatal septicemia.

Clostridium acetobutylicum

Taxonomy

Order	*Eubacteriales*
Family	*Bacillaceae*
Genus	*Clostridium*
Species	*acetobutylicum*

Cellular Characteristics
Morphology—Rods.
Motility—Motile.
Flagella—Peritrichous.
Staining—Gram positive becoming gram negative.
Occurring—Singly and in pairs, not in chains.
Size—0.6 to 0.72 by 2.6 to 4.7 μ.
Habitat—Principally in agricultural soils.
Spores—Clostridial; swelling rods.
Position—Eccentric to subterminal.
Granulose reaction—Positive.
Size—1.3 to 1.6 by 4.7 to 5.5 μ.

Cultural Characteristics
Glucose agar surface colonies—Compact, raised, and regular (anaerobic).
Deep glucose agar colonies—Compact and smooth; agar fragmented by gas.

Physiological Characteristics
Biochemical action
Indole production—Negative.
Hydrogen sulfide—Produced from thiosulfate or sulfite.
Nitrite—Not formed or reduced.
Nitrogen—Fixed.
Protein liquefaction or digestion
Glucose gelatin—Liquefied.
Blood serum—Not liquefied.
Indicator reactions
Litmus milk—Acid, stormy fermentation, casein coagulated, clot broken up but not digested.
Fermentation reactions
Monosaccharides
Arabinose—Acid and gas.
Rhamnose—Acid and gas.
Xylose—Acid and gas.

Glucose—Acid and gas.
Fructose—Acid and gas.
Galactose—Acid and gas.
Mannose—Acid and gas.
Disaccharides
Lactose—Acid and gas.
Sucrose—Acid and gas.
Maltose—Acid and gas.
Melibiose—Acid and gas.
Polyalcohols
Glycerol—Acid and gas.
D-Arabitol—Acid and gas.
Sorbitol—Acid and gas.
Dulcitol—Acid and gas.
Adonitol—Acid and gas.
Growth factors
Oxygen—Anaerobic.
Temperature
Optimum—About 37 C.
Range—20 to 47 C.
Nutrition—Biotin necessary.

Biochemical Characteristics
Enzyme production—Amylases formed.
Vitamin production—Riboflavin produced.
Chemical end products—Butyl alcohol, ethyl alcohol, acetone, acetic acid, hydrogen, and carbon dioxide.

Industrial Utilization
Products—Manufacture of butyl alcohol, ethyl alcohol, and acetone.
Processes — Acetone-butanol fermentation; production of riboflavin; assists lactic acid bacteria to produce *i*-lactic acid.

Addenda. Unfermentable sugar by yeast in the Giordani-Leone process can be used by the organism for the production of butyl alcohol, acetone, and ethyl alcohol.

Bacillus granulobacter pectinovorum gives four times as much acetone as the Fernbach organism. *B. granulobacter pectinovorum* was an early name for *C. acetobutylicum.*

The organism can cause lactic acid bacteria to produce inactive lactic acid.

This organism produces large amounts of water-soluble B vitamin in a whey medium. Metals can affect the synthesis of the vitamins, especially riboflavin.

Amylase and maltase are considered as adaptive enzymes for the organism. It is not activated by chloride ions.

Clostridium botulinum, Type B

Taxonomy
Order — *Eubacteriales*
Family — *Bacillaceae*
Genus — *Clostridium*
Species — *botulinum*
Type — B

Cellular Characteristics
Morphology—Large rods with rounded ends.
Motility—Motile.
Flagella—Peritrichous.
Staining—Gram positive; stains with aniline dyes, nonacid-fast.
Occurring—Singly, in pairs, or in short chains.
Size—0.5 to 0.8 by 3.0 to 8.0 μ.
Spores—Oval.
Position—Central, subterminal; when maturing, terminal with swelling of cell.
Habitat—Probably soil.

Cultural Characteristics
Deep liver agar colonies—Dense center.
Liver agar stroke—No growth.
Nutrient broth—No growth.
Liver broth—Good growth, turbidity, gas.
Brain medium—Not blackened or digested.
Cooked meat medium—Good growth; digestion of medium; gas is formed; blackening occurs.
Blood agar—Alpha type hemolysis.

Physiological Characteristics
Biochemical action
Indole production—Negative.
Hydrogen sulfide production—Positive.
Ammonia—Produced.
Nitrate—No action.
Milk—Acid after a period of time; no gas; no coagulation.
Protein liquefaction or digestion
Blood serum—Not liquefied.
Egg albumin—Not liquefied.
Gelatin—Liquefied.
Fermentation reactions
Monosaccharides
Glucose—Acid and gas.
Fructose—Acid and gas.
Galactose—No fermentation.
Disaccharides
Lactose—Not fermented.
Sucrose—Not fermented.
Maltose—Acid and gas.
Polysaccharides
Dextrin—Acid and gas.
Polyalcohols
Adonitol—Acid and gas.
Growth factors
Oxygen—Strictly anaerobic.
Temperature
Optimum—Between 20 and 30 C; 30 C.
Resistance—Spores are resistant to dry heat for 15 to 20 minutes at 180 C; moist heat for 3 to 5 hours at 100 C.

Serology
Grouping—Species are separated on basis of ovolysis: *C. botulinum* types are nonovolytic; *C. parabotulinum* are ovolytic. *C. botulinum* types B and E affect man; types C and D affect lower animals.
Antitoxin—*C. botulinum* type B toxin is neutralized by antitoxin produced with *C. parabotulinum.*

Biochemical Characteristics
Toxin production—Very potent neurotoxic exotoxin produced; causes hemolysis of human and horse red blood cells. Not affected by gastric juice; may be destroyed by heating at 80 C for 30 minutes or at 100 C for 10 minutes. Maximum toxin production by organism at 28 C.

Pathogenicity
Human beings—Ingestion of food, particularly spoiled canned vegetables and meats containing the toxin results in food poisoning called botulism. The toxin is absorbed from the stomach and intestines. It affects the nerves and muscles.
Animals—Guinea pigs have been killed by a 0.00001 ml dose of toxin; chickens may be affected.

Spoilage
Food—A cause of food spoilage, especially of home canned vegetables and meats.

Clostridium botulinum Type C

Taxonomy

Order	*Eubacteriales*
Family	*Bacillaceae*
Genus	*Clostridium*
Species	*botulinum*
Type	C

Cellular Characteristics—See *C. botulinum* type B.
Morphology—Rods, usually slightly curved.
Size—0.5 to 0.8 by 3.0 to 6.0 μ.

Cultural Characteristics
Glucose agar deep colonies—No central nucleus, fluffy; no gas.
Liver agar deep colonies—Lenticular, then fluffy; gas formed.

Physiological Characteristics
Fermentation reactions
Monosaccharides
Arabinose—Not fermented.
Rhamnose—Not fermented.
Xylose—Not fermented.
Glucose—Acid and gas.
Fructose—Acid and gas.
Galactose—Acid and gas.
Disaccharides
Lactose—Not fermented.
Sucrose—Not fermented.
Maltose—Acid and gas.
Polysaccharides
Raffinose—Not fermented.
Inulin—Not fermented.
Dextrin—Weakly fermented.
Polyalcohols
Glycerol—Acid and gas.
Mannitol—Not fermented.
Dulcitol—Not fermented
Adonitol—Not fermented.
Glucosides
Salicin—Not fermented.
Growth factors
Oxygen—Strictly anaerobic.
Temperature—Good growth at 37 C.
Serology
Antitoxin—Homologous antitoxin will neutralize toxin, but antitoxin of *B. parabotulinum* (Seddon type Cβ) will not.
Biochemical Characteristics
Toxin production—Powerful neurotoxic exotoxin produced.
Pathogenicity
Animals—Pathogenic to animals; causes limberneck in chickens.

Clostridium butylicum

Taxonomy
Order *Eubacteriales*
Family *Bacillaceae*
Genus *Clostridium*
Species *butylicum*
Cellular Characteristics
Morphology—Straight or curved rods, rounded ends.
Motility—Motile.
Flagella—Peritrichous.
Staining—Gram positive becoming gram negative; cells contain glycogen, stain yellow with iodine.
Granulose—Positive in clostridial stage.
Occurring—Singly, in pairs, or in short chains.
Size—0.7 by 5.0 to 7.0 μ.
Habitat—Soils rich in humus; starchy plant materials undergoing natural fermentation.
Spores—Oval.
Position—Eccentric to subterminal.
Size—Large.
Cultural Characteristics
Glucose agar colonies—Circular or slightly irregular, moist creamy-white, raised.
Deep glucose agar—Biconvex, yellowish-white, entire colonies, fragmented by gas.
Glucose broth—Abundant growth, gas turbidity.
Broth, plain—Little growth.
Physiological Characteristics
Biochemical action
Indole production—Negative.
Methyl red—Positive.
Voges-Proskauer—Negative.
Catalase—Negative.
Ammonia—Slight positive.
Nitrogen—Fixed from atmosphere.
Nitrite—Not formed from nitrate.
Protein liquefaction or digestion
Gelatin—Not liquefied.
Glucose gelatin—Not liquefied.
Blood agar—Not hemolyzed.
Coagulated albumin—Probably not liquefied.

Indicator reactions
Litmus milk—Acid; quick coagulation; stormy fermentation.
Fermentation reactions
Monosaccharides
Xylose—Acid and gas.
Glucose—Acid and gas.
Disaccharides
Lactose—Acid and gas.
Sucrose—Acid and gas.
Polysaccharides
Starch, potato—Acid and gas.
Maize mash starch—Not fermented.
Cellulose—Not fermented.
Pectin—Not fermented.
Polyalcohols
Glycerol—Not fermented.
Glycosides
Amygdalin—Not fermented.
Esculin—Fermented.
Salicin—Fermented.
Growth factors
Oxygen—Anaerobic.
Temperature
Optimum—30 C.
This range is for optimum
Range—30 to 37 C.
Biochemical Characteristics
Chemical end products—Acetic acid, butyric acid, ethyl alcohol, isopropyl alcohol, butyl alcohol, and acetone.
Industrial Utilization
Processes—Used in the butanol-acetone fermentation.
Pathogenicity
Animals—Nonpathogenic for guinea pig and rabbit.
Spoilage
Food—Can cause "late gas" defect in cheese; the cheese becomes spoiled because of the cracks, fissures, and holes in the product.

Clostridium histolyticum

Taxonomy
Order *Eubacteriales*
Family *Bacillaceae*
Genus *Clostridium*
Species *histolyticum*
Cellular Characteristics
Morphology—Rods, rounded ends, parallel sides; in older cultures irregular forms.
Motility—Motile.
Flagella—Peritrichous.
Staining—Gram positive in young cultures.
Occurring—Singly and in pairs.
Size—0.5 to 0.7 by 3.0 to 5.0 μ.
Spores—Oval, swelling.
Position—Subterminal, wider than organism.
Habitat—Soil; isolated from war wounds.
Cultural Characteristics
Deep agar colonies—Lenticular, lobate, fluffy.
Blood agar surface colonies—Dew drop, minute and round.
Gelatin stab—Completely liquefied in 24 hours.
Nutrient broth—Turbid, slight precipitate.
Horse blood agar colonies—No hemolysis; irregular round, lobate edge, raised.
Löffler's serum—Digested after 2 weeks.
Cooked meat medium—Good growth; gas, black medium after 2 weeks.
Physiological Characteristics
Biochemical action
Indole production—Negative.
Ammonia—Negative.
Nitrite—Not produced from nitrate.
Voges-Proskauer—Negative.
Protein liquefaction or digestion
Gelatin—Liquefied.
Blood serum—Slowly liquefied, darkened.

Egg-meat medium—Reddish to dark digestion, little gas; tyrosine crystals abundant after 1 week.
Brain medium—Blackened, digested, putrefactive odor.
Indicator reactions
Litmus milk—Soft coagulation, some digestion, little gas.
Methylene blue reduction—Negative.
Fermentation reactions
Carbohydrates—Not fermented.
Growth factors
Oxygen—Microaerophilic.
Temperature
Optimum—37 C.
Thermal death time—Killed in 6 minutes at 105 C (moist) (young cultures).
Biochemical Characteristics
Exotoxin—Produced; cytolytic; local necrosis and sloughing after injections; not toxic on ingestion.
Serology
Antigens—Culture filtrates contain 3 toxic antigens: an α-component that is a necrotizing and lethal toxin; a β-component, namely, collagenase; and a γ-component that is a proteinase which can use processed collagen but not native collagen as a substrate.
Group—Belongs to group three of the proteolytic clostridia.
Biochemical Characteristics
Enzyme and toxin production—Collagenase, proteinase, lethal and necrotizing toxin, and hemolysin produced; the latter two can be produced with a liver digest glucose medium.
Pathogenicity
Animals—Pathogenic for small animals used in the laboratory.

Addenda. Hemolysin is inactivated by surface denaturation, oxidation, heat, agitation, acids, and alkalies and can be absorbed by erythrocytes.

Lethal toxin of organism is resistant to oxidation and surface denaturation; it is inactivated by heating at 55 C for 10 minutes and by treatment with trypsin and papain; it is somewhat more resistant to heat and can withstand agitation.

Iron milk digested and blackened.

Clostridium parabotulinum

Taxonomy
Order *Eubacteriales*
Family *Bacillaceae*
Genus *Clostridium*
Species *parabotulinum*
Cellular Characteristics
Morphology—Rods with rounded ends.
Motility—Motile.
Flagella—Peritrichous.
Staining—Gram positive.
Occurring—Singly, in pairs, or in short chains.
Size—0.5 to 0.8 by 3.0 to 8.0 μ.
Spores—Oval.
Position—Subterminal with distinct swelling of cell.
Habitat—Soil.
Cultural Characteristics
Deep liver agar colonies—Compact discs with dense nucleus at edge.
Liver agar stroke—Anaerobic growth profuse and moist.
Egg yolk agar surface colonies—Raised, irregular edge, lustrous.
Nutrient broth—Abundant growth with some turbidity; some strains agglutinate.
Liver broth—Luxuriant growth, turbidity.
Physiological Characteristics
Biochemical action
Milk—Slow precipitation and curdling followed by digestion and darkening; slightly acid.

Protein liquefaction or digestion
- Gelatin—Liquefied.
- Coagulated egg albumin—Liquefied.
- Brain medium—Digested with production of putrefactive odor, blackened.
- Meat medium—Digested with production of putrefactive odor, blackened; tyrosine crystals not formed.

Fermentation reactions
- Monosaccharides
  - Arabinose—Not fermented.
  - Rhamnose—Not fermented.
  - Xylose—Not fermented.
  - Glucose—Acid and gas.
  - Fructose—Acid and gas.
  - Galactose—Not fermented.
- Disaccharides
  - Lactose—Not fermented.
  - Sucrose—Not fermented.
  - Maltose—Acid and gas.
- Polysaccharides
  - Raffinose—Not fermented.
  - Inulin—Not fermented.
  - Dextrin—Acid and gas.
- Polyalcohols
  - Glycerol—Acid and gas.
  - Mannitol—Not fermented.
  - Dulcitol—Not fermented.
  - Adonitol—Not fermented.
  - Inositol—Not fermented.
- Glucosides
  - Salicin—Acid and gas.

Growth factors
- Oxygen—Anaerobic.
- Temperature
  - Optimum—Between 35 and 37 C.

Serology
- Grouping—*C. parabotulinum* types are proteolytic and ovolytic, with activity of type B on liquefaction of coagulated egg albumin more pronounced than type A as compared with *C. botulinum* types which are nonovolytic; types generally identified by antitoxin protection tests.
- Antitoxin—Toxin neutralized by homologous antitoxin.

Biochemical Characteristics
- Toxin production—Very potent neurotoxic exotoxin produced; type A toxin isolated and crystallized, molecular weight *ca.* 900,000, a mouse MLD is 3.1×10^{-10} g; type B toxin has a molecular weight of about 60,000.

Pathogenicity
- Human beings—Ingestion of food, particularly of spoiled nonacid canned vegetable and meat products containing the toxins of *C. parabotulinum*, results in a type of food poisoning known as botulism. It affects the nerves and muscles.
- Animals—Pathogenic to animals.

Spoilage
- Food—A cause of food spoilage, especially of improperly processed, home canned, nonacid vegetables and meats.

Clostridium perfringens

Taxonomy

Order	*Eubacteriales*
Family	*Bacillaceae*
Genus	*Clostridium*
Species	*perfringens*

Cellular Characteristics
- Morphology—Short, thick rods.
- Motility—Nonmotile.
- Capsules—Present.
- Staining—Gram positive.
- Occurring—Singly and in pairs.
- Size—1.0 to 1.5 by 4.0 to 8.0 μ.
- Habitat—Soil, feces, sewage; isolated from cases of gaseous gangrene.

Spores—Oval, not swelling.
Position—Central to eccentric.

Cultural Characteristics
Agar surface colonies—Circular, raised, opaque, moist, entire.
Broth—Turbid, peptolytic.
Potato—Thin, grayish-white streak; gas.

Physiological Characteristics
Biochemical action
Indole production—Negative.
Nitrite—Produced from nitrate.
Protein liquefaction or digestion
Gelatin—Liquefied and blackened.
Blood serum—Not liquefied.
Coagulated albumin—Not liquefied.
Egg-meat—Abundant gas production in 7 to 10 hours; no digestion.
Brain medium—Not blackened.
Indicator reactions
Litmus milk—Acid, coagulated, gas formed; clot not digested.
Fermentation reactions
Monosaccharides
Glucose—Acid and gas.
Fructose—Acid and gas.
Galactose—Acid and gas.
Mannose—Acid and gas.
Disaccharides
Lactose—Acid and gas.
Sucrose—Acid and gas.
Maltose—Acid and gas.
Polysaccharides
Raffinose—Acid and gas.
Starch—Acid and gas.
Inulin—Variable.
Glycogen—Acid and gas.
Polyalcohols
Glycerol—Variable.
Mannitol—Not fermented.
Growth factors
Oxygen—Anaerobic.
Temperature
Optimum—35 to 37 C.
Range—Up to 50 C.

Biochemical Characteristics
Exotoxin—Produced.

Medical Utilization
Processes—Antitoxin prepared from horses by uses of the exotoxin.

Pathogenicity
Human beings—When absorbed from intestinal tract may cause a fatal enterotoxemia. Causes gangrene.
Animals—Causes an enterotoxemia in cattle and sheep; pathogenic for guinea pigs, pigeons, and mice.

Differentiation
C. perfringens types—Differentiated by fermentation reactions.

	Glycerol	*Inulin*
Type I	+	+
II	−	+
III	+	−
IV	−	−

Addenda. There are six types differentiated on the basis of toxin production. Type A causes human gas gangrene, B lamb dysentery, C sheep "struck," D lamb pulpy kidney and horse grass illness, E enterotoxemia, and F human enteritis necroticans.

Long chains of the organism may be found when the organism comes into contact with penicillin. Filamentous cells may be a result of the organism growing in the absence of magnesium, potassium, and iron.

Induced lysis may be brought on by suspending the organism (washed cells) in a 0.15 *M* phosphate buffer at pH 7.2 at 45 C. Glucose, cysteine, and sodium pyruvate protect the organism from lysis.

Colonies of strain A are surrounded by narrow zones of complete hemolysis. Type F strains do not have an inner zone of complete hemolysis. Strains of types B and C on sheep blood agar may have large zones of hemolysis. In deep shake agar, colonies are usually lenticular or look like commas. The organism can reduce sulfite to sulfide.

Clostridium septicum

Taxonomy
- Order *Eubacteriales*
- Family *Bacillaceae*
- Genus *Clostridium*
- Species *septicum*

Cellular Characteristics
- Morphology—Rod-shaped, rounded ends; from animal body may be boot-shaped, or lemon-shaped, or may form long filaments; pleomorphism on agar.
- Motility—Motile.
- Flagella—Peritrichous.
- Capsules—No capsule.
- Staining—Gram positive when young; gram negative in older cultures.
- Habitat—Soil.
- Spores—Oval, wider than organism.
  - Position—Subterminal.

Cultural Characteristics
- Agar colonies—Not regularly round, filamentous, translucent, honeycombed surface, grayish by reflected light, bluish by transmitted light.
- Nutrient broth—Slight turbidity; moderate growth.
- Horse blood agar—α-Hemolysis in the beginning; β after several days.
- Löffler's serum—Good growth after 2 weeks; no liquefaction.
- Coagulated egg—Good granular growth after 2 weeks; no digestion.

Physiological Characteristics
- Biochemical action
  - Indole production—Negative.
  - Methyl red reaction—Negative.
  - Voges-Proskauer test—Negative.
  - Hydrogen sulfide production—Positive.
  - Ammonia—Slight positive.
  - Nitrate—Reduced to nitrite.
  - Catalase—Negative.
- Protein liquefaction or digestion
  - Gelatin—Liquefied after a week; gas bubbles.
  - Blood serum—Hemolysis on horse blood; hemolysis of human and sheep's blood; not liquefied.
  - Albumin—Not liquefied.
- Indicator reactions
  - Litmus milk—Acid, some gas, clot.
- Fermentation reactions
  - Monosaccharides
    - Glucose—Acid and gas.
    - Fructose—Acid and gas.
    - Galactose—Acid and gas.
  - Disaccharides
    - Lactose—Acid and gas.
    - Sucrose—Not fermented.
    - Maltose—Acid and gas.
  - Polysaccharides
    - Inulin—No acid or gas.
  - Alcohols and polyalcohols
    - Glycerol—No acid or gas.
    - Mannitol—No acid or gas.
  - Glycosides
    - Salicin—Acid and gas.
- Growth factors
  - Oxygen—Strict anaerobe.
  - Temperature
    - Optimum—37 C.
- Color and light characteristics
  - Fluorescence—Green fluorescence on MacConkey agar; differentiation from *C. feseri* and *C. novyi.*

Serology
- Antigenic grouping—Strains are differentiated into 4 groups by O antigen and each group into specific types by H antigen. There is some cross reaction with O antigen of *C. feseri* but not with H antigen.

Biochemical Characteristics
- Enzyme production—Hyaluronidase, col-

lagenase, desoxyribonuclease produced.

Toxin—Hemolytic and lethal exotoxin produced.

Lysin—Fibrinolysin formed.

Pathogenicity

Human beings—Pathogenic; isolated from appendicitis cases and from war wounds.

Animals—Causes edema, swelling, infiltration of cellular tissue in sheep, horses and cattle. Pathogenic experimentally to guinea pigs, rabbits, mice, pigeons. Pathogenicity can be retained for years by subculture.

Addenda. Differentiation of *C. septicum* from *C. chauvoei:*

C. septicum	*C. chauvoei*
Found in wounds	Not found in wound cultures
Pathogenic for laboratory animals	Less pathogenic for laboratory animals
Produces gas (more) in tissues	Produces gas (less) in tissues
Ferments salicin	Ferments sucrose

Clostridium tetani

Taxonomy

Order	*Eubacteriales*
Family	*Bacillaceae*
Genus	*Clostridium*
Species	*tetani*

Cellular Characteristics

Morphology—Rods with rounded ends, drumstick appearance; curved filamentous forms may be produced.

Motility—Motile.

Flagella—Peritrichous.

Staining—Gram positive.

Occurring—Singly, in pairs, long chains or filaments.

Size—0.4 to 0.6 by 4.0 to 8.0 μ.

Habitat—Soils.

Spores—Clostridial, spherical and swelling; stain easily when young.

Position—Terminal.

Cultural Characteristics

Agar colonies—Irregular, glistening, yellowish-gray after 4 days.

Deep agar colonies—Like cotton spheres, fluffy.

Serum agar surface colonies—Small, transparent, and fringed.

Broth—Slightly turbid, gas; sedimentation in some strains.

Horse blood agar colonies—Rounded, translucent, granular surface; hemolysis may occur.

Physiological Characteristics

Biochemical action

Indole production—Positive.

Voges-Proskauer test—Negative.

Nitrite—Not formed from nitrate.

Protein liquefaction or digestion

Gelatin—Slowly liquefied and blackened.

Blood agar—Hemolyzed.

Blood serum—Slowly liquefied.

Brain medium—Blackened, slowly digested.

Coagulated albumin—Slowly liquefied.

Indicator reactions

Litmus milk—Casein precipitated, slowly clotted; little gas.

Methylene blue reductase test—Negative.

Fermentation reactions

Carbohydrates—Not fermented.

Growth factors

Oxygen—Strictly anaerobic.

Temperature

Optimum—37 C.

Thermal death time—105 C for 3 to 25 minutes; spores resist boiling for 1 hour.

Resistance—Killed by 5 per cent phenol.

Biochemical Characteristics
Exotoxin—Formed; extremely poisonous; unstable and destroyed in 5 minutes by heating at 65 C or exposure to acid or alkali; precipitated by ammonium sulfate.

Serology
Antigenic grouping—At least 10 types on basis of H antigen; all types produce lethal exotoxin; type VI is a nonflagellated strain.

Medical Utilization
Products—Toxoid prepared from toxin.
Processes—Antitoxin preparation; despeciated antitoxin preparation; purified toxin; purified toxoid.

Pathogenicity
Human beings—Cause of tetanus or lockjaw; toxin taken up by motor end nerves and then to the central nervous system.
Animals—Toxic on injection but not by feeding.

Clostridium thermosaccharolyticum

Taxonomy

Order	*Eubacteriales*
Family	*Bacillaceae*
Genus	*Clostridium*
Species	*thermosaccharolyticum*

Cellular Characteristics
Morphology—Rods, slender.
Motility—Motile.
Flagella—Peritrichous.
Staining—Gram negative.
Occurring—Singly and in pairs.
Size—0.4 to 0.7 by 3.5 to 7.5 μ.
Spores—Spherical, swollen cells.
Position—Terminal.
Habitat—Soil; isolated from hard swells of canned goods.

Cultural Characteristics
Deep glucose tryptophane agar—Colonies, small, smooth, lenticular.
Liver infusion broth—Turbidity and gas.
Pea-infusion agar—Surface colonies, granular, grayish-white, center raised, feathery edges.

Physiological Characteristics
Biochemical action
Indole production—Negative.
Nitrite—Not formed from nitrate.
Protein liquefaction
Gelatin—Not liquefied.
Blood serum—Not liquefied.
Brain medium—Not digested or blackened.
Indicator reactions
Litmus milk—Reduced, acid, firm coagulation, gas, clot not digested.
Fermentation reactions
Monosaccharides
Arabinose—Acid and gas.
Xylose—Acid and gas.
Rhamnose—Not fermented.
Glucose—Acid and gas.
Galactose—Acid and gas.
Mannose—Acid and gas.
Fructose—Acid and gas.
Disaccharides
Lactose—Acid and gas.
Sucrose—Acid and gas.
Maltose—Acid and gas.
Cellobiose—Acid and gas.
Trehalose—Acid and gas.
Polysaccharides
Raffinose—Weakly fermented.
Starch, corn—Acid and gas.
Dextrin—Acid and gas.
Pectin—Not fermented.
Glycogen—Acid and gas.
Cellulose—Not fermented.
Polyalcohols
Dulcitol—Not fermented.
Glycerol—Not fermented.
Sorbitol—Not fermented.

Erythritol—Not fermented.
Quercitol—Not fermented.
Mannitol—Not fermented.
Inositol—Not fermented.
Glycosides
alpha-Methyl glucoside—Acid and gas.
Esculin—Acid and gas.
Salicin—Acid and gas.
Amygdalin—Acid and gas.
Organic acid salts
Calcium lactate—Not fermented.
Growth factors
Oxygen—Anaerobic.
Temperature
Optimum—55 to 62 C; high-temperature organism.
Spoilage
Food—Produces hard swells in canned goods.

Corynebacterium diphtheriae

Taxonomy
Order *Eubacteriales*
Family *Corynebacteriaceae*
Genus *Corynebacterium*
Species *diphtheriae*
Common Names Klebs-Löffler or diphtheria bacillus

Cellular Characteristics
Morphology—Rods which may be curved; at times swollen at one or both ends.
Motility—Nonmotile.
Staining—Usually staining is unequal; alternate bands of stained and unstained material are observed; older cultures may not be gram positive.
Occurring—Singly.
Size—0.3 to 0.8 by 1.0 to 8.0 μ.
Habitat—Diphtheria cases in man.

Cultural Characteristics
Colony forms
Smooth colony—Round, convex with smooth surface and margin; opaque by transmitted light; glistening and moist; 1 to 3 mm in diameter.
Rough colony—Pitted and uneven surface; little light is reflected from surface; translucent by transmitted light.
Dwarf colony—Very small colonies with round and even margins; convex surface; less than 0.2 mm in diameter.
Intermediate colonies—Incomplete R and S types.
Agar stroke—Grayish, granular translucent growth.
Gelatin colonies—Grayish, small lobate, slow growth.
Gelatin stab—No liquefaction, slow growth.
Blood tellurite medium colonies—Gray to black.
Potato—Whitish, scanty growth.

Physiological Characteristics
Biochemical action
Indole production—Negative.
Nitrite—Produced from nitrate.
Urea—Hydrolyzed.
Protein liquefaction or digestion
Gelatin—Not liquefied.
Indicator reactions
Litmus milk—Steady growth, no change in milk.
Fermentation reactions
Monosaccharides
Glucose—Acid.
Fructose—Acid.
Galactose—Acid with some strains.
Disaccharides
Maltose—Acid with some strains.
Sucrose—Acid with some strains.
Polysaccharides
Dextrin—Acid with some strains.

Polyalcohols
Glycerol—Acid with some strains.
Growth factors
Oxygen—Facultatively aerobic.
Temperature
Optimum—34 to 37 C.
Nutrition—Requires many amino acids and magnesium.

Serology—11 serological types.

Biochemical Characteristics
Enzyme production—Phosphorylase produced.
Toxin production—Powerful exotoxin produced.

Medical Utilization
Products—Toxoid and purified toxoid prepared from toxin.
Processes—Antitoxin preparation; despeciated antitoxin preparation.

Pathogenicity
Human beings—Cause of diphtheria.

Addenda. A method devised to test for the organism in anaerobic cultures combining the Koch and the Clauberg-Hermann plate methods with oxygen reducing pyrogallol soda or potash-silicon earth procedure.

Diphtheria toxin injected into dogs increased the potassium in serum.

The protein fraction of the organism found in the cell wall appears to be different than the fraction of the intercellular components.

The toxin can be produced *in vitro* in a medium having a pH of 7.8 to 8.0, iron concentration (0.14 g/l; 5 g/l is killing), and a large surface area. The toxin is destroyed by a temperature of 75 to 80 C. It deteriorates when exposed to light by means of oxidation. It is also inactivated by digestive juices and a pH of 6 or less. The toxin can also be concentrated by salting out, dialyzing, and dehydration. It will keep at 70 C. A potent and neutralizing antitoxin can be produced by repeated injections (subminimal) of the toxin into experimental animals. A medium containing glutamic acid, cystine, proline, tryptophane, leucine, valine, methionine, glycine, ammonium sulfate, trace metals, inorganic salts, maltose, growth factors (thiamine) can be used to obtain high toxin concentration.

Acetylation at pH 6 destroys the toxicity of the toxin by affecting the ability to combine and flocculate with antitoxin.

A lysogenic phage is responsible for toxin production in so-called "virulent" strains of *C. diphtheriae.*

Mitochondria of the organism show oxidation-reduction activity (not with Nadi reagent); are sudanophilic and nonbasophilic. Metachromatic granules are also sudanophilic, removable only with ribonuclease.

Polyphosphate reaches a peak of accumulation just before cell division and a low at the end of division periods. The increase and decrease of polyphosphate are said to be related to cell division.

Corynebacterium diphtheriae type *gravis*

Taxonomy
Order — *Eubacteriales*
Family — *Corynebacteriaceae*
Genus — *Corynebacterium*
Species — *diphtheriae*
Type — *gravis*

Cellular Characteristics—See *C. diphtheriae;* has few metachromatic granules of small size.

Cultural Characteristics
McLeod's blood-tellurite medium—Dark-gray, daisy-like colonies.
Broth—Pellicle, granular deposit, relatively quick reversal of pH.

Physiological Characteristics
Biochemical action—Nonhemolytic.
Fermentation reactions
Polysaccharides

Starch—Fermented.
Dextrin—Fermented.
Glycogen—Fermented.

Biochemical Characteristics
Toxin production—Potent exotoxin produced; tolerates heat better than *C. diphtheriae* type *mitis.*

Growth factors—See *C. diphtheriae.*
Nutrition—Brewers' yeast contains many factors required for growth.

Pathogenicity
Animals—Pathogenicity for guinea pigs is high, for mice, moderate.

Corynebacterium diphtheriae type *intermedius*

Taxonomy

Order	*Eubacteriales*
Family	*Corynebacteriaceae*
Genus	*Corynebacterium*
Species	*diphtheriae*
Type	*intermedius*

Cellular Characteristics—See *C. diphtheriae;* marked barring of bacilli.

Cultural Characteristics
McLeod's blood-tellurite medium colonies—Small, flat, raised black center, crenated edge.
Broth—Fine granular deposit; no pellicle and no reversal of pH.

Physiological Characteristics
Biochemical action—Nonhemolytic.
Fermentation reactions
Polysaccharides
Starch—Not fermented.
Glycogen—Not fermented.
Dextrin—Variable.

Pathogenicity
Animals—Pathogenicity for mice is low; only about 10 per cent nonpathogenic for guinea pigs.

Corynebacterium diphtheriae type *mitis*

Taxonomy

Order	*Eubacteriales*
Family	*Corynebacteriaceae*
Genus	*Corynebacterium*
Species	*diphtheriae*
Type	*mitis*

Cellular Characteristics—See *C. diphtheriae;* long forms with prominent metachromatic granules.

Cultural Characteristics
McLeod's blood-tellurite medium colonies—Smooth, moist, convex, shiny black, entire.
Broth—Uniform suspensions, diffuse turbidity; pellicle appears late or not at all; later reversal of pH.

Physiological characteristics
Biochemical action—Hemolytic.
Fermentation reactions
Polysaccharides
Starch—Not fermented.
Dextrin—Variable.
Glycogen—Not fermented.

Pathogenicity
Animals—Pathogenic for mice; about 10 to 20 per cent nonpathogenic for guinea pigs.

Corynebacterium murisepticum

Taxonomy

Order	*Eubacteriales*
Family	*Corynebacteriaceae*
Genus	*Corynebacterium*
Species	*murisepticum*

Cellular Characteristics
Morphology—Slender rods, polar granules.
Motility—Nonmotile.
Staining—Gram positive.

Occurring—Can grow into long filaments.
Size—1.2 to 1.5 μ.
Cultural Characteristics
Gelatin stab—Poor growth, fimbriate growth along line of stab.
Löffler's blood serum—Good growth.
Egg glycerol broth—Good growth.
Broth—Turbid.
Potato—Good growth.
Physiological Characteristics
Biochemical action
Indole production—Negative.
Hydrogen sulfide production—Positive.
Indicator reactions
Litmus milk—No coagulation; acid.
Fermentation reactions
Monosaccharides
Arabinose—Not fermented.
Glucose—Acid.
Fructose—Acid.
Galactose—Acid.
Disaccharides
Lactose—Acid.
Sucrose—Acid.
Maltose—Acid.
Polysaccharides
Inulin—Acid.
Alcohols and polyalcohols
Mannitol—Acid.
Isodulcitol—Not fermented.
Growth factors
Oxygen—Facultatively aerobic.
Temperature
Optimum—37 C.
Pathogenicity
Human beings—No evidence of pathogenicity to man.
Animals—Causes septicemia in mice.

Corynebacterium pyogenes

Taxonomy
Order *Eubacteriales*
Family *Corynebacteriaceae*
Genus *Corynebacterium*
Species *pyogenes*
Cellular Characteristics
Morphology—Rods, club forms may be present.
Motility—Nonmotile.
Staining—Gram positive.
Occurring—Chains formed.
Size—0.2 by 0.3 to 2 μ in length; some scarcely visible.
Habitat—Abscesses in cattle, swine, and other domestic animals.
Cultural Characteristics—Does not grow on ordinary agar.
Serum agar colonies—Minute after 2 days. Surface colonies may increase in size to 3 mm in diameter; colonies appear smoky-brown by transmitted light and bluish-white by reflected light.
Bovine blood serum slants—Areas of liquefaction.
Serum bouillon—Flocculent grayish flakes; sediment formed.
Physiological Characteristics
Biochemical action
Indole production—Negative.
Nitrate—Not reduced to nitrite.
Milk—Coagulation after 2 days; acid at bottom; whey separated; peptonization.
Protein liquefaction or digestion
Serum gelatin—Liquefied.
Blood serum—Beta hemolysis; does not utilize hemoglobin.
Löffler's coagulated medium—Liquefied.
Fermentation reactions
Monosaccharides
Xylose—Acid formed in serum bouillon.
Glucose—Acid formed in serum bouillon.
Disaccharides

Lactose—Acid formed in serum bouillon.
Sucrose—Acid formed in serum bouillon.
Polysaccharides
Raffinose—No acid.
Inulin—No acid.
Alcohols and polyalcohols
Mannitol—No acid.
Glucosides
Salicin—No acid.
Growth factors
Oxygen—Aerobic and anaerobic.
Temperature
Optimum—37 C.
Range—20 C and 40 C.
Biochemical Characteristics
Toxin—Produced.
Hemolysin—Heat-labile hemolysin produced.
Pathogenicity
Animals—Fatal to rabbits upon intravenous injection; found in abscesses of pigs, cattle, and human beings.

Coxiella burnetii

Taxonomy

Order	*Rickettsiales*
Family	*Rickettsiaceae*
Tribe	*Rickettsieae*
Genus	*Coxiella*
Species	*burnetii*

Cellular Characteristics
Morphology—Pleomorphic, coccoid to rods; externally appear as lanceolate rods, diplobacilli.
Motility—Nonmotile.
Capsules—Nonencapsulated.
Staining—Gram negative; difficult to stain with ordinary aniline dyes; Giemsa stain used appear reddish-purple; in Macchiavello's stain, appear bright red with blue background.
Occurring—As microcolonies in cytoplasm.
Size—0.25 by 0.4 to 0.5 μ.
Habitat—Ticks, wild and domestic animals; dust in barns.
Cultural Characteristics—Difficult to cultivate; can be cultivated in tissue culture and membranes of chick embryos; plasma tissue culture.
Physiological Characteristics
Filterability—Can pass through Berkefeld N and W filters; the latter filter out rickettsiae of typhus and spotted fever; the former filter out bacteria.
Growth factors
Temperature—Resistant to heat; survives 60 C for 1 hour.
Tolerance—Tolerates 1 per cent phenol for 24 hours in fertile eggs; tolerates 0.5 per cent formalin for 24 hours in fertile eggs; killed by dehydration or stronger chemical antiseptics.
Serology
Antigenic grouping—Has no antigenic factors in common with *Proteus*.
Agglutination—Cross immunity between Australian and American strains of Q fever. Identical by agglutination and agglutinin absorption.
Other—No Weil-Felix reaction. Ninemile fever may be identical.
Academic or Research Utilization—Similar electrophoretic characteristics as bacteria.
Pathogenicity
Human beings—The cause of Q fever in man; febrile reaction often accompanied by pneumonitis.
Animals—Pathogenic for mice and guinea

pigs. The wood tick usually transmits the disease. Ticks and some wild and domesticated animals serve as the natural reservoir. Found in dust in shelters housing infected animals. The tick seldom transmits the disease to man. The illness can also be transmitted through the ingestion of contaminated milk from infected animals. Tetracyclines are effective in the treatment of the disease.

Desulfovibrio aestuarii

Taxonomy
- Order — *Pseudomonadales*
- Suborder — *Pseudomonadineae*
- Family — *Spirillaceae*
- Genus — *Desulfovibrio*
- Species — *aestuarii*

Cellular Characteristics
- Morphology—Greater pleomorphism than *D. desulfuricans*.
- Motility—Motile.
- Flagella—Polar flagellum.
- Staining—Gram negative; easily stained with carbol fuchsin; older cells may appear black because of ferric chloride in the cells.
- Occurring—Singly, in pairs, or chains.
- Size—0.5 to 1.0 by 1 to 5 μ.
- Habitat—Soil, sewage, sea water, oil and salt wells.

Cultural Characteristics
- Agar colonies—Dark, small, slightly raised.
- Sea water—Optimum results obtained with media containing sea water or 3 per cent salt mineral solutions enriched with sulfate and peptone. Slight turbidity produced when oxygen is absent; organisms are found mainly in sediment.

Physiological Characteristics
- Biochemical action
  - Hydrogen sulfide—Produced, 950 mg per liter.
  - Nitrites—Not produced from nitrates.
  - Sulfate—Reduced to hydrogen sulfide.
  - Sulfur—Reduced.
  - Thiosulfate—Reduced.
  - Sulfite—Reduced.
  - Hyposulfite—Reduced.
  - Peptone—Utilized when sulfates are present.
  - Asparagine—Utilized when sulfates are present.
  - Glycine—Utilized when sulfates are present.
  - Alanine—Utilized when sulfates are present.
  - Acetate—Utilized when sulfates are present.
  - Malate—Utilized when sulfates are present.
  - Lactate—Utilized when sulfates are present.
- Protein liquefaction
  - Gelatin—Not liquefied.
- Fermentation reactions
  - Butyl alcohol—Utilized when sulfates are present.
- Growth factors
  - Oxygen—Anaerobic.
  - Temperature
    - Optimum—25 to 30 C.
  - pH
    - Optimum—6 to 7.5.
    - Range—5 to 9.

Academic or Research Utilization—There may be an association between this organism and the formation of petroleum.

Desulfovibrio desulfuricans

Taxonomy
- Order — *Pseudomonadales*
- Suborder — *Pseudomonadineae*
- Family — *Spirillaceae*
- Genus — *Desulfovibrio*
- Species — *desulfuricans*

Cellular Characteristics
- Morphology—Slightly curved rods resembling spirilla; pleomorphic forms may be present.
- Motility—Motile.
- Flagella—Polar flagellum.
- Staining—Gram negative; easily stained with carbol fuchsin; older cells may appear black because of ferric chloride in the cells.
- Occurring—Singly, in pairs, or chains.
- Size—0.5 to 1.0 by 1 to 5 μ.
- Habitat—Soil, sewage, sea water.

Cultural Characteristics
- Peptone glucose agar colonies—Dull, small, slightly raised colonies, circular and entire (no air).
- Sea water—Opalescent turbidity produced in such media enriched with sulfate and peptone in the absence of oxygen.

Physiological Characteristics
- Biochemical action
  - Hydrogen sulfide—Produced, up to 3100 mg per liter.
  - Nitrites—Not produced from nitrates.
  - Phenanthrene—Utilized.
  - Sulfate—Reduced to hydrogen sulfide.
  - Sulfite—Reduced.
  - Thiosulfate—Reduced.
  - Hyposulfite—Reduced.
  - Sulfur—Reduced.
  - Peptone—Utilized as hydrogen donor.
  - Asparagine—Utilized as hydrogen donor.
  - Glycine—Utilized as hydrogen donor.
  - Alanine—Utilized as hydrogen donor.
  - Lactate—Utilized as hydrogen donor.
  - Succinate—Utilized as hydrogen donor.
  - Malate—Utilized as hydrogen donor.
- Fermentation reactions
  - Monosaccharides
    - Glucose—Utilized as hydrogen donor.
  - Alcohols and polyalcohols
    - Propyl alcohol—Utilized as hydrogen donor.
    - Glycerol—Utilized as hydrogen donor.
- Protein liquefaction
  - Gelatin—Liquefied.
- Color and light characteristics
  - Respiratory pigment—Cytochrome elaborated.
- Growth factors
  - Oxygen—Anaerobic.
  - Temperature
    - Optimum—25 to 30 C.
  - Nutrition—The absence of certain growth factors found at times in cell aggregates requires a large inoculum to produce growth.
  - pH
    - Optimum—6 to 7.5.
    - Range—5 to 9.
  - Fresh water—Growth is best in fresh water; difficult, at first, to isolate from sea water.

Academic or Research Utilization—1. The organism was cultured in synthetic Lubing oil field water to test its permeability on cores of Edwards' limestone (from which Lubing crude oil originates) and it was found to reduce the permeability of the core.

2. Lead and iron in zinc plate are attacked by *D. desulfuricans* before the zinc is.

Addenda. D. desulfuricans can be associated with zinc metal corrosion in dilute salt solution. The inhibiting effect of the zinc ions or other products of corrosion may slow down the bacterial activity. The organism attacks zinc best where air, surface, and hydrogen sulfide are in contact with the metal.

A growth factor is needed for cells to grow in a medium. This factor seems tied to the action of ferrous sulfide precipitating colonies. Hydrogenase is produced by the organism and hydrogen is utilized. Carbon dioxide is also reduced. Some strains can produce methane. Nitrogen may also be fixed by some strains.

Diplococcus pneumoniae

Taxonomy

Order	*Eubacteriales*
Family	*Lactobacteraceae*
Tribe	*Streptococceae*
Genus	*Diplococcus*
Species	*pneumoniae*

Cellular Characteristics
- Morphology—Oval or spherical shapes, distal ends are pointed or lancet-shaped.
- Motility—Nonmotile.
- Capsules—Encapsulated; well marked in animal fluid. *In vitro* growth usually loses the capsule.
- Staining—Young cells are gram positive; nonacid fast; special capsule stains needed.
- Occurring—In pairs, sometimes in chains, or singly.
- Size—0.5 to 1.25 μ.
- Habitat—Respiratory tract; may be present in sputum, blood, exudates in pneumonia patients.

Cultural Characteristics
- Infusion agar colonies—Grayish, transparent, small, entire margin.
- Agar stroke—White, difficult to grow, transparent, raised, smooth.
- Gelatin stab—No liquefaction; filiform or beaded growth.
- Blood broth—Growth and turbidity.
- Blood agar colonies—Pinpoint, surrounded by a zone of greenish hemolysis.
- Beef heart infusion broth—Turbidity is uniform and sediment is variable; addition of glucose, serum, whole blood, ascitic fluid, to the medium enhances growth.
- Potato—No growth.

Physiological Characteristics
- Biochemical action
  - Nitrates—Not reduced.
  - Inulin serum water—Acid with coagulation.
  - Bile—10 per cent solution of sodium taurocholate or sodium glycocholate will destroy organism. It is customary to use 0.1 to 0.5 ml of bile for each 0.5 ml of the culture mixture.
- Protein liquefaction or digestion
  - Gelatin—Not liquefied.
- Indicator reactions
  - Litmus milk—Usually acid with coagulation.
- Fermentation reactions
  - Monosaccharides
    - Glucose—Acid, no gas.
  - Disaccharides
    - Lactose—Acid, no gas.
    - Sucrose—Acid, no gas.
  - Polysaccharides
    - Inulin—Acid, no gas (differential test from green streptococci).
- Growth factors
  - Temperature
    - Optimum—37 C.

No growth—18 to 22 C.
Thermal death time—55 C in 20 minutes.
pH—Initial optimum 7.8.
Drying and sunlight—Kill the organism.

Serology—There are over 75 various types of pneumococci based upon antisera determinations. Identification is based upon the Neufeld swelling capsule reaction. If serum and capsule are homogenous, a swelling of the capsule occurs. The swelling is probably due to the carbohydrate-antibody complex. Serological reactions seem to be due to a group specific material which is protein in nature and a type specific substance which is a polysaccharide. Specific soluble substances do not induce the formation of antibodies by themselves. They can produce immune sera when combined with a protein. Immunity is of very short duration. Antibodies may be demonstrated in normal individuals too.

Pathogenicity—The organism is found in cases of lobar pneumonia. Secondary infections may also be caused: pericarditis, meningitis, mastoiditis, peritonitis, tonsillitis.

Addenda. Pneumococci typing can be done by using various methods.

Some bacteria, when grown in the presence of extracts or filtrates of other bacteria, acquire some properties of the other organisms. Transformation in pneumococci was obtained by inoculating mice with some extract of a type II, a rough strain, together with some heat-killed type III smooth culture. The new progeny was of type III smooth variety.

Erwinia amylovora

Taxonomy

Order	*Eubacteriales*
Family	*Enterobacteriaceae*
Tribe	*Erwinieae*
Genus	*Erwinia*
Species	*amylovora*

Cellular Characteristics
- Morphology—Rods.
- Motility—Motile.
- Flagella—Peritrichous.
- Staining—Gram negative.
- Occurring—Singly, in pairs, or in short chains.
- Size—0.7 to 1.0 by 0.9 to 1.5 μ.
- Habitat—Found as the cause of fire blight on pear and apple trees.

Cultural Characteristics
- Gelatin colonies—Whitish, circular, entire; do not have any definite form.
- Gelatin stab—Slow crateriform liquefaction in the upper part of the stab.
- Nutrient broth—Thin granular pellicle, turbid.
- Potato—White, moist, glistening growth; no pigment.

Physiological Characteristics
- Biochemical action
  - Indole production—Negative.
  - Voges-Proskauer test—Positive, acetylmethylcarbinol produced.
  - Ammonia—May be detected in broth with most strains.
  - Nitrite—Not produced from nitrates.
- Protein liquefaction or digestion
  - Gelatin—Slowly liquefied.
- Fermentation reactions
  - Monosaccharides
    - Arabinose—Acid, no gas.
    - Rhamnose—Not fermented.

Xylose—Not fermented.
Glucose—Acid, no gas.
Fructose—Acid, no gas.
Galactose—Variable.
Mannose—Acid, no gas.
Disaccharides
Lactose—Variable.
Sucrose—Acid, no gas.
Maltose—Acid, no gas.
Cellobiose—Acid, no gas.
Polysaccharides
Starch—Not fermented.
Glucosides
Salicin—Acid, no gas.
Amydalin—Acid, no gas.
Growth factors
Temperature
Minimum—3 to 8 C.
Maximum—About 36 C.
pH
Minimum—4.0 to 4.4.
Maximum—8.8.
Optimum—6.8.
Nutrition—Can be grown in synthetic media with diammonium hydrogen phosphate as a source of nitrogen.
Asparagine—Utilized to form an alkaline medium.
Cystine—Not utilized.
Glutamic Acid—Not utilized.
Glycine—Not utilized.
Isoleucine—Not utilized.
Tryptophane—Not utilized.
Tyrosine—Not utilized.
Urea—Not utilized.
Valine—Not utilized.
Inhibition—Apple trees sprayed with streptomycin or thiolutin showed reduced infection.
Pathogenicity
Plants—The cause of soft blight in pear and apple trees. Can cause fire blight disease on raspberry; produces same symptoms as on apple trees.

Erwinia carotovora

Taxonomy

Order	*Eubacteriales*
Family	*Enterobacteriaceae*
Tribe	*Erwinieae*
Genus	*Erwinia*
Species	*carotovora*

Cellular Characteristics
Morphology—Rods.
Motility—Motile.
Flagella—Peritrichous, 1 to 6.
Capsules—None.
Staining—Gram negative; stain well with Löffler's methylene blue.
Occurring—In chains, at times.
Size—0.7 to 0.8 by 1.5 to 5 μ.
Habitat—Various plants.
Cultural Characteristics
Agar colonies—After 48 hours, circular, convex, smooth, moist, glistening, grayish white, entire margin.
Agar stroke—Thin growth, moist glistening butyrous.
Gelatin stab—Surface liquefaction.
Nutrient broth—Pellicle, white flocculent, turbid, slow alkaline production.
Endo agar colonies—Circular, pink turning red with metallic sheen, red medium.
Potato—Creamy-white, thick growth.
Dunham's solution—Little, but persistent turbidity.
Uschinsky's solution—Strong turbidity.
Blood serum—Thin, grayish, moist growth.
Physiological Characteristics
Biochemical action
Indole production—Negative.
Methyl red reaction—Positive.
Voges-Proskauer test—Negative.

Hydrogen sulfide production—Usually negative.
Starch hydrolysis—Negative.
Pectates—Liquefied.
Ammonia—Not produced.
Nitrite—Formed from nitrate.

Protein liquefaction
Gelatin—Liquefied.

Fermentation reactions
Monosaccharides
Arabinose—Acid, sometimes gas.
Rhamnose—Acid, sometimes gas.
Xylose—Acid, sometimes gas.
Glucose—Acid, sometimes gas.
Fructose—Acid, sometimes gas.
Galactose—Acid, sometimes gas.
Disaccharides
Lactose—Acid, sometimes gas.
Sucrose—Acid, sometimes gas.
Maltose—Acid, sometimes gas.
Cellobiose—Acid, sometimes gas.
Polysaccharides
Raffinose—Acid, sometimes gas.
Inulin—Not fermented.
Starch—Not fermented.
Cellulose—Not attacked.
Alcohols and polyalcohols
Ethyl alcohol, 5 per cent solution—Acid, sometimes gas.
Butyl alcohol—Not fermented.
Glycerol—Acid, no gas.
Erythritol—Acid, sometimes gas.
Mannitol—Acid, sometimes gas.
Dulcitol—Acid, sometimes gas.

Growth factors
Oxygen—Aerobic.
Temperature
Optimum—25 to 30 C.
Minimum—6 C.
Maximum—35 to 37 C.
Thermal death range—41 to 51 C.
Nutrition
Sodium hippurate—Utilized.
Sodium malonate—Utilized.
Sodium tartrate—Utilized.
Sodium urate—Utilized.
Nitrogen utilization — Ammonium salts, potassium nitrate, asparagine, yeast extract, gelatin, and peptone utilized.
Aspartic acid—Not utilized.
Tyrosine—Not utilized.
Inhibition—5 per cent sodium chloride slows growth, 7 per cent inhibits.

Biochemical Characteristics
Enzyme production—Pectinase produced; amylase not produced.

Pathogenicity
Plants—Causes soft rot in a variety of plants, such as carrots, cabbage, cucumber, and onion; roots, rhizomes, fruits, and fleshy parts are affected.

Addenda. Methanol is liberated from pectin during growth in a pectin medium.

Polygalacturonase is difficult to demonstrate in cultures, although active in a wide pH range, optimum being 5.8.

The organism in special medium can utilize galacturonic acid.

Endotoxin prepared from the organism has polysaccharide which can cause wilt in sunflowers. Can also cause soft rot in wilt-proof chicory.

Erysipelothrix insidiosa

Taxonomy

Order	*Eubacteriales*
Family	*Corynebacteriaceae*
Genus	*Erysipelothrix*
Species	*insidiosa*
Synonym	*Erysipelothrix rhusiopathiae*

Cellular Characteristics
Morphology—Slender rods to long filaments.
Motility—Nonmotile.
Staining—Gram positive.
Occurring—Singly and in chains.

Size—0.2 to 0.3 by 0.5 to 1.5 μ.
Habitat—Widely distributed.

Cultural Characteristics
Tellurite agar colonies—Gray, minute; in 24 hours become jet-black and larger.
Agar stroke—Moist, even, translucent growth.
Gelatin colonies—Slow growth, bluish-gray, racemose.
Gelatin stab—Fimbriate colonies in stab, no surface growth.
Broth—Gray sediment, slight turbidity.
Bone marrow—Used to culture the organism.

Physiological Characteristics
Biochemical action
Methyl red reaction—Negative.
Voges-Proskauer test—Negative.
Hydrogen sulfide production—Positive.
Protein liquefaction or digestion
Gelatin—Not liquefied.
Blood serum—Zone of hemolysis on blood agar; green zone.
Indicator reactions
Litmus milk—Not changed.
Methylene blue reduction test—Negative.
Fermentation reactions
Carbohydrates—No gas.
Monosaccharides
Arabinose—Acid in favorable media.
Xylose—Acid in favorable media.
Rhamnose—Usually no acid.
Glucose—Acid.
Fructose—Acid.
Galactose—Acid.
Mannose—Acid.
Disaccharides
Lactose—Acid.
Sucrose—No acid.
Maltose—No acid.
Melibiose—Acid in favorable media.
Cellobiose—Acid in favorable media.
Trehalose—No acid.
Polysaccharides
Raffinose—No acid.
Melezitose—No acid.
Starch—No acid.
Inulin—No acid.
Dextrin—No acid.
Alcohols and polyalcohols
Glycerol—No acid.
Mannitol—No acid.
Sorbitol—No acid.
Inositol—No acid.
Glucosides
Salicin—No acid.
Esculin—Not hydrolyzed.
Growth factors
Oxygen—Facultatively anaerobic, microaerophilic.
Temperature
Optimum—37 C; maximum amount of cells, 33 C.
Range—16 to 41 C.
pH
Optimum range—7.4 to 7.8.
Toleration—Phenol, 0.2 per cent; potassium tellurite, 0.05 per cent.
Serology—Pigs vaccinated with the organism bacterin using aluminum hydroxide as an adsorbent were unable to resist the organism when challenged.
Agglutination—Virulent strain of the organism has particular agglutination properties that are specific for it and not the Staub strain.

Biochemical Characteristics
Enzyme production—Catalase not produced.

Pathogenicity
Human beings—Isolated from erysipeloid infections.
Animals—Cause of swine erysipelas. Can be transmitted to mice, rabbits, pigeons.

Addenda. Sea water cannot be used to support growth of the organism. Infections at sea suggest the organism was brought on board boat.

Mortality rate of turkeys was lower in birds vaccinated with bacterin vaccine.

Strains recovered from bone marrow medium were in the R phase with a reduced pathogenicity for mice and pigeons.

Escherichia coli

Taxonomy
- Order — *Eubacteriales*
- Family — *Enterobacteriaceae*
- Tribe — *Escherichieae*
- Genus — *Escherichia*
- Species — *coli*

Cellular Characteristics
- Morphology—Rods, ranging in size from long to coccoid.
- Motility—Motile and nonmotile forms.
- Flagella—Peritrichous on motile forms.
- Staining—Gram negative.
- Occurring—Singly, in pairs, or in short chains.
- Size—0.5 by 1.0 to 3.0 μ.
- Habitat—Intestinal tract of human beings.

Cultural Characteristics
- Agar colonies—White in appearance; color may change; spreading, moist, glistening; atypical colonies may form.
- Agar stroke—White, spreading, moist, glistening.
- Gelatin colonies—Grayish-white, opaque, moist, entire.
- Gelatin stab—Grayish-white, spreading, undulate.
- Nutrient broth—Turbid with grayish sediment.
- Potato—Grayish to yellowish-brown, spreading, abundant growth.
- Blood agar plates—Some strains are hemolytic.

Physiological Characteristics
- Biochemical action
  - Indole production—Usually positive.
  - Methyl red reaction—Positive.
  - Voges-Proskauer test—Negative.
  - Citrate—Not utilized as sole source of carbon.
  - Uric acid—Not utilized as sole source of nitrogen.
  - Uracil—Utilized as sole source of nitrogen.
  - Hydrogen sulfide—Sensitive tests may be positive; none formed in peptone iron agar.
  - Hemolysis—Some strains are hemolytic.
  - Nitrite—Formed from nitrate.
  - Catalase—Positive.
- Protein liquefaction
  - Gelatin—Not liquefied.
- Indicator reactions
  - Litmus milk—Acid formed with gas developed rapidly; coagulation may result with curd broken or not broken, no peptonization of curd; litmus may be reduced.
- Fermentation reactions
  - Monosaccharides
    - Arabinose—Acid and gas.
    - Rhamnose—Acid and gas.
    - Xylose—Acid and gas.
    - Glucose—Acid and gas; almost equal volume of carbon dioxide to hydrogen.
    - Fructose—Acid and gas.
    - Galactose—Acid and gas.
  - Disaccharides
    - Lactose—Acid and gas; some strains of *E. coli* are slow lactose fermenters.
    - Sucrose—May be fermented.
    - Maltose—Acid and gas.
    - Cellobiose—Not fermented.
  - Polysaccharides
    - Starch—Not fermented.
    - Inulin—Rarely fermented.
    - Dextrin—Not fermented.
    - Glycogen—Not fermented.
  - Alcohols and polyalcohols

Glycerol—May be fermented; trimethylene glycol not formed under anaerobic conditions.
Adonitol—Rarely fermented.
Mannitol—Acid and gas.
Dulcitol—May be fermented.
Inositol—Not fermented.
Glycosides
alpha-Methyl glycoside—Not fermented.
Salicin—May be fermented.
Esculin—May be fermented.
Growth factors
Oxygen—Aerobic, facultatively anaerobic.
Temperature
Optimum—30 to 37 C.
Range—10 to 45 C.
Eijkmann test—Positive.
Thermal death time—Usually 60 C for 30 minutes.
Color characteristics
Chromogenesis—Some strains produce a yellow pigment.
Serology
Antigenic grouping—*E. coli* strains divided into 135 O (heat-stable somatic antigen) groups, 75 K antigens, and 40 H (flagellar) antigens to give a large number of serotypes.
Pathogenicity
Human beings—Usually nonpathogenic but can cause infection of the genito-urinary tract.

Addenda. Cytosine and uracil nucleosides prevented growth inhibition by 5-hydroxydeoxyuridine. L-Aspartic acid, folic acid, and adenine failed to prevent growth inhibition. Strain K 12 is inhibited by pentamidine isethionate. The inhibition can be overcome by glutamic acid or alpha-ketoglutaric acid in a competitive manner. Pentamidine also inhibits transamination in dried cells between glutamic acid and alpha-ketovaline. *E. coli* is also inhibited by propamidine. Large doses of riboflavin, thiamine, nicotinic acid and pyridoxine have a retarding and peculiar morphological effect. Reversal of growth inhibition is caused by sulfadiazine but can be overcome by vitamin B_{12} and glycine. Sulfanilamide resistant strains require methionine. Strains resistant to sodium chloroacetate are unable to form gas from sugar. Pipradral inhibited the growth of the organism but this inhibition was reversed by yeast extract.

Strains of coli could be mated with strains of *Shigella;* hybridization showed both coli and shigella characteristics. Coli organisms grown in Tyrode's solution containing the complete antigen of nucleoprotein and the desoxyribonucleic acids of *Bacillus breslau* appeared as variants resembling *B. breslau* after the 30th transfer. *E. coli* exposed to methylcholanthrene and 7,2-dimethylbenz(a)anthracene on agar media were shown to produce an increase in the ribonucleic acids/desoxyribonucleic acids ratio. Other cells showed only a slight variation in the RNA/DNA ratio.

Cellular constituents were released from coli cells after x irradiation and incubation in a phosphate buffer-glucose solution at 37 C. The constituents lost were nucleic acid fragments. The loss of these fragments was inhibited in the absence of phosphate in the surrounding fluid. During bacteriolysis of *E. coli,* beta-D-galactosidase is released by the cells into the surrounding medium. When the cell volume of the organism is large and the glutamic acid concentration of the medium is small, the cell will take up all the glutamic acid.

X rays are more efficient in production of mutations than ultraviolet light and x rays also kill more cells than ultraviolet light. The growth of an irradiated culture depends upon the size of the inoculum used. Catalase treatment appeared to remove the growth inhibiting mutagenic factors. Thus catalase can help a damaged cell to repair itself after exposure to ultraviolet rays. In order to increase the amino acid decarboxylase, cetyltrimethylammonium chloride should be added to the medium.

A strain of biochemical mutants of *E. coli* race K 12 was produced by irradiation. Multiple mutant stocks were produced by causing a single deficiency subsequently a mutant with a double deficiency and then one with a triple deficiency. Some requirements are threonine, leucine, and thiamine.

Sodium desoxycholate, when employed as a mutagenic agent, increased the proportion of virus resistant strains of *E. coli.* Similar experiments with pyronine and acriflavine indicated that these substances were also active. The mutation rate to phage resistance is independent of the generation time in different media. Resistance to bacteriophage is usually absolute or absent in the case of coli. The phage resistant mutants usually fail to absorb the bacteriophage. Some phage resistant mutants also show a biochemical correlation to nutritional deficiencies.

Electron micrographs showed nucleoid bodies in the organisms which resembled chromosomes during mitosis. There is some evidence for at least three chromosomes in the vegetative haploid state of strain K 12.

E. coli communis can produce an antagonistic factor in the medium which can inhibit other organisms such as *Aerobacter aerogenes* and *Streptococcus fecalis.* Filtrates of *E. coli* inhibited the growth of *Salmonella typhosa.* This inhibition was due to a heat labile antagonistic substance formed by the coli.

The cell membrane appears to be permeable by many molecules through a simple mechanism. Material is thought to be transported across the membrane by diffusion. The organism can take up sulfate from a medium in proportion to the increase in cell protein. Penetration of sulfate into the water space of the cell seems to work by diffusion. Phosphorus as phosphate in a sodium phosphate buffer is immediately taken up by the cell. This metabolic activity can take place in the absence of glucose and ammonium salts.

Mutabile strains can be cultivated to ferment lactose. Iron deficiency in *E. coli* can influence the reduction of nitrate but not of nitrite. A strain of the organism can form indole from ammonium salts and glucose. This strain is unable to convert indole into tryptophane. Magnesium ions stimulate the production of the indole. Serine is also essential.

Coliform bacteria were detected using the biuret reaction. Suspensions of the organism were treated with an alkaline solution. The intensity of the color is proportional to the amount of bacteria present.

Polymerase, an enzyme extracted from *E. coli,* can be used to synthesize desoxyribonucleic acids from desoxyribonucleoside-5′-triphosphate with the aid of a small amount of DNA to act as a template. Glutaminases have been found in and obtained from the organism.

Strains of *E. coli* were isolated from the respiratory tract of chickens affected with chronic respiratory disease.

Fusobacterium fusiforme

Taxonomy

Order	*Pseudomonadales*
Suborder	*Pseudomonadineae*
Family	*Bacteroidaceae*
Genus	*Fusobacterium*
Species	*fusiforme*
Synonym	*Fusobacterium plauti-vincenti*

Cellular Characteristics

Morphology—Rods which may be curved with blunt or pointed ends.

Motility—Nonmotile.

Staining—Gram negative.

Occurring—Pairs, chains, or thread-like chains.

Size—1.0 by 8.0 up to 16 μ.
Habitat—Mouth cavities which may be gangrenous and in the normal mouth.

Cultural Characteristics
- Agar—No growth.
- Meat infusion agar—Some growth.
- Serum agar (shake)—Spherical yellow-brown colonies after 40 hours.
- Agar plate with serum—Protein precipitated and growth becomes matted; turbidity where precipitation occurs.
- Gelatin—No growth.
- Broth
  - Peptone—No growth.
  - Liver—Gray-white precipitate.
  - Serum—Turbid.

Physiological Characteristics
- Biochemical action
  - Indole production—Negative.
  - Hydrogen sulfide—Negative.
- Fermentation reactions
  - Monosaccharides
    - Glucose—Acid.
    - Fructose—Acid.
  - Disaccharides
    - Sucrose—Acid.
    - Lactose—Acid variable.
    - Maltose—Acid.
  - Polysaccharides
    - Inulin—No acid.
  - Alcohols and polyalcohols
    - Mannitol—No acid.
- Growth factors
  - Oxygen—Anaerobic.
  - Temperature—Can survive 60 C for only 2 minutes.
  - Nutrition—For isolation purposes the following should be included in a basal medium: pantetheine, pantothenic acid, coenzyme A and, in addition, tryptophane, adenine, and hypoxanthine.

Pathogenicity
- Human beings—Associated with *Borrelia vincentii* in trench mouth or Vincent's angina.
- White mice—Nonpathogenic.

Gaffkya tetragena

Taxonomy

Order	*Eubacteriales*
Family	*Micrococcaceae*
Genus	*Gaffkya*
Species	*tetragena*
Synonym	*Micrococcus tetragena*

Cellular Characteristics
- Morphology—Spheres, typically in groups of four or tetrads; always in tetrads when taken from a body.
- Capsules—Pseuodcapsule around tetrad taken from body fluids.
- Staining—Gram positive.
- Occurring—In tetrads.
- Size—0.6 to 0.8 μ in diameter.
- Habitat—Mucous membranes of respiratory tract.

Cultural Characteristics
- Agar colonies—White, circular, smooth, glistening, and entire; variants may occur.
- Agar stroke—White, glistening, and moist.
- Gelatin colonies—Small, white, and convex.
- Gelatin stab—Thick, white, surface growth.
- Nutrient broth—Gray, viscous sediment.
- Potato—White, viscid.

Physiological Characteristics
- Biochemical action
  - Indole production—Negative.
  - Hydrogen sulfide production—Negative.
  - Starch hydrolysis—Negative.
  - Ammonium salts—Not utilized.

Nitrite—Not formed from nitrate.
Protein liquefaction
Gelatin—Not liquefied.
Indicator reactions
Litmus milk—Slightly acid.
Fermentation reactions
Monosaccharides
Glucose—Acid.
Disaccharides
Lactose—Acid.
Polyalcohols
Glycerol—Acid.
Growth factors
Oxygen—Aerobic, facultatively anaerobic.
Temperature
Optimum—37 C.
Nutrition
Amino acids required—L-Tyrosine, L-glutamic acid.
Vitamins required—Biotin.
Pathogenicity
Human beings—Has been found in spinal fluid in meningitis and in pus in abscesses; may be found in sputum from tuberculosis patients; probably does not invade animal tissue, may gain entry with other organisms.
Animals—Pathogenic for mice and guinea pigs; localized reaction produced in rabbits. Rarely pathogenic for man.

Addenda. The organism was isolated from a case of subacute bacterial endocarditis. Penicillin was used in therapy.

Crystal violet method was used to stain the nucleus. Water soluble crystal violet, mercuric chloride and nigrosin were used. The slide is heated at 50 C for 20 seconds while the stain is applied. Nucleus can be seen in various stages of division.

The cells also have an affinity for stains which color the DNA but not for stains which impart a color to the macronucleotides.

Haemophilus influenzae

Taxonomy

Order	*Eubacteriales*
Family	*Brucellaceae*
Genus	*Haemophilus*
Species	*influenzae*
Common name	Pfeiffer bacillus

Cellular Characteristics
Morphology—Short rods, may have rounded ends; cocci forms may be observed, as well as thread-like forms; strains may differ in morphology; artificial culture may produce pleomorphic forms.
Motility—Usually nonmotile.
Capsules—Some strains encapsulated.
Staining—Gram negative, nonacid fast; with carbol fuchsin stain and alkaline methylene blue staining may be bipolar.
Occurring—Singly, in pairs, in short chains, and in long threads.
Size—1 to 1.5 by 0.3 to 0.4 μ.
Spores—Not formed.
Habitat—Respiratory tract.
Cultural Characteristics
Agar colonies
Blood agar—Drop-like colonies, transparent, entire edges.
Chocolate agar—Drop-like colonies, possibly dome-shaped.
Levinthal's agar—Good growth; pinpoint colonies larger than blood agar colonies.
Filde's agar—Good growth; pinpoint colonies larger than blood agar colonies; typical strains produce a smoother colony. An atypical strain produced granular types of colony. Smooth strains may

give rise to rough strains. Rough strains are not encapsulated. Three forms have been proposed: M—mucoid capsule; S—S form, no capsule, smooth; R—R form, rough.

Physiological Characteristics
  Biochemical action
    Indole production—Positive in some strains.
    Nitrate—Reduced to nitrite.
  Fermentation reactions
    Monosaccharides
      Glucose—Agar medium, plus litmus and glucose: acid produced.
    Disaccharides
      Lactose—Never fermented.
      Maltose—Not fermented.
    Alcohols and Polyalcohols
      Mannitol—Never fermented.
  Growth factors
    Oxygen—Aerobic to facultatively anaerobic.
    Temperature
      Optimum—37 C.
      Minimum—25 to 27 C.
      Maximum—43 C.
      Thermal death time—30 minutes at 55 C.
    Nutrition—Growth factors must be present, notably X and V factors found in blood; X factor is heat stable and can be substituted for by hemin or hemoglobin; V factor phosphopyridine nucleotide which is heat-labile is extracted from yeast; it can be replaced by coenzyme I or II. Carbon dioxide may assist growth.
Serology—Six serological types, a to f, distinguished by use of capsular material to precipitate immune serum; type b is usually associated with cerebrospinal fluid from patients.
Pathogenicity
  Human beings—Cause of acute respiratory illness, pus-type meningitis of children, and acute conjunctivitis.

Halobacterium salinarium

Taxonomy
  Order *Pseudomonadales*
  Family *Pseudomonadaceae*
  Genus *Halobacterium*
  Species *salinarium*
Cellular Characteristics
  Morphology—Rods and spherical forms; club-shaped or clavate, spindle, irregular forms.
  Motility—Motile.
  Flagella—Polar, single or one at each end.
  Staining—Gram negative.
  Occurring—Singly.
  Size—Spheres are 0.8 to 1.4 μ in diameter; rods are 0.6 by 1.5 to 1.0 by 6.0 μ.
  Habitat—Tidal pools, water along the seashore.
Cultural Characteristics
  Codfish agar colonies—Smooth, raised, entire, and pale pink in about 20 per cent salt.
  Milk salt agar colonies—Pink in about 30 per cent salt.
  Codfish agar slant—Growth after one week is raised, smooth, translucent, red, and odorous in about 25 per cent salt.
  Salt gelatin—Slow liquefaction.
  Codfish broth—Pink sediment and pink pellicle in 25 per cent salt.
Physiological Characteristics
  Biochemical action

Indole production—Negative.
Hydrogen sulfide—Positive.
Starch hydrolysis—Negative.
Nitrogen utilization—Cannot utilize inorganic nitrogen as sole source.
Nitrite—Not produced from nitrate.
Nitrate—No gas produced.
Fermentation reactions
Carbohydrates—No action.
Growth factors
Oxygen—Aerobic.
Temperature
Optimum—37 C.
Growth—Will grow at 22 C.
Salinity
Optimum—28 to 32 per cent sodium chloride.
Cells ruptured—8 per cent sodium chloride.
Color characteristics
Chromogenesis—Pale pink to scarlet pigment; produces a reddening in salted fish.

Hydrogenomonas pantotropha

Taxonomy

Order	*Pseudomonadales*
Suborder	*Pseudomonadineae*
Family	*Methanomonadaceae*
Genus	*Hydrogenomonas*
Species	*pantotropha*

Cellular Characteristics
Morphology—Rods with rounded ends.
Motility—Motile.
Flagella—Long polar flagellum.
Capsules—Encapsulated.
Staining—Bipolar in old cultures.
Occurring—In pairs, singly, or in chains.
Size—0.4 to 0.5 by 1.2 to 1.5 μ.
Habitat—Soil.

Cultural Characteristics
Inorganic solutions—May be cultivated under atmosphere of hydrogen, carbon dioxide, and oxygen; liquid becomes turbid without pellicle formation.
Inorganic solid media—Under atmosphere of oxygen, carbon dioxide, and hydrogen, colonies are yellow and slimy, and plates smell like hot soapy water.
Gelatin colonies—Yellow, smooth, rarely greenish.
Gelatin stab—Surface growth only.
Potato—Yellowish, glistening, moist.
Broth—Turbid, pellicle may appear.

Physiological Characteristics
Biochemical action
Indole production—Negative.
Hydrogen sulfide—Not formed.
Nitrite—Not produced from nitrate.
Milk—No coagulation; medium becomes slimy.
Hydrogenase—The organism, although possessing hydrogenase, does not fix nitrogen.
Fermentation reactions—Does not act on carbohydrates.
Growth factors
Oxygen—Aerobic, not sensitive to high concentrations of oxygen.
Temperature
Optimum—28 to 30 C.
Nutrition—Facultatively autotrophic.

Addenda. Can oxidize hydrogen to water and use carbon dioxide as a source of carbon.

Heavy metals introduced into the medium can act as enzymic poisons; potassium cyanide–azide–carbon monoxide and oxygen was used as the H acceptor in Warburg apparatus. Chloroform, ethyl alcohol, and ether inhibit the oxidation of hydrogen and the reduction of methylene blue. Cupric ions at a concentration of 1.25×10^{-4} *M* at pH 5.9 under aerobic conditions can reduce the hydrogenase activity 50 per cent.

Klebsiella pneumoniae

Taxonomy
- Order *Eubacteriales*
- Family *Enterobacteriaceae*
- Genus *Klebsiella*
- Species *pneumoniae*
- Common name Friedländer's pneumobacillus, Friedländer's bacillus
- Synonym *Bacillus mucosus capsulatus*

Cellular Characteristics
- Morphology—Long rods with rounded ends.
- Motility—Nonmotile.
- Capsules—Encapsulated, swell with antisera.
- Staining—Gram negative.
- Occurring—Singly and in pairs.
- Habitat—Associated with the infections of the intestinal genito-urinary and respiratory tract of man.

Cultural Characteristics
- Agar stroke—White, slimy, raised growth.
- Agar colonies—White, smooth, glistening, entire, convex.
- Gelatin colonies—Dirty white, opaque, smooth, entire, slightly raised.
- Gelatin stab—Dirty white on surface. Filiform growth. No liquefaction. Gas bubbles.
- MacConkey's agar—Reddish colonies.
- Horse blood agar plate—Convex white colonies, smooth surface.
- Nutrient broth—Turbid; thick ring or filament.
- Potato—Yellowish growth, slimy, raised; gas formed.
- Colonies—Mucoid when isolated from respiratory tract.

Physiological Characteristics
- Biochemical action
  - Indole—Usually negative.
  - Methyl red reaction—Variable.
  - Voges-Proskauer test—Variable, principally positive.
  - Citrate—Can be used as sole source of carbon, depending on conditions.
  - Hemolysis—Usually none on blood agar.
  - Nitrite—Produced from nitrate.
  - Hydrogen sulfide—Not formed.
- Protein liquefaction
  - Gelatin—Not liquefied.
- Indicator reactions
  - Bromocresol purple milk—No acid or coagulation.
  - Litmus milk—Acid but no coagulation.
- Fermentation reactions
  - Monosaccharides
    - Arabinose—Acid.
    - Rhamnose—Acid.
    - Xylose—Acid.
    - Glucose—Acid and gas.
  - Disaccharides
    - Lactose—Acid and gas may be formed.
    - Sucrose—Acid.
    - Maltose—Acid.
  - Polyalcohols
    - Mannitol—Acid.
    - Sorbitol—Acid.
    - Dulcitol—Acid, variable.
    - Adonitol—Acid.
    - Inositol—Acid.
  - Glucosides
    - Salicin—Acid.
- Growth factors
  - Oxygen—Aerobic.
  - Temperature
    - Optimum—37 C.
    - Range—12 to 43 C.
    - Thermal death time—Killed by moist heat: 55 C for 0.5 hour.

Serology
- Antigenic grouping—Two O antigens and 3 capsular antigens have been identified.

Agglutination—*K. pneumoniae, K. rhinoscleromatis,* and *K. ozaenae* can be differentiated by slide agglutination, capsular swelling.
Strains—Divided into A, B, C, and K.

Lactobacillus acidophilus

Taxonomy
- Order — *Eubacteriales*
- Family — *Lactobacillaceae*
- Tribe — *Lactobacilleae*
- Genus — *Lactobacillus*
- Species — *acidophilus*
- Types — X or R, which produce rough colonies; and Y or S, which produce smooth colonies; R strains may dissociate to form S but the reverse is difficult.

Cellular Characteristics
- Morphology—Rods, rounded ends.
- Motility—Nonmotile.
- Staining—Gram positive; old cultures may turn gram negative.
- Occurring—Singly, in pairs, and in short chains.
- Size—0.6 to 0.9 by 1.5 to 6.0 μ.
- Habitat—Milk products.

Cultural Characteristics
- Wort agar or tomato agar—Surface colonies long and twisted in form; center is dark and thick; deep colonies are irregular with fine radiation.
- Wort agar slant—Scanty growth, dry.
- Wort broth—Fine flocculent sediment after 48 hours.
- Gelatin—No growth at 20 C.

Physiological Characteristics
- Biochemical action
  - Milk—Coagulation from bottom up; slow growth.
  - Sugars—*i*-Lactic acid and volatile organic acids formed.
- Protein liquefaction
  - Gelatin—Not liquefied.
- Fermentation reactions
  - Monosaccharides
    - Arabinose—Not fermented.
    - Rhamnose—Not fermented.
    - Xylose—Not fermented.
    - Glucose—Acid, no gas.
    - Fructose—Acid.
    - Galactose—Acid.
    - Mannose—Acid.
  - Disaccharides
    - Lactose—Acid, no gas.
    - Sucrose—Acid, no gas.
    - Maltose—Acid.
    - Trehalose—Fermentation variable.
  - Polysaccharides
    - Raffinose—Fermentation variable.
    - Dextrin—Some strains, slight action.
  - Polyalcohols
    - Glycerol—Not fermented.
    - Mannitol—Not fermented.
    - Sorbitol—Not fermented.
    - Dulcitol—Not fermented.
    - Inositol—Not fermented.
- Growth factors
  - Oxygen—Microaerophilic.
  - Temperature
    - Optimum—37 C.
    - Maximum—43 to 48 C.
    - No growth—20 to 22 C.
  - Nutrition—In media lacking carbohydrate, no visible growth.
  - pH—Grows in acid media.

Industrial Utilization
- Processes—Acidophilus milk.

Medical Utilization—Therapy of various gastrointestinal disturbances; R strain usually employed.

Pathogenicity
- Animals—Not pathogenic to laboratory animals.

Lactobacillus bulgaricus

Taxonomy
- Order *Eubacteriales*
- Family *Lactobacillus*
- Tribe *Lactobacilleae*
- Genus *Lactobacillus*
- Species *bulgaricus*

Cellular Characteristics
- Morphology—Rods, slender with rounded ends.
- Motility—Nonmotile.
- Staining—Gram positive; old cultures may show unstained portions.
- Occurring—Often in chains.
- Habitat—Milk products.

Cultural Characteristics
- Whey agar colonies—Circular to irregular.
- Whey gelatin—No liquefaction.
- Potato—Yellow-white colonies; sometimes no growth.

Physiological Characteristics
- Biochemical action
  - Indole production—Negative.
  - Nitrite—Not formed from nitrate.
  - Milk—Coagulation at 37 C; no gas; no decomposition of casein; high acidity.
- Fermentation reactions
  - Monosaccharides
    - Arabinose—Not fermented.
    - Rhamnose—Not fermented.
    - Xylose—Not fermented.
    - Glucose—Acid.
    - Fructose (unheated) — Not fermented.
    - Galactose—Acid.
    - Sorbose—Not fermented.
  - Disaccharides
    - Lactose—Acid.
    - Sucrose—Variable.
    - Maltose—Usually no acid.
  - Polysaccharides
    - Starch—Not fermented.
    - Inulin—Not fermented.
    - Dextrin—Not fermented.
  - Polyalcohols
    - Mannitol—Not fermented.
    - Dulcitol—Not fermented.
- Growth factors
  - Oxygen—Aerobic, microaerophilic.
  - Temperature
    - Optimum—45 to 50 C; high-temperature organism.
    - Minimum—22 C.

Industrial Utilization
- Products—Lactic acid.
- Processes—Manufacture of buttermilk, cream cheese, related cheese, yogurt, other fermented milks. Cultures used to prevent wheying off of buttermilk during pasteurization of sour cream. Used to ripen and for gas formation in cheese. Normal fermentation in ensilage.

Lactobacillus casei

Taxonomy
- Order *Eubacteriales*
- Family *Lactobacillaceae*
- Tribe *Lactobacilleae*
- Genus *Lactobacillus*
- Species *casei*

Cellular Characteristics
- Morphology—Rods, short or long.
- Motility—Nonmotile.
- Staining—Gram positive.
- Occurring—In chains.
- Habitat—Milk and cheese products.

Physiological Characteristics
- Biochemical action
  - Milk—Acid with coagulation in 3 to 5 days, sometimes longer.

Protein digestion
  Casein—Utilized.
Fermentation reactions
  Monosaccharides
    Glucose—Acid.
    Fructose—Acid.
    Galactose—Acid.
    Mannose—Acid.
  Disaccharides
    Lactose—Acid.
    Maltose—Acid.
  Polyalcohols
    Mannitol—Acid.
  Glycosides
    Salicin—Acid.
Growth factors—The organism is inhibited when potassium acetate is added to the fatty acid-free medium. Separately they have little effect. The action is reversed if lithium or sodium or other fatty acid salts are added to the medium.
  Oxygen—Microaerophilic.
  Temperature
    Optimum—30 C.
    Minimum—10 C.
    Maximum—37 to 40 C for some strains.

Differentiation — *Lactobacillus casei-plantarum* group can be differentiated by paper chromatography.
  Acid production—Dextrolactic acid is the principal acid formed.
  L. plantarum—L. casei produces dextrolactic acid and ferments lactose more readily than maltose or sucrose.

Biochemical Characteristics
  Enzymes—Proteinase produced on substrate of casein at pH 6.0. Peptidase produced on substrate of glycyl-DL-alanine at pH 8.0. Peptidase produced on substrate of DL-alanylglycine at pH 7.0 to 7.5. Deaminase produced on substrate of serine at pH 7.0 (52 C); pH 8.3 (46 C).

Industrial Utilization
  Product—Lactic acid.
  Processes—Used to ferment milk or whey; *L. casei* is a principal organism of kefir grains used to make kefir-type fermented milk.

Assay Utilization—Used as assay organism for riboflavin, pyridoxine, and pantothenic acid.

Addenda. When the bacterial cells have reached the resting stage and reproduction ceases, the addition of riboflavin to the medium has no effect upon the cell. Bacterial cultures failing to reproduce still show a high rate of metabolism for some time. Because of an insufficient amount of riboflavin, cells can become prematurely old.

Extracts of pancreas contain two growth stimulants, of a peptide nature, for *L. casei.*

When the organism is grown on partly acid-free medium and the concentration of the sodium is low, potassium and acetate, when in combination, can inhibit the organism. Oleic acid can reverse the action.

Lactobacillus delbrueckii

Taxonomy

Order	*Eubacteriales*
Family	*Lactobacillaceae*
Tribe	*Lactobacilleae*
Genus	*Lactobacillus*
Subgenus	*Lactobacillus*
Species	*delbrueckii*

Cellular Characteristics
  Morphology—Rods.
  Motility—Nonmotile.
  Staining—Gram positive.
  Occurring—Singly and in short chains.
  Size—0.5 to 0.8 by 2.0 to 9.0 μ.
  Habitat—Fermenting vegetable and grain mashes.

Cultural Characteristics
Agar colonies—Crenated, small, flat.
Agar stroke—Translucent, narrow, grayish streaks.
Gelatin colonies—Small, gray, circular.
Nutrient broth—Slightly turbid.

Physiological Characteristics
Biochemical action
Nitrite—Not produced from nitrate.
Protein liquefaction or digestion
Gelatin—Not liquefied.
Fermentation reactions
Monosaccharides
Arabinose—No acid.
Rhamnose—No acid.
Xylose—No acid.
Glucose—Acid.
Galactose—Acid.
Fructose—Acid.
Disaccharides
Lactose—No acid.
Sucrose—Acid.
Maltose—Acid.
Trehalose—No acid.
Polysaccharides
Raffinose—No acid.
Starch—No acid.
Inulin—No acid.
Dextrin—Acid.
Alcohols and polyalcohols
Mannitol—No acid.
Glycosides
alpha-Methyl glucoside—No acid.
Growth factors
Oxygen—Microaerophilic.
Temperature
Optimum—45 C; high-temperature organism.

Biochemical Characteristics
Chemical end product—L-Lactic acid.
Fermentation—Homofermentative.

Industrial Utilization
Products—Produces L-lactic acid; converts carbohydrates to lactic acid; forms 1.6 per cent acid in mash.
Processes—Used in the production of white calcium lactate. Used as the initial inoculum in the production of yeast from cereal grain to secure a lactic acid medium.

Academic or Research Utilization
Physiological mechanisms—The organism has the ability to convert hexosediphosphate to methylglyoxal. Lactic acid may arise by this conversion.

Lactobacillus leichmannii

Taxonomy

Order	*Eubacteriales*
Family	*Lactobacillaceae*
Tribe	*Lactobacilleae*
Genus	*Lactobacillus*
Species	*leichmannii*

Cellular Characteristics
Morphology—Rods.
Motility—Nonmotile.
Staining—Gram positive; deeply stained granules.
Occurring—Singly and in short chains.
Size—0.6 by 2.0 to 4.0 μ.
Habitat—Dairy and plant products.

Cultural Characteristics
Agar colonies—Small with white centers.
Agar stroke—Grayish streak, limited growth.
Gelatin stab—No liquefaction.
Nutrient broth—Turbid.

Physiological Characteristics
Biochemical action
Nitrite—Not formed from nitrate.
Lactic acid—Produced, 1.3 per cent in mash.
Protein liquefaction
Gelatin—Not liquefied.
Fermentation reactions

Monosaccharides
- Arabinose—Not fermented.
- Rhamnose—Not fermented.
- Glucose—Acid.
- Fructose—Acid.
- Galactose—Small amount of acid.

Disaccharides
- Lactose—Not fermented.
- Sucrose—Acid.
- Maltose—Acid.
- Trehalose—Acid.

Polysaccharides
- Raffinose—Not fermented.
- Inulin—Not fermented.
- Dextrin—Not fermented.

Polyalcohols
- Mannitol—Small amount of acid.

Glycosides
- alpha - Methyl glucoside — Small amount of acid.

Growth factors
- Oxygen—Microaerophilic.
- Temperature
  - Optimum—36 C.
  - Maximum—40 to 46 C.

Differentiation
- *L. delbrueckii*—May be similar to *L. leichmannii* but has a lower optimum temperature.

Industrial Utilization
- Product—L-Lactic acid.
- Processes—Commercial production of lactic acid; fermentation of maltose or glucose; usually encountered in acetone-butanol fermentations.

Lactobacillus plantarum

Taxonomy

Order	*Eubacteriales*
Family	*Lactobacillaceae*
Tribe	*Lactobacilleae*
Genus	*Lactobacillus*
Species	*plantarum*

Cellular Characteristics
- Morphology—Rods, rounded ends; greater length as acidity of medium increases; short rods may occur; longer rods under adverse conditions.
- Motility—Nonmotile.
- Staining—Gram positive.
- Occurring—Singly or in short chains.
- Size—Usually 0.7 to 1.0 by 3.0 to 8.0 μ.
- Habitat—Distributed widely; commonly in fermenting plant and animal materials.

Cultural Characteristics
- Agar stroke—Slight or no growth.
- Gelatin-yeast extract-glucose stab—Filiform growth.
- Nutrient broth—Turbid or flocculent, depending on strain.

Physiological Characteristics

Biochemical action
- Nitrite—Not formed from nitrate.

Protein liquefaction
- Gelatin—Not liquefied.

Indicator reactions
- Litmus milk—Acid, usually coagulated.

Fermentation reactions

Monosaccharides
- Pentoses—Acetic and lactic acid formed.
- Arabinose—Acid.
- Rhamnose—Not fermented.
- Xylose—Acid, slowly.
- Hexoses—DL-Lactic acid, small quantity acetic acid and carbon dioxide.
- Glucose—Acid.
- Fructose—Acid.
- Galactose—Acid.
- Mannose—Acid.

Disaccharides
- Lactose—Acid.
- Sucrose—Acid.
- Maltose—Acid.

Polysaccharides
Raffinose—Acid.
Starch—Not fermented.
Inulin—Not fermented.
Dextrin—Acid, slowly.
Alcohols and polyalcohols
Glycerol—Acid, slowly.
Mannitol—Acid, slowly.
Sorbitol—Acid, slowly.
Growth factors
Oxygen—Microaerophilic.
Temperature
Optimum—30 C.
Minimum—10 C.
Maximum—40 C.
Thermal death range—65 to 75 C for 15 minutes.
Salt—Tolerates up to 5.5 per cent.

Spoilage
Food—Has been isolated from spoiled tomato products, fermenting potatoes, and other food products.

Biochemical Characteristics
Fermentation—Elaborates up to 1.5 per cent acid in broth.
Chemical end products—Inactive lactic acid.

Industrial Utilization
Processes—*L. plantarum* is the principal member of the third of four groups of organisms involved in kraut fermentation; pickle fermentation.

Leptospira icterohaemorrhagiae

Taxonomy

Order	*Spirochaetales*
Family	*Treponemataceae*
Genus	*Leptospira*
Species	*icterohaemorrhagiae*

Cellular Characteristics
Morphology—Closely wound coils. Difficult to detect, spinning motion. Cells may be hooked at both ends.
Flagella—None.
Staining—Poorly stained with most aniline dyes; Giemsa's stain will stain body red.
Size—0.25 by 6 to 9 μ; sometimes 20 to 25 μ.
Spiral size—0.4 to 0.5 μ, rigid.
Spiral depth—0.3 μ, regular.
Habitat—Kidneys and urine of wild rats; survives in water and slime.

Cultural Characteristics—Can be cultured in Ringer's solution, in a salt solution containing 10 per cent rabbit serum, and in 2 per cent agar.

Biochemical Characteristics
Bile salts, 10 per cent—Easily dissolved.
Saponin, 10 per cent—Resistant to solution.

Physiological Characteristics
Growth factors
Temperature
Range—25 to 37 C; lives longer at 25 C.

Serology—On the basis of serologic studies, 21 serogroups and more than 59 serotypes of *Leptospira* have been found which are pathogenic for man and other animals. *L. icterohaemorrhagiae* was the first recognized species.

Pathogenicity
Human beings—Cause of infectious jaundice or Weil's disease. It is believed infection takes place through a break in the skin or through the mucous membrane. The organism may be present in the urine during the final phases of the disease. The Pfeiffer phenomenon can be demonstrated. Lytic antibodies appear in the

blood shortly after infection. The organism is carried by rats. The disease usually occurs in damp, rat-infested places. Where the soil is acid, no outbreaks occur.

Animals—Pathogenic for guinea pigs and hamsters.

Identification—Guinea pig inoculation, observe for fever, jaundice of eyes, ears, and for *Leptospira* in blood. Spirochetes can be found in the liver and kidneys of dead animals. Dark-field examination. Agglutination and complement-fixation tests are available.

Leuconostoc mesenteroides

Taxonomy
- Order — *Eubacteriales*
- Family — *Lactobacillaceae*
- Tribe — *Streptococceae*
- Genus — *Leuconostoc*
- Species — *mesenteroides*

Cellular Characteristics
- Morphology—Spheres.
- Capsules—Gelatinous membrane of dextran in sucrose solutions.
- Staining—Gram positive.
- Occurring—Pairs, short or long chains.
- Size—0.9 to 1.2 μ in diameter.
- Habitat—Fermenting vegetables and other plant materials.

Cultural Characteristics
- Glucose gelatin colonies—White to grayish-white, small, raised, nodular.
- Glucose gelatin stab—Growth along stab; no liquefaction.
- Sucrose broth—Good growth with formation of slimy substance.
- Potato—No visible growth.
- Beetroot solution—Thick cake formed.
- Grape and cane sugar media—Growth in presence of nitrate and phosphate.
- Gelatin—Zoogloeal mass formed in presence of glucose or sucrose.

Physiological Characteristics
- Biochemical action
  - Indole—Not formed.
  - Voges-Proskauer test—Negative.
  - Nitrite—Not formed from nitrate.
- Protein liquefaction
  - Gelatin—Not liquefied.
- Indicator reactions
  - Methylene blue—Reduced.
- Fermentation reactions
  - Monosaccharides
    - Arabinose—Acid.
    - Xylose—Acid.
    - Glucose—Acid.
    - Fructose—Acid.
    - Galactose—Acid.
    - Mannose—Acid.
  - Disaccharides
    - Lactose—Acid may be formed.
    - Sucrose—Acid; produces slime also.
  - Polysaccharides
    - Starch—Rarely acid.
    - Inulin—Rarely acid.
    - Dextrin—Rarely acid.
- Growth factors
  - Oxygen—Facultatively anaerobic, microaerophilic.
  - Temperature
    - Optimum—21 to 25 C.
  - Nutrition—Certain strains require nicotinic acid and calcium pantothenate.

Biochemical Characteristics
- Enzyme production
  - Oxidase—Negative.
  - Catalase—Negative.
  - Peptidases—Di- and tripeptidases formed.
- Chemical end products—Forms 45 per cent levolactic acid, 20 per cent

carbon dioxide, and 25 per cent other products, such as acetic acid and ethyl alcohol in fermentation of glucose.

Industrial Utilization

Processes—*L. mesenteroides* is the principal member of the second of the four groups of bacteria involved in kraut manufacture; participates in pickle fermentation.

Addenda. Dextran derived from this organism contains 1,6 linkages which are able to activate both potato and muscle phosphorylase.

Listeria monocytogenes

Taxonomy

Order	*Eubacteriales*
Family	*Corynebacteriaceae*
Genus	*Listeria*
Species	*monocytogenes*

Cellular Characteristics

Morphology—Small rods, with rounded ends; V-shaped forms; in some culture media curved forms are found.

Motility—Positive—best observed when grown at room temperature.

Flagella—Peritrichous; nonflagellated mutants occur.

Capsules—None.

Staining—Gram positive; not acid fast.

Occurring—Singly or in parallel pairs; may be in short chains.

Size—0.4 to 0.5 by 0.5 to 2.0 μ.

Habitat—Lesions in organs, blood, cerebrospinal fluid of animals and man.

Cultural Characteristics—Media can be enriched by liver extract or blood.

Sheep liver extract agar colonies—Circular, flattened, smooth, transparent by transmitted light.

Sheep liver extract agar stroke—Flat transparent, viscid.

Gelatin stab—No liquefaction; growth along needle puncture.

Peptone broth—Film, flocculent sediment.

Glycerol-potato—No growth.

Special medium, containing 0. 25 per cent agar, 8.0 per cent gelatin, 1.0 per cent glucose, semisolid finish—Growth of organism along stab in 24 hours; irregular cloudy granular extensions; no spreading.

Inspissated ox serum—Thin transparent film.

Physiological Characteristics

Biochemical action

Indole production—Negative.

Hydrogen sulfide production—Negative.

Nitrite—Not produced from nitrate.

Odor—Unpleasant, acid.

Protein liquefaction or digestion

Blood serum agar—Zone of hemolysis.

Indicator reactions

Litmus milk—Acid to a slight degree; decolorized; no coagulation.

Fermentation reactions

Monosaccharides

Arabinose—Not fermented.

Rhamnose—Acid, no gas.

Xylose—Not fermented.

Glucose—Acid, no gas.

Galactose—Not fermented.

Disaccharides

Lactose—Slight acid produced.

Sucrose—Slight acid or variable.

Maltose—Slight acid produced.

Trehalose—Acid, no gas.

Polysaccharides

Melezitose—Variable.

Inulin—Not fermented.

Dextrin—Variable.
Alcohols and polyalcohols
Glycerol—Variable.
Dulcitol—Not fermented.
Mannitol—Not fermented.
Inositol—Not fermented.
Glucosides
Esculin—Hydrolyzed in 24 hours.
Salicin—Acid, no gas.
Growth factors
Oxygen—Aerobic, facultatively anaerobic.
Temperature
Optimum—37 C.
Thermal death time—58 to 59 C in 10 minutes.
Range—Down to 2.5 C.
Resistance
Sodium chloride solution, 20 per cent —Survives 8 weeks at 4 C.
Serology—Types 1, 2, 3, but not 4A or B share antigens with *Staphylococcus aureus.*
Antigenic grouping—Four types classified by flagellar and somatic antigens.
Agglutination—Different strains may be recognized by agglutination absorption reactions. O somatic antigens are designated as I, II, III, IV, and V; H flagella antigens as a, b, c, and d; there is cross agglutination.
Biochemical Characteristics
Enzyme production—Catalase produced.
Academic or Research Utilization—Host responses were studied after experimental infection of sheep. Reactions were change in body temperature, leucocyte change, production of agglutinating antibodies. Encephalitis was produced in only one of 16 sheep. The bacteria were not found in the sheep 15 days after exposure. Experiments performed with rabbits were the same as those performed with sheep. Some rabbits died; other rabbits harbored the organism in their healthy state.
Pathogenicity
Human beings—Cause of listerosis in man.
Animals—Cause of a monocytosis in 26 species of animals and birds. Injection of rabbits—increase of monocytes in blood. Organisms recovered from fowl were pathogenic for mice but not for fowl.

Addenda. Positive immunization against *L. monocytogenes* can be accomplished by inoculation of sublethal doses of the organism. Challenging by the intraabdominal route showed the most resistance to the infection; intracerebral, the least.

Usually antibiotics and antimicrobial agents do not work, but the following are to some degree effective: Chlorotetracycline, oxytetracycline; and sulfadiazine. Sulfonamides cure experimental infections. Penicillin is less effective. Chlorotetracycline is effective against resistant strains.

Methanomonas methanica

Taxonomy

Order	*Pseudomonadales*
Suborder	*Pseudomonadineae*
Family	*Pseudomonadaceae*
Genus	*Methanomonas*
Species	*methanica*

Cellular Characteristics
Morphology—Short rods; older cultures, organisms nearly spherical.
Motility—Motile in new cultures.
Flagella—Single flagellum, polar.
Membrane—Present when cultivated.

Staining—Gram negative.
Size—0.5 to 0.8 by 2.0 to 3.0 μ.
Habitat—Soil, widely distributed.

Cultural Characteristics
Washed agar—Membranous growth in an atmosphere containing 1 volume of methane per 2 volumes of air, when required salts are present.

Physiological Characteristics
Biochemical action
Methane—Oxidized to form carbon dioxide; organism obtains its energy by this oxidation.

Micrococcus flavus

Taxonomy
- Order *Eubacteriales*
- Family *Micrococcaceae*
- Genus *Micrococcus*
- Species *flavus*

Cellular Characteristics
Morphology—Spheres.
Motility—Generally nonmotile but at times motility is found.
Flagella—Single flagellum.
Staining—Gram variable.
Occurring—Singly, in clumps, or at times in tetrads.

Cultural Characteristics
Agar colonies—Small, yellowish, entire.
Agar stroke—Yellow, dry, raised, entire, and wrinkled.
Gelatin stab—Crateriform liquefaction; yellow, wrinkled surface; slow growth.
Nutrient broth—Turbid, yellowish ring and sediment.
Potato—Slight yellow growth.

Physiological Characteristics
Biochemical action
Indole—Not produced.
Ammonia—Formed from peptone.
Nitrite—Not produced from nitrate.
Protein liquefaction
Gelatin—Liquefied.
Indicator reaction
Litmus milk—Slight acid; soft coagulum formed; slow peptonization.
Fermentation reactions
Monosaccharides
Glucose—Generally acid.
Disaccharides
Lactose—Generally acid.
Color characteristics
Chromogenesis—When organism is grown in light, a yellow pigment is produced; when grown in the dark, it is colorless.
Growth factors
Temperature
Optimum—25 C.

Laboratory Utilization—Assay of bacitracin.

Micrococcus ureae

Taxonomy
- Order *Eubacteriales*
- Family *Micrococcaceae*
- Genus *Micrococcus*
- Species *ureae*

Cellular Characteristics
Morphology—Spheres.
Motility—Nonmotile.
Staining—Gram variable.
Occurring—Singly, in pairs, or in clumps; never in chains.
Habitat—Found in decomposing urine and in soil containing urine.

Cultural Characteristics
Agar colonies—White, slightly raised.
Agar stroke—Grayish-white, raised, glistening, butyrous.

Gelatin colonies—White, translucent, small, slimy.
Gelatin stab—Slight, white growth
Broth—Turbidity, viscid sediment.

Physiological Characteristics
Biochemical action
Indole—Not formed.
Starch—Not hydrolyzed.
Ammonia—Formed from peptone.
Nitrite—Not produced from nitrate.
Ammonium salts—Utilized.
Milk—Acidified.
Urea—Converted to ammonium carbonate; used as sole source of nitrogen.
Protein liquefaction
Gelatin—Slowly liquefied or not at all.
Indicator reaction
Litmus milk—Slightly alkaline reaction; slow reduction.
Fermentation reactions
Monosaccharides
Glucose—Acid.
Disaccharides
Lactose—Acid.
Sucrose—Acid.
Alcohols
Mannitol—Acid.
Growth factors
Oxygen—Aerobic.
Temperature
Optimum—25 C.
Nutrition—Saprophytic.
Color characteristics
Chromogenesis—No color formed on agar media.

Moraxella bovis

Taxonomy

Order	*Eubacteriales*
Family	*Brucellaceae*
Genus	*Moraxella*
Species	*bovis*
Synonym	*Hemophilus bovis*

Cellular Characteristics
Morphology—Short, plump rods.
Motility—Nonmotile.
Capsules—Capsulated.
Staining—Gram negative.
Size—0.5 by 1.5 to 2.0 μ.

Cultural Characteristics
Blood agar colonies—Round, zone of hemolysis, grayish-white in 1 day; colonies are deep and minute; surface colonies flattened at 48 hours; deep colonies ellipsoidal.
Agar stroke—Heavy viscid growth.
Gelatin colonies—Slow liquefaction and growth.
Nutrient broth—Sediment, slow growth, light turbidity.
Potato—No visible growth.

Physiological Characteristics
Biochemical action
Indole production—Negative.
Nitrite—Not formed from nitrate.
Protein liquefaction or digestion
Gelatin—Slowly liquefied.
Coagulated blood serum—Liquefied.
Indicator reactions
Litmus milk—Alkaline, partly coagulated.
Fermentation reactions
Monosaccharides
Glucose—No acid.
Fructose—No acid.
Galactose—No acid.
Mannose—No acid.
Growth factors
Oxygen—Aerobic.
Temperature—Growth in gelatin at 22 C; growth in blood agar at 38 C.
Optimum—36 C.
Thermal death time—Killed at 58 C in a few minutes.

Pathogenicity
Animals—May be the cause of pink eye

in cattle; incubation period 2 to 3 days; disease may be spread by direct contact, flies, etc.; cattle retained the organism up to 139 days after clinical signs subsided; eye secretions from 2 calfs showed bacteriophage action against a seeded culture of the organism; early stages may be treated with 1 per cent chloromycetin.

Not pathogenic for laboratory animals.

Mucor hiemalis

Taxonomy

Class	*Phycomycetes*
Subclass	*Zygomycetes*
Order	*Mucorales*
Family	*Mucoraceae*
Genus	*Mucor*
Species	*hiemalis*

Mycological Characteristics
- Mycelium—Nonseptate.
- Runners or stolons—None formed.
- Spores—Oval.
- Zygospores—Formed, usually heterothallic.
- Sporangia—Have spherical columellae.
- Sporangiophores—Unbranched.
- Chlamydospores—Not formed.
- Oidia—Not formed.

Physiological Characteristics
- Biochemical action
  - Starch—Digested.
- Protein liquefaction or digestion
  - Gelatin—Digested.
- Fermentation reactions
  - Monosaccharides
    - Glucose—Fermented.
  - Disaccharides
    - Sucrose—Not fermented.

Biochemical Characteristics
- Enzyme production—Enzyme that dissolves middle lamella of intercellular substance of flax produced.
- Chemical end products—beta-Carotene.

Industrial Utilization
- Processes—Retting of flax.

Mucor mucedo

Taxonomy

Class	*Phycomycetes*
Subclass	*Zygomycetes*
Order	*Mucorales*
Family	*Mucoraceae*
Genus	*Mucor*
Species	*mucedo*

Mycological Characteristics
- Mycelium—Nonseptate.
- Runners or stolons—Not formed.
- Spores—Smooth, regular, elongated ellipsoid 3 to 6 by 6 to 12 μ.
- Zygospores—Formed, usually heterothallic.
- Sporangia—Sporangial wall covered with fine needles of calcium oxalate; have cylindrical columellae; 100 to 200 μ in diameter.
- Sporangiophores—Unbranched, 30 to 40 μ thick, 2 to 15 cm tall.
- Oidia—Not formed.
- Chlamydospores—Not formed.
- Habitat—Horse manure; retting flax.

Cultural Characteristics—Easily obtained by incubating fresh horse manure.

Physiological Characteristics
- Biochemical action
  - Ammonia—Produced.
- Protein liquefaction or digestion
  - Gelatin—Liquefied.

Fermentation reactions
Monosaccharides
Glucose—Fermented.
Fructose—Fermented.
Disaccharides
Sucrose—Not fermented.
Maltose—Fermented to alcohol.

Biochemical Characteristics
Enzyme production—Lipases and proteases produced.
Chemical end products—Arsines formed; ammonia produced; oxalic acid.

Industrial Utilization
Processes—Ripening of snuff; retting flax.

Pathogenicity
Human beings—Associated with mycotic infection of eye.

Spoilage
Food—Bread and other foods.
Leather—Decomposed.

Mucor racemosus

Taxonomy

Class	*Phycomycetes*
Subclass	*Zygomycetes*
Order	*Mucorales*
Family	*Mucoraceae*
Genus	*Mucor*
Species	*racemosus*

Mycological Characteristics
Mycelium—Nonseptate; fragments to oidia when grown submerged in sugar solutions.
Oidia—Spherical; grow as single cells by budding analogous to yeasts.
Runners or stolons—None.
Spores—Elongated oval.
Sporangia—Sporangial wall; covered with small calcium oxalate crystals; have pear-shaped columellae.
Sporangiophores—Racemose branching.
Chlamydospores—Jet black in aerial mycelium; black in submerged mycelium.

Physiological Characteristics
Fermentation reactions
Sugars—Fermented with formation of ethyl alcohol, carbon dioxide, succinic acid.
Disaccharides
Sucrose—Hydrolyzed.

Biochemical Characteristics
Chemical end products—Glycerol produced; ammonia produced.

Industrial Utilization
Processes—Treatment of tobacco.

Mucor rouxii

Taxonomy

Class	*Phycomycetes*
Subclass	*Zygomycetes*
Order	*Mucorales*
Family	*Mucoraceae*
Genus	*Mucor*
Species	*rouxii*

Mycological Characteristics
Mycelium
Vegetative—Nonseptate; fat globules formed on starch substrates.
Submerged—Thick walled cells and yeast-like cells.
Aerial—Loosely meshed.
Runners or stolons—None.
Spores—Large, oval, colorless, glabrous.
Sporangia—Have spherical columellae; up to 50 μ.
Sporangiophores—Cymose branching; 1 mm long, 7 to 14 μ wide.
Chlamydospores—Black in aerial mycelium.

Physiological Characteristics
- Biochemical action
  - Starch hydrolysis—Yields glucose.
- Protein liquefaction or digestion
  - Gelatin—Slight liquefaction.
- Fermentation reactions
  - Monosaccharides
    - Arabinose—Anaerobic, no alcohol.
    - Rhamnose—Anaerobic, no alcohol.
    - Xylose—Anaerobic, no alcohol.
    - Glucose—Fermented; anaerobic yields alcohol.
    - Fructose—Fermented; anaerobic yields alcohol.
    - Mannose—Fermented; anaerobic yields alcohol.
  - Disaccharides
    - Lactose—Not fermented; anaerobic, no alcohol.
    - Sucrose—Not fermented; anaerobic, no alcohol.
    - Maltose—Fermented; anaerobic yields alcohol.
    - Melibiose—Anaerobic, no alcohol.
    - Trehalose—Fermented; anaerobic yields alcohol.
  - Polysaccharides
    - Raffinose—Anaerobic, no alcohol.
    - Starch—Fermented; anaerobic yields alcohol.
    - Inulin—Anaerobic, no alcohol.
    - Dextrin—Fermented; anaerobic yields alcohol.
  - Glucosides
    - alpha-Methyl glucoside—Fermented; anaerobic yields alcohol.
    - beta-Methyl glucoside—Anaerobic; no alcohol.
- Growth factors
  - Oxygen—Aerobic, facultatively anaerobic.

Biochemical Characteristics
- Enzyme production—Amylase and zymase produced; optimum amylase activity 35 to 38 C, destroyed at 72 C.
- Chemical end products—Lactic acid.

Industrial Utilization
- Products—Ethyl alcohol from starch without malting step.
- Processes—Alcoholic beverages from rice; Amylo process for industrial alcohol.

Mycobacterium marinum

Taxonomy

Order	*Actinomycetales*
Family	*Mycobacteriaceae*
Genus	*Mycobacterium*
Species	*marinum*

Cellular Characteristics
- Morphology—Short, thick, in clumps; long, thin, scattered, beaded or barred rods.
- Mycelium—Absent.
- Motility—Nonmotile.
- Staining—Gram positive; acid-fast, acid-alcohol-fast.
- Occurring—Singly or in clumps.
- Habitat—Salt-water fish.

Cultural Characteristics
- Agar colonies—In a week, smooth, slimy, moist, lemon-yellow to orange.
- Agar stroke—After a week, moist, glistening, elevated, lemon-yellow.
- Dorset's egg medium—Luxuriant growth after 2 weeks.
- Gelatin stab—Not liquefied.
- Glycerol agar colonies—In 2 weeks, grayish-white, moist, elevated with irregular margins.
- Glycerol broth—No pellicle, diffuse growth.
- Nutrient broth—No pellicle, diffuse growth.
- Petroff's egg medium—Luxuriant growth after 2 weeks.

Physiological Characteristics
Biochemical action
Indole production—Negative.
Nitrite—Not formed from nitrate.
Protein liquefaction
Gelatin—Not liquefied.
Indicator reactions
Litmus milk—Acidified and coagulated.
Fermentation reactions
Monosaccharides
Arabinose—Utilized.
Fructose—Utilized.
Galactose—Not fermented.
Polyalcohols
Sorbitol—Not fermented.
Growth factors
Oxygen—Aerobic, facultatively anaerobic.
Temperature
Optimum—18 to 20 C.
No growth—47 C.
Thermal death time—60 C for 1 hour.
Nutrition—Saprophytic.
Color characteristics
Chromogenesis—Lemon-yellow and orange colonies.
Serology
Agglutination—Can be distinguished from *M. ranae* and *M. friedmannii.*
Pathogenicity
Animals—Causes tuberculosis in salt-water fish.

Mycobacterium paratuberculosis

Taxonomy
Order *Actinomycetales*
Family *Mycobacteriaceae*
Genus *Mycobacterium*
Species *paratuberculosis*
Common Name Johne's bacillus
Cellular Characteristics
Morphology—Plump rods; some pleomorphic forms.
Motility—Nonmotile.
Flagella—None.
Staining—Acid-fast with Ziehl-Neelsen stain, gram positive; longer forms may show alternate stained and unstained segments.
Occurring—In clumps, singly and in pairs.
Size—1.0 to 2.0 μ.
Habitat—Intestinal mucosa, the cause of chronic diarrhea in cattle (Johne's disease).
Cultural Characteristics—Difficult to cultivate; grows best when killed acid-fast bacteria are added.
Glycerol agar colonies—Containing heat killed *Mycobacterium phlei:* 4 to 6 weeks dull, white, raised circular colonies.
Dorset's glycerol egg colonies—Containing sheeps' brain and heat killed *M. phlei:* colonies slightly luxuriant growth.
Glycerol broth—Sediment in bottom of tube, clear above; grows in clumps.
Dorset's glycerol egg medium—Containing heat killed *M. phlei:* Colonies dull, white, raised circular with irregular margin after 4 to 6 weeks. Cultures may become adjusted to synthetic medium free from dead added bacteria.

Physiological Characteristics
Growth factors
M. phlei—May contain a growth factor.
Resistance—Sensitive to streptomycin; resistant to isonicotinic acid hydrazide, terramycin.

Serology
  Antigenic structure—Johnin, a preparation similiar to tuberculin gives a positive reaction in cattle with Johne's disease.
Pathogenicity
  Animals—The cause of Johne's disease in cattle and sheep. The cause of chronic diarrhea. Chronic enteritis and emaciation finally ending in death of the animal is the course of the disease. Post-mortem examination reveals specific lesions in the intestinal tract. Bacilli are usually found in the mesenteric glands. The disease cannot be transferred to guinea pigs, rats, and mice. Disease produced experimentally in kids given a diet low in calcium.

Mycobacterium tuberculosis

Taxonomy
- Order *Actinomycetales*
- Family *Mycobacteriaceae*
- Genus *Mycobacterium*
- Species *tuberculosis*

Cellular Characteristics
- Morphology—Rods which may be straight or curved, sometimes swollen or beaded.
- Motility—Nonmotile.
- Capsules—Fatty envelope around organism.
- Staining—Gram positive, acid-fast and alcohol-fast; staining may be uneven; Ziehl-Neelsen and Pappenheim stains are used.
- Occurring—Singly or in threads.
- Size—0.3 to 0.6 by 0.5 to 4.0 μ.
- Habitat—Respiratory discharges and urine of tuberculosis cases; milk.

Cultural Characteristics
- Glycerol agar colonies—Cream colored, raised or thick nodular, wrinkled surface with irregular margin.
- Agar stroke—No growth
- Glyceral agar slant—Cream-colored growth, thick, raised after 3 to 5 weeks.
- Glycerol broth—Cream colored, wrinkled pellicle, granular deposit after 2 months.
- Dorset's egg media—Grayish-yellow separated growth, discrete, slightly raised granular surface after 1 month.
- Glycerol egg—Gray to yellow, luxuriant raised growth.
- Coagulated beef serum—Gray to yellow, thin; effuse, confluent, fine granular growth.
- Glycerol beef serum—Yellow to orange-yellow growth, coarsely granular surface, irregular areas.
- Bordet-Gengou medium—Finely, granular, raised colonies, 1.1 to 3.3 mm in diameter with indented edges.
- Löwenstein's medium—Raised colonies which look like a ball.
- Petragnani medium—Cream colored, good growth, colonies are raised and granular.
- Nutrient broth—No growth.

Physiological Characteristics
- Fermentation reactions
  - Monosaccharides
    - Arabinose—Utilized.
    - Glucose—Utilized.
    - Fructose—Utilized.
    - Galactose—Utilized.
  - Disaccharides
    - Lactose—Not fermented.
    - Sucrose—Not fermented.
- Growth factors
  - Temperature

Optimum—37 C.

Thermal death time—Moist heat will kill the organism at 60 C in 15 to 20 minutes.

Inhibition—Strains of the organism grown in appropriate medium were inhibited by 10^{-5} *M* diethyl-*p*-nitrophenyl phosphate; 5 per cent phenol is not very effective; direct sunlight will kill the organism in a few hours.

pH

Optimum—7.4 to 8.0; other investigation reported 6.0 to 6.5.

Serology—By absorption tests followed by agglutination and for complement fixation the mammalian variety can be distinguished from *M. avium*. Tuberculin is difficult to distinguish, but by cross anaphylactic reactions it is possible to differentiate the two.

Tubercle bacilli wax dissolved in *n*-hexadecane was used as an antigen to immunize mice; subcutaneous and intraperitoneal injections were effective.

Biochemical Characteristics—No true exotoxin produced but a substance called tuberculin is found in filtrates of glycerin broth. Tuberculin injected into a tubercular animal will cause a local inflammation at the site of injection. It is interpreted as a state of hypersensitivity due to the tubercle bacilli or its products. Used as a diagnostic test.

Academic or Research Utilization—The organism contains mycolic acid. There is a high lipid content, of about 40 per cent, containing neutral fat, phospholipids, and waxes; nucleoprotein contributes about ½ dry weight.

Pathogenicity

Human beings—The cause of tuberculosis in man; found in lung lesions of tuberculosis patients and also in sputum; the organisms may spread to other parts of the body.

Animals—Pathogenic for guinea pigs and rabbits, not for fowls. Generalized tuberculosis in guinea pigs is routine but not for rabbits. Can cause tuberculosis in dog, monkey, and parrot.

Differentiation—

Characteristic	Human Type	Bovine Type
Morphological	Long, slim, slightly bent, and may show beading and irregular staining.	Short, thick, and solidly stained.
Cultural	Grows well on media. Growth greatly enhanced by glycerol.	Grows poorly or not at all when freshly isolated on media.
Acid production in glycerol broth	As growth progresses, acidity is increased.	Bouillon becomes less and less acid.
pH of tuberculin	Markedly acid.	Alkaline or slightly acid.
Virulence for rabbits	Slightly virulent for rabbits.	Virulent for rabbits.

Addenda. The concentration of glucose puts a limiting growth on the organism. When ammonium *N* is present in limiting amounts, glucose in excess was proportional to the concentration of ammonium salt. Autolysis, which followed maximum growth using the glucose and ammonium salt as described, was related to the initial glucose in the medium.

Potato medium is best for BCG (a bovine strain) vaccine organism. A small number of virulent strains can produce tuberculosis in mice even if mixed with BCG organisms. The usual pulmonary lesions were observed after 8 weeks.

Species of the organism which are resistant to isonicotinic acid hydrazide fail to grow if hydrogen peroxide is present in the media. Formation of hydrogen peroxide can take place in the autoclave and involves oxygen, citrate, and traces of manganese. delta-Hexachlorocyclohexane at 16 micrograms/ml inhibits the growth of the organism *in vitro*. The inhibitory action disappears in serum.

An ester from the lipids of the tubercle bacilli was found to be methyl phthienoate and was saponified to give phthienoic acid. The absorption spectrum showed this acid to be a 2-alkenoic acid. Three new substances along with phthioceral accompany *M. tuberculosis*. These substances are called phthiotrial, phthiodiolone, and phthiocerolone.

Differences between the virulent and nonvirulent strains can be detected by suspending them in an alkaline buffer and adding neutral red. Virulent strains become rose colored and their lipopolysaccharides become red. Nonvirulent strains are less strongly colored.

2,3,5-Triphenyltetrazolium chloride added to broth and agar induced the growth of variants. Cholesterol found in the nonsaponifiable portion of egg yolk solids was found to be favorable for growth of the organism. A strain of *Fungi Imperfecti* had a stimulating effect on the growth of *M. tuberculosis* var. *hominis.*

Mycoplana dimorpha

Taxonomy
- Order — *Pseudomonadales*
- Suborder — *Pseudomonadineae*
- Family — *Pseudomonadaceae*
- Genus — *Mycoplana*
- Species — *dimorpha*

Cellular Characteristics
- Morphology—Irregular rods, short curved, branching in young cultures and in adults.
- Motility—Variable.
- Flagella—Long polar, variable.
- Staining—Gram negative.
- Size—0.5 to 0.7 by 1.25 to 4.5 μ.
- Habitat—Soil and marine habitats.

Cultural Characteristics
- Agar colonies—Circular, entire, smooth, buff, glistening, convex.
- Agar stroke—White, entire, glistening, filiform, convex.
- Gelatin colonies—Circular, entire, smooth, buff, resinous.
- Gelatin stab—No liquefaction, filiform growth.
- Nutrient broth—Turbid, surface ring.

Physiological Characteristics
- Biochemical action
  - Starch hydrolysis—Positive.
  - Nitrite—Not formed from nitrate but gas evolved in tubes.
  - Phenol—Utilized.
- Protein liquefaction or digestion
  - Gelatin—Not liquefied.
- Fermentation reactions
  - Carbohydrates—No acid.
- Growth factors

Oxygen—Aerobic.
Temperature
Optimum—Below 30 C.
Nutrition—Potassium ion, magnesium ion, and, in some instances, sodium ion were needed for growth. A general testing of 33 marine strains showed 19 were able to grow in a media containing one of several organic compounds; seven strains needed amino acids; 5 of the strains grew in the presence of vitamins.

Neisseria catarrhalis

Taxonomy
- Order — *Eubacteriales*
- Family — *Neisseriaceae*
- Genus — *Neisseria*
- Species — *catarrhalis*

Cellular Characteristics
- Morphology—Spheres, adjacent sides flattened.
- Staining—Gram negative.
- Occurring—Singly, or in pairs or tetrads.
- Habitat—Mucous membranes of the respiratory tract of human beings.

Cultural Characteristics—Grows on artificial media without enrichment.
- Blood agar colonies—Small, circular, grayish-white to dirty white, base margins.
- Nutrient broth—Turbidity with slight pellicle.

Physiological Characteristics
- Fermentation reactions
  - Carbohydrates—No acid.
- Growth factors
  - Oxygen—Aerobic, facultatively anaerobic.
  - Temperature—Can grow at temperatures below 20 C which distinguishes it from *N. meningitidis;* resistant to drying and heat.
    - Optimum—37 C; grows well at 22 C.
- Color and light characteristics
  - Chromogenesis—Forms no pigment.

Pathogenicity
- Human beings—The organism has been isolated from healthy persons as well as persons suffering from catarrhal inflammations.
- Animals—Pathogenic for guinea pigs which die of toxemia in 24 hours after an injection of a large dose of *N. catarrhalis.*

Neisseria gonorrhoeae

Taxonomy
- Order — *Eubacteriales*
- Family — *Neisseriaceae*
- Genus — *Neisseria*
- Species — *gonorrhoeae*
- Common name — gonococcus

Cellular Characteristics
- Morphology—Spheres with flattened sides; cocci form may resemble coffee beans.
- Motility—Nonmotile.
- Capsules—Usually none; some encapsulated forms may appear.
- Staining—Gram negative; safranin and carbol fuchsin used.
- Occurring—Singly and in pairs.
- Size—0.6 to 1.0 μ.
- Habitat—Parasitic, found in discharges of gonorrhea; also found in pus of conjunctival fluid.

Cultural Characteristics—Special media used, such as blood agar and ascitic agar.
- Blood agar colonies—Small, fine in appearance which do not hemolyze the medium.

Serum agar colonies—Grayish-white, round within the edge; glistening surface.
Gelatin stab—No growth.
Blood broth—Slight growth with turbidity.
Potato—No growth.
Chocolate agar (heated blood)—Good growth.

Physiological Characteristics
Biochemical action
Methyl reductase test—Negative.
Oxidase test—Colonies turn black when 1 per cent dimethyl-*p*-phenylenediamine is poured over culture of chocolate agar plate.
Fermentation reactions
Monosaccharides
Glucose—Acid.
Fructose—No acid.
Disaccharides
Sucrose—No acid.
Maltose—No acid.
Alcohols and polyalcohols
Mannitol—No acid.
Growth factors
Oxygen—Aerobic, facultatively anaerobic; increased carbon dioxide tension usually required.
Temperature
Optimum—37 C.
Range—25 to 40 C.
No growth— $<$ 25 C.
Resistance—Room temperature kills cultures; weak disinfectants are destructive.

Serology—Antibodies are produced, but little immunity is conferred.
Antigenic grouping—Two types have been recognized by agglutination and agglutinin absorption tests; the two types are related to two colony types: (*A*) large, irregular flattened, translucent colony with surface pepillation on long incubation. (*B*) small, round, raised opaque, convex with irregular surface.

Pathogenicity
Human beings—Gonococci are the cause of gonorrhea in man. Once contacted, the disease spreads quickly. The organism attacks the urethra in male and female. Newborn infants may contract conjunctivitis during parturition. Credé treatment is given to all newborn infants.
Animals—Nonpathogenic for lower animals. No exotoxin produced.

Addenda. At times L-shaped organisms may be observed. It is believed the L type of organism found in the culture may be a stage in the life cycle of the bacterium. The organism may swell when this occurs. The L organism can be subcultured on an artificial medium for long periods of time without reverting to the bacterial form.

Positive identification of the organism requires several steps to be followed:

1. Direct smear should be made from the suspected infected material, either urethal or conjunctival discharges. Gram stain is employed and the organism examined for general morphological characteristics.

2. Cultures should be made from the exudate. Special media should be used and placed in an atmosphere of 10 per cent carbon dioxide and temperature 32 C.

3. When cultures are examined after a 24-hour period aside from the regular colonial morphological identification, the oxidase test should be used. This consists of a 1 per cent solution of dimethyl or tetramethyl-*p*-phenylenediamine. The solution is poured over the growth and immediately poured off. Colonies of gonococci forming indophenoloxidase will turn pink, and finally black. Subcultures may be made

within 20 minutes after adding solution.

4. Carbohydrate fermentation may take place.

Silver proteinates, such as argyrol and protargol, may prevent infection after exposure.

Neisseria meningitidis

Taxonomy

Order	*Eubacteriales*
Family	*Neisseriaceae*
Genus	*Neisseria*
Species	*meningitidis*
Common name	meningococcus
Synonym	*Neisseria intracellularis*

Cellular Characteristics

Morphology—Spheres, adjacent side flattened, look like coffee beans; from patients intracellular diplococci; extracellular organisms found in early stages of disease.

Capsules—Groups I and II are encapsulated.

Staining—Gram negative; metachromatic granules (Löffler's or Neisser's stain); organism may autolyze.

Occurring—In pairs or occasionally in tetrads.

Size—0.6 to 0.8 μ in diameter.

Habitat—Nasopharynx of human beings.

Cultural Characteristics—Blood media with added glucose are needed for good isolation; frequent transplantation is required for newly isolated cultures. Hydrolyzed casein-starch medium used. Boors' tryptic digest medium. Laboratory cultures can be grown on a medium of glutamic acid, glucose, and mineral salts. Another medium is: glucose or lactate, thiosulfate, glutamate, and mineral salts. After 24 hours on most media: smooth, moist, elevated, bluish colonies.

Blood agar colonies—Small, convex, transparent and glistening.

Physiological Characteristics

Biochemical action

Nitrite—Formed from nitrate.

Oxidase test—Positive. No different from gonococci in the test.

Fermentation reactions

Monosaccharides

Glucose—Acid.

Fructose—No acid.

Disaccharides

Sucrose—No acid.

Maltose—Acid.

Alcohols and polyalcohols

Mannitol—No acid.

Growth factors

Oxygen—Aerobic; 5 to 10 per cent carbon dioxide favorable.

Temperature

Optimum—37 C.

No growth—22 C or $>$ 40 C.

Inhibition—Susceptible to penicillin and sulfonamides; susceptible to cold and drying. Lyophilization best method of preserving organisms.

pH—7.4 to 7.6.

Serology

Antigenic grouping—Contains somatic polysaccharide; cross agglutination with other *Neisseria, Klebsiella,* and pneumococci.

Typing—Type specificity is determined by capsular polysaccharide in Group I; polysaccharide-polypeptide in Group II.

Agglutination—Four main groups of *N. meningitidis* are classified, according to agglutination reactions with immune serum, as A, B, C, D.

Pathogenicity

Human beings—Infects man causing a pharyngitis. Cause of meningitis (epidemic cerebrospinal fever). In progressive infections, organisms gain entrance to blood. Meninges usually affected. Spots may appear called spotted fever. Blood cultures should be made before patient is treated with drugs. Chronic meningococcemia and bacterial endocarditis may result. Endotoxins found in dead meningococci. Shwartzman phenomenon demonstrated a diseased bluish skin area after filtrates were injected.

Animals—Chick embryos can be infected.

Nitrobacter winogradskyi

Taxonomy

Order	*Pseudomonadales*
Suborder	*Pseudomonadineae*
Family	*Nitrobacteraceae*
Genus	*Nitrobacter*
Species	*winogradskyi*

Cellular Characteristics

Morphology—Short rods.

Motility—Nonmotile.

Membrane—Gelatinous.

Staining—Gram negative; difficult to stain.

Size—0.6 to 0.8 by 1.0 to 1.2 μ.

Habitat—Soil (alkaline).

Cultural Characteristics

Washed agar colonies—In a week to 10 days, small, circular to irregular, light brown, becoming darker.

Washed agar slant—Scanty, grayish streak in 7 to 10 days.

Inorganic solution medium—Flocculent sediment after 10 days; sensitive to ammonium salts under alkaline conditions.

Silica gel—Small dense colonies.

Mineral broth—Sediment in 1 week to 10 days.

Physiological Characteristics

Biochemical action

Nitrate—Formed from nitrite.

Ammonia—Oxidized to nitrites (nitrosification).

Growth factors

Oxygen—Aerobic.

Temperature

Optimum—25 to 28 C.

Nutrition—Strictly autotrophic.

Nitrocystis sarcinoides

Taxonomy

Order	*Pseudomonadales*
Suborder	*Pseudomonadineae*
Family	*Nitrobacteraceae*
Genus	*Nitrocystis*
Species	*sarcinoides*

Cellular Characteristics

Morphology—Rods, ellipsoidal or wedge-shaped.

Zoogloeae—Formed.

Occurring—Grouped like sarcinia.

Size—0.5 to 1 μ.

Source—Found in the soil; activated sludge.

Cultural Characteristics

Colonies on silica gel (coated with kaolin)—Appear as warts; may grow up to 5 mm in diameter.

Colonies—Sticky and viscid when young, becoming brown with age; older colonies are like grains of sand; each colony is surrounded by thick slime.

Physiological Characteristics
Biochemical action
Nitrites—Oxidized to nitrates.
Growth factors
Oxygen—Aerobic.

Nitrosomonas europaea

Taxonomy
- Order *Pseudomonadales*
- Suborder *Pseudomonadineae*
- Family *Nitrobacteraceae*
- Genus *Nitrosomonas*
- Species *europaea*

Cellular Characteristics
Morphology—Rods, almost ellipsoidal.
Motility—Motile swarm cells.
Flagella—Polar, 4 to 8 μ in length.
Occurring—Singly or in a mass.
Size—0.9 to 1.0 by 1.1 to 1.8 μ.
Habitat—Soil, widely distributed.

Cultural Characteristics
Aqueous media with salts—Grows readily at bottom in soft masses around magnesium carbonate.
Silica gel colonies—Small, compact, brownish, well defined.

Physiological Characteristics
Biochemical action
Ammonia—Oxidized to nitrite.
Ammonium salts—Oxidized to nitrite.
Growth factors
Oxygen—Aerobic.
Nutrition—Strictly autotrophic; medium must contain ammonium salt, such as ammonium sulfate, magnesium carbonate, and potassium phosphate.
Inhibition—Chelating agents inhibit formation of ammonia.

Nocardia asteroides

Taxonomy
- Order *Actinomycetales*
- Family *Actinomycetaceae*
- Genus *Nocardia*
- Species *asteroides*

Cellular Characteristics
Morphology—Bacillary and coccoid forms may be present, branching mycelium; in disease tissue red or black granules may be observed.
Mycelium
Vegetative—Yellow to red.
Aerial—Not visible.
Staining—Gram positive; some acid-fast forms.

Cultural Characteristics
Czapek's medium—Yellow to orange growth.
Starch—Limited orange growth.
Agar—Many folded light yellow, subsequently marked yellow to yellow-red growth.
Gelatin stab—No growth within stab; growth on surface yellowish.
Glucose broth—Thin yellow pellicle.
Potato—Very wrinkled growth, first white then yellow to red.

Physiological Characteristics
Biochemical action
Starch hydrolysis—Negative.
Neutral red—Negative.
Nitrite—Formed from nitrate.
Protein liquefaction or digestion
Gelatin—Not liquefied.
Growth factors
Oxygen—Aerobic.
Temperature
Optimum—37 C.
Grows—At room temperature.

Nutrition—A strain of the organism was able to metabolize naphthalene, and salicylic and benzoic acids; salicylic acid may be an intermediate in the breakdown of naphthalene.

Resistance—Resistant to streptomycin. Inhibited by aureomycin, chloroamphenicol, terramycin. Subtilin affected the growth of the organism in a 1:1000 dilution. Sulfadiazine used to treat patients.

Color and light characteristics

Chromogenesis—Insoluble pigments formed are cream to yellow and orange.

Biochemical Characteristics

Antibiotic production—An antibiotic produced by a strain of the organism was able to inhibit the tobacco mosaic virus. Cholic acid can be converted to a compound labeled 246 by a strain of the organism.

Chemical end products—Glucose-6-phosphate and both 6-phosphogluconate, dehydrogenase were found in extracts of the cell. When ribose-5-phosphate was used by the cell, hexoses, heptoses, and trioses were formed. The ribose-5-phosphate was inhibited by *M*/60 inorganic phosphate.

Composition of cell wall—Chitin and cellulose were not identified and were not part of the cell wall. This was demonstrated in other organisms belonging to the *Actinomycetales,* which from a chemical point of view, belong to the bacteria, not the true fungi.

Academic or Research Utilization—The organism is similar to *Mycobacterium tuberculosis* (acid-fast staining).

Pathogenicity

Human beings—Causes lesions in man; found in diseases resembling tuberculosis.

Animals—Pathogenic for laboratory animals.

Addenda. A rod-shaped virus (bacteriophage) viewed with the electron microscope entered the organism through holes in the cell membrane and attacked the cytoplasm without attacking the nucleus.

Nocardia opaca

Taxonomy

Order	*Actinomycetales*
Family	*Actinomycetaceae*
Genus	*Nocardia*
Species	*opaca*

Cellular Characteristics

Morphology—Rods or long curved branching filaments; in older cultures rods as short as cocci may be found.

Staining—Gram positive; not acid-fast.

Occurring—Few chains or clumps.

Habitat—Found in the soil.

Cultural Characteristics

Gelatin colonies—Whitish, convex, smooth, shiny, edges slightly arborescent.

Gelatin stab—Whitish, smooth, convex, filiform.

Nutrient broth—Turbid, broken white film or granular suspension; coccoid forms.

Dorset's egg medium—Salmon-colored growth, spreading, smooth and moist.

Löffler's medium—Light, buff-colored,

scanty growth, smooth and moist.
Glycerol potato—Buff-colored growth, or pink; dry, rough, crumpled.
Nutrient agar—Opaque, cream-colored growth.

Physiological Characteristics
Biochemical action
Nitrite—Formed from nitrate.
Phenol—Utilized.
Hydrocarbons (naphthalene, dodecane, tetradecane, octadecane)—Utilized.
Protein liquefaction
Gelatin—Not liquefied.
Indicator reactions
Litmus milk—Slightly alkaline; grayish pellicle.
Fermentation reactions
Monosaccharides
Glucose—No acid.
Disaccharides
Lactose—No acid.
Sucrose—No acid.
Maltose—No acid.
Growth factors
Temperature
Optimum—30 C.
pH
Optimum—6.8 to 7.3.
Nutrition—Oxygen uptake is increased by adding *n*-dodecane to medium. Other hydrocarbons, such as paraffin wax, also increase oxygen uptake.

Differentiation from
N. corallina—*N. opaca* cells much longer.
N. polychromogenes—*N. opaca* cells much shorter.

Nocardia rubra

Taxonomy

Order	*Actinomycetales*
Family	*Actinomycetaceae*
Genus	*Nocardia*
Species	*rubra*

Cellular Characteristics
Morphology—Filaments forming unicellular mycelium.
Mycelium—Produced in young cultures; septa formed which break into short rods, then coccoid forms.
Staining—Gram positive; not acid-fast.
Habitat—Soil.

Cultural Characteristics
Colonies—Bright or dark red, smooth or folded, may be rough.
Nutrient broth—Medium clear; surface ring, sediment.
Potato—Good growth.
Sodium chloride solution—Can grow well in 5 to 10 per cent salt solution.

Physiological Characteristics
Biochemical action
Starch hydrolysis—Negative.
Nitrite—Not formed from nitrate.
Fats—Utilized.
Paraffin—Utilized.
Wax—Utilized less readily than paraffin.
Milk—No coagulation or peptonization.
Protein liquefaction
Gelatin—Not liquefied.
Fermentation reactions
Disaccharides
Sucrose—Not inverted.
Polysaccharides
Cellulose—Not attacked.

Color characteristics
Pigment—Produced; red in color; is a carotenoid; soluble in chloroform, slightly soluble in alcohol and ether.

Growth factors
Nutrition—Hydrocarbons utilized; can grow readily in 5 to 10 per cent sodium chloride solution.

Noguchia granulosis

Taxonomy
- Order — *Eubacteriales*
- Family — *Brucellaceae*
- Genus — *Noguchia*
- Species — *granulosis*

Cellular Characteristics
- Morphology—Rods, involution atypical forms found in older cultures of blood agar.
- Motility—Motile.
- Flagella—Single peritrichous.
- Staining—Gram negative.
- Occurring—Singly.
- Size—0.25 to 0.3 by 0.8 to 1.2 μ.

Cultural Characteristics
- Agar—No growth.
- Blood agar colonies—Initial are grayish, round, raised; subsequent are sticky and opalescent, becoming brown.
- Semisolid *Leptospira* medium—Gray-white forming zones, diffuse.

Physiological Characteristics
- Fermentation reactions
  - Monosaccharides
    - Mannose—Acid.
    - Glucose—Acid.
    - Rhamnose—Small quantity of acid.
    - Fructose—Acid.
    - Galactose—Acid.
    - Xylose—Acid.
  - Disaccharides
    - Sucrose—Acid.
    - Maltose—Acid.
    - Trehalose—Small quanity of acid.
  - Polysaccharides
    - Raffinose—Small quantity of acid.
    - Inulin—Small quantity of acid.
  - Alcohols and polyalcohols
    - Mannitol—Acid.
    - Sorbitol—No acid.
    - Dulcitol—No acid.
  - Glycosides
    - Salicin—Acid.
    - Amydalin—Acid.
- Growth factors
  - Oxygen—Facultatively anaerobic.
  - Temperature
    - Optimum—Between 15 and 30 C.
    - Grows—At body temperature.
  - pH—7.8
- Distinctive characteristics—On *Leptospira* medium and blood medium (agar), when grown at 30 to 37 C, nonmotile forms will appear; on agar plates (horse blood) at 30 C, and motile forms at 15 C on blood agar.

Pathogenicity
- Human beings—The cause of a disease simulating trachoma.
- Animals—Causes conjunctivitis in monkeys and apes.

Pasteurella multocida

Taxonomy
- Order — *Eubacteriales*
- Family — *Brucellaceae*
- Genus — *Pasteurella*
- Species — *multocida*
- Synonyms — Family name known as *Parvobacteriaceae*; *Pasteurella septica*

Cellular Characteristics
- Morphology—Short ellipsoidal rods.
- Motility—Nonmotile.
- Staining—Gram negative, bipolar staining.
- Occurring—Singly and in pairs.
- Size—0.3 to 1.25 μ in length.

Cultural Characteristics—Can usually grow on ordinary media.
- Agar—Translucent growth, odor.

Nutrient broth—Turbidity, odor.
Potato—No growth.

Physiological Characteristics
- Biochemical action
  - Indole production—Positive.
  - Hydrogen sulfide—Produced.
  - Nitrite—Formed from nitrate.
  - Milk—Coagulated.
- Protein liquefaction or digestion
  - Gelatin—Not liquefied.
  - Blood agar—No hemolysis.
- Fermentation reactions
  - Monosaccharides
    - Arabinose—Usually no acid.
    - Rhamnose—No acid.
    - Xylose—Usually acid but no gas.
    - Glucose—Acid, no gas.
    - Fructose—Acid, no gas.
    - Galactose—Acid, no gas.
    - Mannose—Acid, no gas.
  - Disaccharides
    - Lactose—No acid.
    - Maltose—Usually no acid.
    - Sucrose—Acid, no gas.
    - Trehalose—Usually acid but no gas.
  - Polysaccharides
    - Raffinose—No acid.
    - Inulin—No acid.
    - Dextrin—No acid.
  - Alcohols and polyalcohols
    - Glycerol—No acid.
    - Erythritol—No acid.
    - Mannitol—Usually acid but no gas.
    - Sorbitol—Acid, no gas.
    - Dulcitol—No acid.
    - Adonitol—No acid.
  - Glucosides
    - Amygdalin—No acid.
    - Salicin—Usually no acid.
- Growth factors
  - Oxygen—Aerobic to facultatively anaerobic.
  - Temperature
    - Optimum—37 C.
    - Thermal death point—Above 45 C.
  - Inhibition
    - Bile salts—inhibit growth.

Serology—Four types A, B, C, and D.
- Hemagglutination—Types A and B largely from cattle; type A associated with pneumonia; type B associated with epizootic hemorrhagic septicemia.

Pathogenicity
- Animals—Cause of hemorrhagic septicemia in mammals and birds; cause of chicken cholera; virulent for mice and rabbits.

Pasteurella pestis

Taxonomy

Order	*Eubacteriales*
Family	*Brucellaceae*
Genus	*Pasteurella*
Species	*pestis*
Synonyms	Family name known as *Parvobacteriaceae*

Cellular Characteristics
- Morphology—Rods, safety pin, and ring involution forms; involution forms in 3 to 4 per cent sodium chloride solution.
- Motility—Nonmotile.
- Capsules—Gelatinous capsule.
- Staining—Gram negative, polar staining; stain with ordinary dyes like methylene blue, carbol fuchsin.
- Size—1.0 to 2.0 μ by 0.5 to 0.7 μ in breadth.

Cultural Characteristics
- Agar colonies—Translucent, grayish-white, iridescent, undulate.
- Agar stroke—Translucent, grayish, moist, thin; growth expedited by blood or sodium sulfite.
- Gelatin colonies—Flat, gray, granular margin; arborescent in stab; no liquefaction.

Nutrient broth—Turbid or clear; old cultures show pellicle with streamers.
Potato—Scanty grayish growth.

Physiological Characteristics
Biochemical action
Indole production—Negative.
Nitrite—Formed from nitrate.
Protein liquefaction or digestion
Gelatin—Not liquefied.
Indicator reactions
Litmus milk—Slight acidity of medium, no coagulation.
Fermentation reactions
Monosaccharides
Rhamnose—Not fermented.
Glucose—Acid, no gas.
Galactose—Acid, no gas.
Disaccharides
Lactose—Not fermented.
Maltose—Acid, no gas.
Polysaccharides
Raffinose—Not fermented.
Inulin—Not fermented.
Alcohols and polyalcohols
Glycerol—Variable.
Growth factors
Oxygen—Aerobic, facultatively anaerobic.
Temperature
Optimum—25 to 30 C.
Minimum—0 C.
Maximum—43 to 45 C.
Resistance—Resistant to cold, killed in few hours by drying or sunlight.
Tolerance—Killed in a few minutes by 1 per cent Lysol or chloride of lime.

Serology—*P. pestis* and *P. pseudotuberculosis* not differentiated by serologic methods.
Immunity—One attack confers immunity on the individual.

Biochemical Characteristics
Composition—Lipopolysaccharide removed from the cell, purified by ethyl alcohol fractionation and ultracentrifugation, showed by analysis to be 1.6 per cent nitrogen and 2.2 per cent phosphorus.

Pathogenicity
Human beings—The cause of plague in man; plague may be of 3 types: bubonic, spread by flea; pneumonic, spread by contact; septicemic, fatal. Transmitted from rat to rat and from rat to man by rat flea. Pneumonic plague may be spread by droplet infection. Diagnosis—smear from buboes, post-mortum blood of dead guinea pig inoculation.
Animals—Cause of plague in rats and other rodents; infectious for mice, guinea pigs, and rabbits.

Pasteurella septicaemiae

Taxonomy
Order — *Eubacteriales*
Family — *Brucellaceae*
Genus — *Pasteurella*
Species — *septicaemiae*

Cellular Characteristics
Morphology—Small rods.
Motility—Nonmotile.
Staining—Gram negative.
Occurring—Singly, in pairs on threads.
Size—0.5 by 1.5 to 2.0 μ.
Habitat—Found in young geese suffering from fatal septicemia.

Cultural Characteristics
Agar colonies—Circular, smooth, transparent, entire.
Agar stroke—Grayish-white streak, slightly viscid, becoming transparent.
Endo agar—No growth.

Gelatin colonies—Small, white, circular.
Gelatin stab—Infundibuliform liquefaction.
Nutrient broth—Uniform turbidity, slight pellicle.

Physiological Characteristics
Biochemical action
Indole production—After several days positive.
Hydrogen sulfide production—Positive.
Protein liquefaction or digestion
Gelatin—Liquefied.
Blood serum—Yellowish-white streak, medium slowly liquefied.

Fermentation reactions
Monosaccharides
Glucose—Slight acid, no gas.
Disaccharides
Lactose—No acid.
Growth factors
Temperature
Optimum—37 C.

Pathogenicity
Animals—The cause of fatal septicemia in young geese; not pathogenic for chickens, pigeons, white mice, and guinea pigs; may cause illness in ducks.

Pasteurella tularensis

Taxonomy

Order	*Eubacteriales*
Family	*Brucellaceae*
Genus	*Pasteurella*
Species	*tularensis*

Cellular Characteristics
Morphology—Pleomorphic rods; organisms are divided among the cocci, rods, and bipolar forms.
Motility—Nonmotile.
Capsules—May be present when organisms are isolated from tissues or serum.
Staining—Gram negative, stains with carbol fuchsin, gentian violet.
Occurring—Singly.
Size—0.2 by 0.2 to 0.7 μ.
Habitat—Found in rabbits, hares, rodents, and other animals; the disease is transmitted to man by bites of insects or infected animals.

Cultural Characteristics—Organisms need special media for growth and isolation. Enrichment foods, such as egg, blood, serum, or rabbit spleen, are required.
Agar colonies—Various types occur, including rough R, smooth S, and mucoid-like varieties.
Dorset's egg medium—Drop-like colonies, which are transparent, appear in a few days.
Egg yolk medium colonies—Mucoid pinpoint becoming larger on consecutive days.
Serum glucose agar colonies—Drop-like.
Blood glucose cystine agar colonies—Grayish-white, small, viscid, easily emulsified.

Physiological Characteristics
Biochemical action
Hydrogen sulfide—Formed in cystine media.
Sodium ricinoleate—Dissolves growth.
Fermentation reactions
Monosaccharides
Glucose—Slight acid reaction, no gas.
Fructose—Slight acid reaction, no gas.
Disaccharides
Maltose—Slight acid reaction, no gas.
Polysaccharides
Dextrin—Slight acid reaction, no gas.
Alcohols and polyalcohols
Glycerol—Slight acid reaction, no gas.
Growth factors

Oxygen—Strictly aerobic.
Temperature
Optimum—37 C.
Thermal death time—10 minutes at 56 C.
Resistance—Killed by 2 per cent solution of tricresol in 2 minutes. Sunlight is detrimental.

Serology—Two types of antibodies are found in the serum of infected animals, agglutinins and complement-fixing antibodies. Differentiation tests must be performed since there are cross reactions with *Brucella* organisms. There are two reactions to be found: (a) *Brucella abortus* and *B. melitensis* will be agglutinated up to titers of 1/5 to 1/6 of the regular titer of 1 to 2560 or 5210 which agglutinates *P. tularensis*. (b) Members of the *Brucella* group do not absorb agglutinins of *P. tularensis*. Immunity is conferred after one attack.

Pathogenicity—The cause of tularemia, a disease characterized by buboes and necrosis of the skin. The disease is transmitted by infected animals and insects. The disease is of long duration.
Animals—Many animals can become infected with tularemia. It is usually fatal for smaller animals. The organism is found in the spleen, liver, blood, and lymph nodes. Diagnosis can be made by cultures, animal inoculation, and agglutination tests. Agglutination of 1:80 without cross reaction to the *Brucella* group is diagnostic. Streptomycin has been used to treat the disease.

Pediococcus cerevisiae

Taxonomy

Order	*Eubacteriales*
Family	*Lactobacillaceae*
Tribe	*Streptococceae*
Genus	*Pediococcus*
Species	*cerevisiae*

Cellular Characteristics
Morphology—Spheres.
Motility—Nonmotile.
Staining—Gram negative.
Occurring—Singly, or in pairs or tetrads.
Size—1 to 1.3 μ.
Habitat—Fermenting materials, wort, beer, yeast, sauerkraut, and pickles.

Cultural Characteristics—Does not grow in alkaline medium.
Meat extract gelatin stab—Not liquefied; growth along stab, white, raised surface growth.
Wort with calcium carbonate—White colonies, carbonate dissolved.
Potato—Scanty growth.
Peptone meat extract gelatin—Not liquefied. White becoming yellow to yellow-brown.

Physiological Characteristics
Biochemical action
Nitrite—Not formed from nitrate.
Urea—Not utilized.
Indicator reactions
Litmus milk—No growth; some strains cause coagulation.
Fermentation reactions
Monosaccharides
Arabinose—Usually acid.
Rhamnose—Sometimes acid.
Xylose—Sometimes acid.
Glucose—Acid.
Fructose—Acid.
Galactose—Acid.
Mannose—Acid.
Disaccharides
Lactose—Usually acid.

Sucrose—Usually acid.
Maltose—Acid.
Polysaccharides
Raffinose—Usually acid.
Starch—No acid.
Inulin—No acid.
Dextrin—No acid.
Alcohols and polyalcohols
Mannitol—No acid.
Glucosides
Amydalin—Usually acid.
Salicin—Usually acid.
alpha-Methyl glucoside—No acid.

Growth factors
Oxygen—Microaerophilic
Temperature
Optimum—25 to 32 C.
Range—7 to 45 C.
Thermal death time—60 C for 8 minutes.

Nutrition
Alkaline media—No growth.
Amino acid requirements—Required are DL-alanine, L-arginine, L-aspartic acid, asparagine, L-cystine, L-glutamic acid, glycine, L-histidine, DL-isoleucine, DL-leucine, L-proline, DL-phenylalanine, DL-serine, DL-threonine, L-tryptophane, and L-tyrosine. DL-Methionine and DL-lysine have a stimulating effect. Asparagine partially replaces aspartic acid. Aspartic acid can replace asparagine.
Nitrogen requirements—Some strains require purines and pyrimidines, with xanthine and guanine being most effective and thymine and uracil least; some require uracil; some require no pyrimidines or purines.
Vitamin requirements—Niacin, pantothenic acid, and leucovorin are absolute requirements; some strains require riboflavin; biotin and pyridoxine have a stimulating effect.

Biochemical Characteristics
Enzyme production—Usually catalase negative.
Chemical end products—Biacetyl (diacetyl) produced probably by oxidation of acetoin.

Spoilage
Beer—Cause of "sarcina" odor.

Penicillium camemberti

Taxonomy

Class	*Fungi Imperfecti*
Subclass	*Hyphomycetes*
Order	*Moniliales*
Family	*Moniliaceae*
Genus	*Penicillium*
Group	*Asymmetrica*
Subgroup	*Lanata-Typica*
Species	*camemberti*

Mycological Characteristics
Mycelium
Aerial—Abundant, giving colony woolly texture.
Conidia—Appear in center of colony after aerial felt is established; elliptical when formed, becoming subglobose.
Sterigmata—Groups of 2 to 5.
Metulae—Arise at different levels of the penicillus.
Conidiophores—Long, arise from substratum and upon branches from aerial hyphae; walls are roughened; spore bearing parts poorly differentiated.
Penicillus—Branched asymmetrically around axis of conidiophore.

Cultural Characteristics
Czapek's agar solution colonies—After 7 to 8 days cream to pale yellow

with pronounced odor; exudate may be scattered through mycelial mass with penicilli and conidial chains forming irregular masses about 50 to 80 μ in length; after 12 days change from white to green.

Steep agar colonies—Like those on Czapek's agar but grow more rapidly and with heavy spore formation.

Malt extract agar colonies—Rapid growth with condiophores up to 2 mm in length; penicilli are larger than on Czapek's agar.

Biochemical Characteristics

Enzyme production—Large number of enzymes produced; among these are amylases, invertase, maltase, raffinase, lactase, erepsin, lipases, proteases, and nuclease.

Industrial Utilization

Products—Used in the manufacture of Camembert cheese; texture and flavor of cheese depend upon proteolytic activity of *P. camemberti;* the curd is inoculated with the mold and goes from an acid to an alkaline reaction, the ripening proceeding from the outside to the inside of the cheese.

Penicillium chrysogenum

Taxonomy

Class	*Fungi Imperfecti*
Subglass	*Hyphomycetes*
Order	*Moniliales*
Family	*Moniliaceae*
Genus	*Penicillium*
Group	*Asymmetrica*
Subgroup	*Velutina*
Subgroup	*Radiata*
Species	*chrysogenum*

Mycological Characteristics—There are great variations in the morphology of strains of *P. chrysogenum;* in general they exhibit characteristics of the *Asymmetrica* group of the penicillia.

Conidia—Produced; have ability to grow after long periods of desiccation.

Sterigmata—Generally groups of 2 to 5.

Conidiophores—Smooth wall in virtually all strains.

Penicillus—Smooth wall, branched asymmetrically around axis of conidophore; many strains distorted.

Cultural Characteristics—Valuable strains capable of submerged culture.

Physiological Characteristics

Color characteristics

Chromogenesis—Most strains produce yellow pigment.

Biochemical Characteristics

Antibiotic production—Major producer of penicillin; principal strains NRRL 1951.B25; Stanford 25099, Stanford 35217 and other variants of NRRL 1951.B25, including Wisconsin series.

Industrial Utilization

Products—Penicillin.

Penicillium notatum

Taxonomy

Class	*Fungi Imperfecti*
Subclass	*Hyphomycetes*
Order	*Moniliales*
Family	*Moniliaceae*
Genus	*Penicillium*
Group	*Asymmetrica*
Species	*notatum*

Mycological Characteristics—There are great variations in the morphology of strains of *P. notatum;* in general, they exhibit the characteristics of the *Asymmetrica* group of the penicillia.
- Conidia—Numerous forming radial furrows resembling a wheel.
- Conidiophores—Smooth wall.
- Sterigmata—In clusters.
- Metulae—Vertical.
- Penicillus—Smooth wall.

Cultural Characteristics
- Czapek's agar solution colonies—Grow rapidly with good growth in 10 to 12 days at room temperature; blue-green shades, yellow to amber in color with white to yellowish margins; older colonies become brown; abundant spores.
- Steep agar colonies—Rapid growth, velvety appearance, abundant spores, radial pattern, exudate produced.
- Malt agar colonies—Rapid growth in 10 to 12 days, no furrows, clear blue, green exudate lacking.

Biochemical Characteristics
- Antibiotic production—Penicillin produced by nearly all strains; NRRL 1249.B21 principal strain for surface culture production; NRRL 832.A2 used for submerged culture production.

Industrial Utilization
- Products—Formerly used as principal means of production of penicillin.

Penicillium roqueforti

Taxonomy

Class	*Fungi Imperfecti*
Subclass	*Hyphomycetes*
Order	*Moniliales*
Family	*Moniliaceae*
Genus	*Penicillium*
Group	*Asymmetrica*
Subgroup	*Velutina*
Subgroup	*Stellata*
Species	*roqueforti*

Mycological Characteristics
- Mycelium
  - Vegetative—Submerged hyphae have granular walls.
  - Aerial—Velvety appearance.
- Conidia—Abundant, green.
- Conidiophores—Generally short, ascending, aerial loops.
- Penicillus—Varies from verticils of metulae and sterigmata to compact branching.

Cultural Characteristics
- Czapek's agar colonies—Spreading, heavy sporing in 10 to 12 days at room temperature; surface smooth, margin is broad, thin, and white; radiating hyphae on surface or just below surface; conidial areas are green forming at margin; no exudate in most strains.
- Malt extract agar colonies—Growth more rapid than on Czapek's agar; other characteristics similar, although conidiophores and metulae may be rougher.

Biochemical Characteristics
- Enzyme production—Lipase formed.

Industrial Utilization
- Products—Manufacture of Roquefort cheese. Curd is inoculated with *P. roqueforti* and is ripened by growth of mold; pungent taste of cheese is due to fatty acids like caproic, caprylic, and cap-

ric acids liberated from milk fat by lipase of the mold. Because mold is aerobic, holes are punched in curd to give some air to mold.

Peptostreptococcus magnus

Taxonomy
- Order — *Eubacteriales*
- Family — *Lactobacillaceae*
- Genus — *Peptostreptococcus*
- Species — *magnus*
- Synonym — *Diplococcus magnus;* family name *Lactobacteriaceae*

Cellular Characteristics
- Morphology—Large spherical cells.
- Staining—Gram negative.
- Occurring—Usually in pairs or small clumps.
- Size—1.5 to 1.8 μ in diameter.
- Habitat—Digestive tract of man.

Cultural Characteristics
- Deep agar colonies—Lenticular, granular growth after 24 to 30 hours, margin is fine.
- Gelatin colonies—Slow, retarded growth.
- Broth—Turbid, upon clearing a thick mass is produced.
- Peptone broth—Slightly turbid.
- Sterilized urine—Turbidity in 72 to 96 hours; ammonium carbonate formed from the urea.

Physiological Characteristics
- Biochemical action
  - Indole production—Negative.
  - Ammonia—Produced; marked alkali producing property.
  - Milk—No action.
- Protein liquefaction or digestion
  - Proteoses—Ammonia liberated; digested, yielding ammonium carbonate.
  - Gelatin—Not liquefied.
  - Fibrin—Not digested.
- Fermentation reactions
  - Carbohydrates—Not fermented.
- Growth factors
  - Oxygen—Anaerobic.
  - Temperature
    - Optimum—37 C.
    - Range—18 to 37 C.
    - Thermal death time—30 minutes at 60 C; boiling kills organism.
  - pH
    - Optimum—7.0.
    - Range—5.5 to 8.5

Pathogenicity—Nonpathogenic, found, however, in case of acute appendicitis.

Spoilage
- Food—Found in putrefying meat.

Propionibacterium arabinosum

Taxonomy
- Order — *Eubacteriales*
- Family — *Propionibacteriaceae*
- Genus — *Propionibacterium*
- Species — *arabinosum*

Cellular Characteristics
- Morphology—Spherical cells in neutral lactate media; ellipsoidal and swollen spherical cells in acid media.
- Motility—Nonmotile.
- Staining—Gram positive; metachromatic granules present.
- Occurring—Pairs and short chains.

Size—Principally 2.0 by 3.0 to 3.5 μ, but size is dependent upon the medium.

Cultural Characteristics

Yeast agar lactate stab—Cream-colored growth, orange-yellow colored surface.

Yeast gelatin lactate stab—No liquefaction.

Liquid medium—Turbid in early stages, cream-colored smooth sediment.

Physiological Characteristics

Biochemical action

Indole production—Negative.

Catalase—Barely positive.

Protein liquefaction

Gelatin—Not liquefied.

Indicator reactions

Litmus milk—No coagulation.

Fermentation reactions

Monosaccharides

D-Arabinose—Propionic acid, acetic acid, and carbon dioxide formed.

L-Arabinose—Propionic acid, acetic acid, and carbon dioxide formed.

Rhamnose—No acid.

Xylose—No acid.

Glucose—Propionic acid, acetic acid, and carbon dioxide formed.

Fructose—Propionic acid, acetic acid, and carbon dioxide formed.

Galactose—Propionic acid, acetic acid, and carbon dioxide formed.

Disaccharides

Lactose—Probably no acid.

Sucrose—Propionic acid, acetic acid, and carbon dioxide formed.

Cellobiose—Propionic acid, acetic acid, and carbon dioxide formed.

Polysaccharides

Raffinose—Propionic acid, acetic acid, and carbon dioxide formed.

Starch—Probably no acid.

Inulin—No acid.

Alcohols and polyalcohols

Glycerol—Propionic acid, acetic acid, and carbon dioxide formed.

Mannitol—Propionic acid, acetic acid, and carbon dioxide formed.

Sorbitol—Acid.

Dulcitol—No acid.

Glucosides

Salicin—No acid.

Acids

Lactic acid—Propionic acid, acetic acid, and carbon dioxide formed.

Pyruvic acid—Propionic acid, acetic acid, and carbon dioxide formed.

Alcohol-keytone

Dihydroxyacetone—Propionic acid, acetic acid, and carbon dioxide formed.

Growth factors

Oxygen—Anerobic.

Nutrition—Biotin and pantothenic acid required; thiamine aids growth; *p*-aminobenzoic acid not required.

Industrial Utilization

Processes—Production of propionic acid.

Propionibacterium freudenreichii

Taxonomy

Order	*Eubacteriales*
Family	*Propionibacteriaceae*
Genus	*Propionibacterium*
Species	*freudenreichii*

Cellular Characteristics

Morphology—Small spherical cells; aerobic growth show irregular, branched, and club-shaped organisms; slight morphological differences between organisms growing in anaerobic solid media and those growing in neutral or acid liquid media.

Motility—Nonmotile.

Staining—Gram positive; metachromatic granules present.

Occurring—Pairs or chains.

Size—Small cells 0.5 to 0.6 μ in diameter.

Habitat—Milk products.

Cultural Characteristics

Yeast agar lactate stab—Grayish with dirty appearance; slight surface growth.

Yeast gelatin lactate stab—No liquefaction.

Liquid media—Turbid; grayish-creamy, ropy sediment.

Physiological Characteristics

Biochemical action

Indole production—Negative.

Nitrite—Not formed from nitrate.

Catalase—Positive.

Protein liquefaction

Gelatin—Not liquefied.

Indicator reactions

Litmus milk—Slight reduction; not coagulated.

Fermentation reactions

Monosaccarides

D-Arabinose—No acid.

L-Arabinose—No acid.

Rhamnose—No acid.

Xylose—No acid.

Glucose—Propionic acid, acetic acid, and carbon dioxide formed.

Fructose—Propionic acid, acetic acid, and carbon dioxide formed.

Galactose—Propionic acid, acetic acid, and carbon dioxide formed.

Mannose—Propionic acid, acetic acid, and carbon dioxide formed.

Disaccharides

Lactose—No acid.

Sucrose—No acid.

Maltose—No acid.

Melibiose—No acid.

Polysaccharides

Raffinose—No acid.

Melezitose—No acid.

Inulin—No acid.

Dextrin—No acid.

Glycogen—No acid.

Alcohols and polyalcohols

Glycerol—Propionic acid, acetic acid, and carbon dioxide formed.

Erythritol—Acid.

Adonitol—Acid.

Mannitol—No acid.

Dulcitol—No acid.

Inositol—Acid.

Perseitol—No acid.

Glycosides

Amygdalin—No acid.

Esculin—Acid.

Acids

Lactic acid—Propionic acid, acetic acid, and carbon dioxide formed.

Pyruvic acid—Propionic acid, acetic acid, and carbon dioxide formed.

Alcohol-ketone

Dihydroxyacetone—Propionic acid, acetic acid, and carbon dioxide formed.

Growth factors

Oxygen—Anaerobic; aerotolerant.

Vitamins—Pantothenic acid required; thiamine and *p*-aminobenzoic acid not required; some strains need biotin.

Differentiation—Cannot ferment disaccharides in yeast extract—sugar media

Industrial Utilization
Processes—Manufacture of emmentaler and Swiss cheese. Produces propionic acid.

Addenda. One of the group of propionic acid bacteria.

The organism produces vitamin B_{12}. Lactic acid substrates were more favorable to the formation of the vitamin than glucose.

Protaminobacter alboflavus

Taxonomy
- Order *Pseudomonadales*
- Suborder *Pseudomonadineae*
- Family *Pseudomonadaceae*
- Genus *Protaminobacter*
- Species *alboflavus*

Cellular Characteristics
- Morphology—Rods.
- Motility—Nonmotile.
- Staining—Gram negative.
- Habitat—Soil, water.

Cultural Characteristics
- Agar colonies—Red or yellow, light gray or colorless, circular opaque.
- Amine agar colonies—White to dark yellow, circular.
- Gelatin colonies—Light yellow or colorless, circular, dry.

Physiological Characteristics

Biochemical action
- Alkylamines—Dissimulated.

Protein liquefaction or digestion
- Gelatin—Not liquefied.

Growth factors
- Oxygen—Facultatively aerobic.
- Temperature
  - Optimum—30 C.
- Nutrition—The nutritive utilization of a number of organic acids, amino compounds, and amines by varieties of this organism have been investigated. On this basis 4 varieties α, β, γ, and δ, have been characterized. Thus all use ethyl alcohol but only α, β, and γ use glucose.

Color characteristics
- Chromogenesis—

Variety	*Gelatin*	*Agar*	*Amine agar*
α	Light yellow	Bright red	Yellow
β	Light yellow	Yellow	Dark yellow
γ	Light yellow	Light gray	Yellow
δ	Colorless	Colorless	White

Biochemical Characteristics
- Enzyme production—Catalase formed.

Proteus morganii

Taxonomy
- Order *Eubacteriales*
- Family *Enterobacteriaceae*
- Tribe *Proteeae*
- Genus *Proteus*
- Species *morganii*
- Common name Morgan's bacillus

Cellular Characteristics
- Morphology—Rods.
- Motility—Motile.
- Flagella—Peritrichous.
- Staining—Gram negative.
- Occurring—Singly; characteristic swarming in culture.
- Size—0.4 to 0.6 by 1.0 to 2.0 μ.
- Habitat—Intestinal tract.

Cultural Characteristics
- Agar colonies—Blue-gray, at times, whitish, smooth and entire growth.

Agar stroke—Gray-like white growth, glistening and smooth.
Gelatin colonies—Blue-gray growth, smooth, entire.
Nutrient broth—Turbidity.
Potato—When growth occurs it is a dirty white.

Physiological Characteristics
Biochemical action
Indole production—Positive.
Voges-Proskauer test—Negative.
Citrate utilization—Not as sole source of carbon.
Hydrogen sulfide production—Negative.
Nitrite—Formed from nitrate.
Phenylalanine—Yields phenylpyruvic acid.
Leucine—Becomes alkaline.
Protein liquefaction or digestion
Gelatin—Not liquefied.
Indicator reactions
Litmus milk—Neutral or becomes alkaline.
Fermentation Reactions
Monosaccharides
Arabinose—No acid or gas.
Rhamnose—No acid or gas.
Xylose—Rarely yields acid or gas.
Glucose—Acid and some gas.
Fructose—Acid and some gas.
Galactose—Acid and some gas.
Mannose—Acid and some gas.
Disaccharides
Lactose—No acid or gas.
Sucrose—No acid or gas.
Maltose—No acid or gas.
Polysaccharides
Raffinose—No acid or gas.
Dextrin—No acid or gas.
Alcohols and polyalcohols
Mannitol—No acid or gas.
Sorbitol—No acid or gas.
Dulcitol—No acid or gas.
Adonitol—No acid or gas.
Inositol—No acid or gas.
Glucosides
Salicin—No acid or gas.
Growth factors
Oxygen—Aerobic, facultatively anaerobic.
Temperature
Optimum—37 C.
Resistance—Sensitive to fumagillin.

Biochemical Characteristics
Enzyme production—A kinase product of *P. morganii* has a tendency to phosphorylate pantothenic acid, pantothine, and pantotheine. Product formed from pantothenic acid is 4′-phosphopantothenic acid.

Academic or Research Utilization—Cell-free extracts can metabolize pyruvate to alpha-acetolactic acid + carbon dioxide. This is done anaerobically. DPN and magnesium or manganese ion are also required.

Arsenite, succinate, and malonate injected into mice served to enhance the infection of the animal by the organism.

Pathogenicity
Human beings—*P. morganii* was isolated from infants afflicted with summer diarrhea. May cause a fever like salmonella infection. Found in cases of food poisoning from eating fried or boiled sardines.

Addenda. The drug furadantin, when given to rats infected with the *P. morganii,* increased the survival rate of the rats. *Proteus* infection of the body has a tendency for stone formation. This was not true when high dosage of the drug was administered.

There is a tendency to mistake *P. morganii* for *Salmonella* or *Shigella* sp. on the basis of combined indole urease test media. It is a contaminant, and ambiguous results are obtained from the dual-purpose media.

Proteus vulgaris

Taxonomy
- Order — *Eubacteriales*
- Family — *Enterobacteriaceae*
- Genus — *Proteus*
- Species — *vulgaris*
- Strains — OX2, OX19, OXK, X

Cellular Characteristics
- Morphology—Rods; old cultures show variation.
- Motility—H forms are motile; O forms are nonmotile.
- Flagella—Peritrichous.
- Staining—Gram negative.
- Occurring—Singly, in pairs, as chains.
- Size—0.5 to 1.0 by 1.0 to 3.0 μ.

Cultural Characteristics—Swarm on solid media.
- Agar colonies—Gray, opaque, spreading.
- Agar stroke—Bluish-gray, thin, spreading easily over the agar.
- Gelatin colonies—Irregular, spreading.
- Gelatin stab—Stratiform liquefaction.
- Nutrient broth—Turbidity and possible thin pellicle.
- MacConkey's agar—Three phases of growth: (a) smooth colony, (b) smaller smooth, (c) felt.

Physiological Characteristics
- Biochemical action
  - Indole production—Positive.
  - Voges-Proskauer test—Negative.
  - Citrate—Usually used as sole source of carbon.
  - Hydrogen sulfide—Formed from cystine, cysteine, and related organic sulfur compounds; also from sulfur and thiosulfates.
  - Nitrate—Reduced to nitrite.
  - Phenylpyruvic acid—Formed from phenylalanine.
  - Ammonia—Formed.
  - Urea—Utilized.
  - Odor—Putrefactive odor produced.
- Protein liquefaction or digestion
  - Gelatin—Liquefied.
  - Fibrin—Peptonized.
- Indicator reactions
  - Litmus milk—Alkaline, some strains coagulate casein; litmus is reduced.
  - Methylene blue reduction—Positive, decolorized slowly.
- Growth factors
  - Oxygen—Aerobic; under anaerobic conditions enzymic activity may be suppressed.
  - Temperature
    - Optimum—37 C.
    - Minimum—10 C.
    - Maximum—43 C.
  - Nutrition—Nicotinic acid required in media; adenosine triphosphate has stimulating effect on the multiplication of *P. vulgaris*.
  - Inhibition—Cobalt ions added to nutrient broth prevent growth; pentosenucleic acid concentration is increased as if cells were continuing to grow.

    Inhibited by several pentacyano compounds but not by hexacyano compounds.
- Fermentation reactions
  - Monosaccharides
    - Glucose—Acid and gas.
    - Fructose—Acid and gas.
    - Galactose—Acid and gas.
  - Disaccharides
    - Lactose—No acid or gas.
    - Sucrose—Acid and gas.
    - Maltose—Acid and gas.
  - Polysaccharides
    - Dextrin—No acid or gas.
  - Polyalcohols
    - Mannitol—No acid or gas.

Serology
- Antigens—Somatic and flagellar antigens present; nonswarming strains do

not have H antigen; O antigen of OX19 strain has two receptors, one alkali labile and the other alkali stable which is responsible for Weil-Felix reaction; *Rickettsia prowazekii* has same receptor; O antigen is resistant to heating at 95 C in ethyl alcohol.

Agglutination—X strains agglutinated by typhus serum.

Biochemical Characteristics

Enzyme production—Catalase produced; chrondrosulfatase formed, has mucopolysaccharase activity.

Hemolysin—Produced, acts on horse blood and rabbit blood.

Academic or Research Utilization

Physiological mechanisms—H and O variants first described in connection with this organism.

Differentiation—Production of hydrogen sulfide and hydrolysis of urea distinguishes *P. vulgaris* from other gram-negative, gelatin-liquefying rods.

Pathogenicity

Human beings—Generally nonpathogenic but may be encountered in cystitis, infantile diarrhea, and suppurative lesions.

Animals—Virulent cultures can cause death of rabbits and guinea pigs in a few hours.

Addenda. Swarming on media can be inhibited by morphine, chloral hydrate, and 5 or 6 per cent ethyl alcohol.

P. vulgaris can be used to test cutting oils; gram-negative bacteria survive longer than gram-positive bacteria; hence cutting oils should contain inhibitors.

The flagella of the organism can be demonstrated under fluorescent microscopy by staining with a mixture of Auramine O and a mordant, such as a solution containing aluminum sulfate.

Pseudomonas aeruginosa

Taxonomy

Order	*Pseudomonadales*
Suborder	*Pseudomonadineae*
Family	*Pseudomonadaceae*
Genus	*Pseudomonas*
Species	*aeruginosa*
Synonym	*Pseudomonas pyocyanea*
Common name	Blue pus organism

Cellular Characteristics

Morphology—Rods.

Motility—Motile with one to three polar flagella; some authorities believe the organism to be monotrichous.

Staining—Gram negative.

Occurring—Singly, in pairs, or in chains.

Size—0.5 to 0.6 by 1.5 μ.

Habitat—Found in polluted water and sewage.

Cultural Characteristics—Cultures have a noticeable odor of trimethylamine.

Agar colonies—Neutral shade of green, large, spreading, grayish to dark center, irregular with translucent edge.

Agar stroke—Medium turning green, brown, or black, abundant thin growth.

Gelatin colonies—Yellow to green, liquefaction; fringed, irregular, and granular.

Broth—Yellowish-green to blue with fluorescence; heavy turbidity with pellicle and sediment.

Potato—Dirty brown becoming green; good growth.

Potassium gluconate medium—Slime formed.

Physiological Characteristics

Biochemical action
- Indole production—Usually negative.
- Nitrate—Reduced to nitrite.

Protein liquefaction or digestion
- Gelatin—Liquefied.
- Blood serum—Liquefied, liquid is yellow, surface of medium is green.
- Blood—Hemolyzed.

Indicator reactions
- Litmus milk—Soft coagulum, rapid peptonization and reduction of litmus, alkaline.

Fermentation reactions
- Monosaccharides
  - Arabinose—Not fermented.
  - Glucose—Oxidized to gluconic acid, 2-ketogluconic acid.
  - Fructose—Not fermented.
  - Galactose—Not fermented.
- Disaccharides
  - Lactose—Not fermented.
  - Sucrose—Not fermented.
  - Maltose—Not fermented.
- Polysaccharides
  - Dextrin—Not fermented.
  - Inulin—Not fermented.
- Polyalcohols
  - Glycerol—Not fermented.
  - Mannitol—Not fermented.
  - Dulcitol—Not fermented.

Color and light characteristics
- Chromogenesis—Pyocyanine, a blue pigment, formed by some strains.
- Fluorescence—Fluorescein produced by some strains.

Growth factors
- Oxygen—Facultatively aerobic.
- Temperature
  - Optimum—37 C.
  - Good growth—42 C.
- Nutrition—Can utilize hydrocarbons.

Spoilage
- Food—Causes decay and aerobic decomposition.
- Milk—Cause of blue-green milk.

Pathogenicity
- Human beings—May cause lesions.
- Animals—Pathogenic for rabbits, mice, guinea pigs.

Addenda. Hemolysin production of the organism cannot be used for identification purposes of the organism. Several strains of the organism which were known to be producers of high titers of hemolysin were poor producers of pyocyanine. The hemolysin produced by the organism is more heat resistant and can act more rapidly on the erythrocytes than the hemolysin produced by *P. aureofaciens* or *P. chlororaphis.*

Uroconic acid can be metabolized to glutamic acid. The metabolism is nonoxidative.

Histadine adapted cells can partially convert uroconic acid into succinic monoureide (oxidatively) in the presence of ethylenediaminetetraacetate.

Washed cell suspension oxidized glycine and glyoxalic acid, isoniazid inhibited oxidation of glycine. The activity of aged cells was stimulated by adenosine triphosphate and pyridoxal.

The organism can produce hyaluronic acid.

It has been suggested that in the early oxidation of cyclohexane, peroxide was formed. Concerning the utilization of hydrocarbons, magnesium and phosphate concentrations are important. Calcium and zinc are not. The organism can utilize hydrocarbons at 37 C, whereas other bacteria have their optimum temperature at 20 to 30 C. The organism is usually found in oily locations and has been isolated from industrial oils. Often isolated from contaminated oils.

The metabolic pathway of toluene in the organism is as follows: toluene ⟶ benzyl alcohol ⟶ benzaldehyde ⟶ benzoic acid ⟶ pyrocatechol.

When glucose is metabolized to carbon dioxide and water, it is metabolized by way of gluconic and 2-ketogluconic acid.

Pyocyanine, pyrorubin, and fluorescein are formed in broth culture.

Pseudomonas fluorescens

Taxonomy
- Order — *Pseudomonadales*
- Suborder — *Pseudomonadineae*
- Family — *Pseudomonadaceae*
- Genus — *Pseudomonas*
- Species — *fluorescens*

Cellular Characteristics
- Morphology—Rods.
- Motility—Motile.
- Flagellum—Polar.
- Staining—Gram negative.
- Occurring—Singly and in pairs.
- Size—0.3 to 0.5 by 1.0 to 1.8 μ.
- Habitat—Water and soil.

Cultural Characteristics
- Agar stroke—Abundant, reddish layer.
- Gelatin colonies—Circular,with greenish center, liquefaction.
- Gelatin stab—Infundibuliform liquefaction, whitish to reddish-gray sediment.
- Nutrient broth—Yellowish-green pellicle, gray sediment, turbid.
- Potato—Thick, grayish-yellow, spreading.

Physiological Characteristics
- Biochemical action
  - Indole production—Negative.
  - Nitrate—Reduced to nitrite and ammonia.
- Protein liquefaction or digestion
  - Gelatin—Liquefied.
  - Blood serum—Liquefied.
- Indicator reactions
  - Litmus milk—Alkaline; no coagulation.
- Fermentation reactions
  - Monosaccharides
    - Glucose—Acid.
  - Polysaccharides
    - Cellulose—Not fermented.
- Growth factors
  - Oxygen—Aerobic.
  - Temperature
    - Optimum—20 to 25 C.
    - Maximum—37 C poor growth or none.
- Color and light characteristics
  - Fluorescence—Forms green fluorescent pigment.

Biochemical Characteristics
- Chemical end products—Produces alpha-ketoglutaric acid and 2-ketogluconic acid. The organism also produces L-arabonic acid, D-xylonic acid, and D-ribonic acid.

Pathogenicity—Not pathogenic.

Addenda. *p*-Aminosalicylic acid can inhibit the oxidation of *p*-aminobenzoic acid; oxygen consumed remains stable. Less than 0.35 per cent of acidities in churning butter inhibited the organism. When added to cream the organism was also inhibited. When lactic acid was added the organism grew. Pyocyanine stopped the action of a number of substrates at the keto acid level when tested against *P. fluorescens*.

Pseudomonas fragi

Taxonomy
- Order — *Pseudomonadales*
- Suborder — *Pseudomonadineae*
- Family — *Pseudomonadaceae*
- Genus — *Pseudomonas*
- Species — *fragi*

Cellular Characteristics
- Morphology—Rods.
- Motility—Motile.
- Flagella—Polar flagellum.
- Staining—Gram negative.
- Occurring—Singly in pairs or chains.
- Size—0.5 to 1.0 by 0.75 to 4 μ.
- Habitat—Soil and water; may be isolated from raw milk.

Cultural Characteristics

Agar colonies—Convex, occasionally viscid, glistening, butyrous, rough forms are less proteolytic; not as active in the hydrolysis of fat.
Agar stroke—Abundant, spreading growth.
Gelatin stab—Crateriform to stratiform liquefaction, raised white, shining, butyrous, sweet odor.
Nutrient broth—Turbidity, pellicle, sediment.
Potato—Raised, glistening, white growth becoming brown.

Physiological Characteristics
Biochemical action
Indole production—Negative.
Hydrogen sulfide production—Negative.
Ammonia—Formed from peptone.
Nitrate—Not reduced to nitrite.
Fats—Usually hydrolyzed.
Acetylmethylcarbinol—Not formed.
Protein liquefaction or digestion
Gelatin—Liquefied.
Indicator reactions
Litmus milk—Acid ring and coagulation at surface, some digestion, sweet odor like strawberry.
Fermentation reactions
Monosaccharides
Arabinose—Variable acid.
Glucose—Acid.
Fructose—No acid.
Galactose—Acid.
Disaccharides
Lactose—No acid.
Maltose—No acid.
Sucrose—No acid.
Polysaccharides
Raffinose—No acid.
Inulin—No acid.
Alcohols and polyalcohols
Glycerol—No acid.
Mannitol—No acid.
Glucosides
Salicin—No acid.
Growth factors
Oxygen—Aerobic.
Temperature
Range—10 to 30 C.
No growth—37 C, sensitive to heat.
Tolerance—Sensitive to low concentration of chlorine.

Biochemical Characteristics
Enzyme production—Lipase produced using a coconut oil substrate at a pH optimum of 7.0 to 7.2.
Chemical end products—Acid production is inhibitory to the release of tyrosine and tryptophane active compounds.

Industrial Utilization
Processes—When the organism is grown in butter, high water-insoluble acids may be obtained; also high butyric acid values may be obtained.

Spoilage
Food—Often isolated in rancid cream and butter. In cottage cheese a fruity ester-like odor is produced, as well as a white gelatinous film. Aroma of cottage cheese can be destroyed. Organism slightly retarded by churning acidities in butter production.

Pseudomonas oleovorans

Taxonomy
Order *Pseudomonadales*
Suborder *Pseudomonadineae*
Family *Pseudomonadaceae*
Genus *Pseudomonas*
Species *oleovorans*

Cellular Characteristics
Morphology—Short rods.

Motility—Motile.
Staining—Gram negative.
Occurring—Singly and in pairs.
Size—0.5 by 0.8 to 1.5 μ.
Habitat—Oil-soaked soils.

Cultural Characteristics
Agar colonies—Creamy; after 1 day, 1 to 2 mm in diameter; fluorescent, smooth, convex; entire edge in young colonies.
Deep agar colonies—Buff colored, lens-shaped, nonfluorescent, 0.5 by 1.0 to 1.5 mm.
Agar stroke—Raised growth, smooth, fluorescent.
Gelatin colonies—Growth up to 1 mm in diameter, fluorescent.
Gelatin stab—No liquefaction.
Nutrient broth—Moderate turbidity after 1 day; yellowish, viscid sediment; no pellicle or ring.
Potato—Good growth.

Physiological Characteristics
Biochemical action
Indole production—Negative.
Starch hydrolysis—Positive.
Nitrite—Formed from nitrate.
Indicator reactions
Litmus milk—No change.
Fermentation reactions
Monosaccharides
Xylose—No acid.
Glucose—No acid.
Galactose—No acid.
Disaccharides
Lactose—No acid.
Sucrose—No acid.
Growth factors
Oxygen—Aerobic.
Temperature
Optimum—25 to 37 C.
Nutrition—Can utilize cutting oils as sole source of energy.
Color and light characteristics
Fluorescence—Fluorescent colonies on agar or gelatin; nonfluorescent deep agar colonies; fluorescence not found in the culture media.

Industrial Aspects—Found as a contaminant in cutting oils.

Academic or Research Utilization—Petroleum hydrocarbons utilized.

Pathogenicity—Cause of cutting oil dermatitis.

Pseudomonas ovalis

Taxonomy

Order	*Pseudomonadales*
Suborder	*Pseudomonadineae*
Family	*Pseudomonadaceae*
Genus	*Pseudomonas*
Species	*ovalis*

Cellular Characteristics
Morphology—Rods.
Motility—Motile.
Flagellum—Polar.
Staining—Gram negative.
Occurring—Singly.
Size—0.3 to 0.7 by 0.7 to 1.3 μ.
Habitat—Soil; found in the intestinal canal.

Cultural Characteristics
Agar colonies—entire and circular, opaque, greenish fluorescence.
Agar stroke—Abundant growth white, becoming greenish fluorescent.
Gelatin colonies—Irregular, lobate, slightly granular.
Nutrient broth—Turbid, pellicle.
Potato—Abundant, dirty brown.

Physiological Characteristics
Biochemical action
Indole—Negative.
Nitrite—Not produced.
Starch—Not hydrolyzed.
Protein liquefaction or digestion
Gelatin—Not liquefied.
Blood serum—Not liquefied.
Indicator reactions
Litmus milk—Alkaline; no coagulation; not reduced.
Fermentation reactions

Monosaccharides
Glucose—Acid.
Growth factors
Oxygen—Facultatively aerobic.
Temperature
Optimum—25 C.
Maximum—37 C; poor growth or none.
Color and light characteristics
Fluorescence—Forms green fluorescent pigment.

Biochemical Characteristics
Chemical end products—Gluconic acid, ketogluconic acid, D-xylonic acid, and D-ribonic acid produced.

Pathogenicity—Not pathogenic.

Pseudomonas putida

Taxonomy

Order	*Pseudomonadales*
Suborder	*Pseudomonadineae*
Family	*Pseudomonadaceae*
Genus	*Pseudomonas*
Species	*putida*

Cellular Characteristics
Morphology—Rods, with rounded ends.
Motility—Motile.
Flagella—Single polar.
Staining—Gram negative.
Habitat—Found in putrefying materials and water.

Cultural Characteristics
Agar colonies—Raised, smooth, circular colonies, entire, amorphous; fluorescent zone around edges.
Agar slant—Yellow-green layer.
Gelatin colonies—Growth around a dark center, fluorescence within a yellow zone, granular, small.
Gelatin stab—Surface growth is dirty white, becoming greenish, fluorescent; no liquefaction.
Nutrient broth—Fluorescence observable, turbid.
Potato—Slimy layer of thin growth, grayish to brownish.

Physiological Characteristics
Biochemical action
Indole—Not formed.
Nitrite—Formed from nitrate.
Trimethylamine—Formed.
Protein liquefaction or digestion
Gelatin—Not liquefied.
Indicator reactions
Litmus milk—Not changed.
Growth factors
Oxygen—Facultatively aerobic.
Temperature
Optimum—25 C.
Range—Will grow at 37 C.
Color and light characteristics
Fluorescence—In gelatin and agar colonies—greenish.

Academic or Research Utilization
Physiological mechanisms—Can utilize 77 different organic compounds in its respiration processes.
Other—According to some authorities it is identical with *P. fluorescens* Migula with the exception of gelatin liquefaction.

Pseudomonas savastanoi

Taxonomy

Order	*Pseudomonadales*
Suborder	*Pseudomonadineae*
Family	*Pseudomonadaceae*
Genus	*Pseudomonas*
Species	*savastanoi*

Cellular Characteristics
Morphology—Rods.

Motility—Positive.
Flagella—Polar, 1 to 4.
Staining—Gram negative.
Size—0.4 to 0.8 by 1.2 to 3.3 μ.

Cultural Characteristics
Beef-agar colonies—White, smooth, flat; margin erose to entire.
Gelatin stab—No liquefaction.
Nutrient broth—Turbid, no pellicle or ring.

Physiological Characteristics
Biochemical action
Hydrogen sulfide production—Negative.
Starch hydrolysis—Positive.
Nitrite—Not formed from nitrate.
Milk—Becomes alkaline.
Protein liquefaction
Gelatin—Not liquefied.
Fermentation reactions
Monosaccharides
Glucose—Acid, no gas.
Galactose—Acid, no gas.
Disaccharides
Sucrose—Acid, no gas.
Growth factors
Oxygen—Aerobic.
Temperature
Optimum—23 to 24 C.
Minimum—1 C.
Maximum—32 C.
pH
Optimum—6.8 to 7.0.
Minimum—5.6.
Maximum—8.5.
Color characteristics
Fluorescence—Green in culture media.

Industrial Utilization
Products—Gluconic acid from glucose solution.

Pathogenicity
Plants—Cause of galls on olives.

Variety—A variety, which is pathogenic to and produces a canker on ash, is not pathogenic to the olive.

Pseudomonas schuyllkilliensis

Taxonomy

Order	*Pseudomonadales*
Suborder	*Pseudomonadineae*
Family	*Pseudomonadaceae*
Genus	*Pseudomonas*
Species	*schuyllkilliensis*

Cellular Characteristics
Morphology—Short, rounded rods.
Motility—Motile.
Flagella—Polar, single.
Staining—Gram negative.
Occurring—In pairs, singly, or in chains.
Habitat—Water.

Cultural Characteristics
Agar slant—Grayish, translucent growth.
Gelatin colonies—Grayish-white becoming bluish-green; radiate margin.
Gelatin stab—Slow crateriform liquefaction.
Broth—Slight pellicle, blue-green fluorescence, stringy sediment.
Potato—Spreading growth, viscid, brownish.

Physiological Characteristics
Biochemical action
Indole production—Slight positive.
Protein liquefaction or digestion
Gelatin—Liquefied.
Indicator reactions
Litmus milk—Made alkaline, coagulated, slow reduction of litmus, peptonized.
Growth factors
Oxygen—Facultatively anaerobic.
Temperature—No growth at 35 to 36 C.

Puccina graminis

Taxonomy
- Class — *Basidiomycetes*
- Subclass — *Heterobasidiomycetes*
- Order — *Uredinales*
- Family — *Pucciniaceae*
- Genus — *Puccina*
- Species — *graminis*

Mycological Characteristics
- Mycelium—Carry plus and minus mating factors, bipolar and heterothallic; mature mycelium penetrates leaf.
- Sterigmata—Produced by promycelium upon which basidiospores are formed.
- Spores
  - Teleutospores—Two celled, produced in summer; germination produces basidiospores.
  - Sexual—Spermatization by insect vectors.
  - Dikaryotization—Followed by aecia and aeciospore formation.
- Life cycle
  - Stages (5)
    - Stage 0—Spermagonia are plus and minus, spermatia and receptive hyphae present.
    - Stage I—Aecium with aeciospores, mycelium in host.
    - Stage II—Uredium and urediospores.
    - Stage III—Telium and teleuspore, plus and minus strains, meiosis.
    - Stage IV—Basidospores, host plant infected by germ tube.

Physiological Characteristics
- Growth factors—alpha-Naphthaleneacetic acid (potassium salt) and 2,4,-D (sodium salt) were used to test the germinating effect. Dilutions of 2000 had to be used to get the growth started. In smaller dilutions there was no growth or sporulation.

Academic or Research Utilization
- Genetics—When examined during mitosis the chromosome number of 6 was observed during the metaphase.
- Other—When an experimental infection of barberry is inoculated with aeciospores, uredia and abortive pycinia are produced.

  Uredia were formed on albino barley leaves and fed sucrose solution. The sori were smaller than normal, but the urediospores were not. Sori also developed on sugar-fed plants in the dark. There was no loss of pathogenicity.

Pathogenicity
- Plants—In the uredinal stage, causes stem rust of bluegrass. The cause of cereal rust disease.

Rhizobium phaseoli

Taxonomy
- Order — *Eubacteriales*
- Family — *Rhizobiaceae*
- Genus — *Rhizobium*
- Species — *phaseoli*

Cellular Characteristics
- Morphology—Rods; bacteriods, at times vacuolated, some branched forms.
- Motility—Motile.
- Flagella—Peritrichous.
- Staining—Gram negative.
- Habitat—Found in soils in which beans grow.

Cultural Characteristics
- Mannitol agar stroke—Rapid spreading growth; streak is raised, semi-translucent.

Physiological Characteristics
- Fermentation reactions
  - Monosaccharides
    - Glucose—Slight acid formation.
    - Galactose—Slight acid formation.
    - Mannose—Slight acid formation.
  - Disaccharides
    - Lactose—Slight acid formation.
    - Sucrose—Slight acid formation.
- Growth factors
  - Oxygen—Aerobic.
  - Temperature
    - Optimum—25 C.

Biochemical Characteristics
- Nitrogen fixation—Grow symbiotically on root nodules of the kidney bean *Phaseolus vulgaris,* bean *Phaseolus augustifolius,* scarlet runner *Phaseolus multiflorus.*

Rhizopus delemar

Taxonomy

Class	*Phycomycetes*
Subclass	*Zygomycetes*
Order	*Mucorales*
Family	*Mucoraceae*
Genus	*Rhizopus*
Species	*delemar*

Mycological Characteristics
- Mycelium—Nonseptate.
- Runners—Present.
- Spores—Irregular.
- Sporangia—Have hemispherical columellae.
- Sporangiophores—Arise from holdfasts.

Physiological Characteristics
- Biochemical action
  - Starch—Saccharified.

Biochemical Characteristics
- Chemical end products—Ethyl alcohol.

Industrial Utilization
- Processes—Saccharified starches.

Rhizopus japonicus

Taxonomy

Class	*Phycomycetes*
Subclass	*Zygomycetes*
Order	*Mucorales*
Family	*Mucoraceae*
Genus	*Rhizopus*
Species	*japonicus*

Mycological Characteristics
- Mycelium—Nonseptate.
- Runners or stolons—Present.
- Spores—Irregular.
- Sporangia—Have hemispherical columellae.
- Sporangiophores—Arise from holdfasts.

Physiological Characteristics
- Biochemical action
  - Starch—Saccharified.

Biochemical Characteristics
- Enzyme production—Amylases produced.
- Chemical end products—Fumaric acid, lactic acid.

Industrial Utilization
- Products—Accompanies *Aspergillus flavus-oryzae* in koji.
- Processes—Used in hydrolysis of corn meal prior to alcoholic fermentation; saccharification of starches.

Rhizopus nigricans

Taxonomy

Class	*Phycomycetes*
Subclass	*Zygomycetes*
Order	*Mucorales*
Family	*Mucoraceae*
Genus	*Rhizopus*
Species	*nigricans*
Synonym	Common bread mold

Mycological Characteristics
- Mycelium—Nonseptate.
- Runners or stolons—Formed.
- Rhizoids—Formed.
  - Sexual
    - Zygospores—Formed.
  - Asexual
    - Sporangiophores—Grow from nodes of stolons at points where rhizoids on holdfasts are formed; end in an apophysis.
    - Sporangia—Have flattened columellae.

Cultural Characteristics
- Agar colonies—Grow rapidly in Petri plate cultures, climbing up sides and cover by stolons.

Physiological Characteristics
- Fermentation reactions
  - Monosaccharides
    - Glucose—Strain of *R. nigricans* can convert 40 to 50 per cent to fumaric acid.
  - Disaccharides
    - Sucrose—Not fermented.
    - Maltose—Not fermented.
- Growth factors
  - Dehydration—Viable after being in dried soil for more than 5 years.
  - Nutrition—Requires zinc for growth and fumaric acid production.
  - Inhibition—Inhibited by 1.5 per cent ethyl alcohol, by Actidione, and by quinine sulfate.

Biochemical Characteristics
- Enzyme production—Forms pectinase.
- Chemical end products—Oxalic acid, succinic acid, fumaric acid, fatty acids, alpha-ketoglutaric acid; aerated mycelium yielded trioses, pyruvic acid, acetaldehyde.
- Processes—Production of fumaric acid; in the Kane-Finlay-Amann process fumaric acid is produced with only traces of other acids.

Spoilage
- Food—Cause of leak in strawberries and damage to other fruits, such as peaches; cause of soft rot in sweet potatoes and other vegetables, such as carrots; bread mold; browning and death of sugar beet seedlings on blotter tests; associated with infection of sweet cider.

Rickettsia prowazekii

Taxonomy

Order	*Rickettsiales*
Family	*Rickettsiaceae*
Tribe	*Rickettsieae*
Genus	*Rickettsia*
Species	*prowazekii*

Cellular Characteristics
- Morphology—Many shapes including coccoid, ellipsoidal and ovoid forms to short rods; at times long rods and filamentous forms are observed. Organisms may vary in size and shape depending upon the media of growth. In yolk sacs they may appear coccoid; this appearance is also

dominant in highly infected tissues. In lightly infected tissues they may resemble rods or minute bacteria.

Motility—Nonmotile.

Staining—Colored purple with Giemsa's stain; individuals of a pair may have a zone of lightly stained material connecting them. Colored blue-purple with Castaneda stain. Bright red organisms are seen with a blue background in Machiavello's stain.

Occurring—In pairs and sometimes found in chains.

Size—Single elements are 0.25 by 0.4 to 0.3 by 0.45 μ; in pairs the size may be 0.25 by 0.7 to 0.3 by 1.1 μ.

Cultural Characteristics

Can be cultured on the following:

1. Plasma tissue of mammalian cells.
2. Louse intestine.
3. Modified Maitland medium with or without agar.
4. Chorio-allantoic membrane.
5. Yolk sac of chick embryo.

Physiological Characteristics

Temperature

Optimum—32 C in plasma tissue culture; 35 C in chick embryo cells.

Thermal death time—50 C for 30 minutes.

Resistance—Inactivated by heat and chemical agents; 0.5 per cent phenol and 0.1 per cent formalin are lethal.

Serology—The Weil Felix agglutination test is diagnostic in serum of 1:50 to 1:50,000 dilution using *Proteus* strain OX19. Other strains from different parts of the world are closely related by the complement fixation reaction. Can be distinguished from other rickettsia by various serological tests; shares a common antigenic factor with *Proteus* OX19. Lasting immunity is conferred after recovery, and vaccines have also been successful.

Pathogenicity—The cause of typhus fever and spread from man to man by the body louse.

Addenda. The organism does not pass through bacterial filters. They can be seen with the ordinary microscope.

Saccharomyces carlsbergensis

Taxonomy

Class	*Ascomycetes*
Subclass	*Plectomycetes*
Order	*Endomycetales*
Family	*Endomycetaceae*
Tribe	*Saccharomyceteae*
Genus	*Saccharomyces*
Species	*carlsbergensis*
Group	Bottom yeasts

Cellular Characteristics—See S. *cerevisiae.*

Physiological Characteristics

Fermentation reactions

Monosaccharides

Glucose—Fermented.

Galactose—Fermented.

Disaccharides

Sucrose—Fermented.

Maltose—Fermented.

Melibiose—Fermented.

Polysaccharides

Raffinose—Fermented.

Growth factors—See S. *cerevisiae.*

Differentiation—Bottom yeasts like S. *carlsbergensis* ferment melibiose and all of raffinose.

Biochemical Characteristics

Enzyme production—See S. *cerevisiae;* in addition to the carbohydrases sucrase and maltase, melibiase and raffinase are formed.

Industrial Utilization
Processes—Manufacture of beer.

Saccharomyces cerevisiae

Taxonomy

Class	*Ascomycetes*
Subclass	*Plectomycetes*
Order	*Endomycetales*
Family	*Endomycetaceae*
Tribe	*Saccharomyceteae*
Genus	*Saccharomyces*
Species	*cerevisiae*
Group	Top yeasts

Cellular Characteristics
Morphology—Cells in young wort cultures are round, oval, egg- or pear-shaped; buds generally oval.
Mycelium—No mycelium formed.
Hyphae—May be developed by nutritional variants.
Staining
Acid fuchsin-methyl green—Chromosomes dark green, cyptoplasm pink, centrosomes red.
Giemsa's stain—Chromosomes purple-red, cytoplasm pale blue.
Heidenhain's hematoxylin—Chromosomes black, cytoplasm gray.
Volutin-metaphosphate stain—Volutin red, basophilic protein light blue.
Alkali-toluidine—Cytoplasm colorless, heterochromatin stands out as well as filaments of desoxyribosenucleoprotein.
Dead cell stain—Methylene blue stains dead yeast cells, whereas live cells stain only slightly.
Flemming's solution—Fat globules brown to black.
Sudan III—Fat globules red.
Dimethylaminoazobenzene—Fat globules yellow.
Dimethyl-*p*-phenylenediamine plus alpha or beta naphthol in weak alkaline solution—Fat globules blue.
Iodine in potassium iodide solution—Glycogen red-brown; starch blue-violet.
Polychrome methylene blue—Volutin nucleoprotein blue.
Zinc chloroiodide—Cellulose blue.
Neutral red, 1 per cent solution—Metachromatic particles and vacuoles light pink to red.
Occurring—Singly, twos, threes, small clusters.
Size—Generally 4 to 6 μ in diameter, range from 1 to 5 μ in width to 1 to 10 μ in length; S. *cerevisiae* var. *ellipsoideus* are usually elongated oval.
Spores—Round, smooth, 2 to 4 per ascus.
Staining—Delafield's hematoxylin makes cell walls stand out.
Habitat—Widely distributed; found on grapes and other fruits.

Physiological Characteristics
Fermentation reactions
Monosaccharides
Glucose—Fermented.
Galactose—Fermented.
Disaccharides
Sucrose—Fermented.
Maltose—Fermented.
Lactose—Not fermented.
Melibiose—Not fermented.
Polysaccharides
Raffinose—One-third fermented.
Growth factors
Nutrition
Unsaturated acids—Oleic and linoleic acids required for anaerobic growth.

Vitamins—Ergosterol, biotin, thiamine, and *p*-aminobenzoic acid are required.

Carbon—Supplied principally by sugars, impure maltose being best; aldehydes, some organic acid salts, glycerol, and ethyl alcohol can also be used.

Nitrogen—Can be supplied by ammonia, ammonium salts, amino acids, peptones, and peptides.

Amino acids—Asparagine, aspartic acid, glutamic acid, glycine, and leucine are good sources of nitrogen for yeasts.

Mineral requirements—Phosphorus, copper, iron, and manganese are necessary.

Serology

Antigenic grouping—Absorption techniques can be used to determine the antigenic composition; serological tests indicate that allelic genes may control the production of two specific antigens.

Differentiation—Top yeasts, such as S. *cerevisiae,* are distinguished from bottom yeasts, like S. *carlsbergensis,* in that they ferment only one-third of raffinose and do not ferment melibiose; S. *cerevisiae* is distinguished from S. *cerevisiae* var. *ellipsoideus* in that its cells are rounder and it cannot use ethyl alcohol as sole source of carbon as efficiently as S. *ellipsoideus.*

Biochemical Characteristics

Enzyme production—Large number of enzymes formed. These can be placed into two major groups: hydrolases and desmolases; among the hydrolases there are the carbohydrases sucrase and maltase, proteolytic enzymes such as proteases and peptidases, phosphatases, and amidases like asparaginase; the zymase group is representative of the desmolases.

Industrial Utilization

Processes—Used in the manufacture of bakery, distillery, and ale yeasts, that is, the group of top yeasts; S. *cerevisiae* var. *ellipsoideus* (commonly termed S. *ellipsoideus*) is the yeast used in the manufacture of wines.

Salmonella choleraesuis

Taxonomy

Order	*Eubacteriales*
Family	*Enterobacteriaceae*
Tribe	*Salmonelleae*
Genus	*Salmonella*
Species	*choleraesuis*

Cellular Characteristics

Morphology—Short rods.

Motility—Motile.

Flagella—Peritrichous.

Staining—Gram negative, nonacid fast; stains with aniline dyes.

Occurring—Singly.

Size—0.6 to 0.7 by 2.0 to 3.0 μ.

Habitat—The hog is the natural host.

Cultural Characteristics

Agar colonies—Moist, grayish, smooth, translucent, round.

Agar stroke—Moist, grayish, smooth, translucent.

Gelatin colonies—Smooth, grayish, glistening, flat, with irregular margin.

Gelatin stab—Flat, gray surface; no liquefaction.

Nutrient broth—Turbid, gray-thin pellicle.

Potato—Gray growth along streak becoming brown.

Physiological Characteristics

Biochemical action
- Indole production—Negative.
- Hydrogen sulfide production—Positive to variable.
- Nitrate—Is reduced to nitrite.
- Trimethylamine oxide—Reduced.

Protein liquefaction or digestion
- Gelatin—Not liquefied.

Indicator reactions
- Litmus milk—Acid becoming alkaline; as the organism continues to grow, there is an opalescence to yellowish-gray growth.

Fermentation reactions
- Monosaccharides
  - Arabinose—Not fermented.
  - Rhamnose—Acid and gas, variable.
  - Xylose—Acid and gas.
  - Glucose—Acid and gas.
  - Fructose—Acid and gas.
  - Galactose—Acid and gas.
  - Mannose—Acid and gas.
- Disaccharides
  - Lactose—Not fermented.
  - Sucrose—Not fermented.
  - Maltose—Acid and gas.
  - Trehalose—Not fermented.
- Polysaccharides
  - Inulin—Not fermented.
  - Dextrin—Acid and gas.
- Alcohols and polyalcohols
  - Mannitol—Acid and gas.
  - Dulcitol—Acid and gas, variable.
  - Sorbitol—Acid and gas.
  - Inositol—Not fermented.
  - Adonitol—Not fermented.
- Glucosides
  - Salicin—Not fermented.
- Acids
  - D-Tartrate—Variable.
  - L-Tartrate—Variable delayed fermentation.
  - DL-Tartrate—Variable delayed fermentation.
  - Mucate—Variable delayed fermentation.

Growth factors
- Oxygen—Aerobic, facultatively anaerobic.
- Temperature
  - Optimum—37 C.
  - Thermal death time—1 hour at 56 C; 20 minutes at 58 C.
- Resistance—Formalin, phenol, chloramine kill organism in 15 minutes.

Serology
- Antigenic grouping—VI, VII: c: 1, 5.
- Typing—Serologically similar to *S. typhisuis*.
- Agglutination—Cross agglutination with other species.

Pathogenicity
- Human beings—Causes food poisoning in man; can cause acute-gastroenteritis and enteric fever.
- Animals—Commonly found in hog intestine, may become pathogenic; fatal to rabbits, mice, guinea pigs.

Salmonella gallinarum

Taxonomy

Order	*Eubacteriales*
Family	*Enterobacteriaceae*
Tribe	*Salmonelleae*
Genus	*Salmonella*
Species	*gallinarum*
Synonym	*Salmonella pullorum*

Cellular Characteristics
- Morphology—Short rods.
- Motility—Nonmotile.
- Staining—Gram negative.
- Occurring—Singly.
- Size—0.3 to 0.5 by 1.0 to 2.5 μ.

Cultural Characteristics

Agar colonies—Grayish-white, smooth, glistening, entire to undulate margins.
Agar stroke—Discreet, translucent colonies.
Gelatin colonies—Grayish-white, moist, lobate.
Gelatin stab—No liquefaction; gray surface if growth occurs.
Nutrient broth—Turbid, flocculent sediment.
Potato—Gray colony if any growth.

Physiological Characteristics
Biochemical action
Indole production—Negative.
Hydrogen sulfide production—Positive.
Nitrite—Formed from nitrate.
Trimethylamine oxide—Reduced to trimethylamine.
Indicator reactions
Litmus milk—No coagulation, acid becoming alkaline.
Fermentation reactions
Monosaccharides
Arabinose—Acid, no gas.
Xylose—Possibility of late fermentation.
Glucose—Acid, no gas.
Fructose—Acid, no gas.
Galactose—Acid, no gas.
Mannose—Acid, no gas.
Disaccharides
Lactose—Not fermented.
Sucrose—Not fermented.
Maltose—Acid, no gas.
Polysaccharides
Dextrin—Not fermented.
Polyalcohols
Mannitol—Acid, no gas.
Sorbitol—Acid, no gas.
Dulcitol—Variable.
Inositol—Not fermented.
Adonitol—Not fermented.
Glucosides
Salicin—Not fermented.
Growth factors
Oxygen—Aerobic, facultatively anaerobic.
Temperature
Optimum—37 C.

Serology
Antigenic grouping—The antigenic structure of the organism is I, IX, XII:—;—. The complete antigenic formula is IX, XII, XII_2, XII_3; antigenic XII_2 is variable.
Agglutination—Agglutination tests are employed to diagnose the disease; a liter of 1:100 is significant.

Pathogenicity
Human beings—May produce food poisoning and gastroenteritis in man.
Animals—The cause of white diarrhea in chicks. May infect the ovaries of adult birds. It is transmitted by the egg. The ovaries are attacked, after which the organism travels to the intestine.

Salmonella typhimurium

Taxonomy

Order	*Eubacteriales*
Family	*Enterobacteriaceae*
Tribe	*Salmonelleae*
Genus	*Salmonella*
Species	*typhimurium*

Cellular Characteristics
Morphology—Rods.
Motility—Motile.
Flagella—Peritrichous.
Staining—Gram negative.
Occurring—Singly.

Cultural Characteristics
Agar colonies—Grayish, small, circular, entire, undulate.
Agar slant—Grayish, filiform, moist, entire.
Gelatin colonies—Grayish, small, circu-

lar, granular, become yellowish-brown.
Gelatin stab—Growth on surface, flat.
Nutrient broth—Turbid.
Potato—Grayish streak.

Physiological Characteristics
Biochemical action
Indole production—Negative.
Citrate utilization—Variable.
Hydrogen sulfide production—Positive.
Nitrite—Formed from nitrate.
Trimethylamine—Yields trimethylamine oxide.
Indicator reactions
Litmus milk—Slightly acid; subsequently becomes alkaline.
Fermentation reactions
Monosaccharides
Arabinose—Acid and gas.
Rhamnose—Variable.
Xylose—Variable.
Glucose—Acid and gas.
Disaccharides
Lactose—Not fermented.
Sucrose—Not fermented.
Maltose—Acid and gas.
Trehalose—Variable.
Alcohols and polyalcohols
Mannitol—Acid and gas.
Sorbitol—Acid and gas.
Dulcitol—Variable.
Adonitol—Not fermented.
Inositol—Variable.
Glucosides
Salicin—Not fermented.
Acid salts
Mucate—Fermented.
L-Tartrate—Fermented.
DL-Tartrate—Variable.
D-Tartrate—Variable.
Growth factors
Oxygen—Aerobic to facultatively anaerobic.
Temperature
Optimum—37 C.

Serology
Antigenic grouping—I, IV, (V), XII: i: 1, 2.

Pathogenicity
Human beings—A cause of food poisoning.
Animals—Attacks rodents and causes a typhoid-like disease; pathogenic for mammals and birds.

Salmonella typhosa

Taxonomy

Order	*Eubacteriales*
Family	*Enterobacteriaceae*
Tribe	*Salmonelleae*
Genus	*Salmonella*
Species	*typhosa*

Cellular Characteristics
Morphology—Rods.
Motility—Motile.
Flagella—Peritrichous, usually about 12.
Capsules—Noncapsulated.
Staining—Gram negative.
Occurring—Singly, in pairs, short chains.
Size—0.6 to 0.7 by 2.0 to 3.0 μ.
Habitat—Found in stools of convalescents, carriers, and patients afflicted with typhoid fever.

Cultural Characteristics
Agar colonies—Gray, transparent to opaque growth.
Agar stroke—Grayish-white, glistening, toothed margins.
Gelatin colonies—Grayish, leaf-like structure, transparent to opaque.
Gelatin stab—White, thin opalescent growth.
Nutrient broth—Turbid, pellicle and sediment in old cultures.
Potato—Little growth.
Endo medium—Colorless colonies.
Brilliant Green Agar—Snowflake appearance.
Selenite F—No coliform growth with exception of typhoid group.

Wilson-Blair—Black colonies.
Krumwiede's triple sugar—Acid in butt only.
Desoxycholate citrate agar—Gray, translucent, round glistening.

Physiological Characteristics
Biochemical action
Indole—Not formed.
Citrate utilization—Variable.
Hydrogen sulfide—Usually formed.
Nitrate—Reduced to nitrite.
Trimethylamine—Formed from trimethylamine oxide.
Protein liquefaction or digestion
Gelatin—Not liquefied.
Indicator reactions
Litmus milk—First slightly acid; becomes alkaline.
Fermentation reactions
Monosaccharides
Arabinose—Variable.
Rhamnose—Not fermented.
Xylose—Variable.
Glucose—Acid, no gas.
Fructose—Acid, no gas.
Disaccharides
Lactose—Not fermented.
Sucrose—Not fermented.
Maltose—Acid, no gas.
Cellobiose—Acid, no gas.
Trehalose—Acid, no gas.
Polysaccharides
Raffinose—Acid, no gas.
Inulin—Not fermented.
Alcohols and polyalcohols
Glycerol—Acid, no gas.
Mannitol—Acid, no gas.
Sorbitol—Acid, no gas.
Dulcitol—Variable.
Inositol—Variable.
Adonitol—Not fermented.
Glucosides
Salicin—Not fermented.
Acid salts
D-Tartrate—Variable.
L-Tartrate—Not fermented.
DL-Tartrate—Not fermented.
Mucate—Late variable.
Growth factors
Oxygen—Aerobic, facultatively anaerobic.
Temperature
Optimum—37 C.

Serology
Antigenic grouping—IX, XII, (Vi): d_1: d_2; fifty or more Vi-phage types.

Pathogenicity
Human beings—The cause of typhoid fever in man; it is transmitted by water, milk, food.
Animals—Pathogenic to laboratory animals by way of parenteral inoculation.

Sarcina lutea

Taxonomy

Order	*Eubacteriales*
Family	*Micrococcaceae*
Genus	*Sarcina*
Species	*lutea*

Cellular Characteristics
Morphology—Spheres, packed formation.
Staining—Gram positive.
Size—1.0 to 1.5 μ.
Habitat—Air, soil, water, skin.

Cultural Characteristics
Agar colonies—Circular, raised, yellow, granular, moist, glistening, entire margin.
Agar stroke—Smooth, soft, sulfur to chrome yellow.
Gelatin colonies—Circular, sulfur-yellow, penetrating into medium.
Gelatin stab—Slow infundibuliform liquefaction.
Nutrient broth—Clear, yellow sediment.
Potato—Raised, sulfur to yellow.

Physiological Characteristics
Biochemical action
Indole production—Slight.
Hydrogen sulfide—Formed.
Nitrite—Generally formed from nitrate.
Urea—Not changed to ammonium carbonate.
Indicator reactions
Litmus milk—Coagulated, becoming alkaline.
Fermentation reactions
Monosaccharides
Glucose—No acid.
Disaccharides
Lactose—No acid.
Sucrose—No acid.
Growth factors
Oxygen—Aerobic.
Temperature
Optimum—25 C.
Nutrition—Not halophilic.
Color characteristics
Chromogenesis—Yellow pigment produced.

Serratia marcescens

Taxonomy

Order	*Eubacteriales*
Family	*Enterobacteriaceae*
Tribe	*Serratieae*
Genus	*Serratia*
Species	*marcescens*

Cellular Characteristics
Morphology—Rods, short; may be spherical.
Motility—Motile.
Flagella—Usually 4 peritrichous; at 20 to 25 C, one cell may have 8 to 10 flagella.
Staining—Gram negative.
Occurring—Singly or as chains of 5 or 6.
Habitat—Water, soil, milk, food, silkworms.

Cultural Characteristics
Agar colonies—White then red, circular, thin, granular; R and S forms with mucoid variants.
Agar stroke—White, smooth, orange-red to magenta; sometimes with metallic sheen.
Gelatin colonies—Thin, gray becoming red, circular, slightly granular, sometimes undulate margin.
Gelatin stab—Infundibuliform liquefaction; usually red on top; sediment in liquefied portion.
Nutrient broth—Turbid, red ring or slight pellicle at surface, gray sediment.
Potato—White lines gradually turning red; growth is luxuriant.
Sodium formate broth—Cultures do not show visible gas.

Physiological Characteristics
Biochemical action
Indole production—Negative.
Acetylmethylcarbinol production—Positive.
Hydrogen sulfide production—Positive from organic sulfur-bearing compounds like cystine and cysteine and from sulfur; negative from sulfates, sulfites, or thiosulfates.
Nitrite—Formed from nitrate.
Trimethylamine—Formed.
Milk—Rancidity produced; red color often formed.
Protein liquefaction
Gelatin—Liquefied; no or inconspicuous pellicle.
Indicator reactions
Litmus milk—Acid reaction with soft coagulum; red surface growth.
Fermentation reactions
Monosaccharides
Glucose—Formic, succinic, acetic,

L-lactic acid, ethyl alcohol, 2,3-butylene glycol, acetylmethylcarbinol, carbon dioxide, and a slight amount of hydrogen produced; no visible gas.

Growth factors

Oxygen—Aerobic, facultatively anaerobic.

Temperature

Optimum—25 to 30 C.

No growth—37 C.

Nutrition—Poor or no growth in distilled water containing urea, glucose, and potassium chloride.

Color characteristics

Chromogenesis—Orange-red pigment produced which is soluble in alcohol, ether, chloroform, benzene, carbon disulfide; the pigment may diffuse through agar indicating some solubility in water; because S. *marcescens* is slow growing, other organisms which grow faster may inhibit pigment formation.

Biochemical Characteristics

Antibiotic production—Prodigiosin is formed.

Enzyme production—Some strains produce a choline phosphatase.

Chemical end products—A mixture of meso- and dextrorotatory 2,3-butanediol (2,3-butylene glycol) is produced with the latter form comprising about 2 per cent of the total amount of glycol formed.

Addenda. Older cells are usually white and are more susceptible to toxins used as surface agents than are younger red cells. Mutant strains were obtained from aging cells grown in peptone or gelatin.

Cells that have lost their chromogenic ability may be reactivated by exposure to ultraviolet light.

Usual drying method resulted in a loss of viability; a medium containing 2 per cent dextran, 0.5 per cent ascorbic acid, and 0.5 per cent thiourea permitted about 50 per cent survival. When the organism is dried, most of the killing is obtained during the initial stages of water removal; killing is increased when air and steam temperatures are raised; at a given point, however, no loss of viability is obtained.

Egg albumen inhibited the growth of strains of S. *marcescens;* the longer the albumen was incubated the less the antibacterial action.

Lysozyme and trypsin lysed the organism when used together.

Consumption of oxygen is higher in growing cells. Resting cells are supported by nitrogen sources, such as alanine, urea, and ammonia.

The organism can be adapted to resist quaternary ammonium compounds, but resistance is accompanied by loss of pigment.

The endotoxin of the organism can inhibit human leucocyte migration.

Dinitrophenol can block the oxidation of 2, 6, and 7 carbon fatty acids.

Infection produced by injecting the organism into the udder of cows did not last, indicating that the udder has a natural tendency to ward off attack by certain organisms.

Shift in pH can cause mutation in pigmentation; changes can also occur in production of somatic antigens and in cell morphology; color variation may be due to a metabolic factor.

When streptomycin is produced under anaerobic conditions, its effect on S. *marcescens* is reduced.

A strain of S. *marcescens* has been isolated with a high degree of selectivity for the hydrolysis of egg lecithin. The hydrolysis is due to choline phosphatase and the egg lecithin emulsion must be buffered at a pH of 8.8 with sodium tetraborate. Boron in the culture media may cause morphological changes.

Shigella boydii

Taxonomy
- Order — *Eubacteriales*
- Family — *Enterobacteriaceae*
- Tribe — *Salmonelleae*
- Genus — *Shigella*
- Species — *boydii*

Cellular Characteristics
- Morphology—Rods.
- Motility—Nonmotile.
- Staining—Gram negative.
- Capsules—Most types and strains have no capsule; some strains of serotype 2 encapsulated.
- Habitat—Cases of dysentery.

Cultural Characteristics—Grows well in common laboratory media.

Physiological Characteristics
- Biochemical action
  - Indole production—Formed by serotypes 5, 7, and 11.
  - Hydrogen sulfide—Not formed.
  - Nitrate—Reduced to nitrite.
- Fermentation reactions
  - Monosaccharides
    - Rhamnose—No acid.
    - Xylose—Usually acid.
    - Glucose—Acid, no gas.
    - Arabinose—Acid, no gas.
  - Disaccharides
    - Lactose—No acid.
    - Sucrose—Occasionally acid, no gas.
    - Maltose—Occasionally acid, no gas.
  - Polyalcohols
    - Mannitol—Acid, no gas.
- Growth factors
  - Oxygen—Aerobic, facultatively anaerobic.
  - Temperature
    - Optimum—37 C.
    - Minimum—10 C.
    - Maximum—40 C.
  - pH
    - Range—6.4 to 7.8.

Serology
- Serotypes—11.
- Agglutination—Agglutinated by polyvalent serum.

Pathogenicity
- Human beings—Produces bacillary dysentery in man but is found in only a small proportion of such cases.

Shigella dysenteriae

Taxonomy
- Order — *Eubacteriales*
- Family — *Enterobacteriaceae*
- Tribe — *Salmonelleae*
- Genus — *Shigella*
- Species — *dysenteriae*

Cellular Characteristics
- Morphology—Rod.
- Motility—Nonmotile.
- Staining—Gram negative.
- Occurring—Singly.
- Size—0.4 to 0.6 by 1.0 to 3.0 μ.
- Habitat—Intestinal tract of bacillary dysentery cases.

Cultural Characteristics—Grows well in ordinary culture media.
- Agar stroke—Gray smooth growth; inhibited by brilliant green.
- Gelatin colonies—Grayish, smooth, homogeneous growth.
- Gelatin stab—Grayish growth on surface; no liquefaction.
- Nutrient broth—Grayish sediment, slight turbidity.
- Kligler's medium—Reddish slope, yellowish butt; no gas evolved.

Physiological Characteristics
- Biochemical action

Indole production—Negative.
Hydrogen sulfide—Not produced.
Nitrates—Reduced to nitrites.
Catalase—Not produced.
Trimethylamine oxide—Not reduced.

Indicator reactions
Litmus milk—Acid, turning alkaline.

Fermentation reactions
Monosaccharides
Arabinose—Not fermented.
Rhamnose—Not fermented.
Xylose—Not fermented.
Glucose—Acid, no gas.
Fructose—Acid, no gas.
Galactose—Acid, no gas.
Disaccharides
Lactose—Not fermented.
Sucrose—Not fermented.
Maltose—Not fermented.
Polysaccharides
Raffinose—Acid, no gas.
Alcohols and polyalcohols
Glycerol—Acid, no gas.
Mannitol—Not fermented.
Dulcitol—Not fermented.
Adonitol—Not fermented.
Glucosides
Salicin—Not fermented.

Growth factors
Oxygen—Aerobic; facultatively anaerobic.
Temperature
Optimum—37 C.
No growth—45 C.
pH
Range—6.4-7.8.

Serology
Antigenic structure—O antigen consists of a toxic protein plus a polysaccharide; R variants do not have O antigen.

Biochemical Characteristics
Toxin production—The organism produces a potent exotoxin. Toxoid can be prepared from exotoxin.

Pathogenicity
Human beings—Produces bacillary dysentery in man. The organism is found in the mucous membranes of the intestine. Convalescent persons become carriers of the organism.
Animals—The exotoxin can produce paralysis in rabbits. When injected into rabbits there is marked respiratory failure and diarrhea.

Shigella flexneri

Taxonomy

Order	*Eubacteriales*
Family	*Enterobacteriaceae*
Tribe	*Salmonelleae*
Genus	*Shigella*
Species	*flexneri*

Cellular Characteristics
Morphology—Rods; irregular and filamentous in old cultures.
Motility—Nonmotile.
Capsules—None.
Staining—Gram negative.
Occurring—Singly, filaments.
Size—0.5 by 1.0 to 1.5 μ.
Habitat—Cases of bacillary dysentery.

Cultural Characteristics—Grows well in common laboratory media.
Broth—Abundant growth.

Physiological Characteristics
Biochemical action
Indole production—Positive; type 6 negative.
Hydrogen sulfide—Not formed.
Nitrate—Reduced to nitrite.
Trimethylamine oxide—Not reduced.
Protein liquefaction or digestion
Gelatin—Not liquefied.
Fermentation reactions
Monosaccharides
Arabinose—Acid, no gas.

Rhamnose—Variable.
Xylose—No acid.
Glucose—Acid, no gas.
Disaccharides
Lactose—Not fermented.
Sucrose—Variable.
Maltose—Variable.
Polyalcohols
Mannitol—Acid.
Dulcitol—No acid.
Sorbitol—Not fermented.
Adonitol—Not fermented.
Glucosides
Salicin—Not fermented.
Growth factors
Oxygen—Aerobic, facultatively anaerobic.
Temperature
Optimum—37 C.
No growth—45.5 C.
pH
Range—6.4 to 7.8.
Serology
Serotypes—1a, 1b, 2a, 2b, 3, 4a, 4b, 5, 6, X, Y.
Antigenic composition—Somatic antigen is a protein-phospholipid-carbohydrate complex that can be extracted by diethylene glycol.
Pathogenicity
Human beings—The most common of bacteria involved in bacillary dysentery; a cause of infantile gastroenteritis.

Shigella sonnei

Taxonomy
Order — *Eubacteriales*
Family — *Enterobacteriaceae*
Tribe — *Salmonelleae*
Genus — *Shigella*
Species — *sonnei*
Cellular Characteristics
Morphology—Rods.
Motility—Nonmotile.
Staining—Gram negative.
Habitat—Cases of bacillary diarrhea.
Cultural Characteristics
Agar colonies
Phase I—Smooth glistening, gray, convex, circular, entire edge, 2 to 4 mm in diameter; readily emulsifiable in normal salt solution.
Phase II—Granular glistening, irregular, translucent edge, 5 mm in diameter; readily emulsifiable in normal salt solution.
Phase IIr—Like Phase II.
Phase IIs—Smooth glistening, small 1 to 2 mm in diameter.
Broth—Many strains turbid; some strains heavy flakes.
SS agar
Phase II—No growth.
Desoxycholate agar
Phase II—No growth.
Physiological Characteristics
Biochemical action
Indole production—Negative.
Nitrate—Reduced to nitrite.
Trimethylamine oxide—Reduced to trimethylamine.
Milk—Coagulation produced in 4 to 30 days.
Protein liquefaction or digestion
Gelatin—Not liquefied.
Fermentation reactions
Monosaccharides
Arabinose—Acid in 24 hours.
Rhamnose—Acid in 24 hours.
Glucose—Acid in 24 hours.
Galactose—Acid in 24 hours.
Fructose—Acid in 24 hours.
Xylose—Not fermented.
Disaccharides
Lactose—Acid, no gas, in 2 to 30 days.
Sucrose—Acid in 24 hours.

Maltose—Acid in 24 hours.
Polysaccharides
Raffinose—Acid in 24 hours.
Polyalcohols
Mannitol—Acid in 24 hours.
Adonitol—Not fermented.
Dulcitol—Not fermented.
Inositol—Not fermented.
Growth factors
Oxygen—Aerobic; facultatively anaerobic.
Temperature
Optimum 37 C.
Good growth—45.5 C.
pH
Range—6.4 to 7.8.
Serology
Antigenic composition—Antigens extracted from Phase I by an aqueous solution of glycerol and from Phase IIs by 50 per cent pyridine solution are protein-lipid-carbohydrate complexes of nearly the same composition.
Agglutination—Positive with specific serum; living organism serum of Phase I agglutinates both Phase I and Phase II, whereas that of Phase II agglutinates only Phase II.
Antiserum of Phase II agglutinates Phase IIs and Phase IIr but not Phase I.
Pathogenicity
Human beings—Cause of bacillary dysentery in man.

Spirillum volutans

Taxonomy

Order	*Pseudomonadales*
Suborder	*Pseudomonadineae*
Family	*Spirillaceae*
Genus	*Spirillum*
Species	*volutans*

Cellular Characteristics
Morphology—Spirals, ends slightly attenuated.
Motility—Motile.
Flagella—10 to 15.
Staining—Gram negative; volutin granules prominent; dark volutin granules in cytoplasm.
Size—1.5 μ in diameter; largest of spirilla.
Wave length—13 to 15 μ.
Spiral width—4 to 5 μ.
Habitat—Stagnant water.
Cultural Characteristics—No artificial cultivation.
Growth factors
Temperature
Optimum—35 C.

Staphylococcus aureus

Taxonomy

Order	*Eubacteriales*
Family	*Micrococcaceae*
Genus	*Staphylococcus*
Species	*aureus*
Synonym	*Micrococcus pyogenes* var. *aureus*

Cellular Characteristics
Morphology—Cocci.
Motility—Nonmotile.
Capsules—Nonencapsulated.
Staining—Gram positive, stains with aniline dyes.
Occurring—Singly, in pairs, in short chains and in clumps or clusters.
Size—0.8 to 1.0 μ.
Habitat—Found on the skin, in the air, on mucous membranes, and in pus.
Cultural Characteristics

Agar colonies—Yellowish to orange glistening growth; smooth, circular, butyrous.
Agar stroke—Yellowish to orange, smooth, flat, moist, growth.
Blood agar—Usually beta hemolysis.
Gelatin stab—Yellow to orange sediment, yellowish pellicle, saccate liquefaction.
Nutrient broth—Yellowish ring, turbidity and sediment.
Potato—Orange, abundant growth.

Physiological Characteristics
Biochemical action
Indole production—Negative.
Hydrogen sulfide production—Slight.
Sodium hippurate—Hydrolyzed sometimes.
Starch hydrolysis—Negative.
Ammonia—Formed from peptone and arginine.
Nitrite—Formed from nitrate.
Indicator reactions
Litmus milk—Acid and coagulated.
Fermentation reactions
Monosaccharides
Glucose—Acid.
Disaccharides
Lactose—Acid.
Sucrose—Acid.
Polysaccharides
Raffinose—No acid produced.
Inulin—No acid produced.
Alcohols and polyalcohols
Glycerol—Acid.
Mannitol—Acid.
Growth factors
Oxygen—Aerobic; facultatively anaerobic.
Temperature
Optimum—37 C.
Minimum—10 C.
Maximum—45 C.
Thermal death time—About 60 C for 10 minutes.
Nutrition
Nitrogen—Amino acids required as nitrogen source; cannot use ammonium dihydrogen phosphate as sole source of nitrogen.
Vitamins—Niacin and thiamine are necessary.
Other—S. *aureus* does not grow well in raw milk but does grow in pasteurized and condensed milk.
Inhibition—Moderately resistant to drying and disinfectants. 8-Azoquinoline inhibits the formation of beta-galactosidase and catalase; the inhibition can be reversed by the addition of guanine or xanthine.
Color and light characteristics
Chromogenesis—Pigment formation yellow to orange; free access to oxygen is required.

Serology—There is a degree of natural immunity to the organism. Autogenous vaccines have been employed with some success. Antiserum may be used on local dressings.

Biochemical Characteristics
Enzyme and toxin production—Catalase formed; various toxic products are elaborated: (a) hemolysin causes the hemolysis of red blood cells; can be inactivated by heat at 60 C for 2 minutes; (b) leucocidin causes the destruction of white blood cells; (c) enterotoxin causes gastroenteritis when ingested; (d) coagulase, an enzyme given off by the more pathogenic strains, causes coagulation of blood; (e) fibrinolysin causes the dissolution of human blood fibrin; (f) dermonecrotic toxin produces necrosis when injected under the skin.

Pathogenicity
Human beings—Produces infection when it gains entrance through the

broken skin. Pus is formed and there is an accumulation of polymorphonuclear leucocytes in the infected area.

Addenda. S. citreus (*Micrococcus citreus*) and *S. albus* (*Micrococcus pyogenes* var. *albus*) are considered variants of *S. aureus* differing only in chromogenesis, *S. citreus* forming more yellow colonies and *S. albus* white varieties. Pigments are produced by the organism when it is exposed to various nutritional and cultural environments. There is a relationship between pigment formation and the chemical requirements in the media. Variations in the conditions of lighting also contribute to variations in pigment formation. The most suitable medium for pigment formation contained 1 per cent potassium citrate, 0.005 per cent ammonium hydrogen phosphate, 0.15 per cent dipotassium hydrogen phosphate, 0.05 per cent potassium carbonate, 2 per cent potato peptone, 1 per cent lactose, 1.5 per cent glycerol monophosphate, 1.5 per cent agar, and pH 7.2. Glycerol inhibits pigment formation whereas glycerol monophosphate enhances it. Several strains after being subcultured on liquid media, containing lithium chloride, became white. The white variants were of the same age group as the parent.

Studies have shown that it is not possible to derive capsulated strains from unencapsulated strains.

S. aureus is more resistant than *Escherichia coli* strain B B/r C-30 to sound fields. Certain ultraviolet resistant strains were susceptible; this would appear to indicate that oxidative individuality was affected little by vibratory energy.

Cells, after becoming streptomycin-resistant, exhibited noticeable variations in at least three characteristics, namely, they were enlarged, sugar fermentation was repressed, and hemolytic and plasma coagulation properties were diminished.

It has been suggested that there are two pathways involved in the oxidation of pyruvate in this organism. A by-product of the alternative system is acetoin. Methylene blue or oxygen exert an inhibitory effect that may be overcome by thiamine or magnesium.

After the release of protoplasts from the cell wall, the cells look like small spherical shells, which account for the greater part by weight of the cell wall.

Glutamine synthesis is inhibited by crystal violet, methyl green, fuchsin or pararosaniline, and malachite green.

Young cells treated with macro anions do not yield coagulase and hyaluronidase readily.

Streptococcus agalactiae

Taxonomy

Order	*Eubacteriales*
Family	*Lactobacillaceae*
Tribe	*Streptococceae*
Genus	*Streptococcus*
Species	*agalactiae*
Group	Pyogenic group of *Streptococcus* genus
Family synonym	*Lactobacteriaceae*

Cellular Characteristics

Morphology—Spherical or ovoid cells.

Staining—Gram positive.

Occurring—In chains, which may look like paired cocci; seldom less than four cells.

Size—0.4 to 1.2 μ in diameter.

Habitat—Udder of cattle with mastitis.

Cultural Characteristics

Nutrient agar colonies—Small, gray.

Gelatin stab—No liquefaction; gray filiform growth.

Nutrient broth—Growth may adhere to

side of tube, supernatant clear. Long chains upon microscopic examination.
Starch broth—Yellow to orange sediment may be produced.

Physiological Characteristics
Biochemical action
Indole production—Negative.
Hemolysis—Beta hemolytic, some strains; alpha hemolytic, some strains.
Ammonia—Formed from peptone and arginine.
Nitrite—Not formed from nitrate.
Bile—Not soluble; not inhibited by 10 to 35 per cent bile.
Sodium hippurate—Hydrolyzed.
Protein liquefaction or digestion
Gelatin—Not liquefied.
Blood—Many strains produce a clear zone of hemolysis; some hemolysis looks green.
Humin fibrin—Not digested.
Indicator reactions
Litmus milk—Acid and curdling; reduction from bottom to top.
Fermentation reactions
Monosaccharides
Arabinose—No acid.
Rhamnose—No acid.
Xylose—No acid.
Glucose—Acid.
Fructose—Acid.
Galactose—Acid.
Mannose—Acid.
Disaccharides
Lactose—Most strains produce acid.
Sucrose—Acid.
Maltose—Acid.
Trehalose—Acid.
Polysaccharides
Raffinose—No acid.
Inulin—No acid.
Dextrin—Acid.
Starch—Not hydrolyzed.
Alcohols and polyalcohols
Glycerol—Acid under aerobic conditions.
Mannitol—No acid.
Sorbitol—No acid.
Glycosides
Esculin—Not hydrolyzed.
Salicin—Variable.
Growth factors
Temperature
Optimum—37 C.
Range—Between 15 and 40 C.
Minimum—No growth at 10 C.
Maximum—45 C.
Thermal death time—No survival after 30 minutes at 60 C.
pH—Glucose broth 4.2 to 4.6; no growth at 9.6.
Tolerance—Growth in 4 per cent sodium chloride but not in 6 per cent; no growth in milk containing 0.1 per cent methylene blue; usually grows in blood agar containing 40 per cent bile.

Serology
Antigenic grouping—Lancefield's Group B.
Typing—Three antigenic types which have their specificity tied up to the carbohydrate fraction.
Hemolysis—Beta group of hemolysis after Smith and Brown.

Biochemical Characteristics
Erythrogenic toxin—Not formed.
Hemolysin—Many strains produce an oxygen-stable, filterable hemolysin, different from streptolysin O and S.

Academic or Research Utilization—The Camp test can be used to identify organism.

Pathogenicity—Can cause mastitis in cattle.

Addenda. Cows suffering from mastitis showed improvement when changed from machine milking to hand milking. Milk levels also returned to good levels.

It has been demonstrated that the plate count of milk is more dependent on the handling and production than on the presence of S. *agalactiae*. The presence of the organism in milk is not indicative that there is going to be a high count. The organism is in a large way responsible for udder infections. The Hotis test can be used to detect the presence of the organism. When growing anaerobically, the organism is sensitive to many conditions. Peptone added to milk can overcome many environmental conditions.

Streptococcus cremoris

Taxonomy
- Order — *Eubacteriales*
- Family — *Lactobacillaceae*
- Tribe — *Streptococceae*
- Genus — *Streptococcus*
- Species — *cremoris*
- Group — Lactic group of *Streptococcus* genus
- Family synonym — *Lactobacteriaceae*

Cellular Characteristics
- Morphology—Spheres.
- Staining—Gram positive.
- Occurring—In long chains, sometimes in pairs.
- Size—0.6 to 1.0 μ in diameter.
- Source—Raw milk and milk products.

Cultural Characteristics—Does not grow on artificial media.

Physiological Characteristics
- Biochemical action
  - Starch hydrolysis—Negative.
  - Hemolysis—Alpha (slight) to gamma (no) hemolysis.
  - Ammonia—Not formed from 4 per cent peptone or from arginine.
  - Sodium hippurate—Not hydrolyzed.
- Protein liquefaction or digestion
  - Gelatin—Not liquefied.
  - Blood—No hemolysis on blood plate.
- Indicator reactions
  - Litmus milk—Acid, reduction complete before curdling; red line on top; separation of clot milk becomes slimy; no digestion of casein.
- Fermentation reactions
  - Monosaccharides
    - Arabinose—Not fermented.
    - Xylose—Not fermented.
    - Glucose—Acid.
  - Disaccharides
    - Lactose—Acid.
    - Sucrose—Seldom fermented.
    - Maltose—May be fermented.
    - Trehalose—Variable.
  - Polysaccharides
    - Raffinose—Seldom fermented.
    - Inulin—Not fermented.
  - Alcohols and polyalcohols
    - Glycerol—Not fermented.
    - Mannitol—Seldom fermented.
    - Sorbitol—Not fermented.
  - Glucosides
    - Esculin—Not hydrolyzed.
    - Salicin—Variable.
- Growth factors
  - Oxygen—Facultatively aerobic.
  - Temperature
    - Optimum—30 C.
    - Minimum—10 C.
    - Maximum—37 C.
    - Thermal death time—65 C to 70 C; may survive 60 C for 30 minutes.
  - pH—Final pH in glucose broth 4.6 to 4.0; inhibited at 9.2 and 9.6.
  - Tolerance
    - Methylene blue—Tolerates 0.01 per cent and may tolerate 0.1; seldom will tolerate 0.3 per cent.
    - Penicillin—Sensitive.
    - Sodium chloride—No growth in broth containing 4 per cent; not inhibited by 2 per cent.

Bile—Blood agar with 40 per cent bile: grows.

Serology

Antigenic grouping—Contains group specific, Group N antigen of *S. lactis.*

Typing—Many serological types.

Biochemical Characteristics

Antibiotic production—Produces an antibiotic which is different than nisin made by *S. lactis.*

Chemical end products—If fermentable sugar is present, utilizes citric acid producing acetic acid, biacetyl, and carbon dioxide.

Industrial Utilization

Processes—Used in commercial lactic starters because it is an acid producer.

Addenda. Viruses which phage the bacteria are of special concern since the bacterial destruction means no lactic acid production. Bacteriophages active against *S. cremoris* have diameters of 70 mμ and tails of 150 to 160 mμ by 7.0 mμ in thickness and an overall length of 220 to 230 mμ.

Streptococcus equi

Taxonomy

Order	*Eubacteriales*
Family	*Lactobacillaceae*
Tribe	*Streptococceae*
Genus	*Streptococcus*
Species	*equi*
Group	Pyogenic group of *Streptococcus* genus
Family synonym	*Lactobacteriaceae*

Cellular Characteristics

Morphology—Oval or spherical; bacillary form may appear; in pus long axis of cells transverse to the chain.

Staining—Gram positive.

Occurring—In pairs or in short or long chains; long chains in broth cultures.

Size—0.6 to 1 μ in diameter.

Habitat—Found in strangles of horses.

Cultural Characteristics—Depth in medium may help in growth.

Nutrient agar—Poor growth, small, convex, transparent colonies grayish-white or yellowish; growth may be increased by horse protein.

Gelatin stab—No liquefaction.

Nutrient broth—Poor growth; serum may increase growth; no change in infusion broth.

Blood agar—Small colonies, beta hemolysis.

Blood serum broth—Hemolysis of blood corpuscles of horse; little hemolysis of blood corpuscles of rabbit and guinea pig.

Physiological Characteristics

Biochemical action

Hemolysis—Beta.

Ammonia—Formed from arginine.

Sodium hippurate—Not hydrolyzed.

Protein liquefaction or digestion

Gelatin—Not liquefied.

Fibrin—Not digested.

Indicator reactions

Litmus milk—Not changed.

Fermentation reactions

Monosaccharides

Arabinose—No acid.

Glucose—Acid.

Disaccharides

Lactose—No acid.

Sucrose—Acid, no viscous polysaccharide produced.

Maltose—Acid.

Trehalose—Not fermented.

Polysaccharides

Raffinose—No acid.
Inulin—No acid.
Alcohols and polyalcohols
Glycerol—No acid.
Mannitol—No acid.
Sorbitol—Not fermented.
Glucosides
Salicin—Acid.
Esculin—Not hydrolyzed.
Growth factors
Temperature
Optimum—37 C.
Minimum, slow growth—20 C.
Maximum—45 C.
No growth— < 10, > 45.
Thermal death time—60 C for 30 minutes.
pH—4.8 to 5.5 in glucose broth; 9.6 no growth.
Tolerance—Does not tolerate 6.5 per cent sodium or 0.01 to 0.1 per cent methylene blue; no growth on blood agar containing 40 per cent bile.

Serology
Antigenic grouping—Lancefield's Group C.
Agglutination—Poor antigens for production of agglutinating serum.
Hemolysin—Beta group of hemolysis by Smith and Brown classification.

Biochemical Characteristics
Hemolysin—Produced, different from streptolysins O and S.
Toxin—Necrosis caused after subcutaneous injection.

Differentiation—Does not ferment lactose, trehalose, glycerol, or sorbitol.

Pathogenicity
Animals—Causes strangles in horses; mice are susceptible to toxin. Pathogenicity high for white mice. Immunized rabbit serum may protect mice from infection. Little or no virulence for guinea pigs or rabbits.

Streptococcus lactis

Taxonomy

Order	*Eubacteriales*
Family	*Lactobacillaceae*
Tribe	*Streptococceae*
Genus	*Streptococcus*
Species	*lactis*
Family synonym	*Lactobacteriaceae*
Group	Lactic group of *Streptococcus* genus

Cellular Characteristics
Morphology—Spheres, many cells elongated.
Motility—Nonmotile.
Flagella—None.
Capsules—None.
Staining—Gram positive.
Occurring—In pairs and short chains.
Size—0.5 to 1 μ.
Habitat—Milk and milk products.

Cultural Characteristics
Nutrient agar colonies—Small, round, gray and entire.
Gelatin stab—Filiform to beaded growth, no liquefaction.
Glucose broth—Turbidity.

Physiological Characteristics
Biochemical action
Starch hydrolysis—Negative.
Hemolysis—Negative, may show some slight green.
Ammonia—Formed from 4 per cent peptone.
Tyrosine—Not decarboxylated.
Protein liquefaction or digestion
Gelatin—No liquefaction.
Indicator reactions
Litmus milk—Complete reduction before curdling, acid; young cul-

tures reduce indicator with red band on top; no digestion or gas.

Fermentation reactions

Monosaccharides

Xylose—Variable.

Glucose—Acid.

Disaccharides

Lactose—Acid.

Maltose—Acid.

Polysaccharides

Raffinose—No acid; some strains variable.

Inulin—No acid.

Alcohols and polyalcohols

Glycerol—No acid.

Mannitol—Variable.

Sorbitol—No acid.

Growth factors

Oxygen—Facultatively anaerobic.

Temperature

Growth—10 C; 40 C.

No growth—45 C; some strains may survive 60 C for 30 minutes.

pH—Will grow at pH 9.2 but not at 9.6.

Tolerance

Sodium chloride—Growth in 2 per cent and 4 per cent saline solutions; will not grow in 6.5 per cent.

Bile—Does not inhibit growth; does not have lytic action.

Methylene blue—Tolerates up to 0.3 per cent.

Serology

Antigenic grouping—A species-specific serum has been produced, termed Group N.

Biochemical Characteristics

Enzyme production—Proteinase produced on substratum of α-casein. pH optimum 6.5.

Industrial Utilization

Products—Produces D-lactic acid.

Processes—Used as a starter in the making of sauerkraut. The organism is also used in preparing cultured buttermilk. Important in the ripening and curing of Cheddar cheese. Employed in the propionic acid fermentation as an associate organism.

Addenda. Lysis of the organism due to phage can cause great economic loss. Destruction of the organism means loss of lactic acid production. Phage active against *S. lactis* has a head size of about 7 mμ, tail of 150 to 160 mμ by 7 mμ in thickness; overall length is 220 to 230 mμ.

Several strains were able to oxidize noncarbohydrate substances. The reaction can be inhibited by glucose and ascorbic acid. Sodium fluoride can stimulate oxidative reactions.

Streptococcus pyogenes

Taxonomy

Order	*Eubacteriales*
Family	*Lactobacillaceae*
Tribe	*Streptococceae*
Genus	*Streptococcus*
Species	*pyogenes*
Family synonym	*Lactobacteriaceae*
Group	Pyogenic group of *Streptococcus* genus

Cellular Characteristics

Morphology—Spherical or oval cocci; spherical formation usually in blood or exudates.

Motility—Nonmotile.

Flagella—None.

Capsules—Present.

Staining—Gram positive, stains with the basic aniline dyes.

Occurring—Chains and pairs.

Size—0.6 to 1 μ.

Habitat—Found on man, in the air, on animals.

Cultural Characteristics
- Agar colonies—Small, discrete, translucent, convex colonies with entire edge.
- Agar stroke—Grayish-white, pinpoint colonies which may flow together; growth increased with addition of enrichments, such as blood.
- Gelatin stab—No liquefaction, light growth, opaque colonies.
- Nutrient broth—Flocculent sediment, no pellicle; sediment often looks like tangled chains.
- Potato—Growth.
- Löffler's blood serum—Good growth with isolated colonies.

Physiological Characteristics
- Biochemical action
  - Starch—Not hydrolyzed; some strains positive.
  - Hemolysis—Beta hemolytic.
  - Ammonia—Formed from arginine.
  - Sodium hippurate—Not hydrolyzed.
- Protein liquefaction or digestion
  - Gelatin—Not liquefied.
  - Fibrin—Fribrinolytic.
  - Casein—Not digested.
- Indicator reactions
  - Litmus milk—Reduced slowly or no reduction; acid, milk not curdled.
- Fermentation reactions
  - Monosaccharides
    - Arabinose—No acid.
    - Glucose—Acid.
  - Disaccharides
    - Lactose—Acid; few strains negative.
    - Sucrose—Acid.
    - Maltose—Acid.
    - Trehalose—Acid; few strains negative.
  - Polysaccharides
    - Raffinose—No acid.
    - Inulin—No acid.
  - Alcohols and polyalcohols
    - Glycerol—No acid.
    - Mannitol—No acid; few strains positive.
    - Sorbitol—No acid.
    - Dulcitol—No acid.
  - Glucosides
    - Salicin—Acid.
    - Esculin—Hydrolyzed.
- Growth factors
  - Temperature
    - Optimum—37 C.
    - No growth— $\leq$ 10 C; $\geq$ 45 C.
    - Thermal death time— $\geq$ 60 C for 30 minutes.
  - pH (glucose broth)—4.8 to 6.0.
  - Tolerances
    - Broth adjusted to pH 9.6—No growth.
    - Blood agar, 40 per cent bile—No growth.
    - Skim milk, 0.1 per cent methylene blue—Inhibited.
    - Sodium chloride, 6.5 per cent—Inhibited.

Serology
- Antigens—Capsular protein M, which is associated with the virulence of the organism, and capsular substance T, which is not associated with the virulence of S. *pyogenes.* M-bearing and T-bearing strains are independent. More than 40 serotypes have been identified. Assigned to Lancefield Group A.
- Precipitin tests—Based on M antigen.
- Agglutinin tests—Based on T antigen.

Biochemical Characteristics
- Erythrogenic toxin—Produced by most strains.
- Hemolysins (streptolysins)—Produced in fluid cultures.
  - Streptolysin O—Reversibly oxygen-labile.
  - Streptolysin S—Stable to oxygen, sensitive to light and heat.

Enzyme production—Some strains produce extracellular proteinase; digests type specific M-antigen.

Pathogenicity
Human beings—Cause of scarlet fever, fatal septicemias, pus formation.

Streptomyces aureofaciens

Taxonomy
- Order — *Actinomycetales*
- Family — *Streptomycetaceae*
- Genus — *Streptomyces*
- Species — *aureofaciens*

Mycological and Cellular Characteristics
Mycelium
Vegetative—Hyaline, yellow becoming golden-tan; does not fragment.
Aerial—White, becoming brown to dark gray.
Spores—Spherical or ellipsoid.
Size—Long diameter, 1.5 μ.
Sporophores—Straight but not rigid; no turns.
Habitat—Soil.

Cultural Characteristics
Agar—Light brown; no aerial mycelium.
Asparagine-meat extract-glucose agar—Hyaline, becoming yellow-orange.
Potato—Wrinkled, yellow-orange.

Physiological Characteristics
Biochemical action
Milk—Not peptonized or coagulated; sparse yellow-brown.
Protein liquefaction or digestion
Gelatin—Not liquefied.
Growth factors
Nutrition—Saprophytic.
Color characteristics
Chromogenesis—Soluble golden-yellow pigment produced; no soluble pigment on agar.

Biochemical Characteristics
Antibiotic production—Chlorotetracycline (Aureomycin) produced.

Streptomyces griseus

Taxonomy
- Order — *Actinomycetales*
- Family — *Streptomycetaceae*
- Genus — *Streptomyces*
- Species — *griseus*

Mycological Characteristics
Mycelium
Vegetative—Colorless, folded or smooth growth turning olive-tan; not fragmented.
Aerial—Light green, powdery, profuse.
Spores—Spherical to ellipsoid.
Size—0.8 by 0.8 to 1.7 μ.
Sporophores—Tufts formed.

Cultural Characteristics
Agar colonies—Cream to transparent, profuse.
Gelatin stab—Green-yellow or cream with brown tint.
Gelatin agar—Cream to orange, raised, center, radiate, erose margin.
Starch agar—Transparent, spreading.
Glucose broth—Yellow, folded, profuse pellicle with green tint.
Synthetic agar—Colorless, then olive-tan, spreading, thin; light-green, abundant, powdery, aerial mycelium.
Potato—Yellow, wrinkled, covered with white aerial mycelium.

Physiological Characteristics
Biochemical action
Starch hydrolysis—Positive.
Nitrite—Formed from nitrate.

Protein liquefaction or digestion
Gelatin—Rapidly liquefied.
Indicator reactions
Litmus milk—Coagulated; peptonization rapid, becomes alkaline; cream ring.
Growth factors
Oxygen—Aerobic.
Temperature
Optimum—37 C.
Color characteristics
Chromogenesis—Light green to gray insoluble pigment.
Biochemical Characteristics
Antibiotic production—Depending on strain, streptomycin, actidione, grisein, and candicidin are produced.

Streptomyces rimosus

Taxonomy

Order	*Actinomycetales*
Family	*Streptomycetaceae*
Genus	*Streptomyces*
Species	*rimosus*

Mycological Characteristics
Mycelium
Vegetative—Smooth, flat, edge irregular; does not fragment.
Aerial—Sparse; center opaque, edge buff; many spirals.
Spores
Conidia—Cylindrical, 0.6 to 0.7 by 0.8 to 1.4 μ.
Habitat—Soil.

Cultural Characteristics
Agar colonies—Light yellow, sparse; no aerial mycelium.
Gelatin colonies—White aerial mycelium.
Czapek's synthetic agar—Sparse, colorless, submerged with no aerial mycelium.
Starch agar colonies—Poor growth; sparse aerial mycelium; off-cinnamon color.
Asparagine agar colonies—White to pale-tan aerial mycelium.
Glucose agar colonies—Yellow-brown; cracked, dry appearance; gray aerial mycelium.

Physiological Characteristics
Biochemical action
Starch hydrolysis—Weak positive.
Cellulose hydrolysis—Negative.
Nitrite—Readily formed from nitrate.
Milk—Not peptonized; no pH change; gray-white mycelium; thick pellicle.
Protein liquefaction or digestion
Gelatin—Not liquefied.
Growth factors
Temperature—Psychrophilic or mesophilic.
Nutrition—Saphrophytic.
Color characteristics
Chromogenesis—Yellow, soluble pigment; no soluble pigment formed with Czapek's synthetic agar.
Biochemical Characteristics
Antibiotic production—Oxytetracycline produced.

Thiobacillus novellus

Taxonomy

Order	*Pseudomonadales*
Suborder	*Pseudomonadineae*
Family	*Thiobacteriaceae*
Genus	*Thiobacillus*
Species	*novellus*

Cellular Characteristics
Morphology—Ellipsoidal or short rods.

Motility—Nonmotile.
Staining—Gram negative.
Size—0.4 to 0.8 by 0.6 to 1.8 μ.
Habitat—Soils.

Cultural Characteristics
- Agar slant—Fairly abundant growth, raised, moist, shining, white in reflected light, brown in transmitted light.
- Thiosulfate agar plate—Slow growth, becoming white from precipitated sulfur; calcium sulfate crystals; small, moist surface colonies.
- Gelatin stab—At point of stab mucoid growth; slow liquefaction.
- Broth—Slightly turbid, gelatinous pellicle; network of streamers extending from surface to bottom.
- Thiosulfate solution medium—Uniform turbidity; acid in a few days; no growth in sulfur solution medium (slightly alkaline).
- Potato slant—Limited growth, moist, shining, slightly brown.

Physiological Characteristics
- Biochemical action
  - Free sulfur—Not oxidized.
  - Thiosulfate—Oxidized to sulfate and sulfuric acid with increased acidity; tetrathionate not formed.
- Protein liquefaction or digestion
  - Gelatin—Slowly liquefied.
- Indicator reactions
  - Litmus milk—Slight alkalinity, develops slowly.
- Growth factors
  - Oxygen—Aerobic.
  - Nutrition—Facultatively autotrophic.
  - pH—Limited within 5.0 to 9.0.

Thiobacillus thiooxidans

Taxonomy

Order	*Pseudomonadales*
Suborder	*Pseudomonadineae*
Family	*Thiobacteriaceae*
Genus	*Thiobacillus*
Species	*thiooxidans*

Cellular Characteristics
- Morphology—Short rods, rounded ends.
- Motility—Motile.
- Flagella—Single polar flagellum.
- Staining—Gram negative.
- Occurring—Singly, in pairs, or in chains.
- Size—0.5 by 1.0 μ.
- Habitat—Soil.

Cultural Characteristics
- Thiosulfate agar colonies—Almost transparent; scant growth.
- Liquid sulfur-bearing medium—No surface growth; uniform turbidity, no sediment, very acid.
- Liquid thiosulfate medium—Uniform turbidity; becomes acid, sulfur precipitated.

Physiological Characteristics
- Biochemical action
  - Ammonia—Utilized.
  - Nitrate—Not utilized.
  - Asparagine—Not utilized.
  - Urea—Not utilized.
  - Peptone—Not utilized.
  - Acid—Produced by oxidation of sulfur.
- Growth factors
  - Oxygen—Strictly aerobic.
  - Temperature
    - Optimum—28 to 30 C.
    - Growth—Rate diminished at 18 and 37 C.
    - Thermal death point—Between 55 and 60 C.
  - Nutrition—Strictly autotrophic; energy obtained from oxidation of sulfur and thiosulfate yielding sulfuric acid as product; carbon dioxide of atmosphere utilized as source of carbon.

pH
Optimum—2.0 to 3.5.
Range—0.5 to 6.0.
Acidity—This organism can live in a more acid medium, as low as pH 0.5, and produce more acid than any other organism isolated.

Treponema pallidum

Taxonomy

Order	*Spirochaetales*
Family	*Treponemataceae*
Genus	*Treponema*
Species	*pallidum*

Cellular Characteristics
Morphology—Spirals of fine protoplasmic constituents; 3 to 12 convolutions; terminal filament present.
Motility—Slow motion, rarely rotating, flexible, movement bending along spiral.
Staining—Poorly stained with most aniline dyes. Can be stained with Giemsa (rose-red stain), Burri India ink (negative staining), Fontana-Tribondeau (silver impregnation), Noguchi's method.
Size—0.25 to 0.3 by 6 to 14 μ; nonfilterable in pore size of membrane of 0.4 μ.
Spiral size—1.0 μ.
Spiral depth—0.5 to 1.0 μ.
Habitat—Man.

Cultural Characteristics—Cannot be cultivated in artificial media but may be maintained alive for several days. Difficult to cultivate in ascitic fluid with fresh rabbit kidney under strict anaerobiosis.

Physiological Characteristics
Biochemical action
Trypsin digestion—Resistant for many days.
Bile salts, 10 per cent—Disintegration complete.
Saponin, 10 per cent—Broken up in time.

Growth factors
Oxygen—Strict anaerobe.
Temperature—Killed at 50 to 55 C in 30 minutes; destroyed by temperatures below that of the human body. When frozen under special conditions at −80 C, a number of cells remain viable for years.
Resistance—Quickly destroyed by exposure to sunlight, drying, and disinfectants. Dies in stored blood, unless frozen. Rapidly immobilized by arsenicals, bismuth compounds, and mercurials. Penicillin is treponemicidal.

Serology
Complement fixation tests—Positive in 2 to 4 weeks after onset of primary lesions; cerebrospinal fluid could be positive even if blood is negative in tertiary form of disease. Positive tests are not always indicative of a history of the disease.
Flocculation and precipitation tests—Can be carried out by mixing serum and reagents; if positive flocculation or precipitation occurs. Positive tests are not always indicative of the disease.

Research Utilization—The disease can be transmitted to monkeys. The organism can be kept virulent in mice or rabbits but its virulence cannot be maintained *in vitro*.

Pathogenicity
Human beings—Cause of syphilis in man. The exudate contains many spi-

rochetes. Serological diagnosis is usually negative during the chancre stage. The organism can penetrate the placenta.

Animals—Monkeys and chimpanzees are susceptible. The disease can be transmitted to apes. Mice can harbor the organisms for a long period of time, without gross lesions. Rabbits can be infected by inoculation into testicles; inoculation into the anterior chamber of the eye also causes the disease.

Differentiation—The organism is distinguished from *T. pertenue* (cause of yaws) by the following characteristics:

Characteristic	*T. pallidum*	*T. pertenue*
Transmission	Sexual contact, congenital	Person to person, not congenital
Site of lesion	Genitalia	Any exposed area
Late stages	Any organ, nervous system, liver	Skin, bone

Veillonella alcalescens

Taxonomy
- Order — *Eubacteriales*
- Family — *Neisseriaceae*
- Genus — *Veillonella*
- Species — *alcalescens*
- Synonym — *Micrococcus gazogenes*

Cellular Characteristics
- Morphology—Spheres.
- Staining—Gram negative.
- Occurring—Irregular masses, short chains, singly.
- Size—0.3 to 0.7 μ.
- Habitat—Found in saliva of man and animals; also isolated from various other sources, such as tonsils, appendix, scarlet fever.

Cultural Characteristics
- Deep agar colonies—Punctiform, turning lenticular; gas bubbles in less than a day.
- Peptone broth—Gas, slightly alkaline; no rancid odor.
- Blood agar plate—Nonhemolytic, minute colonies.

Physiological Characteristics
- Biochemical action
  - Indole production—Negative.
  - Hydrogen sulfide production—Negative.
  - Hemolysis—Negative.
  - Ammonia—Slightly positive.
  - Nitrite—Not formed from nitrate.
  - Sodium chloride solution, 5 per cent—Slow plasmolysis.
  - Milk—Gas, no acid, no coagulation.
  - Hydrogen—Small amount formed.
- Protein liquefaction or digestion
  - Gelatin—Not liquefied.
  - Coagulated blood serum—Negative.
  - Egg albumin—Negative.
- Fermentation reactions
  - Carbohydrates—Not fermented.
- Growth factors
  - Oxygen—Strictly anaerobic.
  - Temperature
    - Optimum—37 C.
    - Minimum—22 C for some strains.
    - Thermal death time—56 C in 1 hour.
  - pH
    - Optimum—6.0 to 8.0.
    - Minimum—Growth in broth at 5.5.
- Color characteristics
  - Chromogenesis—Some strains may form green pigment.

Academic or Research Utilization—Strains of this genus were found to be morphologically and biochemically identical with *Neisseria.*

Differentiation—Will not ferment sugars; *Veillonella parvula* will ferment sugars.

Pathogenicity

Animals—Some strains are pathogenic for rabbits; generally nonpathogenic.

Veillonella parvula

Taxonomy

Order	*Eubacteriales*
Family	*Neisseriaceae*
Genus	*Veillonella*
Species	*parvula*

Cellular Characteristics

Morphology—Small spheres.

Staining—Gram negative.

Occurring—In masses, at times in small chains.

Size—0.2 to 0.4 μ.

Habitat—Found in natural cavities, such as the digestive tract and mouth.

Cultural Characteristics

Semisolid agar colonies—Punctiform becoming lenticular with diameter of 2 mm; gas bubbles formed.

Agar stroke—Transparent, minute, bluish colonies.

Gelatin stab—No liquefaction.

Peptone broth—Turbid with fine sediment.

Glucose broth—Turbid, fetid odor; gas produced containing carbon dioxide, hydrogen, and hydrogen sulfide.

Blood agar colonies—Usually surrounded by a halo, weakly hemolytic.

Broth serum—Very abundant growth.

Physiological Characteristics

Biochemical action

Indole production—Slight.

Hydrogen sulfide production—Positive.

Hemolysis—Blood hemolyzed.

Ammonia—Not produced.

Nitrite—Formed from nitrate.

Milk—No acid, no coagulation; some strains produce gas.

Protein liquefaction or digestion

Coagulated protein—Not attacked.

Fermentation reactions

Monosaccharides

Glucose—Acid and gas.

Fructose—Small amount of acid.

Galactose—Small amount of acid.

Disaccharides

Sucrose—Small amount of acid.

Maltose—Some strains may attack weakly.

Polysaccharides

Inulin—Some strains may attack weakly.

Growth factors

Oxygen—Strictly anaerobic.

Temperature

Optimum—37 C.

Minimum—Feeble growth at 22 C.

Thermal death time—55 C for 1 hour.

pH

Optimum—6.5 to 8.0.

Biochemical Characteristics

Chemical end products—Can ferment polypeptides to produce hydrogen, carbon dioxide, hydrogen sulfide, and indole.

Pathogenicity

Human beings—Occasionally pathogenic; normally a harmless parasite.

Varieties—*V. parvula* var. *minimus,* smaller in size; var. *branhamii,* serologically different; and var. *thomsonii,* requires growth factor.

Vibrio comma

Taxonomy
- Order — *Pseudomonadales*
- Suborder — *Pseudomonadineae*
- Family — *Spirillaceae*
- Genus — *Vibrio*
- Species — *comma*

Cellular Characteristics
- Morphology—Slightly curved rods; cells may be long, thin, short or thick; curved form may be lost on artificial media; long forms in older cultures; involution forms when glycerine is added to media; globoid bodies in the presence of penicillin.
- Motility—Motile.
- Flagella—Single polar flagellum.
- Staining—Gram negative.
- Occurring—Singly and in spiral chains.
- Size—0.3 to 0.6 by 1.0 to 5.0 μ.
- Habitat—Intestinal content of cholera carriers.

Cultural Characteristics
- Agar colonies—Whitish-brown, circular, entire, raised, moist, translucent glistening.
- Agar stroke—Brownish-gray, moist, glistening.
- Gelatin colonies—Small, yellowish to white.
- Gelatin stab—Liquefaction rapid; napiform.
- Nutrient broth—Slight turbidity, wrinkled pellicle, flocculent precipitate.
- McConkey's medium—Good growth; colorless after inoculation, but soon pinkish; medium becomes a darker red.
- Peptone water—Rapid growth at surface where a delicate membrane is formed.
- Potato—Dirty white to yellowish, moist, spreading, glistening.
- Blood agar—Pigment digested forming greenish zone around colonies (El Tor strain produces a soluble hemolysin).
- Dieudonne's medium—For isolation, a pH of 9.0 to 9.6 is required.

Physiological Characteristics
- Biochemical action
  - Indole production—Positive; cholera red reaction depends upon this.
  - Hydrogen sulfide—Produced.
  - Starch hydrolysis—Positive in alkaline media.
  - Hemolysis—Does not produce filterable hemolysin. El Tor strains produce soluble hemolysin.
  - Nitrate—Reduced to nitrite when sulfuric acid is added to medium.
  - Cholera red reaction—Positive.
  - Milk—Not coagulated.
  - Benzene ring compounds—Not attacked.
  - Oxalates—Not oxidized.
  - Agar—Not digested.
- Protein liquefaction or digestion
  - Gelatin—Liquefied.
- Fermentation reactions
  - Monosaccharides
    - Arabinose—Not fermented by Group I of Heiberg.
    - Glucose—Acid, no gas.
    - Fructose—Acid, no gas.
    - Galactose—Acid, no gas.
    - Mannose—Fermented by Group I of Heiberg.
  - Disaccharides
    - Lactose—Not attacked.
    - Sucrose—Acid, no gas.
    - Maltose—Acid, no gas.
  - Polysaccharides
    - Inulin—Not attacked.
  - Alcohols and polyalcohols
    - Glycerol—Very slow acid formation.
    - Mannitol—Acid, no gas.

Dulcitol—Not attacked.

Growth factors

Oxygen—Aerobic.

Temperature

Optimum—37 C.

Maximum—42 C.

Minimum—14 C.

pH—High alkali but low acid tolerance; 7.6 to 8.0 or 6.4 to 9.6.

Inhibition—Penicillin does not inhibit growth; streptomycin inhibits growth.

Color and light characteristics—Not luminescent.

Serology—Groupings of cholerigenic and nonpathogenic vibrios based on somatic O and flagellar H antigens have been attempted; a polysaccharide-lipid complex identical with somatic O antigen has been isolated.

Biochemical Characteristics

Enzyme production—Forms mucinase which can destroy virus receptors of red cells.

Toxin production—No exotoxin is formed, but endotoxin is produced.

Pathogenicity

Human beings—Cause of cholera.

Addenda. When the organism was inoculated into sterilized skim milk at 86 F it was not inhibited; it grew rapidly. However, at 59 F the organism did not grow. At temperature of 131 F the organism was inhibited.

Vibrio fetus

Taxonomy

Order	*Pseudomonadales*
Suborder	*Pseudomonadineae*
Family	*Spirillaceae*
Genus	*Vibrio*
Species	*fetus*

Cellular Characteristics

Morphology—Curved rods, some forms as curved S-shaped lines; others filamentous; older cultures may show granules.

Motility—Motile.

Flagella—One polar flagellum; rarely two, one at each pole in S-forms.

Capsules—Occasionally.

Staining—Gram negative.

Size—0.2 to 0.5 by 1.5 to 5.0 μ.

Habitat—Abortive cattle.

Cultural Characteristics

Subsurface agar colonies—Yellow, small, opaque.

Agar stroke—No growth from isolated strains; when growth occurs it is grayish-white.

Nutrient broth—Viscid pellicle may appear, faint clouding, filmy.

Potato—No growth.

Physiological Characteristics

Biochemical action

Indole production—Negative.

Hydrogen sulfide—Not formed.

Nitrate—Formed from nitrite.

Protein liquefaction or digestion

Gelatin—Not liquefied.

Blood serum slant—Not liquefied; very slight growth.

Fermentation reactions

Carbohydrates—No gas.

Monosaccharides

Arabinose—No acid.

Glucose—No or slight acid.

Fructose—No acid.

Galactose—No acid.

Disaccharides

Lactose—No or slight acid.

Sucrose—No or slight acid.

Trehalose—No acid.

Polysaccharides

Raffinose—No acid.

Inulin—No acid.

Alcohols and polyalcohols

Mannitol—No acid.

Sorbitol—No acid.
Dulcitol—No acid.
Glucosides
Salicin—No acid.
Growth factors
Oxygen—Microaerophilic, aerobic.
Temperature
Optimum—37 C.
Minimum—15 C.
Maximum—40.5 C.
Resistance—Withstands 55 C for 5 minutes.
Tolerance
Sodium chloride—Tolerates 1.5 to 2.0 per cent in semisolid media.
Bile—All strains grow in 5 per cent ox bile; most strains grow in semisolid media with 10 per cent fresh ox bile.

Biochemical Characteristics
Enzyme production—Catalase produced by pathogenic strains.

Pathogenicity
Animals—Causes abortion in cattle and sheep.

Vibrio indicus

Taxonomy

Order	*Pseudomonadales*
Suborder	*Pseudomonadineae*
Family	*Spirillaceae*
Genus	*Vibrio*
Species	*indicus*
Synonym	*Pseudomonas phosphorescens*

Cellular Characteristics
Morphology—Thick rods, small, rounded cells, 2 to 3 times longer than wide; some irregular filamentous forms.
Motility—Motile.
Staining—Light stain with aniline dyes.
Habitat—Dead crustacea, fish, and sea water.

Cultural Characteristics
Cooked fish—Good growth, bluish-white phosphorescence, slimy.
Gelatin colonies—Growth after 36 hours; small, circular, gray-white, punctiform liquefaction; bluish to green phosphorescence in 4 to 6 days.
Acid broth—No turbidity, no phosphorescence.
Alkaline broth—Pellicle in 72 hours; some turbidity in 24 hours.
Potato—Growth after 2 to 3 days, thin white layer.

Physiological Characteristics
Biochemical action—No gas formed.
Milk—No growth.
Nitrates—Not reduced.
Protein liquefaction or digestion
Gelatin—Liquefied.
Blood serum—Gray-white, slimy growth.
Indicator reactions
Indigo blue—Not reduced easily.
Growth factors
Oxygen—Aerobic.
Temperature
Optimum—30 to 32 C.
Minimum—15 C.
Nutrition—3 per cent salt solution is optimum for good growth and phosphorescence.
Color and light characteristics
Phosphorescence—Blue to green, persists for 1 to 2 weeks. Fluorescein formed.

Pathogenicity
Human beings—Not pathogenic; has been found in war wounds but causes no harmful effect.
Animals—Not pathogenic for laboratory animals.

Vibrio piscium

Taxonomy
- Order — *Pseudomonadales*
- Suborder — *Pseudomonadineae*
- Family — *Spirillaceae*
- Genus — *Vibrio*
- Species — *piscium*

Cellular Characteristics
- Morphology—Curved rods.
- Motility—Motile.
- Flagella—Polar flagellum.
- Staining—Gram negative.
- Size—0.3 to 0.5 by 2.0 μ.
- Habitat—Epidemic infection in fish.

Cultural Characteristics
- Agar colonies—Yellowish, smooth, entire, circular, iridescent.
- Agar stroke—Yellow, transparent streak.
- Gelatin colonies—Circular, granular, opaque.
- Gelatin stab—Napiform liquefaction.
- Nutrient broth—Slight turbidity, thin pellicle.
- Potato—Brownish-red streak.

Physiological Characteristics
- Biochemical action
  - Indole—Formed.
  - Hydrogen sulfide—Formed.
  - Nitrite—Not formed from nitrate.
- Protein liquefaction or digestion
  - Gelatin—Liquefied.
- Indicator reactions
  - Litmus milk—Soft coagulum, peptonized, alkaline.
- Fermentation reactions
  - Carbohydrates—Not attacked.
- Growth factors
  - Oxygen—Facultatively aerobic.
  - Temperature
    - Optimum—18 to 20 C.

Pathogenicity
- Animals—Pathogenic for frogs; causes disease in fresh-water fishes.

Xanthomonas campestris

Taxonomy
- Order — *Pseudomonadales*
- Suborder — *Pseudomonadineae*
- Family — *Pseudomonadaceae*
- Genus — *Xanthomonas*
- Species — *campestris*

Cellular Characteristics
- Morphology—Rods.
- Motility—Motile.
- Flagella—Polar.
- Capsules—Present.
- Staining—Gram negative.
- Size—0.3 to 0.5 by 0.7 to 2.0 μ.

Cultural Characteristics
- Beef agar colonies—Round, smooth, entire margins, wax-yellow, translucent.
- Broth—Turbid, yellow rim, pellicle sometimes.

Physiological Characteristics
- Biochemical action
  - Indole production—Slight.
  - Pectate medium—Hydrolyzed.
  - Nitrite—Not formed from nitrate.
  - Milk—Casein digested, tyrosine crystals formed; alkaline.
- Protein liquefaction or digestion
  - Gelatin—Liquefied.

Physiological Characteristics
- Fermentation reactions
  - Monosaccharides
    - Glucose—Acid, no gas.
  - Disaccharides
    - Lactose—Acid, no gas.
    - Sucrose—Acid, no gas.

Alcohols and polyalcohols
Glycerol—Acid, no gas.
Mannitol—Acid, no gas.
Growth factors
Oxygen—Aerobic.
Temperature
Optimum—28 to 30 C.
Maximum—36 C.
Color characteristics
Chromogenesis—Yellow colonies, pigment insoluble in water. No brown pigment in beef extract agar.
Biochemical Characteristics
Enzyme production—Produces a lipase.
Pathogenicity
Plants—Attacks genera of the family *Cruciferae;* pathogenic to cabbage, cauliflower, causing a vascular infection. Originally isolated from diseased rutabagas.
Varieties—A variety pathogenic to horseradish causes leaf spot and does not liquefy pectin.

Xanthomonas cucurbitae

Taxonomy

Order	*Pseudomonadales*
Suborder	*Pseudomonadineae*
Family	*Pseudomonadaceae*
Genus	*Xanthomonas*
Species	*cucurbitae*

Cellular Characteristics
Morphology—Rods.
Motility—Motile.
Flagella—Single polar flagellum.
Staining—Gram negative.
Size—0.45 to 0.6 μ by 0.5 to 1.3 μ.
Habitat—Diseased plants.
Cultural Characteristics
Beef agar slant—Moderate growth, mustard yellow, undulating margins viscid to butyrous.
Broth turbid—Ring and yellow sediment.
Physiological Characteristics
Biochemical action
Indole—Not formed.
Hydrogen sulfide production—Positive.
Starch hydrolysis—Positive.
Pectate medium—Not liquefied.
Nitrite—Not formed from nitrate.
Milk—Precipitation of casein and digestion, alkaline.
Protein liquefaction or digestion
Gelatin—Liquefied.
Fermentation reactions
Monosaccharides
Glucose—Acid.
Fructose—Acid.
Galactose—Acid.
Disaccharides
Lactose—Acid.
Sucrose—Acid.
Maltose—Acid.
Alcohols and polyalcohols
Glycerol—Acid.
Mannitol—No acid.
Growth factors
Oxygen—Aerobic.
Temperature
Optimum—25 to 30 C.
Maximum— 35 C.
Nutrition—Salt solution, 5 per cent; weak growth.
pH
Optimum—6.5 to 7.0.
Range—5.8 to 9.0.
Color and light characteristics
Chromogenesis—Yellow colonies, pigment insoluble in water. No brown pigment in beef-extract agar.
Pathogenicity
Plants—Attacks genera of the family *Cucurbitaceae,* causes leaf spot of squash; spots and localized infections usually restricted to small areas. First isolated from squash.

Xanthomonas phaseoli

Taxonomy
- Order — *Pseudomonadales*
- Suborder — *Pseudomonadineae*
- Family — *Pseudomonadaceae*
- Genus — *Xanthomonas*
- Species — *phaseoli*

Cellular Characteristics
- Morphology—Rods.
- Motility—Motile.
- Flagella—Polar flagellum.
- Staining—Gram negative.
- Size—0.87 by 1.9 μ.
- Habitat—Leguminous plants.

Cultural Characteristics
- Beef extract-agar colonies—Butyrous, smooth, yellow, circular, entire edge.
- Nutrient broth—Turbid in 1 day; yellow ring.
- Beef broth, 4 per cent salt—Slight growth.

Physiological Characteristics
- Biochemical action
  - Indole production—Negative.
  - Hydrogen sulfide production—Positive.
  - Starch hydrolysis—Positive.
  - Nitrite—Not formed from nitrate.
  - Milk—Casein precipitated; tyrosine crystals formed.
  - Pectate—Not liquefied.
- Protein liquefaction or digestion
  - Gelatin—Liquefied.
  - Casein—Digested.
- Fermentation reactions
  - Monosaccharides
    - Arabinose—Acid, no gas.
    - Xylose—Acid, no gas.
    - Glucose—Acid, no gas.
    - Fructose—Acid, no gas.
    - Galactose—Acid, no gas.
  - Disaccharides
    - Lactose—Acid, no gas.
    - Sucrose—Acid, no gas.
    - Maltose—Acid, no gas.
  - Polysaccharides
    - Raffinose—Acid, no gas.
  - Polyalcohols
    - Glycerol—Acid, no gas.
    - Mannitol—Not fermented.
    - Dulcitol—Not fermented.
  - Glycosides
    - Salicin—Not fermented.
  - Acids
    - Formic—Not fermented.
    - Tartaric—Not fermented.
  - Organic acid salts
    - Acetate—Alkaline reaction.
    - Malate—Alkaline reaction.
    - Succinate—Alkaline reaction.
    - Citrate—Alkaline reaction.
- Growth factors
  - Oxygen—Aerobic.
- Color characteristics—Yellow pigment, insoluble in water, formed.

Biochemical Characteristics
- Enzyme production—Lipases produced.

Pathogenicity
- Plants—Cause of bean blight; pathogenic to bean, *Phaseolus vulgaris*, and other beans; not pathogenic to soybean, *Glycine max*. or cowpea.

Variety
- *X. phaseoli* var. *sojensis*—Infects soybean.

TABLE 2. CLASSIFICATION OF BACTERIA, RICKETTSIA, AND VIRUSES

TABLE 3. CLASSIFICATION OF BACTERIA AFTER KRASSILNIKOV

TABLE 4. SOME DISTINGUISHING CHARACTERISTICS OF COMMON AND IMPORTANT BACTERIA

TABLE 5. CONDENSED CLASSIFICATION OF FUNGI

TABLE 2. CLASSIFICATION OF BACTERIA,[a, b] RICKETTSIA, AND VIRUSES

Kingdom *PLANTS*

Phylum (Division) *PROTOPHYTA*

- Class *SCHIZOMYCETES*
  - Order *PSEUDOMONADALES*
    - Suborder *RHODOBACTERIINEAE*
      - Family *THIORHODACEAE*
        - Genera
          - *Thiosarcina*
          - *Amoebobacter*
          - *Thiopedia*
          - *Thiopolycoccus*
          - *Thiocapsa*
          - *Thiospirillum*
          - *Thiodictyon*
          - *Rhabdomonas*
          - *Thiothece*
          - *Rhodothece*
          - *Thiocystis*
          - *Chromatium*
          - *Lamprocystis*
      - Family *ATHIORHODACEAE*
        - Genera
          - *Rhodopseudomonas*
          - *Rhodospirillum*
      - Family *CHLOROBACTERIACEAE*
        - Genera
          - *Chlorobium*
          - *Chlorobacterium*
          - *Pelodictyon*
          - *Chlorochromatium*
          - *Clathrochloris*
          - *Cylindrogloea*
    - Suborder *PSEUDOMONADINEAE*
      - Family *NITROBACTERACEAE*
        - Genera
          - *Nitrosomonas*
          - *Nitrosogloea*
          - *Nitrosococcus*
          - *Nitrobacter*
          - *Nitrosospira*
          - *Nitrocystis*
          - *Nitrosocystis*
      - Family *METHANOMONADACEAE*
        - Genera
          - *Methanomonas*
          - *Carboxydomonas*
          - *Hydrogenomonas*
      - Family *THIOBACTERIACEAE*
        - Genera
          - *Thiobacterium*
          - *Thiospira*
          - *Macromonas*
          - *Thiobacillus*
          - *Thiovulum*
      - Family *PSEUDOMONADACEAE*
        - Genera
          - *Pseudomonas*
          - *Zymomonas*
          - *Xanthomonas*
          - *Protaminobacter*
          - *Acetobacter*
          - *Alginomonas*
          - *Aeromonas*
          - *Mycoplana*
          - *Photobacterium*
          - *Zoogloea*
          - *Azotomonas*
          - *Halobacterium*
      - Family *CAULOBACTERACEAE*
        - Genera
          - *Caulobacter*
          - *Siderophacus*
          - *Gallionella*
          - *Nevskia*
      - Family *SIDEROCAPSACEAE*
        - Genera
          - *Siderocapsa*
          - *Naumanniella*
          - *Siderosphaera*
          - *Ochrobium*
          - *Sideronema*

[a] After R. S. Breed, E. G. D. Murray, and N. R. Smith, *Bergey's Manual of Determinative Bacteriology*, 6th ed. (1948) and 7th ed., Williams & Wilkins, Baltimore, 1957.

[b] The genera belong to the ranking tribe or family, the tribes to the ranking family, the families to the ranking order, etc.

Siderococcus
Ferribacterium
Siderobacter
Sideromonas
Ferrobacillus
Family *SPIRILLACEAE*
Genera
Vibrio
Microcyclus
Desulfovibrio
Spirillum
Methanobacterium
Paraspirillum
Cellvibrio
Selenomonas
Cellfacicula
Myconostoc
Order *CHLAMYDOBACTERIALES*
Family *CHLAMYDOBACTERIACEAE*
Genera
Sphaerotilus
Toxothrix
Leptothrix
Family *PELOPLOCACEAE*
Genera
Peloploca
Pelonema
Family *CRENOTRICHACEAE*
Genera
Crenothrix
Clonothrix
Phragmidiothrix
Order *HYPHOMICROBIALES*
Family *HYPHOMICROBIACEAE*
Genera
Hyphomicrobium
Rhodomicrobium
Family *PASTEURIACEAE*
Genera
Pasteuria
Blastocaulis
Order *EUBACTERIALES*
Family *AZOTOBACTERACEAE*
Genus *Azotobacter*
Family *RHIZOBIACEAE*
Genera
Rhizobium
Chromobacterium
Agrobacterium
Family *ACHROMOBACTERACEAE*
Genera
Alcaligenes
Agarbacterium
Achromobacter
Beneckea
Flavobacterium
Family *ENTEROBACTERIACEAE*
Tribe *ESCHERICHIEAE*
Genera
Escherichia
Paracolobactrum
Aerobacter
Alginobacter
Klebsiella
Tribe *ERWINIEAE*
Genus *Erwinia*
Tribe *SERRATIEAE*
Genus *Serratia*
Tribe *PROTEEAE*
Genus *Proteus*
Tribe *SALMONELLEAE*
Genera
Salmonella
Shigella
Family *BRUCELLACEAE*
Genera
Pasteurella
Actinobacillus
Bordetella
Calymmatobacterium
Brucella
Moraxella
Haemophilus
Noguchia
Family *BACTEROIDACEAE*
Genera
Bacteroides
Sphaerophorus
Fusobacterium
Streptobacillus
Dialister

Family *MICROCOCCACEAE*
Genera
Micrococcus
Sarcina
Staphylococcus
Methanococcus
Gaffkya
Peptococcus
Family *NEISSERIACEAE*
Genera
Neisseria
Veillonella
Family *BREVIBACTERIACEAE*
Genera
Brevibacterium
Kurthia
Family *LACTOBACILLACEAE*
Tribe *STREPTOCOCCEAE*
Genera
Diplococcus
Leuconostoc
Streptococcus
Peptostreptococcus
Pediococcus
Tribe *LACTOBACILLEAE*
Genera
Lactobacillus
Ramibacterium
Eubacterium
Cillobacterium
Catenabacterium
Family *PROPIONIBACTERIACEAE*
Genera
Propionibacterium
Zymobacterium
Butyribacterium
Family *CORYNEBACTERIACEAE*
Genera
Corynebacterium
Microbacterium
Listeria
Cellulomonas
Erysipelothrix
Arthrobacter
Family *BACILLACEAE*
Genera
Bacillus
Clostridium
Order *CARYOPHANALES*
Family *CARYOPHANACEAE*
Genera
Caryophanon
Simonsiella
Lineola
Family *OSCILLOSPIRACEAE*
Genus *Oscillospira*
Family *ARTHROMITACEAE*
Genera
Arthromitus
Coleomitus
Order *ACTINOMYCETALES*
Family *MYCOBACTERIACEAE*
Genera
Mycobacterium
Mycococcus
Family *ACTINOMYCETACEAE*
Genera
Nocardia
Actinomyces
Family *STREPTOMYCETACEAE*
Genera
Streptomyces
Thermoactinomyces
Micromonospora
Family *ACTINOPLANACEAE*
Genera
Actinoplanes
Streptosporangium
Order *BEGGIATOALES*
Family *BEGGIATOACEAE*
Genera
Beggiatoa
Thiothrix
Thiospirillopsis
Thioploca
Family *VITREOSCILLACEAE*
Genera
Vitreoscilla
Microscilla
Bactoscilla
Family *LEUCOTRICHACEAE*
Genus *Leucothrix*

Family *ACHROMATIACEAE*
Genus *Achromatium*
Order *MYXOBACTERALES*
Family *CYTOPHAGACEAE*
Genus *Cytophaga*
Family *ARCHANGIACEAE*
Genera
Archangium
Stelangium
Family *SORANGIACEAE*
Genus *Sorangium*
Family *POLYANGIACEAE*
Genera
Polyangium
Podangium
Synangium
Chondromyces
Family *MYXOCOCCACEAE*
Genera
Myxococcus
Angiococcus
Chondrococcus
Sporocytophaga
Order *SPIROCHAETALES*
Family *SPIROCHAETACEAE*
Genera
Spirochaeta
Cristispira
Saprospira
Family *TREPONEMATACEAE*
Genera
Borrelia
Leptospira
Treponema
Order *MYCOPLASMATALES*
Family *MYCOPLASMATACEAE*
Genus *Mycoplasma*
Class *MICROTATOBIOTES*
Order *RICKETTSIALES*
Family *RICKETTSIACEAE*
Tribe *RICKETTSIEAE*
Genera
Rickettsia
Coxiella
Tribe *EHRLICHIEAE*
Genera
Ehrlichia
Neorickettsia
Cowdria
Tribe *WOLBACHIEAE*
Genera
Wolbachia
Rickettsiella
Symbiotes
Family *CHLAMYDIACEAE*
Genera
Chlamydia
Colettsia
Colesiota
Miyagawanella
Ricolesia
Family *BARTONELLACEAE*
Genera
Bartonella
Haemobartonella
Grahamella
Eperythrozoon
Family *ANAPLASMATACEAE*
Genus *Anaplasma*
Order *VIRALES*
Suborder *PHAGINEAE*
Family *PHAGACEAE*
Genus *Phagus*
Suborder *PHYTOPHAGINEAE*
Family *CHLOROGENACEAE*
Genera
Chlorogenus
Aureogenus
Carpophthora
Galla
Morsus
Fractilinae
Family *MARMORACEAE*
Genera
Marmor
Nanus
Acrogenus
Rimocortius
Corium
Adelonosus
Family *ANNULACEAE*
Genus *Annulus*
Family *RUGACEAE*
Genus *Ruga*

Family *SAVOIACEAE*
Genus *Savoia*
Family *LETHACEAE*
Genus *Lethum*
Suborder *ZOOPHAGINEAE*
Family *BORRELINACEAE*
Genera
Borrelina
Morator
Family *BORRELIOTACEAE*
Genera
Borreliota
Hostis
Briareus
Moliter
Scelus
Family *ERRONACEAE*
Genera
Erro
Formido
Legio
Family *CHARONACEAE*
Genera
Charon
Tortor
Tarpeia
Family *TRIFURIACEAE*
Genus *Trifur*
Family *RABULACEAE*
Genus *Rabula*

TABLE 3. CLASSIFICATION OF BACTERIA AFTER KRASSILNIKOV[a, b]

Kingdom *PLANTS*

Phylum *THALLOPHYTA*

Division *PROTOPHYTA*

- Class *ACTINOMYCETES*
  - Order *ACTINOMYCETALES*
    - Family *ACTINOMYCETACEAE*
      - Genera
        - *Actinomyces*
        - *Proactinomyces*
    - Family *MICROMONOSPORACEAE*
      - Genus *Micromonospora*
  - Order *MYCOBACTERIALES*
    - Family *MYCOBACTERIACEAE*
      - Genera
        - *Mycobacterium*
        - *Lactobacterium*
        - *Mycococcus*
        - *Pseudobacterium*
        - *Propionibacterium*
  - Order *COCCALES*
    - Family *COCCACEAE*
      - Genera
        - *Micrococcus*
        - *Neisseria*
        - *Nitrosococcus*
        - *Streptococcus*
        - *Diplococcus*
        - *Sarcina*
- Class *EUBACTERIAE*
  - Order *EUBACTERIALES*
    - Family *PLANOCOCCACEAE*
      - Genera
        - *Planococcus*
        - *Planosarcina*
    - Family *PSEUDOMONADACEAE*
      - Genera
        - *Pseudomonas*
        - *Nitrosomonas*
        - *Rhizobium*
        - *Sulfomonas*
        - *Acetobacter*
        - *Rhodopseudomonas*
        - *Azotomonas*
    - Family *BACTERIACEAE*
      - Genera
        - *Bacterium*
        - *Thiobacterium*
        - *Chromobacterium*
        - *Photobacterium*
        - *Azotobacter*
    - Family *CHLOROBACTERIACEAE*
      - Genera
        - *Chlorobium*
        - *Pelodictyon*
    - Family *SPIRILLACEAE*
      - Genera
        - *Vibrio*
        - *Thiospirillum*
        - *Spirillum*
        - *Rhodospirillum*
        - *Thiospira*
    - Family *BACILLACEAE*
      - Genera
        - *Bacillus*
        - *Clostridium*
  - Order *CHLAMYDOBACTERIALES*
    - Family *CHLAMYDOBACTERIACEAE*
      - Genera
        - *Sphaerotilus*
        - *Beggiatoa*
        - *Leptothrix*
        - *Thiothrix*
        - *Crenothrix*
        - *Thioploca*
    - Family *OSCILLOSPIRACEAE*
      - Genera
        - *Pontothrix*
        - *Arthromitus*
        - *Anabaeniolum*
        - *Caryophanon*

[a] Krassilnikov, *Guide to the Bacteria and the Actinomycetes*, Moscow, 1949.

[b] The genera belong to the ranking family, the families to the ranking order, etc.

Oscillospira
Order *FERRIBACTERIALES*
Family *FERRIBACTERIACEAE*
Genera
Gallionella
Sideromonas
Siderocapsa
Ochrobium
Order *THIOBACTERIALES*
Family *ACHROMATIACEAE*
Genera
Achromatium
Thiosphaerella
Thiophysa
Thiovolum
Family *THIOCAPSACEAE*
Genera
Thiocystis
Amoebobacter
Thiocapsa
Thiothece
Thiosarcina
Thiodictyon
Thiopedia
Thiopolycoccus
Lamprocystis
Family *CHROMATIACEAE*
Genera
Chromatium
Rhabdochromatium
Family *RHODOCAPSACEAE*
Genera
Rhodocapsa
Rhodothece

Class *MYXOBACTERIAE*
Order *MYXOBACTERIALES*
Family *ARCHANGIACEAE*
Genera
Archangium
Stelangium
Family *SORANGIACEAE*
Genus *Sorangium*
Family *POLYANGIACEAE*
Genera
Polyangium
Podangium
Synangium
Chondromyces
Melittangium
Family *MYXOCOCCACEAE*
Genera
Myxococcus
Angiococcus
Chondrococcus
Family *PROMYXOBACTERIACEAE*
Genera
Sporocytophaga
Cytophaga
Class *SPIROCHAETAE*
Order *SPIROCHAETALES*
Family *SPIROCHAETACEAE*
Genera
Spirochaeta
Saprospira
Cristispira
Treponema
Borrelia
Leptospira

TABLE 4. SOME DISTINGUISHING CHARACTERISTICS OF COMMON AND IMPORTANT BACTERIA[a]

The table illustrates the kinds of morphological and physiological characteristics which serve to identify bacteria. Additional information, determined by other biochemical tests, animal inoculation, and serological tests, is necessary for the complete identification of bacterial species.

The Cocci

(Free cells are spherical)

Characteristic Cell Grouping		Genus	Characteristics	Species
Pairs	Gram −	Genus *Neisseria*	Fermentation of glucose +; maltose +	*N. meningitidis*
			Fermentation of glucose +; maltose −	*N. gonorrhoeae*
			Fermentation of glucose −; maltose −	*N. catarrhalis*
	Gram +	Genus *Diplococcus*	Alpha hemolysis (green discoloration) on blood agar; soluble in bile	*D. pneumoniae*
Chains		Genus *Streptococcus*	Alpha hemolysis (green discoloration) on blood agar; insoluble in bile: streptococci of the Viridans Group, *e.g.*	*S. mitis*
			Beta hemolysis (clear zone) on blood agar: streptococci of the Pyogenic Group and certain enterococci, *e.g.*	*S. pyogenes*
			No change produced on blood agar: certain streptococci of the Lactic Group, *e.g.*	*S. cremoris*
			Growth in 6.5% NaCl: streptococci of the Enterococcus Group, *e.g.*	*S. faecalis*
Cubical packets		Genus *Sarcina*	Color of colony: gold	*S. lutea*
Irregular clusters		Genus *Staphylococcus*	Color of colony: usually orange, sometimes white, sometimes lemon-yellow	*S. aureus*

The Bacilli

(Unbranched, rod-shaped bacteria)

Non-spore-forming; Gram negative; Intestinal bacilli and relatives (Enteric Group):

Lactose	Glucose	Sucrose	Mannitol	Production of Indole	Liquefaction of Gelatin	Motility	Methyl Red Test	Voges-Proskauer test	Growth in Citrate Medium	Genus	*e.g.*
Fermentation of Carbohydrates											
AG[b]	AG	AG or −	AG	+	−	+	+	−	±	*Escherichia*	*E. coli*[c]
AG	AG	AG	AG	−	−	+	−	+	+	*Aerobacter*	*A. aerogenes*
AG or −	AG	AG	−	±	−	−	Short, plump encapsulated rods			*Klebsiella*	*K. pneumoniae*
−	AG	−	AG	−	−	+				*Salmonella*	*S. paratyphi*, *S. schottmülleri*, *S. enteritidis*
−	A	−	A	−	−	+					*S. typhosa*
−	A	A or −	A or −	±	−	−				*Shigella*	*S. dysenteriae*, *S. paradysenteriae*
−	AG	AG	−	+	+	+				*Proteus*	*P. vulgaris*
alk	alk	alk	alk	−	−	+				*Alcaligenes*	*A. faecalis*

Non-spore-forming	Group	Characteristics	Genus	*e.g.*
Gram negative	Chromogenic bacilli; majority saprophytic	Common water bacilli; produce red pigment which is slightly soluble in water	*Serratia*	*S. marcescens*
		Soil and water bacilli; produce water-soluble, yellowish or bluish-green pigments	*Pseudomonas*	*P. aeruginosa*
		Water bacilli; produce water-insoluble, violet pigment	*Chromobacterium*	*C. violaceum*
		Soil and water bacilli; produce yellow to orange, water-insoluble pigments	*Flavobacterium*	*F. aquatile*
	Very small parasitic bacilli	Bipolar staining, coccoid to bacillary forms; ferment carbohydrates (A)	*Pasteurella*	*P. pestis*, *P. tularensis*
		Coccoid to bacillary forms; do not show bipolar staining; do not ferment carbohydrates	*Brucella*	*B. melitensis*, *B. abortus*, *B. suis*
		Pleomorphic, coccoid to filamentous forms. Require growth factors found in blood or/and plants on primary isolation.	*Haemophilus*, *Bordetella*	*H. influenzae*, *B. pertussis*
	Obligate anaerobes	Spindle or crescent-shaped rods with more or less pointed ends; common in oral cavity	*Fusobacterium*	*F. fusiforme*
		Rods morphologically like bacilli of the enteric group; some require enriched media	*Bacteroides*	*B. fragilis*
Gram positive		Long, slender, nonmotile, microaerophilic to anaerobic rods; produce lactic acid from carbohydrates; grow in acid media	*Lactobacillus*	*L. acidophilus*

[a] Modified from F. C. Kelly and K. E. Hite, *Microbiology*, Appleton-Century-Crofts, New York, 1949.
[b] A.G., acid and gas; A, acid but no gas; —, neither acid nor gas produced; alk, alkaline reaction.
[c] Further tests are necessary to differentiate the various species of nonsporulating bacilli.

TABLE 4. SOME DISTINGUISHING CHARACTERISTICS OF COMMON AND IMPORTANT BACTERIA (*Continued*)

Spore-forming	Aerobic	Genus *Bacillus*	Large motile rods producing small, central endospores; colonies circular to amoeboid in shape	*B. subtilis*
Spore-forming	Aerobic	Genus *Bacillus*	Large motile rods producing large central endospores; spreading, arborescent or root-like colonies	*B. cereus*
Spore-forming	Aerobic	Genus *Bacillus*	Large nonmotile rods producing central endospores; irregular colonies composed of long chains of bacilli forming wavy or curled borders	*B. anthracis*
Spore-forming	Anaerobic	Genus *Clostridium*	Long slender motile bacilli which produce terminal spores wider than the vegetative rods; brain medium blackened	*C. tetani*
Spore-forming	Anaerobic	Genus *Clostridium*	Short nonmotile rods not swollen at sporulation; central to excentric endospores; many carbohydrates fermented (AG); brain medium not blackened or digested	*C. perfringens*
Spore-forming	Anaerobic	Genus *Clostridium*	Motile bacilli producing subterminal endospores which swell the vegetative rods; many carbohydrates fermented (AG); fermentation products include acetone, butyl alcohol, ethyl alcohol, butyric acid and acetic acid	*C. acetobutylicum*
THE SPIRILLA (Curved or spiral rods; cells rigid; motile with flagella)				
Short, comma-shaped cells; one polar flagellum		Genus *Vibrio*[d]	Gelatin liquefied; nitrates reduced to nitrites; indole formed; milk not coagulated	*V. comma*
Long, many curved to spiral cells; several polar flagella		Genus *Spirillum*	Spirals 1.5 to 2 by 30 to 50 μ; gelatin liquefied; no pigment formed	*S. volutans*
Long, many curved to spiral cells; several polar flagella		Genus *Rhodospirillum*	Spirals 0.5 to 1.5 by 2 to 50 μ; gelatin not liquefied; red pigment produced. One of the photosynthetic sulfur bacteria	*R. rubrum*
THE ACTINOMYCETES (Branching, mold-like bacteria)				
Straight to slightly curved bacilli which branch occasionally; rudimentary or no mycelium formed	Acid-fast	Genus *Mycobacterium*	Parasitic in warm-blooded animals; grows slowly on enriched (egg, glycerol, serum, etc.) media; pale-yellow to orange colonies; produces tuberculosis in guinea pigs	*M. tuberculosis*
Straight to slightly curved bacilli which branch occasionally; rudimentary or no mycelium formed	Acid-fast	Genus *Mycobacterium*	Saprophytic; grows rapidly on most media producing yellow to orange colonies; survives 60 C for 1 hour; grows at 47 C	*M. phlei*
Straight to slightly curved bacilli which branch occasionally; rudimentary or no mycelium formed	Nonacid-fast, pleomorphic, club-shaped rods	Genus *Corynebacterium*[e]	Human parasites; uneven staining showing metachromatic granules with methylene blue and special stains: Ferments glucose (A) and dextrin (A), but not sucrose; produces exotoxin; pathogenic for guinea pig and rabbit	*C. diphtheriae*
Straight to slightly curved bacilli which branch occasionally; rudimentary or no mycelium formed	Nonacid-fast, pleomorphic, club-shaped rods	Genus *Corynebacterium*[e]	Human parasites; uneven staining showing metachromatic granules with methylene blue and special stains: Does not ferment glucose, dextrin, or sucrose; nonpathogenic	*C. pseudodiphtheriticum*
Straight to slightly curved bacilli which branch occasionally; rudimentary or no mycelium formed	Nonacid-fast, pleomorphic, club-shaped rods	Genus *Corynebacterium*[e]	Human parasites; uneven staining showing metachromatic granules with methylene blue and special stains: Ferments glucose (A) and sucrose (A); may or may not ferment dextrin; nonpathogenic	*C. xerosis*
Branching filaments form mycelium	Vegetative mycelium fragments to form arthrospores; conidia not produced	Anaerobic to microaerophilic; parasitic in man and animals; not acid-fast. Genus *Actinomyces*	Crooked, sometimes branching filaments about 0.5 μ thick; gram positive; slowly liquefies gelatin and peptonizes milk; white fuzzy colonies in broth and solid media; old growth becomes yellowish to brown; experimental animals resist infection	*A. bovis*
Branching filaments form mycelium	Vegetative mycelium fragments to form arthrospores; conidia not produced	Aerobic; many species acid-fast; sometimes pathogenic for man and animals. Genus *Nocardia*	Fine, usually straight, filaments 0.2 μ thick; gram positive; grows rapidly on laboratory media forming yellow to orange colonies; does not liquefy gelatin or peptonize milk; pathogenic for guinea pig and rabbit	*N. asteroides*
Branching filaments form mycelium	Vegetative mycelium does not fragment to form arthrospores; conidia produced; generally saprophytic	Chains of conidia borne on aerial hyphae. Genus *Streptomyces*	One of several species causing potato scab	*S. scabies*

[d] There are other genera of curved bacteria which possess a single polar flagellum, including the cellulose-oxidizing organisms *Cellvibrio* and *Cellfalcicula*.

[e] The genus *Corynebacterium* is classified with the *Eubacteriales* in R. S. Breed, E. G. D. Murray, and N. R. Smith, Bergey's *Manual of Determinative Bacteriology*, 7th ed., Williams & Wilkins, Baltimore, 1957.

TABLE 4. SOME DISTINGUISHING CHARACTERISTICS OF COMMON AND IMPORTANT BACTERIA (*Continued*)

THE SPIROCHETES

(Slender, flexible spirals; motile without flagella)

Cell 45 to 500 μ long; majority free living	No crista or longitudinal ridge along cell	Protoplast spirally wound around an axial filament	Genus *Spirochaeta*	*S. plicatilis*
		No discernible axis filament	Genus *Saprospira*	*S. grandis*
	Crista or longitudinal ridge present		Genus *Cristispira*	*C. balbianii*
Average length of cells, 4 to 16 μ; majority parasitic	Open, irregular coils; active lashing and slow rotary movements; stain readily with ordinary aniline dyes		Genus *Borrelia*	*B. recurrentis*
	Close, permanently wound coils; stain poorly with most aniline dyes	Pitch of coils 1 μ or less; bending movements and rotation along spiral	Genus *Treponema*	*T. pallidum*
		Pitch of coil 0.5 μ or less; rapid spinning and lashing movements; cells hooked at one or both ends	Genus *Leptospira*	*L. icterohaemorrhagiae*

TABLE 5. CONDENSED CLASSIFICATION OF FUNGI[a]

Kingdom *PLANTS*

Phylum *THALLOPHYTA*

Subphylum *FUNGI*

Division *EUMYCETES*

- Class *PHYCOMYCETES*
  - Subclass *ZYGOMYCETES*
    - Order *MUCORALES*
      - Family *MUCORACEAE*
        - Genera
          - *Rhizopus*
          - *Zygorrhynchus*
          - *Absidia*
          - *Circinella*
          - *Mucor*
          - *Pirella*
          - *Parasitella*
      - Family *THAMNIDIACEAE*
        - Genus *Thamnidium*
      - Family *CHAENPHORACEAE*
      - Family *CEPHALIDACEAE*
        - Genus *Syncephalastrum*
      - Family *MORTIERELLACEAE*
        - Genus *Haplosporangium*
      - Family *ENDOGONACEAE*
    - Order *ENTOMOPHTHORALES*
      - Family *ENTOMOPHTHORACEAE*
        - Genera
          - *Empusa*
          - *Entomophthora*
  - Subclass *ARCHIMYCETES*
    - Order *CHYTRIDALES*
      - Genera
        - *Olpidium*
        - *Rhizophydium*
        - *Synchytrium*
        - *Rhinosporidium*
        - *Cladochytrium*
      - Family *CHYTRIDIACEAE*
        - Genus *Chytridium*
    - Order *BLASTOCLADIALES*
      - Genus *Allomyces*
    - Order *MONOBLEPHARIDALES*
      - Genus *Monoblepharis*
  - Subclass *OOMYCETES*
    - Order *LAGENIDIALES*
      - Family *LAGENIDIACEAE*
        - Genera
          - *Lagenidium*
          - *Olpidiopsis*
    - Order *SAPROLEGNIALES*
      - Family *SAPROLEGNIACEAE*
        - Genera
          - *Saprolegnia*
          - *Dictyuchus*
          - *Achlya*
    - Order *LEPTOMITALES*
      - Family *LEPTOMITACEAE*
        - Genus *Sapromyces*
    - Order *PERONOSPORALES*
      - Family *ALBUGINACEAE*
        - Genus *Albugo*
      - Family *PERONOSPORACEAE*
        - Genera
          - *Plasmopara*
          - *Peronospora*
          - *Pythium*
          - *Phytophthora*
- Class *BASIDIOMYCETES*
  - Subclass *HOMOBASIDIOMYCETES*
    - Order *EXOBASIDIALES*
      - Genus *Exobasidium*
  - *HYMENOMYCETES*
    - Order *AGARICALES*
      - Family *AGARICACEAE*
        - Genera
          - *Amanita*
          - *Agaricus* (*Psalliota*)

[a] The genera belong to the ranking tribe or family, the tribes to the ranking family, the families to the ranking order, etc.

GASTROMYCETES
Order *LYCOPERDALES*
Family *LYCOPERDACEAE*
Genus *Lycoperdon*
Order *PHALLALES*
Family *PHALLACEAE*
Genus *Phallus*
Subclass *HETEROBASIDIOMYCETES*
Order *DACROMYCETALES*
Genus *Dacromyces*
Order *TREMELLALES*
Family *TREMELLACEAE*
Genus *Tremella*
Order *AURICULARIALES*
Genus *Auricularia*
Order *SEPTOBASIDIALES*
Genus *Septobasidium*
Order *UREDINALES*
Family *PUCCINIACEAE*
Genera
Puccinia
Uromyces
Order *USTILAGINALES*
Family *USTILAGINACEAE*
Genera
Ustilago
Urocystis
Family *TILLETIACEAE*
Genus *Tilletia*
Class *ASCOMYCETES*
Subclass *HEMIASCOMYCETES*
Order *ENDOMYCETALES*
Family *ENDOMYCETACEAE*
Subfamily *EREMASCOIDEAE*
Genus *Eremascus*
Subfamily *ENDOMYCOIDEAE*
Genera
Endomyces
Schizosaccharomyces
Subfamily *SACCHAROMYCOIDEAE*
Tribe *ENDOMYCOPSEAE*
Genus *Endomycopsis*
Tribe *SACCHAROMYCETEAE*
Genera
Saccharomyces
Hansenula
Torulaspora
Debaryomyces
Pichia
Schwanniomyces
Tribe *NADSONIEAE*
Genera
Saccharomycodes
Nadsonia
Hanseniaspora
Zygosaccharomycodes
Subfamily *NEMATOSPOROIDEAE*
Genera
Monosporella
Coccidiascus
Nematospora
Order *TAPHRINALES*
Genus *Taphrina*
Subclass *EUASCOMYCETES*
PLECTOMYCETES
Order *PLECTASCALES*
Family *GYMNOASCACEAE*
Genera
Ctenomyces
Myxotricum
Gymnoascus
Family *ASPERGILLACEAE*
Genus *Alescheria*
Order *ERYSIPHALES*
Family *ERYSIPHACEAE*
Genus *Erysiphe*
PYRENOMYCETES
Order *SPHAERIALES*
Family *PLEOSPORACEAE*
Genera
Pleospora
Neurospora
Family *CHAETOMIACEAE*
Genus *Chaetomium*
Order *LABOULBENIALES*
Family *LABOULBENIACEAE*
Genera
Laboulbenia
Stigmatomyces
Order *CLAVICEPTALES*
Family *CLAVICEPTACEAE*
Genus *Claviceps*

Order *DOTHIDEALES*
Family *DOTHIDEACEAE*
Genera
Phyllacora
Plowrightia

DISCOMYCETES
Order *PEZIZALES*
Family *PEZIZACEAE*
Genera
Peziza
Helvella
Pyronema
Order *TUBERALES*
Family *TUBERACEAE*
Genus *Tuber*

Class *FUNGI IMPERFECTI*
Order *MONILIALES*
Family *MONILIACEAE*
Subfamily *AMEROSPORAE*[b]
Tribe *ASPERGILLEAE*
Genera
Aspergillus
Gliocladium
Penicillum
Scopulariopsis
Paecilomyces
Tribe *CEPHALOSPORIEAE*
Genera
Cephalosporium
Hyalopus
Trichoderma
Corethropsis
Tribe *BOTRYTIDEAE*
Genera
Botrytis
Monosporium
Acladium
Histoplasma
Sporotrichum
Sepedonium
Blastomyces
Chaetoconidium
Acremonium
Tribe *VERTICILLIEAE*
Genera
Verticillium
Acrostalagmus

[b] The ending "ae" denotes a section of a family.

Subfamily *TRICHOPHYTONAE*
Genera
Trichophyton
Microsporum
Epidermophyton
Achorion
Subfamily *DIDYMOSPORAE*
Genera
Trichothecium
Diplosporium
Arthrobotrys
Family *CRYPTOCOCCACEAE*
Subfamily *CRYPTOCOCCOIDEAE*
Genera
Kleockera
Cryptococcus
Trigonopsis
Mycoderma
Pityrosporum
Schizoblastosporion
Subfamily *CANDIDOIDEAE*
Genera
Candida
Geotrichum
Trichosporon
Family *NECTAROMYCETACEAE*
Genus *Nectaromyces*
Family *RHODOTORULACEAE*
Genus *Rhodotorula*
Family *SPOROBOLOMYCETACEAE*
Genera
Sporobolomyces
Bullera
Family *DEMATIACEAE*
Subfamily *AMEROSPORAE*
Genera
Acromoniella
Madurella
Pullularia
Hemispora
Haplographium
Nigrospora
Dematium
Monotospora
Cladosporium

Glenospora
Phialaphora
Stachybotrys
Subfamily *PHRAGMOSPORAE*
Genera
Acrothecium
Helminthosporium
Spondylocladium
Subfamily *DICTYOSPORAE*
Genera
Alternaria
Stemphylium
Macrosporium
Family *STILBACEAE*
Genera
Dendrostilbella
Styanus
Family *TUBERCULARIACEAE*
Genera
Fusarium
Epicoccum
Order *SPHAEROPSIDALES*
Family *SPHAERIOIDACEAE*
Genus *Phoma*
Family *NECTRIOIDACEAE*
Genus *Plenozythia*
Order *MELANCONIALES*
Family *MELANCONIACEAE*

TABLE 6. ANTIBIOTICS

TABLE 6. ANTIBIOTICS

Abikoviromycin—Derived from *Streptomyces rubescens* and *S. abikoensis*. Readily destroyed by acid, heat, and exposure. Has antiviral activity against Western and Eastern encephalomyelitis but not against Venezuelan. Has little action against fungi and bacteria.

Achromycin—See **tetracycline.**

Actidione—See **cycloheximide.**

Actinobolin—Derived from *Streptomyces* sp. Probably $C_{13}H_{20\text{-}22}N_2O_6$; forms crystalline acetate and sulfate; active against some gram-positive and gram-negative bacteria *in vitro;* active against transplanted mice leukemias with some development of resistance; nontoxic to mice.

Actinomyces Lysozyme—Derived from *Streptomyces* sp. Insoluble in benzene, chloroform, and ether. Active against micrococci.

Actinomycetin—Derived from *Streptomyces albus*. May be composed of an enzyme and a bactericidal fatty acid fraction. Soluble in water and precipitated by protein precipitants. Active against some gram-positive living bacteria and gram-negative dead bacteria exhibiting a lytic action.

Actinomycin—Derived from *Streptomyces antibioticus* and *S. parvus* in **tryptone** medium. $C_{41}H_{56}N_8O_{11}$(?); vermilion-red platelets, slightly soluble in water and ether; soluble in acetone, alcohol, and benzene; insoluble in petroleum ether. Active against gram-positive and to some degree against gram-negative bacteria as well as fungi. Does not influence the blood pressure; quickly disappears from the blood stream. Some cytostatic activity; high toxicity.

Actinomycin A—See **actinomycin.**

Actinomycin B—See **actinomycin.**

Actinomycin C—Derived from *Streptomyces chrysomallus*. A weakly basic substance, $C_{64}H_{90}N_{12}O_{16}$, forming red crystals. It is slightly soluble in water and soluble in alcohol and acetone. Because it has cytostatic activity and destroys proliferating cells, it has been used in the treatment of sarcoma and myelomas. It has some toxicity.

Actinorhodine—Derived from *Actinomyces* sp. $C_{24}H_{22}O_{11}$; fine red needles; slightly soluble in alcohol, acetone, and dioxane; soluble in pyridine; blue color in alkaline solutions and red in acetone. Active against *Staphylococcus aureus.*

Actinorubin—Derived from actinomycetes like *Actinomyces erythreus* with characteristic red mycelia; also *A. albosporeus, A. californicus, A. fradii.* $C_6H_{14}N_3O_2$ or $C_9H_{22}N_5O_4$; positive biuret, reduces Fehling's solution, negative Sakaguchi and Molisch reactions; soluble in methyl alcohol, precipitated by ether. Active against gram-positive and gram-negative bacteria *in vitro;* 0.8 per cent sodium chloride solution reduces activity $\frac{1}{128}$.

Aerosporin—Belongs to the polymyxin group. It is also known as polymyxin A and contains D-leucine in addition to the constituents common to the group.

Agrimycin—A 15 per cent-1.5 per cent combination of **streptomycin** and **oxytetracycline** used to control celery blight and downy mildew of cucumber.

Agrocybin—Derived from *Agrocybe dura*, a member of the *Basidiomycetes*. A crystalline material, $CH_2OH \cdot C \vdots C \cdot C \vdots C \cdot C \vdots C \cdot CONH_2$, that is slightly soluble in water and soluble in alcohol and a number of organic solvents. Is active against *Staphylococcus aureus* and *Escherichia coli*. It is inactivated by blood and is very toxic.

Alazopeptin—Derived from *Streptomyces griseoplanus.* Peptide-type compound, probably $C_{15}H_{21}N_7O_6$. Soluble in water and aqueous solutions of organic solvents. Decomposes readily. Has antitumor activity.

Albamycin—See **novobiocin sodium.**

Albomycin—Derived from *Actinomyces subtropicus.* Cyclic peptide containing iron. The sulfate is a red amorphous powder readily soluble in water with a bright orange color. Has activity against penicillin-resistant strains of staphylococci and pneumococci. It may be administered subcutaneously or intravenously; it has a low toxicity equivalent to that of penicillin.

Allicin—Derived from garlic, *Allium sativum.* $(CH_2{:}CH \cdot CH_2)_2SO \cdot S$; colorless liquid; soluble in water; miscible with alcohol, ether, and benzene; insoluble in Skellysolves. Active against gram-positive and gram-negative bacteria.

Allistatin—See **allicin.**

Alternaric Acid—Derived from *Alternaria solani.* Colorless crystals, dibasic acid. Active against fungi; inhibits spore germination of some fungi.

Aluminum Penicillin G—The aluminum salt of **penicillin G.** It is a slightly yellowish powder with a characteristic taste and odor and is slightly soluble in water. Used for oral administration of penicillin.

Alvein—Derived from *Bacillus alvei.* It is probably a polypeptide; soluble in water and stable in pH below 7, unstable at pH 9; soluble in acetone, chloroform, and ether. Active against *Staphylococcus aureus, Escherichia coli, Bacillus anthracis,* and *Mycobacterium tuberculosis;* hemolytic to red cells.

Amidomycin—Derived from a *Streptomyces* sp. A 24-member cyclic ring of valine and alpha-hydroxyvaleric acid units. Easily soluble in most organic solvents; insoluble in water. Has activity against yeasts.

Amphomycin—Derived from *Streptomyces canus.* Stable polypeptide, soluble in water and alcohol; insoluble in nonpolar compounds. Has activity against gram-positive bacteria. Causes hemolysis, hence used only topically against dermatoses.

Amphotericin B—Derived from a *Streptomyces* sp. Yellow, crystalline, polyene compound, $C_{46}H_{73}NO_{20}$, containing mycosamine, an aminodeoxyhexose; insoluble in neutral water, soluble in acid dimethylformamide. Has antimycotic properties. Used against cryptococcal meningitis and other mycoses. May cause severe reactions.

Anemonin—Derived from *Anemone pulsatilla* L. and other *Ranunculaceae,* such as *Ranunculus acer, R. sceleratus,* etc. $C_{10}H_8O_4$; crystals, slightly soluble in cold water, soluble in hot water and hot alcohol; can be recrystallized from chloroform. Active against molds and fungi: *Mucor stolonifer, Aspergillus niger, Geotrichum candidum.* May cause irritation of the throat.

Anhydrotetracycline—An antibiotic related to **tetracycline, chlorotetracycline** (Aureomycin), and **oxytetracycline** (Terramycin).

Anisomycin—Derived from a streptomycete. Crystalline material, $C_{14}H_{19}NO_4$; soluble in water and ethyl alcohol; acid salts are very soluble. Has activity against *Endamoeba histolytica* and *Trichomonas.* Used intravaginally in treatment of trichomonal vaginitis and to protect bean leaves against infection by *Uromyces phaseoli* var. *typica.*

Antimycin A—Derived from *Streptomyces* sp. $C_{28}H_{40}N_2O_9$ (?); crystals from methyl alcohol; insoluble in water; soluble in alcohol, methyl acetate, pyridine, ether, and acetone. Slightly soluble in petroleum ether, benzene, and carbon tetrachloride. Active against fungi. Has a half-life of about 4 days on apple leaves.

Anti-Smegmatis Factor—Derived from *Actinomyces* sp. A-82, like *Actinomyces lavendulae.* Probably a base. Active against *Bacillus subtilis, Mycobacterium phlei, Mycobacterium tuberculosis* (nonpathogenic). Activity increases as alkalinity increases; cultures not inactivated by 100 C at pH 7 for 30 minutes, less than 50 per cent of activity lost at 121 C for 15 minutes.

Asiaticoside—Derived from Madagascar varieties of *Centella asiatica.* Antibiotic activity is oxyasiaticoside. Insoluble in water; soluble in pyridine. Active against *Mycobacterium tuberculosis.*

Aspergillic Acid—Derived from *Aspergillus flavus.* 3,6-Di-*sec*-butyl-1-hydroxy-2-piperazone, $C_{12}H_{20}N_2O_2$; crystals, melting at 93 C, pale yellow with black-walnut odor; soluble in hot water, alcohol, acetone, ether, benzene, chloroform, and pyridine, insoluble in cold water. Active against *Micrococcus, Streptococcus, Clostridium* sp. Pure aspergillic acid is probably responsible for only part of the activity of the commercial product. Activity is reduced by iron, increased by nickel, zinc, and bismuth.

Aspergillin—A designation given to several antimicrobial materials derived from *Aspergillus* sp.; possibly most appropriately assigned to a pigment obtained from *Aspergillus niger.* See also **aspergillic acid.**

Aureomycin—See **chlorotetracycline.**

Avenacein—Derived from *Fusarium avenaceum.* $C_{25}H_{44}N_2O_7$; melting at 139 C, crystalline. Sparingly soluble in water; freely soluble in organic solvents. Active against *Mycobacterium phlei.*

Ayfivin—Derived from *Bacillus licheniformis.* Probably a mixture of polypeptides. Amorphous; soluble in water, alcohol, and butyl alcohol. Insoluble in ether. Precipitated by picric acid and a number of protein precipitants. Active against *Clostridium, Micrococcus, Hemophilus,* and *Vibrio* sp.; *Mycobacterium tuberculosis.* Some evidence of kidney damage.

Azomycin—Derived from a streptomycete that is similar to *Nocardia mesenterica.* Crystalline compound, $C_3H_3N_2 \cdot NO_2$, 2-nitroimidazole. Soluble in alkaline water and ethyl alcohol; insoluble in acid water and ether. Has activity *in vitro* against *Staphylococcus aureus, Bacillus subtilis,* members of the colon-salmonella-shigella group, and *Mycobacterium phlei.* Is not antimycotic. May irritate the skin. Is one of the few antibiotics containing a nitro group.

Bacilipin—Derived from *Bacillus subtilis.* Bacilipin A and B have been described. Soluble in benzene, chloroform, and ether; insoluble in petroleum ether. Bacteriostatic activity against *Staphylococcus aureus, Bacillus anthracis, Salmonella typhosa, Escherichia coli, Corynebacterium diphtheriae.* Activity lost in drying: heat labile.

Bacillin—Derived from *Bacillus subtilis.* Amorphous precipitate; soluble in water and 90 per cent alcohol; insoluble in organic solvents; heat stable. Active against *Escherichia coli, Salmonella.* Activity reduced by brain-heart media, rabbit blood.

Bacillomycin—Derived from *Bacillus subtilis.* Amorphous precipitate; soluble in water at pH 8, insoluble at pH 2.5; soluble in methyl alcohol, alcohol, acetone, and butyl alcohol; precipitated by ammonium sulfate; not affected by trypsin or pepsin. Has fungistatic activity.

Bacillosporin—See **polymyxin.**

Bacilysin—Derived from *Bacillus subtilis.* Amorphous white powder, possibly a peptide; soluble in water, ethyl alcohol, and methyl alcohol; insoluble in ether, benzene, and acetone. Is inactivated at pH 2 or pH 9 but is stable in aqueous solution, pH 7, at 100 C for 5 minutes. It has synergistic action (*in vitro*) with penicillin against alpha-, beta-hemolytic streptococci.

Bacitracin—An antibiotic derived from *Bacillus licheniformis.* Polypeptide; grayish-white powder; soluble in water, ethyl and other alcohols; insoluble in acetone, ether, and chloroform. Relatively stable in acid solutions; unstable at pH above 9 and above 56 C. Active against many gram-positive bacteria, including staphylococci, streptococci, pneumococci, anaerobic cocci, clostridia of the gas gangrene group, corynebacteria, syphilis spirochetes and mouth spirochetes, and *Actinomyces israelii;* also active against gram-negative cocci, such as meningococci and gonococci; and *Endamoeba histolytica.* It has no activity against most aerobic gram-negative bacilli. Very useful in treatment of susceptible staphylococci. May cause reactions. Used as a growth factor for poultry and hogs. Maximum concentration must not exceed 11 ppm.

Benzathine Penicillin G—A complex of **penicillin G** and the compound $C_6H_5CH_2 \cdot NHCH_2CH_2NH \cdot CHC_6H_5$; an odorless, tasteless, white, crystalline powder; slightly soluble in water and alcohol; yields a saturated aqueous solution with a pH in the range 5.0 to 7.5. Because of its low solubility it exhibits somewhat longer activity than more soluble penicillin preparations. Low frequency of hypersensitivity. Given orally and parenterally.

Biformic Acid, Biforminic Acid—Acid form of biformin. Soluble in water, acidified chloroform, and ether. Active against *Bacillus subtilis, Mycobacterium* sp., *Escherichia coli, Staphylococcus aureus, Pseudomonas aeruginosa.*

Biformin—Derived from the fungus, *Polyporus biformis.* Isolated in solution only. Moderately soluble in water; soluble in alcohol, methyl isobutyl ketone, ether, chloroform. Decomposes on drying. Active against gram-positive and gram-negative bacteria, mycobacteria, and fungi.

Borrelidin—Derived from *Streptomyces rochei.* $C_{28}H_{43}O_6N$ (proposed formula). Active against *Borrelia.* Synergistic action with **penicillin G** against syphilis in rabbits and beta-hemolytic streptococci infection.

Bostrycoidin—Derived from *Fusarium bostrycoides.* Stable, red, crystalline substance, $C_{18}H_{14}O_7$; soluble in sodium carbonate solution, ethyl alcohol, and corn oil. Has activity *in vitro* against *Mycobacterium tuberculosis.*

Brevin—Derived from *Bacillus brevis.* Polypeptide, whitish powder, soluble in dilute sodium hydroxide solution, slightly soluble in water and ethyl alcohol. Has *in vitro* activity against *Mycobacterium tuberculosis* and some gram-positive organisms.

Bryamycin—Derived from *Streptomyces hawaiiensis.* Crystalline sulfur-bearing polypeptide insoluble in water and ethyl alcohol, soluble in formamide. Has activity against gram-positive organisms. Low toxicity for mice.

Candicidin A—Derived from a strain of *Streptomyces griseus.* Red-brown powder soluble in water and ethyl alcohol. Has powerful antimycotic activity against most of the fungi pathogenic to man except the dermatophytes and *Coccidioides immitis;* strong activity against yeasts and yeast-like fungi like *Candida albicans.*

Candidin—Derived from *Streptomyces viridoflavus.* Yellow, crystalline material, possibly $C_{40}H_{75}NO_{17}$; insoluble in water; soluble in ethyl alcohol. Has *in vitro* activity against dermatophytes and other pathogenic fungi like *Blastomyces dermatitidis, Sporotrichum schenckii,* and *Candida albicans.*

Candidulin—Derived from *Aspergillus candidus.* Soluble in ethyl and methyl alcohols and ether. Active against gram-positive and gram-negative organisms. Inactivated by whole blood.

Carbomycin—Derived from *Streptomyces halstedii.* White, odorless, bitter powder; soluble in alcohol; slightly soluble in water; monobasic; active against gram-positive cocci such as staphylococci, pneumococci, and hemolytic streptococci. Low toxicity to animals; it may cause gastrointestinal distress. Carbomycin is a lactone with 18 atoms in the ring connected to mycaminose, a dimethylamino sugar, and mycarose, a deoxy sugar. In addition to the antibiotic activity noted, it is also active against *Endamoeba histolytica,* the virus of psittacosis, some gram-negative cocci, and some rickettsiae.

Cassic Acid—Derived from the leaves of *Cassia reticulata.* Yellow needle-like crystals decomposing at 330 C. Slightly soluble in water, ethyl alcohol, and ether; insoluble in petroleum ether. Yellow in acid, red in alkaline solution. Active against *Mycobacterium* sp., *Escherichia coli, Klebsiella pneumoniae, Bacillus cereus, Staphylococcus aureus.*

Celesticetin—Derived from *Streptomyces caelestis.* Sulfur-bearing amorphous basic compound, $C_{24}H_{36\text{-}40}N_2O_9S$; insoluble in neutral or slightly alkaline water; soluble in acidic or strongly alkaline water. Stable in slight acid solution. The oxalate and sulfate are soluble in water. It is related to the **carbomycin-erythromycin** group of antibiotics. Has activity against plant pathogens like *Xanthomonas pruni, X. stewartii,* and *Corynebacterium fascians.* Displays little phytotoxicity.

Chetomin—Derived from the **fungus** *Chaetomium cochliodes* and possibly from *C. elatum* and *C. funiculum.* Amorphous red powder. Insoluble in water and petroleum ether; slightly soluble in ethyl alcohol and ether; soluble in acetone, ethyl acetate, and chloroform. Active against gram-positive bacteria. Inactive *in vivo.*

Chlamydosporin—Derived from a species of *Fusarium.* Has *in vitro* activity against gram-positive organisms including *Mycobacterium tuberculosis* and many gram-negative organisms. Has little phytotoxicity.

Chloroamphenicol, Chloramphenicol—Derived from *Streptomyces venezuelae* or made by chemical synthesis, D-(-) Threo-1-(*p*-nitrophenyl)-2-dichloroacetamido-1,3-propanediol, $NO_2C_6H_4 \cdot CHOH \cdot CHNH(CO \cdot CHCl_2)\ CH_2OH$; crystals, melting at 150.5 to 151.5 C. Soluble in water 2.5 mg/ml at 25 C. Very soluble in methyl, ethyl, and butyl alcohols; insoluble in benzene. Negative biuret, Molisch and Benedict reactions. Active against *Brucella, Clostridium, Salmonella, Pasteurella, Shigella, Mycobacterium tuberculosis.* Effective against Rocky Mountain spotted fever and typhoid.

Chloroamphenicol (Chloramphenicol) Palmitate—Palmitic acid ester of chloroamphenicol. Has same activity and relatively same potency but does not have the bitterness.

Chloromycetin—See **chloroamphenicol.**

Chloroprocaine Penicillin O—A salt of **penicillin O** and 2-chloroprocaine. A stable, white, crystalline powder that is nearly insoluble in water. Its antimicrobial activity is similar to that of other penicillin O salts.

Chlororaphin—Derived from *Pseudomonas chlororaphis* or made synthetically. 1-Carbamylphenazyl, $C_{13}H_{10}N_3O$, green crystals, melting at 228 to 230 C. Insoluble in water; slightly soluble in alcohol; insoluble in benzene and other common organic solvents. Active against *Staphylococcus aureus, Salmonella typhosa, Streptococcus pyogenes.*

Chlorotetracycline, Chlortetracycline—An antibiotic derived from *Streptomyces aureofaciens.* Free base and hydrochloride soluble in water, methyl alcohol, and acetone. Active against many gram-positive and gram-negative bacteria, such as *Salmonella, Escherichia,* and *Neisseria* sp., rickettsiae, some protozoa, and some viruses. Activity decreased by increase in pH. Increased resistance of bacteria after 14 transfers.

Cinnamycin—Derived from *Streptomyces cinnamoneus.* Stable polypeptide; soluble in water and 50 per cent alcohol. Has activity *in vitro* against *Mycobacterium tuberculosis* and *Clostridium botulinum.*

Circulin—Derived from *Bacillus circulans.* Soluble in water and lower alcohols; insoluble in hydrocarbons. Positive biuret reaction. Active against *Salmonella, Brucella abortus, Escherichia coli, Neisseria catarrhalis, Shigella dysenteriae.*

Citrinin—Derived from *Aspergillus niveus* and *A. terreus;* also from *Penicillium citrinum, P. expansum,* and *P. levidium.* $C_{13}H_{14}O_5$; yellow crystals melting at 168 C. Insoluble in water; soluble in sodium hydroxide solution giving cherry red at pH 9.9; lemon-yellow at pH 4.6. Soluble in alcohol and dioxane. Green-yellow under ultraviolet light. Bacteriostatic action enhanced by 1 per cent glucose. Toxic to mice, rats, guinea pigs.

Clavacin—See **patulin.**

Claviformin—See **patulin.**

Clitocybine—Derived from the fungus *Clitocybe* (*Aspropaxillus*) *gigantea* var. *candida.* Probably a mixture of several compounds, most active clitocybine B. Powder; soluble in water and organic solvents. Active against *Salmonella typhosa, S. paratyphi, Escherichia coli, Brucella abortus, Mycobacterium tuberculosis, Bacillus anthracis.* Gives some protection in guinea pigs against foot-and-mouth disease and streptococcus infections.

Colicine—An antibiotic (possibly more than one compound) derived from *Escherichia coli.* Probably a peptide. Odorless, soluble in water and acetic acid; insoluble in most organic solvents; thermostable in acid solution; decomposed by pepsin and trypsin. Active against enterobacteria, *Vibrio comma, Shigella paradysenteriae, S. sonnei, S. dysenteriae, Salmonella enteritidis.*

Colistatin—Derived from aerobic, sporulating bacilli isolated from soil. Crude product is soluble in hydrochloric acid–methyl alcohol solution and is precipitated at pH 6.5. Active against *Staphylococcus aureus,* pneumococci, *Shigella dysenteriae.*

Collinomycin—Derived from *Streptomyces collinus.* Orange crystals insoluble in water and slightly soluble in alcohol. Has *in vitro* activity against *Staphylococcus aureus.*

Crepin—Derived from *Crepis taraxacifolia.* Crystalline material, $C_{14}H_{16}O_4 \cdot H_2O$, darkening at 300 C without melting. Soluble in water, alcohol, ether, glycerol, and pyridine. Gives a negative Fehling test. Active against *Staphylococcus aureus, Streptococcus pyogenes, Bacillus subtilis, Salmonella typhosa.* Its activity is reduced by human serum.

Cycloheximide—Derived from *Streptomyces griseus.* $C_{15}H_{23}NO_4$; colorless crystals (plates) soluble in water, methyl alcohol, acetone, chloroform, ether and amyl acetate; active against some yeast and bacteria. *Saccharomyces pastorianus* increased in resistance from initial concentration of 0.06 microgram/ml to 4.08 micrograms/ml in 3 transfers. Commercial agricultural fungicide; also used to treat cryptococcic meningitis.

Cycloserine—Derived from *Streptomyces orchicaceus* or *S. garyphalus.* D-4-Amino-3-isoxalzolidinone. It is a broad spectrum oral

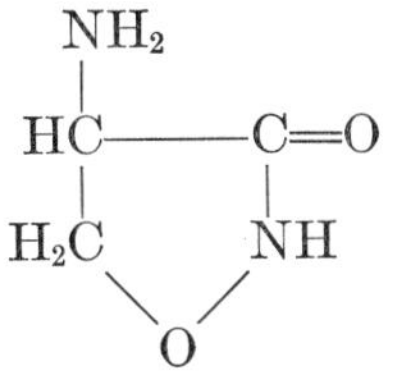

antibiotic inhibiting the growth of both gram-positive and gram-negative bacteria. It is useful against staphylococci, streptococci, *Escherichia coli,* and *Aerobacter aerogenes,* but it does not inhibit *Proteus vulgaris, Pseudomonas,* nor gonococci. It has some *in vivo* activity against *Mycobacterium tuberculosis* but is less effective than **streptomycin,** isoniazid, and *p*-aminosalicylic acid. It has some toxicity and therefore must be watched when administered.

Cytovirin—Isolated from culture filtrates of an unidentified *Streptomyces* sp. Characterized as a potent agent for combatting local lesions and systemic plant virus infections; prevents southern bean mosaic virus and tobacco mosaic virus diseases.

Dicoumarol—An antibacterial substance originally derived from spoiled sweet clover. $C_9H_5O_3 \cdot CH_2 \cdot C_9H_5O_3$; tiny crystals soluble in alkaline solutions. Active against streptococci, and also *Staphylococcus aureus, Bacillus anthracis, Brucella abortus, Clostridium perfringens, Salmonella typhosa, S. paratyphi.* Antibiotic activity reduced by cysteine, rutin. Used principally as an anticoagulant.

Dihydrostreptomycin—An antibiotic made from **streptomycin.**

Diplococcin—Derived from lactic-acid streptococci. Probably a protein similar to **gramicidin** or **tyrocidine.** It is soluble in water; gives a negative Molisch test and positive arginine and tyrosine tests. Active against streptococci.

Diploicin—Derived from the lichen *Buellia canescens.* Colorless substance, $C_{16}H_{10}Cl_4O_5$, melting at 232 C. Insoluble in water; soluble in most organic solvents. Active against *Mycobacterium tuberculosis.*

Duomycin—See **chlorotetracycline.**

Duramycin—Derived from *Streptomyces cinnamoneus* var. *azacoluta.* Amorphous polypeptide, soluble in ethyl alcohol; hydrochloride soluble in water. Has activity against plant pathogens.

Echinomycin—Derived from *Streptomyces echinatus.* Hygroscopic crystalline polypeptide, $C_{50}H_{60}N_{12}O_{12}S_2$, soluble in fat solvents. Has activity against gram-positive bacteria.

Elaiomycin—Derived from *Streptomyces hepaticus.* Light yellow oil, D-*threo*-4-

methoxy-3-(1-octenylazoxy)-2-butanol, $C_6H_{13}CH:CH \cdot N(O):NCH(CH_2OCH_3)CHOH \cdot CH_3$; slightly soluble in water, soluble in common organic solvents. Stable in neutral or slightly acid water solutions. Has *in vitro* activity against *Mycobacterium tuberculosis.*

EL_5—An antibiotic derived from *Streptomyces* sp. It resembles **actinorubin.**

Endomycin—Derived from *Streptomyces endus*. Brownish powder soluble in neutral and alkaline water. Has *in vitro* activity against bacteria and fungi.

Endosubtilysin—Derived from *Bacillus subtilis.* Probably an organic acid capable of forming a water-soluble sodium salt. Yellow powder, soluble in alcohol and chloroform. Active against *Staphylococcus aureus, Escherichia coli, Salmonella typhosa, Mycobacterium tuberculosis.* Low toxicity to man.

Enniatin A—Derived from the fungus, *Fusarium orthoceras* var. *enniathinum.* $C_{24}H_{42}N_2O_6$; crystals melting at 122 C. Slightly soluble in water. Soluble in organic solvents. Decomposed rapidly by alkali and more slowly by acid; thermostable. Active against *Mycobacterium* sp., *Escherichia coli, Staphylococcus aureus.*

Enniatin B—Derived from a variety of fusaria. $C_{22}H_{38}N_2O_6$; crystals, melting at 174 to 176 C. Slightly soluble in water; soluble in most organic solvents. Active against mycobacteria.

Enniatin C—Derived from fusaria. Crystals melting at 152 to 153 C.

L-Ephenamine Penicillin G.—A compound of **penicillin G** and L-*N*-methyl-1,2-diphenyl-2-hydroxyethylamine. Its antimicrobial activity is similar to that of other penicillin G compounds.

Erdin—Derived from *Aspergillus terreus.* $C_{16}H_{10}Cl_2O_7 \cdot 2H_2O \cdot C_4H_8O_2$; yellow crystals decomposing at 211 C. Solubility is similar to **geodin** but erdin is only slightly soluble in chloroform. It reacts as a dibasic acid and is decomposed by alkali.

Erythrin—Derived from erythrocytes. Active against diphtheroids, micrococci, streptococci, as well as cholera, intestinal bacteria, and the rickettsiae causing typhus. Insoluble in water, soluble in acetone; thermostable.

Erythromycin—Derived from *Streptomyces erythreus.* White to slightly yellowish, odorless bitter crystalline powder; slightly soluble in water, soluble in alcohol; pH of saturated aqueous solution has a range of 8.0 to 10. Effective against gram-positive organisms, such as staphylococci, pneumococci, and beta-hemolytic streptococci. It may be administered orally. May be substituted for penicillin in the treatment of venereal disease.

Erythromycin Ethyl Carbonate—An ethyl carbonate ester of **erythromycin** produced by *Streptomyces erythreus.* White, odorless, slightly bitter powder; readily soluble in alcohol, practically insoluble in water. Antibiotic properties analogous to erythromycin.

Erythromycin Glucoheptonate—A glucoheptonic acid salt of **erythromycin.** White, crystalline, odorless powder. Soluble in water and alcohol. Antibiotic properties analogous to erythromycin. A 2 per cent aqueous solution is neutral with a pH range of 6.0 to 7.5.

Erythromycin Lactobionate—A lactobionate salt of **erythromycin.** White, virtually odorless powder. Readily soluble in alcohol and water. A 2 per cent aqueous solution is neutral in acidity with a pH range of 6.0 to 7.5.

Eulicin—Derived from a streptomycete. The trihydrochloride, $C_{24}H_{52}N_8O_2 \cdot 3HCl$, is a whitish powder soluble in water. Has antimycotic activity.

Eumycin—Derived from *Bacillus subtilis.* Amorphous precipitate; soluble in water, ethyl and butyl alcohols, and acetone; insoluble in ether and amyl acetate. It is thermostable but is decomposed at pH above 8. Active against *Mycobacterium tuberculosis, Corynebacterium diphtheriae in vitro,* and some fungi.

Filipin—Derived from *Streptomyces filipinensis.* Yellow crystalline material, $C_{30}H_{50}O_{10}$, insoluble in water, soluble in dimethylformamide; is affected by light. Has antimycotic activity.

Flavacin—See **penicillin.**

Flavatin—See **penicillin.**

Flaveolin—Derived from a streptomycete. Basic substance; hydrochloride is a yellowish powder that is soluble in water and alcohol. Has an activity against gram-positive organisms greater than streptomycin.

Flavicidin—See **penicillin.**

Fomesin A—Derived from *Fomes juniperinus,* a basidiomycete. Cream to orange, crystalline substance, $C_8H_8O_5$, slightly soluble in water, somewhat soluble in ethyl alcohol; stable in neutral or acid solution. Has activity against *Staphylococcus aureus, Bacillus subtilis, B. cereus* var. *mycoides, Pseudomonas aeruginosa, Klebsiella pneumoniae, Escherichia coli, Mycobacterium smegmatis.*

Framycetin—Derived from *Streptomyces lavendulae.* Water-soluble basic substance related to **streptomycin;** hydrochloride and sulfate are soluble in water. Has activity against gram-positive and gram-negative bacteria; has been used for topical applications and treatment of coccidiosis.

Fulvicin—See **griseofulvin.**

Fumagillin—Derived from *Aspergillus fumigatus* H-3. $C_{27}H_{36}O_7$ (?); light-yellow crystals melting at 189 to 194 C. Insoluble in water, dilute acid, and saturated hydrocarbons; soluble in most of the other organic solvents. Active against amoeba, particularly against *Entamoeba histolytica* both *in vitro* and *in vivo.* Side effects frequently encountered at high-dose levels.

Fumigacin—Derived from *Aspergillus fumigatus.* Also known as helvolic acid. $C_{32}H_{44}O_8$; needle crystals, melting at 215 to 220 C; monobasic acid. Insoluble in water; soluble sodium salt; soluble in organic solvents. Bacteriostatic action against clostridia, *Salmonella, Bacillus, Shigella,* micrococci, *Escherichia coli.* Activity is decreased by serum, whole blood, and yeast extract. It is absorbed from the gastrointestinal tract.

Fumigatin—Derived from *Aspergillus fumigatus* and made synthetically. 6-Hydroxy-5-methoxy-*p*-toluquinone, $C_8H_8O_4$; maroon crystals, melting at 114 C. Moderately soluble in water and petroleum ether; soluble in acetone, ether, and benzene. Active against micrococci, *Bacillus, Vibrio comma, Streptococcus mitis, Escherichia coli.*

Fungichromatin—Derived from *Streptomyces cellulosae;* active against fungi *in vitro.* Similar to **fungichromin.**

Fungichromin—Derived from *Streptomyces cellulosae;* active against fungi *in vitro.*

Fuscin—Derived from *Oidiodendron fuscum.* It is a pigment with a quinonoid structure; $C_{15}H_{16}O_5$; orange crystals, melting at 230 C. Insoluble in water; soluble in alkali solution with a deep-purple color; soluble in most organic solvents except petroleum ether. Active against micrococci, *Salmonella,* clostridia, *Mycobacterium phlei, M. smegmatis, Vibrio comma, Shigella paradysenteriae.*

Geodin—Derived from *Aspergillus terreus.* Dextrorotary isomeride of an optically inactive erdin monomethyl ether, $C_{17}H_{12}Cl_2O_7$; pale-yellow needles, melting at 235 C. Insoluble in water and petroleum ether; soluble in alcohol and ethyl acetate; slightly soluble in ether and benzene; soluble in chloroform and acetone. Green-brown color is produced in alcohol with ferric chloride. Active against *Bacillus subtilis, Staphylococcus aureus, Escherichia coli, Streptococcus pyogenes, Vibrio comma, Mycobacterium, Shigella dysenteriae.*

Geomycin—Derived from *Streptomyces xanthophaeus.* Crystalline helianthate and hydrochloride, $(C_6H_{12}N_2O_2 \cdot HCl)_n$. Has activity against *Entamoeba histolytica.* Has some toxic action on the kidney.

Gigantic Acid—See **penicillin.**

Gladiolic Acid—Derived from *Penicillium gladioli.* $C_{11}H_{10}O_5$; needles, melting at 150 C; monobasic acid. Soluble in hot water. Active against *Staphylococcus aureus, Escherichia coli, Salmonella typhosa.* It also has fungistatic properties.

Gliotoxin—Derived from *Aspergillus fumigatus* and other molds. Stable in acid, unstable in alkali; sensitive to heat and oxidation. Active against micrococci, *Salmonella, Bordetella pertussis,* and other organisms.

Globicin—Derived from *Bacillus subtilis* strain *globigii.* The sodium salt is a tan powder readily soluble in water. Has *in vitro* activity against gram-positive and acid-fast bacteria like *Mycobacterium avium* and *M. phlei, Staphylococcus aureus, Bacillus cereus;* does not have activity against coli-aerogenes group, *Pseudomonas aeruginosa, Proteus vulgaris, Serratia marcescens.*

Glutinosin—Derived from *Metarrhizium glutinosum.* Crystals melting over 300 C. Soluble in water and alcohol. Stable solution at pH 2.9 to 7.6. Active against molds.

Gramicidin—See **tyrothricin.**

Gramicidin C—See **gramicidin S.**

Gramicidin D—Separated from **tyrothricin.** A cyclopeptide; crystals, melting at 229 to 230 C. Very slightly soluble in water; soluble in lower alcohols and acetic acid; virtually insoluble in hydrocarbons and ether; moderately soluble in dry acetone. Active against gram-positive and gram-negative cocci.

Gramicidin Dubos—See **gramicidin D.**

Gramicidin S—Derived from a strain of *Bacillus brevis.* A cyclopentapeptide or cyclodecapeptide; crystals, melting at 268 to 270 C. Insoluble in water, acids, and alkalies; soluble in alcohol; slightly soluble in acetone. Active against gram-negative bacilli and gram-positive cocci.

Gramidinic Acid—See **tyrothricin.**

Graminic Acid—See **tyrothricin.**

Grisein—Derived from *Streptomyces griseus.* Amorphous precipitate, $C_{40}H_{61}N_{10}O_{20}SFe$ (?). Soluble in water; insoluble in most common organic solvents; slightly soluble in 95 per cent alcohol. Active against *Salmonella gallinarum, Shigella dysenteriae, Bacillus, Staphylococcus aureus, Mycobacterium tuberculosis, Klebsiella pneumoniae.* Increased acidity lowers activity.

Griseofulvin—Derived from *Penicillium griseofulvum* and *P. janczewskii.* Also known as the curling factor; $C_{17}H_{17}ClO_6$ (?); crystals, melting at 220 C. Insoluble in water; slightly soluble in a number of organic solvents. Thermostable. A yellow color is produced with sulfuric acid. Has broad antifungal action. Inhibits growth in *Zygomycetes, Ascomycetes, Basidiomycetes.*

Griseomycin—Derived from *Streptomyces griseolus.* Basic crystalline substance and hydrochloride soluble in water and alcohol. Has activity against gram-positive bacteria and neisseria.

Griseovirdin—A broad-spectrum antibiotic derived from *Streptomyces griseus;* active against a variety of bacteria *in vitro* and highly effective against experimental pertussis in mice.

Grisic Acid—An antibiotic derived from *Basidiomycetes* sp.

Helenine—Derived from *Penicillium funiculosum.* Possibly a nucleoprotein. Has antiviral activity.

Herquein—Derived from *Penicillium herquei.* $C_{19}H_{20}O_8$; yellow-brown crystals, decomposing at 129 C; slightly soluble in water yielding an orange color; readily soluble in alkali with a green fluorescence; soluble in organic solvents. Active against *Vibrio comma, Staphylococcus aureus, Shigella dysenteriae, Streptococcus pyogenes, Mycobacterium phlei.*

Hirsutic Acids—Antibiotics derived from the fungus, *Stereum hirsutum.* Hirsutic acid A, $C_{15}H_{20}O_4$ (?); crystals, melting at 179.5 C. Soluble in hot water and most organic solvents. Active against *Staphylococcus aureus, Corynebacterium diphtheriae, Streptococcus pyogenes, Bacillus anthracis, Vibrio comma, Bacillus subtilis.*

Homomycin—Derived from *Streptomyces noboritoensis.* White powder readily soluble in water and alcohol. Has *in vitro* activity against *Mycobacterium tuberculosis.*

Humulon—Derived from hops, *Lupulus humulus.* $C_{21}H_{30}O_5$; crystals, melting at 65 to 66.5 C; monobasic acid. Slightly soluble in boiling water; soluble in most organic solvents. The sodium salt is readily soluble in water. Has bacteriostatic action against *Staphylococcus aureus.* See also **lupulon.**

Hydrabamine Phenoxymethylpenicillin—A mixture of the *N,N'*-bis-(dehydroabietyl)-ethylenediamine salt of phenoxymethylpenicillin with lesser amounts of the dihydro- and tetrahydro-derivatives. Has similar activity and uses as phenoxymethylpenicillin. Administered orally.

Hydroxymycin—Derived from a streptomycete. Has antimicrobial activity and has been used in the treatment of trichomoniasis.

Hygromycin—Derived from *Streptomyces hygroscopicus.* Stable, white, amorphous powder, $C_{23}H_{29}NO_{12}$, readily soluble in water and alcohol. Has broad antibiotic activity. Used as an anthelminthic in swine feed.

Inolomin—Derived from *Inoloma traganum.* Yellow substance; soluble in water. Inactivated by autoclaving. Active against *Micrococcus* sp.

Iodinin—Derived from *Chromobacterium iodinum.* 1,4-Dihydroxyphenazine di-*N*-oxide, $C_{12}H_8N_2O_4$. Purple crystals with coppery glint decomposing at 236 C. Insoluble in water; soluble in concentrated acid; soluble in alkali with blue color; soluble in chloroform. Active against *Staphylococcus aureus, Streptococcus pyogenes, Salmonella typhosa, Escherichia coli, Proteus vulgaris.*

Irpexin—Derived from *Basidiomycetes* sp.

Javancin—Derived from *Fusarium javanicum.* $C_{15}H_{14}O_6$; red crystals with a metallic luster which decompose at about 208 C. Soluble in 10 per cent sodium hydroxide solution with a deep-violet color. Active against *Staphylococcus aureus, Escherichia coli, Bacillus subtilis, Mycobacterium tuberculosis, Streptococcus pyogenes, Clostridium perfringens.* Decomposed by blood.

Kanamycin—Obtained from a strain of *Streptomyces* isolated from Japanese soil. Attacks both gram-positive and gram-negative bacteria. Has been proposed as an antituberculosis agent. Described as less toxic than neomycin or streptomycin.

Kojic Acid—Derived from *Aspergillus* sp., such as *A. oryzae, A. flavus, A. glaucus.* 5-Hydroxy-2-(hydroxymethyl)-4-pyrone, $C_6H_6O_4$; crystals, melting at 152 C. Soluble in water and alcohol; sparingly soluble in ether. Gives a red color with ferric chloride; reduces Fehling's solution. Active against *Staphylococcus aureus, Leptospira canicola;* inhibits gram-negative bacteria and also some gram-positive bacteria. Human leucocytes are killed at 1:100 dilution.

Koluophthisin—Derived from *Streptomyces floridae.* The base, possibly $C_{18}H_{32}N_9O_8$, and sulfate and dihydrochloride are freely soluble in water. It has both *in vitro* and *in vivo* activity against *Mycobacterium tuberculosis* but little activity against many other organisms.

Lactaroviolin—Pigment derived from the fungus *Lactarius deliciosus.* Purple-red crystals melting at 53 C. Soluble in common organic solvents. Active against *Mycobacterium tuberculosis.*

Lateritiin I and **II**—See **lateritiin group.**

Lateritiin Group—A group of antibiotics derived as follows: Lateritiin I (which may be enniatin) from *Fusarium lateritium,* $C_{21}H_{38}N_2O_5$, melting at 121 to 122 C; lateritiin II from *F.* sp., $C_{20}H_{36}N_2O_5$, melting at 125 C; avenacein from *F. avenaceum,* $C_{25}H_{44}N_2O_7$, melting at 139 C; fructigenin from *F. fructigenum,* $C_{26}H_{44\text{-}46}N_2O_7$, melting at 129 C; sambucinin from *F. sambucinin,* $C_{24}H_{42}N_2O_7$, melting at 85 to 86 C. The five substances are crystalline; sparingly soluble in water; freely soluble in organic solvents.

Laterosporin—Derived from *Bacillus laterosporus.* Probably composed of laterosporin A and B which are isolated as the hydrochlorides. Soluble in water; insoluble in ether; possibly precipitated by sodium chloride or 0.2 *M* phosphate buffer solution. Active against *Staphylococcus aureus, Streptococcus pyogenes, Mycobacterium tuberculosis, Salmonella typhosa, Escherichia coli.*

Laterosporin A and **B**—See **laterosporin.**

Lavendulin—Derived from *Actinomyces* sp., variant *A. lavendulae.* Derivatives are soluble in water. Gives a positive biuret and a negative Molisch test. Active against *Escherichia coli, Bacillus anthracis, Diplococcus pneumoniae, B. subtilis, Staphylococcus aureus, Streptococcus pyogenes, Shigella dysenteriae.* Sodium chloride reduces its activity.

Licheniformin—Derived from *Bacillus licheniformis.* An amorphous white powder. Soluble in water and methyl alcohol; slightly soluble in ethyl alcohol; insoluble in most organic solvents. Gives a positive biuret. Active against *Mycobacterium tuberculosis, Corynebacterium, Streptococcus* groups A, B, C, O, *Brucella abortus, Shigella dysenteriae, Diplococcus pneumoniae, Escherichia coli, Vibrio comma.* Activity increases with increased pH.

Litmocidin—Pigment derived from *Proactinomyces cyaneus* var. *antibioticus.* Red (acid form) turning to blue on neutralization. Slightly soluble in water; soluble in alcohol. Has bacteriostatic and bactericidal action. Active against *Staphylococcus aureus, Streptococcus pyogenes, Shigella dysenteriae, Salmonella typhosa, S. schottmuelleri, Escherichia coli, Mycobacterium tuberculosis.*

Lupulon—β-Bitter acid, $C_{26}H_{38}O_4$. Derived from hops, *Humulus lupulus.* Crystals, having a bitter taste, melting at 92 to 94 C. Slightly soluble in acidic or neutral aqueous solution; readily soluble in sodium salt; soluble in ethyl alcohol. Active against bacilli, micrococci, mycobacteria, yeast, fungi, and many gram-negative bacteria. See also **humulon.**

Magnamycin—See **carbomycin.**

Marasmic Acid—Derived from *Marasmius conigenus.* Soluble in water and acetone. Reduces Fehling's solution. Active against *Bacillus subtilis, Staphylococcus aureus, Mycobacterium smegmatis, Escherichia coli, Klebsiella pneumoniae, Trichophyton mentagrophytes.*

Maxipen—See **alpha-phenoxyethylpenicillin.**

Methymycin—Derived from a streptomycete. Has a macrolide structure with a lactone ring of 12 atoms, $C_{25}H_{43}NO_7$; insoluble in water; soluble in ethyl alcohol. The sulfate and acid sulfate are soluble in water.

Micromonosporin—Derived from *Micromonospora* sp. A pigmented protein, like an albumin, associated with a carbohydrate. Gives a positive Molisch test. Active against *Staphylococcus aureus, Bacillus subtilis, B. mycoides, Sarcina lutea.* No antibiotic activity against gram-negative bacteria.

Miramycin—Derived from *Streptomyces mirabilis.* Has *in vitro* activity in slight acid solution against gram-negative and gram-positive bacteria; among these are *Escherichia coli, Bacillus subtilus, Serratia marcescens, Azotobacter chroococcum.*

Mitomycin C—Derived from *Streptomyces caespitosus* as deep blue-violet crystals which do not melt or decompose at 360 C. The tentative formula is $C_{54}H_{61}N_{13}O_{19}$ corresponding to a molecular weight of 1120. It is soluble in water, methyl alcohol, acetone, butyl acetate, and cyclohexane; it is sparingly soluble in benzene, carbon tetrachloride, and ether; and is insoluble in petroleum ether.

Mitomycin C gives positive reactions with Fehling solution, hydroxylamine hydrochloride, biuret, Ehrlich, ferric chloride, nitrous acid, and Liebermann reagents and decolorizes potassium permanganate solution. It gives doubtful reactions with bromine, 2,4-dinitrophenylhydrazine, and Janovsky reagents. Benedict, Tollen, fuchsin sulfate, ninhydrin, Millon, and Raymond reagents give negative tests. These reactions indicate double bonds, amine, phenol, and ketone groups are probably present.

The absorbance of mitomycin C at 360 millimicrons is unique in the mytomycin complex. The crystalline form can be heated at 100 C for 4 hours without loss of activity but when heated in solution at pH 7, 80 per cent of the activity is lost after 3 hours. Activity is also lost when heated in solution at pH below 5 and above 12.

Mitomycin C is blue-violet in color in alkaline solution, red in weak acid, and yellow in stronger acids.

Mitomycin C has been found to have chemotherapeutic activity against a number of malignant tumors in mice and rats, including sarcoma 180, carcinomas 755, 63, and 1025, adenocarcinoma E0771. The Wagner and Ridgway osteogenic sarcoma, Jensen rat sarcoma, Walker carcinosarcoma 256, Murphy lymphosarcoma, Flexner-Jobling carcinoma, Yoshida sarcoma, and the Dunning leukemia (IRC/741). The antitumor activity spectrum is one of the broadest known for experimental animals.

Mitomycin C has strong activity against bacteria, rickettsia, and viruses. The minimum concentration for inhibition of *Bacillus subtilis* was 0.025 microgram per ml. It inhibited the growth of many gram-positive and gram-negative bacteria at concentrations of less than 1 microgram per ml.

This agent cured mice infected with *Diplococcus pneumoniae, Salmonella enteritidis,* and *Rickettsia tsutsugamushi* and cured guinea pigs with *Leptospira icterohaemorrhagiae.* Mice infected with toxoplasma organisms were not cured.

Mice inoculated with virus pneumonia of sheep were effectively protected by a total of 8.3 mg/kg administered intraperitoneally but the agent had no effect on mice inoculated with influenza A, Newcastle disease, or Japanese encephalitis viruses.

Moldin—Derived from a streptomycete. Insoluble in water; soluble in alcohol. Has antimycotic activity against *Candida, Trichophyton, Cryptococcus* (*Torula*) *utilis, T.* (*Achorion*) *gypseum, Cryptococcus neoformans.*

Musarin—An antibiotic from the banana plant *Musa sapientum* derived from Meredith's actinomycete. Active against spore germinating species.

Mycelianamide—Derived from *Penicillium griseo-fulvum.* A weak acid; $C_{22}H_{28}N_2O_5$; crystals, decomposing at 170 to 172 C. Soluble in acetone; slightly soluble in common organic solvents; soluble in sodium carbonate solution but not in sodium bicarbonate solutions. Thermostable but destroyed by acids and alkalies. Active against *Staphylococcus aureus, Bacillus anthracis, Streptococcus pyogenes.* Not active against gram-negative bacteria.

Mycetin—Derived from *Streptomyces violaceus.* Slightly soluble in water; deep-violet color in alcohol; insoluble in ether. Active against gram-positive bacteria.

Mycobacidin—Derived from a streptomycete resembling *Streptomyces lavendulae.* Monobasic acid $C_9H_{15}NSO_3$. Has *in vitro* activity against mycobacteria.

Mycocidin—Derived from an *Aspergillus.* It may be identical with **fumigacin.** It is insoluble in acid; the acid precipitate is soluble in water and ether. Active against *Mycobacterium tuberculosis* var. *hominis.*

Mycolutein—Derived from a streptomycete. Yellow, crystalline substance, insoluble in water, soluble in alcohol. Has *in vitro* activity against *Candida albicans, C. tropicalis, Geotrichum.*

Mycomycin—Derived from *Nocardia acidophilus.* It is soluble in amyl acetate and ether. Active against *Bacillus subtilis* and *Mycobacterium tuberculosis.* Its activity is not inhibited by serum. It has been shown to be 3,5,7,8-tridecatetraene-10,12-diynoic acid, $HC{:}C\cdot C{:}CCH{:}C{:}CHCH{:}CHCH{:}$-$CHCH_2COOH$.

Mycosubtilin—An antibiotic and fungicide derived from *Bacillus subtilis.*

NA7M10—Isolated from an unidentified species of *Actinomyces.* Used in urinary and intestinal tract infections.

Narbomycin—Derived from *Streptomyces narbonensis.* Crystalline substance, $C_{28}H_{47}NO_7$. Has high *in vitro* activity against gram-positive bacteria but no *in vivo* action.

Nebularin—Derived from *Clitocybe (Agaricus) nebularis.* Powder; heat stable; readily soluble in water; sparingly soluble in nonpolar solvents. Active against mycobacteria.

Neomycin—A group of antibiotics derived from *Streptomyces fradiae.* Three components, neomycin A, B, and C, have been isolated. Composition of neomycin B and C probably $C_{29}H_{58}N_8O_{16}$. Neomycin base is amorphous, soluble in water, slightly soluble in methyl alcohol, insoluble in common organic solvents.

Neomycin Sulfate—A white to slightly yellow, thermostable, odorless, crystalline, water-soluble powder. It is affected by light and is hygroscopic. Active against gram-negative and gram-positive bacteria, particularly against *Staphylococcus aureus,* possibly against *Mycobacterium tuberculosis.* Neomycin sulfate has a wider bacterial spectrum than penicillin, streptomycin, and bacitracin. It is more active against staphylococci than streptococci. Useful for topical application and for an intestinal antiseptic. Can be given orally. It is also used intramuscularly for systemic infections of *Klebsiella pneumoniae, Proteus vulgaris, Pseudomonas aeruginosa,* and *Haemophilus influenzae;* and urinary infections of *Aerobacter aerogenes, Escherichia coli, P. vulgaris,* or *P. aeruginosa.*

Nisin—A group of antibiotics derived from *Streptococcus lactis.* Stable polypeptides soluble in dilute acids. The dry powder is used to prevent spoilage in cheese and bread caused by clostridia.

Nocardamin—Derived from a *Nocardia* sp. Crystalline, nonbasic, heterocyclic substance, $C_9H_{14}N_2O_3$, soluble in water. Has *in vitro* bacteriostatic activity against mycobacteria which is greatly diminished by presence of serum or egg.

Nocardianin—Derived from a *Nocardia* sp. Red, crystalline substance, probably $C_{66}H_{100}N_{18}O_{15}$, slightly soluble in water. Has activity against gram-positive bacteria like *Staphylococcus aureus;* no action against gram-negative organisms like *Salmonella typhosa* or acid-fast mycobacteria.

Nocardine—Derived from *Nocardia coeliaca.* It is soluble in water and alcohol and is active against *Mycobacterium tuberculosis in vitro.*

Noformicin—Derived from *Nocardia formica.* 2-*N*-(2-Amidinoethyl)carbamoyl-5-iminopyrrolidine, $HN \cdot C_4H_5NH \cdot CONHCH_2CH_2C(NH)NH_2$; hydrochloride soluble in water. Has antiviral activity.

Novobiocin Calcium—The calcium salt of a substance with antibacterial properties derived from *Streptomyces niveus* or *S. spheroides.* It is analogous to **novobiocin sodium** in its antimicrobial activity. It forms more stable suspensions than the analogous sodium compound.

Novobiocin Sodium—The sodium salt of a substance with antibacterial properties separated from cultures of *Streptomyces niveus* or *S. spheroides.* Moderate antibiotic spectrum; active against gram-positive bacteria, especially *Staphylococcus aureus;* has little activity against gram-negative bacteria except the coliform group and *Proteus vulgaris.* Used for treatment of staphylococcic infections. Resistance is developed to this antibiotic.

Nybomycin—Derived from a streptomycete. Crystalline substance, $C_8H_7NO_2$, slightly soluble in water. Has antibacterial and antiphage activity.

Nystatin—Derived from *Streptomyces noursei.* Pale yellow, microcrystalline powder, soluble in alcohol and aqueous alcohol solutions but insoluble in water. Used for the treatment of infections with *Candida albicans* and other fungi and yeasts, but *in vivo* usefulness for organisms other than *C. albicans* has not been well substantiated.

Oleandomycin Phosphate—The phosphate salt of an antibiotic derived from strains of *Streptomyces antibioticus.* It has an empirical formula $C_{35}H_{61}NO_{12} \cdot H_3PO_4$. Active (*in vitro*) against gram-positive bacteria, especially against staphylococci, streptococci, and pneumococci and a few gram-negative organisms, for instance, gonococci, meningococci, and *Haemophilus influenzae.* No activity against coliforms and other enteric bacteria. Useful in treatment of staphylococcic infections, particularly those resistant to penicillin, streptomycin, the tetracyclines, and erythromycin. Given orally and intravenously, sometimes intramuscularly. Resistant strains of staphylococci can occur. Oleandomycin is permitted in poultry feeds; its concentration must not exceed 1.1 ppm.

Oleandomycin Triacetate—The triacetate ester of oleandomycin derived from *Streptomyces antibioticus.* Same activity and uses as **oleandomycin phosphate.** Given orally.

Oligomycin—Derived from a streptomycete similar to *Streptomyces diastatochromogenes.* A group of crystalline antibiotics having formulas (A) $C_{24}H_{40}O_6$, (B) $C_{22}H_{36}O_6$, and (C) $C_{28}H_{46}O_6$. Oligomycin A is a crystalline substance, very slightly soluble in water, soluble in absolute alcohol. Has activity against *Blastomyces dermatitidis.*

Oxytetracycline—An antibiotic derived from *Streptomyces rimosus.* $C_{22}H_{24}N_2O_9$ or $C_{22}H_{26}N_2O_9$. The hydrochloride is very soluble in water. Active against staphylococci, beta-hemolytic streptococci, *Bacteriodes, Brucella,* pneumococci, *Escherichia coli, Aerobacter aerogenes.*

Patulin—Derived from a number of species of fungi, such as *Aspergillus clavatus* and *Penicillium patulum.* $C_7H_6O_4$, soluble in water and a number of organic solvents.

Penatin—Derived from *Penicillium notatum* and *P. resticulosum.*

Penicidin—Derived from *Penicillium* sp. It is active against gram-positive and gram-negative organisms. Soluble in ether and benzene. It gives a negative biuret reaction.

Penicillic Acid—Derived from *Penicillium* sp. and *Aspergillus* sp. $C_8H_{10}O_4$; crystals, monohydrate melting at 58 to 64 C; anhydrous, melting at 83 to 84 C. Acid reaction. Moderately soluble in water; very soluble in hot water and alcohol. Active against *Proteus vulgaris,* micrococci, streptococci, *Salmonella typhosa.*

Penicillin—A term used for a group of antibiotic compounds. The general formula is $NaOOC \cdot C_8H_{10}O_2N_2SR$, in which R represents a radical different for each penicillin, the most important being penicillin G, isolated from strains of *Penicillium notatum, P. chrysogenum* and other species of *Penicillium.* See also **penicillins G, F, X, K, dihydro F, flavicidin.** The most important commercial antibiotic.

Penicillin, Dihydro F. See **gigantic acid.**

Penicillin F—Pentenylpenicillin. An antibiotic not as effective as **penicillin G** in inhibiting certain microorganisms.

Penicillin G—Sodium benzylpenicillin, an antibiotic obtained commercially from *Penicillium chrysogenum* and *P. notatum*, $NaOOC \cdot C_8H_{10}O_2N_2S \cdot CH_2C_6H_5$; crystals very soluble in water and alcohol. One international unit is equal to 0.6 microgram of benzylpenicillin, and 1 mg of this penicillin is equal to 1667 I.U. Active against pneumococci, streptococci, micrococci, *Neisseria,* clostridia, and *Treponema.* Inactive against gram-negative bacteria.

Penicillin K—*n*-Heptylpenicillin. Inactivated more rapidly in the body than **penicillins F, G,** and **X.**

Penicillin V—Phenoxymethylpenicillin.

Penicillin X—*p*-Hydroxybenzylpenicillin. Deemed more active than **penicillin G** for streptococci and *Treponema pallidum.*

Phagolessin A 58—Derived from a streptomycete. Hygroscopic, light-yellow powder, stable under refrigeration. Readily soluble in water; soluble in alcohol. Has antiphage activity against bacterial viruses. Used to kill the phage of infected strains of *Streptomyces griseus.*

Phalamycin—Derived from *Streptomyces noursei.* Yellowish powder only slightly soluble in water, soluble in alcohol. Has *in vitro* activity against saprophytes and gram-positive pathogens like *Mycobacterium tuberculosis* and *Nocardia.* Protected mice against *Streptococcus hemolyticus.*

Phenicin—Derived from *Penicillium phoeniceum* and *P. rubrum.* Yellow-brown, crystalline substance, 3,3′-dihydroxy-5,5′-dimethylbiquinone, $(C_7H_5O_3)_2$; slightly soluble in water, soluble in alcohol.

alpha-Phenoxyethylpenicillin—A semisynthetic **penicillin** made from 6-aminopenicillanic acid, the nucleus of penicillin, which is prepared by biosynthetic methods and subsequently reacting this substance with alpha-phenoxypropionic acid. This penicillin derivative is twice as effective in producing high blood concentrations as other penicillins. *In vitro* tests show that alpha-phenoxyethylpenicillin is active against strains of staphylococci that are resistant to other penicillins.

It is a colorless, crystalline material that is very soluble in water. It resists decomposition by acids and is not readily affected by air and light. It is not destroyed as readily by penicillinase as other penicillins.

The 6-aminopenicillanic acid may be obtained from *Penicillium notatum* and then extracted by ion-exchange methods.

Pimaricin—Derived from *Streptomyces natalensis.* A light-sensitive macrolide having 25 atoms in the ring, $C_{34}H_{49}NO_{14}$; slightly soluble in water. Has antimycotic activity.

Pleocidin—Derived from a streptomycete resembling *Streptomyces lavendulae.* The hydrochloride is a hygroscopic white powder soluble in water and ethyl alcohol. Has antimicrobial activity against organisms causing skin infections. Has high toxicity by parenteral route.

Pleomycin—Derived from *Streptomyces pleofacians.* Acid substance soluble in ethyl alcohol; alkaline salts soluble. Has *in vitro* activity against many organisms. High toxicity to mammals.

Pleuromutilin—Derived from *Pleurotus mutitus* and *P. passeckerianus,* basidiomycetes. Crystalline substance, $C_{22}H_{34}O_5$, soluble in ethyl alcohol. Has activity against gram-positive bacteria. May cause urticaria in human beings on repeated application.

Plumericin—Derived from the roots of *Plumeria multiflora.* Crystalline substance, $C_{15}H_{14}O_6$, insoluble in water, slightly soluble in alcohol. Has *in vitro* activity against some gram-negative bacteria, some gram-positive bacteria like *Mycobacterium tuberculosis,* and some fungi.

Polymyxin—A group of antibiotics derived from *Bacillus polymyxa.* They are polypeptides containing L-threonine and other amino acids: D-leucine in polymyxin A; serine in polymyxin D. Soluble in water and methyl alcohol. Active against gram-negative bacteria. Polymyxin B sulfate is used for the treatment of infections caused by gram-negative bacteria. It has a nephrotoxic action.

Potassium Penicillin G—The potassium salt of **penicillin G.** It is an odorless, colorless to light yellowish, hygroscopic crystalline powder, or colorless crystals, that are very soluble in water. It is soluble in and is inactivated by ethyl alcohol. It is decomposed at 100 C, by acids, alkalies, and oxidizing agents, and loses activity on storage at room temperature but is relatively stable at or below 15 C. Potassium penicillin is spoiled by light or air. Principally active against gram-positive organisms, such as streptococci, pneumococci, and clostridia; and some gram-negative bacteria, such as gonococci and meningococci. Penicillinase producing staphylococci are resistant. Potassium penicillin G may produce toxic reactions.

Potassium Penicillin O—The potassium salt of allylmercaptomethylpenicillin. White crystalline powder that is readily soluble in water. It has an onion-like odor. The antimicrobial activity is similar to that of **penicillin G.**

Procaine Penicillin G—A complex of **penicillin G** and procaine. White to slightly yellowish, odorless, microcrystalline powder or crystals. Soluble in water and ethyl alcohol. Inactivated by acids, alkalies, and oxidizing agents.

Prodigiosin—Derived from *Serratia marcescens.* Red, lustrous crystals, CH_3-$(CH_2)_4 \cdot C_4H_2N(CH_3) \cdot C(C_4H_4N):C_4H_2$-$N \cdot OCH_3$, practically insoluble in water, moderately soluble in alcohol. Used in the treatment of coccidiomycosis.

Propionyl Erythromycin Lauryl Sulfate—A derivative of **erythromycin** that is practically tasteless. Its antibiotic properties are analogous to those of the parent compound.

Pyribenzamine Penicillin G—A compound of **penicillin G** and *N,N*-dimethyl-*N′*-benzyl-*N′*-(α-pyridyl)ethylenediamine. Its antimicrobial activity is similar to that of other penicillin G complexes.

Pyridomycin—Derived from *Streptomyces albidofuscus.* Crystalline substance, $C_{28}H_{32}$-N_2O_8, insoluble in water, soluble in alcohol; hydrochloride soluble in water. Has *in vitro* inhibiting action against *Mycobacterium tuberculosis, M. phlei;* has no activity against gram-positive organisms.

Raisnomycin—Derived from *Streptomyces kentuckensis.* Yellow, basic material insoluble in water, soluble in alcohol. Has activity against some organisms resistant to the tetracyclines, streptothricin, and erythromycin.

Resistomycin—Derived from *Streptomyces resistomycificus.* Yellow, weak acidic substance, $C_{23}H_{18}O_6$, slightly soluble in water, soluble in alcohol. Has activity against *Staphylococcus aureus, Mycobacterium tuberculosis,* and *Bacillus subtilis.*

Rhodocidin—Derived from *Streptomyces phoenix.* Red, soluble material, easily inactivated by acids and alkalies. Has *in vitro* activity against staphylococci, streptococci, mycobacteria, *Klebsiella, Bacillus subtilis, Brucella abortus, Proteus vulgaris, Salmonella typhosa, Pseudomonas aeruginosa.* Very highly toxic.

Rhodomycetin—Derived from a red mutant of *Streptomyces griseus.* Red acid form insoluble in water, soluble in alcohol; blue alkaline form soluble but unstable in water. Has *in vitro* activity against gram-positive organisms; has no *in vivo* action.

Rimocidin—Derived with oxytetracycline from *Streptomyces rimosus.* Is an amphoteric compound having both acidic and basic groups thus forming soluble sodium and sulfate salts. Has antimycotic activity against most pathogenic fungi; has activity against pathogenic protozoa, such as *Endamoeba histolytica* and the hemoflagellates *Leishmania donovani, L. tropica, Trypanosoma cruzi.* Is hemolytic.

Ristocetin—Derived from *Nocardia lurida.* Consists of two components, ristocetin A and B, whose chemistry has not been clarified. It is active against gram-positive cocci, in order of decreasing susceptibility: streptococci, enterococci, pneumococci, and staphylococci. It is given only by intravenous route. It produces a number of side effects, such as reduction in white blood cell count and irritation of the intima of the veins.

Rotaventin—Derived from *Streptomyces reticuli.* Has antimycotic action against the yeasts *Saccharomyces sake, Torula rubra,* and against *Penicillium glaucum, Aspergillus niger.* Has no action against *Staphylococcus aureus, Escherichia coli* and the pathogenic fungi like *Trichophyton interdigitale, Candida albicans, Botrytis bassiana.*

Rubromycin—Derived from *Streptomyces collinus.* Red, crystalline substance, practically insoluble in water and slightly soluble in alcohol. Has *in vitro* activity against staphylococci, streptococci, *Corynebacterium diphtheriae,* and *Bacillus subtilis.*

Sarcidin—Derived from *Streptomyces achromogenes.* Crystalline substance soluble in water and alcohol. Bacteriostatic action against *Sarcina lutea.*

Sarkomycin—Derived from a strain of *Streptomyces erythrochromogenes.* An acid, oily substance soluble in water and alcohol. Has antitumor activity.

Seromycin—See **cycloserine.**

Sodium Penicillin G—The sodium salt of **penicillin G.** The physical and inactivation properties are similar to those of **potassium penicillin G.**

Spiramycin—Derived from *Streptomyces ambofaciens.* Basic amorphous substance soluble in alcohol, slightly soluble in water. The sulfate is soluble in water and alcohol. The spiramycins are macrolide compounds, $C_{45-48}H_{78-82}N_2O_{15-16}$. Spiramycin has activity against gram-positive bacteria and rickettsiae. Has been used in the treatment of infections of such organisms. May cause gastrointestinal distress.

Streptomycin—Derived from *Streptomyces griseus.* White granules or powder, $C_{21}H_{39}N_7O_{12}$, hydrochloride, double salt with calcium chloride, sulfate, or phosphate; very soluble in water; soluble in acid alcohol and methyl alcohol; insoluble in alcohol and butyl alcohol. Active against *Mycobacterium tuberculosis in vivo,* gram-negative and some gram-positive bacteria. With dihydrostreptomycin, it is the second most important commercial antibiotic.

Streptovariun—Tested for the treatment of tuberculosis. Did not prove better than treatment with isoniazid alone. Produced nausea in some cases.

Streptovitacin—Derived from *Streptomyces* sp. Composed of streptovitacins A and B, white crystalline solids, $C_{15}H_{23}NO_5$. Inhibits some mouse tumors but induces toxic symptoms at high dosage levels.

Stylomycin—Puromycin. Used in the control of sleeping sickness caused by *Trypanosoma gambiense.*

Subtilin—Derived from *Bacillus subtilis* NRRL No. B-543. Amorphous cyclic peptide, $C_{144}T_{226}N_{38}O_{39}S_5$; slightly soluble in water, soluble in alcohol and dilute acids. Subtilin was the first antibiotic used experimentally for the preservation of canned goods. It failed to live up to original expectations.

Syncillin—See **alpha-phenoxyethylpenicillin.**

Synnematin—Derived from a strain of *Cephalosporium salmosynnematum* which produces a mixture of active components, one of which is a type of **penicillin,** named synnematin B. It differs from the common penicillins in that it is hydrophilic in character. It has been identified as D-4-amino-4-carboxybutylpenicillin. It has a low toxicity and has been used experimentally in the treatment of salmonellosis in mice and chicks and typhoid fever in human beings.

Syntetrin—*N*-(Pyrrolidinomethyl)tetracycline, a derivative of tetracycline that can be administered by injection. Its antibiotic properties are analogous to those of the tetracyclines.

Teleomycin—Extremely potent against gram-positive bacteria, a class which includes staphylococci, streptococci, pneumococci, and diplococci. It has proved a better weapon than either penicillin or erythromycin in combatting staphylococci.

Tennecetin—Derived from *Streptomyces chattanoogensis,* a relatively newly characterized streptomycete found in the soil of Tennessee. It is a broad-spectrum antifungal agent having activity against more than 80 species of fungi. It is toxic to test animals on injection but, in 1959 tests, did not appear to be toxic by oral administration. Its chemical composition has not been determined.

Terramycin—See **oxytetracycline.**

Tertiomycin—Derived from *Streptomyces eurocidicus.* Member of the **erythromycin-carbomycin** group. Basic crystalline substance insoluble in water, soluble in alcohol. Has activity against gram-positive bacteria. Toxicity is of the same order as erythromycin.

Tetracycline—A generic name assigned to the four-ring skeleton of a group of related antibiotics. This compound has antibiotic activity and may be made from chlorotetracycline by removing the chlorine atom. The group of tetracyclines, including **oxytetracycline** (Terramycin), **chlorotetracycline** (Aureomycin), tetracycline (Achromycin), form the third most important antibiotic.

Thiolutin—Derived from *Streptomyces albus.* Yellow, crystalline, bicyclic compound, 3-acetamido-5-methylpyrrolin-4-one[4,3-d]-1,2-dithiole, $CH_3 \cdot C_5HNOS_2 \cdot NHCOCH_3$, slightly soluble in water, soluble in alcohol. Has wide antimicrobial activity with action against gram-negative and gram-positive bacteria, pathogenic fungi, amoebae, and hemoflagellates. It has greater activity *in vivo* against some plant pathogens than *in vitro.* Has been used to stop growth of microorganisms in beer.

Trichothecin—Derived from *Trichothecium roseum.* Crystalline. Neutral reaction. Very soluble in water and alcohol. Has antifungal activity.

Trichomycin—Derived from *Streptomyces hachijoensis.* Yellow, acidic, crystalline substance; the sodium salt is soluble in water. Has activity against pathogenic protozoa, fungi, and bacteria such as *Trichomonas vaginalis, Candida, Trichophyton,* some yeasts, and *Treponema pallidum.* Used in the treatment of trichomoniasis and candidiasis.

Tylosin—Derived from *Streptomyces fradiae.* Crystalline substance, probably $C_{45}H_{79}NO_{17}$, soluble in water, stable in acid solution. Suggested as an antibiotic for poultry and swine diseases.

Tyrocidine—Obtained from *Bacillus brevis.* It is the major component of the mixture known as tyrothricin. It is a basic cyclic polypeptide containing chlorine.

Tyrothricin—Derived from *Bacillus brevis.* It is a mixture of polypeptides, the principal ones being tyrocidine (40 to 60 per cent) and gramicidin (10 to 20 per cent). It is effective against gram-positive bacteria.

Valinomycin—Derived from *Streptomyces fulvissimus.* Macrocyclic compound composed of units of L-valine, D-valine, L-lactic acid, and D-alpha-hydroxyisovaleric acid with 24 atoms in the ring, $C_{36}H_{60}N_4O_{12}$; nearly insoluble in water. Has *in vitro* activity against *Mycobacterium tuberculosis.*

Vancomycin—Derived from *Streptomyces orientalis.* White, solid hydrochloride soluble in water. Has activity against gram-positive bacteria. Used in treatment of antibiotic-resistant staphylococci.

Viomycin—A strongly basic polypeptide derived from *Streptomyces puniceus,* whose chemical structure has not been determined. Viomycin sulfate is an odorless, somewhat hygroscopic, white to light yellowish powder that is soluble in water and only slightly soluble in alcohol. It is active against *Mycobacterium tuberculosis,* both streptomycin sensitive and resistant strains and isoniazid sensitive and resistant strains. It is less potent than streptomycin but is more potent than *p*-aminosalicylic acid.

Viridogrisein—Derived from *Streptomyces griseus;* active against a variety of bacteria *in vitro.*

Viscosin—Derived from *Pseudomonas viscosa.* Crystalline acidic polypeptide, insoluble in water, soluble in alcohol. Has antiviral activity.

Xanthocillin X—Derived from *Penicillium notatum.* Yellow, crystalline substance, $[HO \cdot C_6H_4CH{:}C(NC)]_2$, insoluble in water but has a soluble dipotassium salt. Has wide-spectrum activity. Used in feed.

TABLE 7. CULTURE MEDIA AND METHODS

TABLE 7. CULTURE MEDIA AND METHODS

A. C. Broth—Used for sterility tests for the detection of strictly aerobic contaminants in biologicals and other products. It is also used for pathogenic and saprophytic microorganisms. It is prepared by dissolving 3 g each of beef, malt, and yeast extracts, 5 g of glucose, 20 g of proteose peptone No. 3 Difco, and 0.2 g of ascorbic acid in a liter of water. The final pH should be adjusted to 7.2. The dehydrated medium is commercially available.

Ammonium Sulfate Solution—Used to demonstrate the disappearance of ammonia and the appearance of nitrites caused by bacteria. It consists of 1 g ammonium sulfate, 1 g dipotassium phosphate, 2 g sodium chloride, 0.5 g magnesium sulfate, a trace of ferrous sulfate, an excess of magnesium carbonate, and a liter of water.

Anaerobic Cultivation—Anaerobes grown only in the complete or nearly complete absence of air. All methods are based on the fact that oxygen is detrimental to the anaerobes. Among the methods used for the exclusion of air are **Roux's, Wright's,** and the **deep agar method.**

Ascitic Fluid Agar—Used for the cultivation of *Neisseria meningitidis.*

Avery's Sodium Oleate Agar—Used for the cultivation of *Hemophilus influenzae.* The sodium oleate inhibits gram-positive cocci present in nasal secretions.

Azotobacter Culture Medium—Dissolve 0.2 g dipotassium hydrogen phosphate, 15 g mannitol, 9.2 g crystallized magnesium sulfate, 0.02 g calcium chloride, 0.05 g ferric chloride (from a 10 per cent aqueous solution), and a trace of molybdenum salt in a liter of water. Adjust the pH to 7.2. For a solid medium add 15 g agar.

BAGG Broth—Buffered azide glucose glycerol broth. A medium used for the detection of fecal streptococci. Dissolve 20 g tryptose, 5 g glucose, 5 g sodium chloride, 5 ml glycerol, 4 g dipotassium monohydrogen phosphate, 1.5 g monopotassium dihydrogen phosphate, 0.5 g sodium azide, and 0.015 g bromocresol purple in water and dilute to 1 liter. Adjust the pH to 6.9. Distribute in tubes, 10 ml per tube, and sterilize in an autoclave at 116 C (10 pounds pressure for 15 minutes). The dehydrated medium is commercially available. However, it does not contain glycerol, and therefore this component of the mixture must be added when the dehydrated medium is reconstituted.

Barnes' Medium—Used as an alternative to **Czapek's medium,** particularly for molds not readily using sucrose. It is prepared by dissolving 10 g each of glucose, tripotassium phosphate, ammonium nitrate, and potassium nitrate in 1 liter of water. A solid medium can be prepared by the addition of agar.

Beef Extract—An extract of beef containing the soluble mineral components used in preparation of media, such as **nutrient broth.**

Beef Extract-Peptone Broth—See **nutrient broth.**

Beef Lactose Agar—A medium prepared by suspending 45 g of a dehydrated mixture of 450 g beef-heart infusion, 10 g lactose, 15 g agar, and 5 g proteose-peptone in 1 liter cold water, boiling for 1 minute, and sterilizing for 20 minutes in an autoclave at 15 pounds pressure (121 C). Final pH should be 6.8 ± 0.1.

Beef Liver Infusion—A medium used for the cultivation of anaerobes. The fat is removed from 500 g of fresh beef liver, which is ground and heated with stirring in 1 liter of water for 1 hour by flowing steam. The mixture is cooled and strained through cheesecloth. The volume is again made up to 1 liter, and 10 g of peptone and 1 g of dipotassium hydrogen phosphate are added. The remaining tissue is dried quickly at 55 C and the broth is tubed over some pieces of the tissue. The infusion is used at full strength or is diluted with 4 volumes of water and is sterilized at 121 C for 20 minutes.

Blood Agar—Agar to which blood has been added for enrichment or to differentiate hemolytic colonies. Generally 5 per cent of horse, rabbit, sheep, or human blood is added to a carbohydrate-free agar containing 0.85 per cent sodium chloride.

Blood Glucose Cystine Agar—Used for the cultivation of *Pasteurella tularensis.* Add 10 g glucose and 1.0 g powdered cystine to 1000 ml of sterile, fresh beef infusion agar. Melt the agar in flowing steam and cool to 50 C after solution. Add 5 to 8 per cent sterile, whole or defibrinated rabbit blood. Heat the mixture in a water bath at 60 C for 2 hours. Transfer the prepared medium from the flask or with the aid of a sterile funnel to tubes or plates. Incubate to test for sterility. Avoid condensation of water on the surface of the medium.

Blood Tellurite Medium—A medium for the cultivation of *Corynebacterium diphtheriae.* Add 1.5 ml defibrinated rabbit's blood and 1.5 ml 2 per cent solution of potassium tellurite to 15 ml **nutrient agar** at a pH of 7.6. The agar should be cooled before adding the other components. After mixing, pour into Petri dishes using sterile precautions. *C. diphtheriae* colonies are black.

Brain Medium—Used for the cultivation of clostridia. Proteolytic activity is demonstrated by disintegration of particles of brain tissue, blackening of the reaction medium, and the production of putrefactive odors. The membranous tissue and blood are removed from uninjured sheep or calf brains and brain tissue remaining is boiled for 0.5 hour with an equal weight of distilled water. The brains are then riced with the aid of a potato ricer. One per cent of peptone and 0.1 per cent of glucose are added to the brain mixture which is heated to dissolve these components. The mixture is distributed in tubes in (containing a strip of iron wire) in deep columns making certain that an even distribution is obtained. The tubes are sterilized at 121 C for 30 minutes and must be checked for sterility.

Brewer's Modified Broth—See **thioglycollate broth.**

Brilliant Green Agar—Used for the differentiation and isolation of *Salmonella. S. paratyphi* and *S. schottmuelleri* grow without inhibition. It is not used or recommended for *S. typhosa.* Suspend 10 g each of proteose peptone No. 3 Difco, lactose, and sucrose, 5 g sodium chloride, 3 g yeast extract, 0.08 g phenol red, 0.0125 g brilliant green, and 20 g agar in a liter of water. Heat to boiling to dissolve, transfer to tubes or flasks and sterilize in an autoclave at 121 C (15 pounds pressure) for 15 minutes.

Brilliant Green Lactose Bile 2%—Used for a confirmatory test for the presence of the coliform group in water, milk, and dairy products. It consists of 10 g peptone, 10 g lactose, 20 g ox gall and 0.0133 g brilliant green dissolved in a liter of water, tubed and sterilized for 15 minutes at 121 C. An alternative method of preparation is to dissolve 10 g peptone and 10 g lactose in somewhat less than 500 ml water. Add a solution of 20 g dehydrated ox gall in 200 ml water, adjusting the pH to between 7.0 and 7.5. Add sufficient water to increase the volume to 975 ml and readjust the pH to 7.4. Add 13.3 ml of 0.1 per cent aqueous brilliant green solution and bring the volume up to 1 liter. Mix and filter through cotton. Tube and sterilize at not more than 121 C (15 pounds pressure) for no longer than 15 minutes.

Broth—A culture medium for heterotrophic bacteria consisting of the essential nutrient requirements. The broth may be a meat extract type consisting of 3 g beef extract, 5 g sodium chloride, 10 g peptone, and 1000 ml distilled water. Fresh meat can be substituted for beef extract in meat infusion broth media. 500 g of ground lean beef are soaked in a liter of water for 2 to 24 hours. The mixture is heated to 80 C and the juice filtered off. Sediment is allowed to settle and fat is removed. Volume of water lost is made up. Sodium chloride and peptone are again added as above.

Buffered Azide Glucose Glycerol Broth—See **BAGG broth.**

Chapman's Medium—A medium for the isolation of the chromogenic staphylococci causing food poisoning. Suspend and dissolve 75 g of ammonium sulfate, 55 g sodium chloride, 30 g gelatin, 15 g agar, 10 g peptone, 10 g mannitol, 5 g dipotassium hydrogen phosphate, 2 g yeast extract, and 6 ml of 10 per cent sodium hydroxide solution in 1 liter of water. Sterilize and after sterilization, stir, in order, to resuspend any precipitate.

Chick-Embryo Technique—A procedure used to cultivate viruses or rickettsiae. There is the preliminary technique in which the eggs are prepared, that is, candling, drilling. The chick embryo is then ready for inoculation. Different parts of the chick embryo are used for different virus isolation: chorio-allantoic—lymphocytic choriomeningitis; amnion—infectious hepatitis; allantoic—influenza; yolk sac—rickettsiae.

Chocolate Agar—Heated blood agar; a medium for the cultivation of *Haemophilus influenzae*. The blood is added at 80 C so that the proteins coagulate and give the medium a chocolate color.

Citrate Medium—See **Koser's citrate medium.**

Citrate Test Medium—Used in the citrate differential test. Dissolve 3.0 g crystalline sodium citrate, 1.5 g sodium ammonium phosphate or microcosmic salt, 1 g potassium dihydrogen phosphate, and 0.2 g magnesium sulfate in water and dilute to 1 liter. Place 5-ml aliquots in tubes and sterilize in an autoclave at 121 C (15 pounds pressure) for 20 minutes.

Conn's Asparagine Medium—Used for the isolation of nonpathogenic actinomycetes. It is prepared by dispersing 15 g agar and dissolving 10 ml of glycerol, 1 g of asparagine neutralized with sodium hydroxide solution, and 1 g of dipotassium monohydrogen phosphate in 1 liter of water.

Corn-Meal Agar—Used for the morphological study of *Candida*, particularly *Candida albicans*. It is prepared by heating 62.5 g corn meal in 1500 ml water for 1 hour at 60 C, filtering, adjusting to the original volume, adding 19 g agar, and subsequently sterilizing in an Arnold sterilizer.

Cystine-Tellurite Blood Agar—Used for the isolation of *Corynebacterium diphtheriae*. To a 2 per cent solution of infusion agar add 15 ml of a sterile 0.3 per cent solution of potassium tellurite. (Agar should be cool and potassium tellurite can be autoclaved.) Add aseptically 5 ml blood. Add 4 g powdered cystine and mix well. This medium will inhibit other bacteria.

Czapek's Medium (Dox and Thom Modification)—A broth medium for the cultivation of fungi, comprising 30.0 g sucrose, 2.0 g sodium nitrate, 1.0 g dipotassium hydrogen phosphate, 0.5 g magnesium sulfate, 0.5 g potassium chloride, 0.01 g ferrous sulfate dissolved in sufficient water to make 1 liter. Agar is added to make the medium solid.

Deep Agar Method—A method of cultivating anaerobic bacteria. Melt glucose infusion agar, cool to 50 C and inoculate with the organism. Mix and solidify quickly by placing in cool water. To isolate colonies, heat sides of tube to melt agar in contact with the glass. Place mouth of tube in a sterile dish and heat back of tube to force out the agar. Slice agar where the colony has grown.

Desoxycholate Lactose Agar—A selective medium used for the direct counting of coliform organisms. Suspend 10 g peptone, 10 g lactose, 5 g sodium chloride, 2 g sodium citrate, 0.5 g sodium desoxycholate, 0.03 g neutral red, and 15 g agar in a liter of water; dissolve by boiling; distribute in tubes or flasks; and sterilize at 121 C for 15 minutes; pH about 7.1.

Dieudonne's Alkaline Blood Agar—Used for the cultivation of *Vibrio comma.* Mix 150 ml defibrinated beef blood, and 150 ml *N* potassium hydroxide solution and steam for 30 minutes. Melt 700 ml nutrient 3 per cent agar, pH 6.8, and add it to the mixture. Pour plates, allow them to harden uncovered but protected with paper, and place strips of filter paper between each dish and cover to absorb ammonia and moisture. Incubate for 15 hours at 37 C before use.

Dorset's Egg Medium—Used for the cultivation of *Mycobacterium tuberculosis* and related acid-fast organisms. It is preferable to use commercial preparations.

Egg Yolk Agar—A medium used for the identification of pathogenic members of the *Clostridium* family and of aerobic sporeformers. Fresh hen's eggs are washed with a disinfectant and then the white and yolk are withdrawn asceptically. The yolk is diluted with an equal volume of 0.85 per cent sodium chloride solution. A separate solution of 40 g peptone, 5 g disodium hydrogen phosphate, 1.0 g of monopotassium dihydrogen phosphate, 20 g sodium chloride, 0.1 g magnesium phosphate, 2 g glucose, and 25 g agar in 1 liter of water is prepared and its pH adjusted to 7.6. This solution is sterilized and 1 ml of egg yolk mixture is added to each 9 ml of sterilized medium.

Eijkman Test Medium—Used to obtain cultures for the Eijkman test. Dissolve 15 g tryptose, 5 g sodium chloride, 4 g dipotassium hydrogen phosphate, 3 g lactose, 1.5 g potassium dihydrogen phosphate in water and make up to 1 liter. Distribute in tubes and sterilize by heating in an autoclave at not over 121 C (15 pounds pressure) for no longer than 12 minutes; the total heating time should not exceed 60 minutes.

E.M.B. Agar—See **eosin-methylene blue agar.**

Endo Agar—Used for the confirmation of the presumptive test for coliform bacteria in water. Coliform organisms fermenting lactose become red and color the surrounding medium. Nonlactose fermenters appear clear and colorless against the faint pink background. Prepare a beef extract base by suspending 30 g agar, 10 g peptone, and 5 g beef extract in water and boiling until the agar dissolves. Make up the water lost by evaporation. Adjust the pH to 7.4. Add 10 g lactose, mix to dissolve, distribute in 100-ml aliquots in flasks or tubes and sterilize at not over 121 C (15 pounds pressure) for no longer than 15 minutes. Dissolve 3 g of basic fuchsin or pararosaniline in 100 ml of 95 per cent ethyl alcohol, allow to stand for 24 hours, and filter. Melt a 100-ml aliquot of lactose agar and add 1 ml of 3 per cent basic fuchsin or pararosaniline solution and a freshly prepared solution of 0.125 g sodium sulfite in 5 ml of water. Mix well and pour plates.

The Robinson and Rettger modification is prepared by adding 10 ml of 10 per cent sodium bicarbonate to a liter of beef-extract base containing 10 g peptone, 5 g beef extract, 2 g dipotassium hydrogen phosphate, and 25 g agar (prepared as directed under eosin-methylene blue agar), mixing, and adjusting the pH to 7.6 to 7.8. After steaming for 10 minutes, add 10 g lactose, 10 ml 10 per cent aqueous sodium bisulfite solution, and 0.4 g basic fuchsin or pararosaniline. Transfer to flasks and sterilize by heating in an autoclave at 116 C (10 pounds pressure) for 20 minutes. Pour into plates.

Enterococci Presumptive Agar—Used as indicated under **enterococci presumptive broth.** The same ingredients are used as in enterococci presumptive broth with the addition of 15 g agar and the replacement of the bromothymol blue by 0.01 g methylene blue. The dehydrated medium is available commercially.

Enterococci Presumptive Broth—Used for the detection of enterococci. Sodium azide is a component. Incubation is carried out at 45 C, and presumptive results are acid and growth. Dissolve 5 g each of glucose, tryptone, and yeast extract, 0.4 g sodium azide, and 0.032 g bromothymol blue in a liter of water. Place 8-ml aliquots in tubes and sterilize in an autoclave at 121 C (15 pounds pressure) for 15 minutes. A medium having 5 times this concentration can also be prepared, but 2 ml each is then distributed in tubes for sterilization. The dehydrated medium is available commercially.

Eosin-Methylene Blue Agar (Levine Modification)—Used to differentiate the organisms in the colon-typhoid-dysentery group: (1) *Escherichia coli* colonies have a metallic sheen with a dark center; (2) *Aerobacter aerogenes* colonies have a brown center; (3) nonlactose fermenting organisms appear pink. To prepare the medium, dissolve 10 g peptone, 5 g beef extract, 2 g dipotassium hydrogen phosphate, and 20 g agar in 1 liter of water by boiling, making up the loss of water. Divide into aliquots. Prior to use add to each 100 ml melted stock agar, 5 ml 20 per cent sterile lactose solution, 2 ml 2 per cent aqueous eosin solution, and 1.3 ml 0.5 per cent aqueous methylene blue solution. Mix thoroughly, pour into Petri dishes, allow to harden, and check for sterility.

Formate-Ricinoleate Broth—Used in the "completed test" to check presence of coliform group. Add 5 g each of peptone, lactose, and sodium formate and 1 g sodium ricinoleate to 900 ml water. Heat on a water bath, stirring constantly to dissolve the components. Cool and make to 1 liter with water. Adjust the pH to the range 7.3 to 7.5. Place in fermentation tubes and sterilize in an autoclave at 117 to 119 C (11 to 13 pounds pressure) for 15 minutes.

Gard Technique—A method by which isolation is possible of a particular phase of *Salmonella* by cultivating one phase in soft agar containing antiserum for that phase. It is used where the organisms are biphasic. The antiserum will immobilize one phase and the other will migrate in the soft agar.

G. C. Medium—A medium for the detection of *Neisseria gonorrhoeae* in exudates of acute and chronic cases of gonorrhea.

Glucose Agar—A medium consisting of 3 g beef extract, 5 g peptone, 10 g glucose, 15 g agar, 1000 ml water; pH between 6.7 and 7.0. To this, various indicators, such as 10 ml Andrade's indicator solution, can be added.

Glucose Broth—Prepared in a manner similar to **glucose agar** but without the agar.

Glucose Cystine Blood Agar—Used for *Pasteurella tularensis.* It is prepared by dissolving and autoclaving meat infusion or trypticase soy agar; 0.1 per cent cystine is added and the mixture is heated for 2 hours in flowing steam with occasional shaking. After cooling below 60 C, 5 per cent sterile defibrinated horse or rabbit blood is added and the mixture is heated at 60 C for 2 hours, swirling from time to time to keep the ingredients mixed. After the addition of 1 per cent glucose from a 50 per cent sterile solution, the medium is placed in sterile tubes aseptically.

Gorodkowa's Medium—Used for the sporulation of yeasts. It consists of 10 g agar, 10 g meat extract, 5 g sodium chloride, and 2.5 g glucose in a liter of water.

Graham and Hastings' Tubes—Used to hasten sporulation of yeasts. Mix equal parts of anhydrous calcium sulfate or plaster of Paris and water, transfer to test tubes, allow to solidify in a slanting position, dry at 50 C for 24 hours, and autoclave. Pour 1 ml of water over a 3-day growth of yeast on **Lindegren's presporulation medium** and allow to stand for 10 minutes. Make a thick suspension and pour over the upper portion of the slant with a sterile pipette. Adjust the pH of water to 4.0 with acetic acid and transfer 3 ml of this dilute acetic acid to the lower part of the plaster of Paris slant. Incubate for 1 to 2 days.

Henneberg's Medium—Used for evaluating nitrogen utilization. It consists of 3 g ammonium sulfate, 3 g potassium phosphate, 2 g magnesium sulfate, 20 g glucose, and a liter of water.

Hiss Medium—See **serum-water medium.**

Hoyer's Solution—A solution used to determine the nitrogen requirements of an organism, consisting of 0.1 g ammonium phosphate, 0.1 g primary phosphate, 0.1 g magnesium phosphate, 0.1 g sodium acetate, 3 ml alcohol, and 100 ml water.

Jordan's Tartrate Agar—Used to determine tartrate utilization. Suspend and dissolve 20 g agar, 10 g peptone, 10 g sodium potassium tartrate, 5 g sodium chloride, and 12 ml of a 0.2 per cent alcoholic solution of phenol red in a liter of water. Adjust the pH of the medium to 7.4, distribute into tubes, and sterilize in an autoclave. Test the medium with known cultures of *Salmonella typhimurium, S. enteritidis, S. paratyphi,* and *S. schottmuelleri* before adopting for routine use.

Kligler's Iron Agar—Used for the differentiation of some gram-negative intestinal organisms on the basis of glucose and lactose fermentation and hydrogen sulfide production. Suspend 15 g peptone, 10 g lactose, 5 g proteose peptone Difco, 5 g sodium chloride, 3 g beef extract, 1 g glucose, 0.3 g sodium thiosulfate, 0.2 g ferrous sulfate, 12 g agar, and 0.024 g phenol red in a liter of water and dissolve by heating to boiling. Place in tubes and stopper with loose caps or with cotton plugs. Sterilize by heating in an autoclave at 122 C (15 pounds pressure for 15 minutes). Allow medium in tubes to solidify to form a slant. The pH should be 7.4.

Koser's Citrate Medium—Used to differentiate the colon-aerogenes organisms. *Escherichia coli* and coli type fail to grow, whereas *Aerobacter aerogenes* readily use the citrate and ammonium of the medium as the principal sources of carbon and nitrogen, respectively. It is prepared by dissolving 3 g sodium citrate, 1.5 g sodium ammonium phosphate, 1 g potassium dihydrogen phosphate, and 0.2 g magnesium sulfate in a liter of water. It is tubed and sterilized by autoclaving for 15 minutes at 121 C.

Kracke Blood Culture Medium—Used for the culturing of organisms from blood, as in bacteremias. It consists of 165 g beef heart, 55 g beef brain, 10 g peptone, 10 g glucose, 4 g sodium chloride, 2 g dipotassium phosphate, and 1 g sodium citrate. This will make about 3 liters of medium.

Lactose Broth—Add sufficient lactose to nutrient broth to make a 0.5 per cent solution, that is, 0.5 g for each 100 ml. Adjust the pH so that it will be 6.9 after sterilization. Sterilize, after distributing in tubes, by heating in an autoclave at not more than 121 C (15 pounds pressure) for no longer than 12 minutes. The total time the medium is subjected to heating should not exceed 60 minutes.

Lauryl Tryptose Broth—Used in the "confirmed" or "completed" test to determine the sanitary quality of water. Dissolve 20 g tryptose, 5 g lactose, 5 g sodium chloride, 2.75 g dipotassium hydrogen phosphate, 2.75 monopotassium dihydrogen phosphate, and 0.1 g sodium lauryl sulfate (Duponol W A Flakes) in a liter of cold water. Place in tubes and sterilize in an autoclave by heating at no higher than 121 C (15 pounds pressure) for no longer than 12 minutes. The pH should be adjusted so that after sterilization it will be 6.8.

Lead Acetate Agar—An agar medium used to test for hydrogen sulfide production. Dissolve 20 g tryptone and 15 g agar in 1 liter water. Adjust the pH to between 6.7 and 7.0. Add 4 ml 25 per cent aqueous glucose solution and 100 ml 0.5 per cent lead acetate solution. Tube and autoclave. The medium is not slanted after sterilization. The medium may be made as a semisolid agar. See also **hydrogen sulfide production tests.**

Lindegren's Presporulation Medium—Used for inducing the formation of spores in yeasts. It consists of 350 ml canned apricot juice, 200 ml of an extract of beet roots made by autoclaving 150 g beet roots and 1500 ml of water, 165 ml grape juice, 100 ml of an extract of beet leaves prepared by autoclaving 450 g beet leaves and 1500 ml of water, 25 ml of glycerol, 20 g dried yeast, 30 g agar, 10 g calcium carbonate, and sufficient water to make 1 liter. The mixture is heated on a steam bath until dissolved, placed in tubes and sterilized. Faster production of spores is obtained by transfer of the medium to plaster of Paris blocks.

Litmus Milk—A medium consisting of skim milk and **litmus solution.** Can be sterilized by heating for 10 to 12 minutes at 121 C. Excessive heat causes caramelization of the milk that results in difficulty in obtaining clear-cut results when bacteria are inoculated.

Litmus Solution. A solution consisting of 5 g azolitmin placed in a mortar to which 50 ml boiling water is added. After grinding, the fluid is decanted and an additional 50 ml water is added. After being ground and decanted, the two portions are mixed together. To use in milk, use 10 ml per liter. If acid, neutralize with 1.0 *N* sodium hydroxide.

Loeffler's Medium—A blood serum medium for the cultivation of *Corynebacterium diphtheriae*. The typical morphology of the diphtheria bacillus is based on this medium, but the **blood tellurite medium** is preferable.

Long's Medium—A synthetic protein-free medium for the preparation of tuberculin. It consists of 5 g ammonium citrate, 3 g acid potassium phosphate, 3 g sodium carbonate, 2 g sodium chloride, 1 g magnesium sulfate, 0.05 g ferric ammonium citrate, 50 g glycerol, and 1000 ml water.

Löwenstein-Jensen's Medium—A medium for the cultivation of *Mycobacterium tuberculosis.*

Löwenstein's Medium—Used for the cultivation of *Mycobacterium tuberculosis.* To prepare, add 150 ml of a solution consisting of 1 g sodium citrate, 1 g monopotassium phosphate, 3 g asparagin, 1 g magnesium sulfate, 60 ml glycerol, and 1000 ml water to 6 g of potato flour. Mix and boil for 15 minutes, always shaking. Keep at 56 C for 1 hour. Add 4 whole eggs and yolk of 1. (Eggs should be washed in tap water and placed in phenol for 15 minutes; then neutralized by washing in alcohol.) After shaking, add 5 ml sterile 2 per cent aqueous solution of Congo red. Filter, tube, and inspissate for 2 hours at 80 to 85 C on 2 successive days.

MacConkey's Agar—Used to isolate *Shigella* and *Salmonella,* that is, all types of dysentery, typhoid, and paratyphoid bacteria from stools, urine, and other specimens containing these organisms, particularly for isolating strains of S. *typhosa* from other members of the coliform group. Suspend and dissolve 17 g peptone, 13.5 g agar, 10 g lactose, 5 g sodium chloride, 3 g Difco proteose peptone, 0.03 g neutral red, and 0.001 g crystal violet in a liter of cold distilled water and heat to boiling. Transfer to tubes and sterilize in an autoclave at 121 C for 15 minutes. If it is to be used the same day as prepared, this medium need not be sterilized. It is commercially available in dehydrated form.

Maitland Medium—Used for the cultivation of vaccina virus and other viruses. Composed of fragments of fowl's kidney suspended in **Tyrode's solution** and fowl serum.

Mallein Broth—Used for the production of mallein endotoxin. Lean veal is macerated in 1 liter of water and left at room temperature overnight. It is then heated for 1 hour at about 47 C, and strained. One per cent Fairchild's peptone and 0.5 per cent sodium chloride are added and the ingredients dissolved by boiling; pH adjusted to between 6 and 6.4 and autoclaved for 15 minutes. After filtering through cotton, add 5 per cent glycerol. Distribute in quart Blake bottles or liter flasks and autoclave for 30 minutes at 15 pounds.

Malt Extract Broth—A medium consisting of 15 g malt extract, 1 g dipotassium phosphate, 1 g ammonium chloride, 15 ml citric acid (1.0 *N*), and 1000 ml water.

Meat Extract Agar—A culture medium for bacteria. It consists of agar, peptone, beef extract, sodium chloride, and water; pH is adjusted to between 6.8 and 7.0. Sterilize in autoclave. See **nutrient agar.**

Meat Extract Broth—The same medium as meat extract agar without the agar.

Meat Infusion—Chopped meat (beef or veal) in water is left to infuse in an icebox from 12 to 24 hours. See **meat infusion broth.** Generally, 500 g meat is steeped in 1000 ml water.

Meat Infusion Agar—Agar (20 g) is added to each 1000 ml of meat infusion broth. Sterilize in an autoclave.

Meat Infusion Broth—Meat infusion filtered through gauze after permitting the whole meat to stand in water for 12 to 18 hours. Peptone (10 g) and sodium chloride (5 g) are added to the infusion obtained from 500 g meat and 1 liter water. Sterilize in an autoclave.

Motility Sulfide Medium—A semisolid medium for determining motility and production of hydrogen sulfide, from L-cystine. Suspend 80 g gelatin, 10 g peptone, 4 g agar, 5 g sodium chloride, 3 g beef extract, 2 g sodium citrate, 0.2 g L-cystine, and 0.2 ferrous ammonium citrate in 1000 ml of water. Heat carefully to boiling to dissolve; place 4-ml aliquots in tubes; and sterilize at 117 C for 10 minutes. The pH is about 7.3.

Nile Blue Sulfate Fat Agar—Used for the detection of lipolytic activity of bacterial colonies. Fat is stained pink by nile blue sulfate. Organic acids yield a dark-blue color. Consequently colonies surrounded by dark-blue zones imply that the bacteria yield lipases, that is, fat-splitting enzymes. A fat emulsion is prepared by mixing 3 ml of cottonseed oil, 0.5 g agar, and 100 ml water and sterilizing the mixture in an autoclave at 121 C (15 pounds pressure) for 20 minutes. To prepare the medium, 4 ml of sterile fat emulsion and 5 ml of 0.2 per cent aqueous nile blue sulfate solution are added to 100 ml of sterile, melted and cooled, nutrient agar. After mixing, the medium is poured into plates.

Nitrate Broth—Used for the detection of the reduction of nitrates to nitrites. Dissolve 1 g pancreatic digest of casein or peptone and 0.1 g nitrite-free potassium nitrate in 100 ml ammonia-free distilled water by heating; adjust the pH to 7.0; place in tubes and autoclave. This broth is also prepared by adding 0.1 g potassium nitrate to nutrient broth.

Nitrosomonas Culture Medium—Dissolve 2.0 g ammonium sulfate $(NH_4)_2SO_4$, 1 g dipotassium hydrogen phosphate K_2HPO_4, 0.5 g magnesium sulfate $MgSO_4$, 0.4 g ferrous sulfate $FeSO_4$, and 0.4 g sodium chloride NaCl in 100 ml water. The pH of the medium is alkaline.

Noguchi-Wenyon Semi-Solid Medium—A medium for the isolation of *Leptospira*.

Novy Jar Method—A method of cultivating anaerobic bacteria in which a bell-shaped jar with a double stopcock at the top is used. Culture plates are placed on the bottom of the jar and air is exhausted by a vacuum pump and replaced by some inert gas, such as nitrogen. At the same time hydrogen is admitted from a Kipp generator.

Nutrient Agar—A medium consisting of 3 g beef extract, 5 g peptone, 15 g agar, and 1000 ml water, pH 6.8 to 7.0.

Nutrient Broth—A medium consisting of 3 g beef extract, 5 g peptone, and 1000 ml water, pH 6.8 to 7.0. Heat on a water bath to dissolve and make up water lost by evaporation. Distribute in tubes and sterilize at 121 C (15 pounds pressure) for 20 minutes or use for preparation of other media.

Nutritive Caseinate Agar—A medium consisting of 3 g casein, 7 g peptonized milk, and 12 g agar in a liter of water. It is used for the differentiation of strong and weak acid-forming colonies and peptonizing colonies in milk.

Omeliansky's Solution—A reagent for the detection of cellulose utilization. The solution consists of 1.0 g ammonium sulfate, 1.0 g dipotassium phosphate, 0.5 g magnesium sulfate, 2.0 g calcium carbonate, a trace of sodium chloride, and 1 liter of water.

Pennsylvania Medium—Used for the cultivation of fungi. It consists of American crude dextrose, imported French peptone, and agar in water.

Peptone Medium—Used to obtain cultures for the methyl red and Voges-Proskauer differential tests. Add 5 g each of glucose, proteose peptone Difco, and dipotassium hydrogen phosphate to 800 ml water. Heat on a steam bath for 20 minutes, stirring occasionally. Filter through a pleated filter, cool to 20 C, and make up to 1 liter with water. Place 10-ml aliquots in tubes and sterilize in an Arnold sterilizer by heating to 100 C for 20 minutes on 3 successive days.

Petragnani's Medium—Used for the cultivation of *Mycobacterium tuberculosis.* Mix 150 ml skimmed milk, 75 g peeled potato cut into small pieces, 10 g peptone, and 6 g potato flour and heat in a double boiler for 10 minutes, stirring constantly. Heat for 1 hour after the mixture becomes pasty. Add sterile distilled water to make up for any loss in volume, cool to 50 C and add 4 whole eggs, 1 egg yolk, 12 ml of glycerol, and 10 ml of a 2 per cent aqueous solution of malachite green. Mix thoroughly and filter through sterile gauze into a sterile distributing funnel. Place in tubes, slant, and inspissate for 2 hours at 70 to 75 C on 3 successive days.

Pia's Medium—A medium consisting of sterile saline and coagulated eggs for the cultivation of *Corynebacterium diphtheriae.*

Plating Method—Used for the primary isolation of organisms from their natural habitat or for enumerating viable bacteria. Matter containing the organism is streaked on a Petri dish containing a medium, or mixed with the medium and poured into the Petri dish for cultivation.

Proteose Tryptone Agar—Used for determining the bacterial count in certified milk. Suspend 3 g beef extract, 5 g peptone, 5 g tryptone, 5 g sodium chloride, 1 g glucose, and 15 g agar in 1 liter cold water. Heat to boiling to dissolve. Place in tubes or flasks and autoclave for 15 minutes at 121 C.

Roux's Method—A method of cultivating anaerobic bacteria. Draw up the inoculated medium (agar or gelatin) into a narrow tube and seal off both ends in a flame. Incubate until growth occurs. Recover the organisms by breaking the tube and fishing.

Russell's Double Sugar Agar—Employed in the primary identification of the organisms in the colon—typhoid–salmonella–dysentery group. Lactose, glucose and phenol red are the differentiating components of the medium. The colon organisms ferment glucose and lactose, showing acid and gas in the butt and acid in the slant. The salmonella group will ferment glucose with acid and gas in the butt and show no reaction on the slant. *Salmonella typhosa* will show an initial acid slant only. *Shigella* will ferment glucose with an acid reaction in the butt.

Sabouraud's Fluid Medium—Used for sterility testing. Dissolve 20 g of glucose, 5 g of pancreatic digest of casein, and 5 g of peptic digest of animal tissue in a liter of water with the aid of gentle heat. Adjust the pH of the medium so that after sterilization it will be 5.7 ± 0.1. Filter if required, distribute, in culture tubes, and autoclave at 121 C for 20 minutes.

Sabouraud's Glucose Agar—Used for the growth of yeast and molds. Suspend 20 g agar in 1 liter water by boiling. Add 40 g glucose and 10 g peptone. Restore the mixture to the original volume and adjust the pH to between 5.8 to 6.0. Autoclave at 121 C for 30 minutes. The final pH is 5.2 to 5.6.

Selenite Broth—An enrichment medium used for the isolation of the *Salmonella* group. It is preferred over tetrathionate broth for routine work. Suspend 23 g of a mixture consisting of 4 g sodium selenite, 10 g disodium hydrogen phosphate, 5 g tryptose, and 4 g lactose in a liter of water and heat to boiling. Place in sterile tubes. Do not sterilize by autoclaving.

Serum-Water Medium—A medium consisting of 1 part of clear beef serum to 2 or 3 parts of water. Heat in an Arnold sterilizer for 15 minutes at 100 c. To this, 1 ml of 1.6 per cent alcoholic solution or 1 per cent **Andrade's solution** and 1 per cent concentrations of various sugars may be added.

Simmons Citrate Agar—A medium for the differentiation of *Escherichia coli* and *Aerobacter aerogenes;* the latter uses citrate as the sole source of carbon. It can also be used for the *Salmonella*–typhoid–dysentery group. *A. aerogenes, S. schottmuelleri, S. enteritidis,* and *S. typhimurium* utilize the citrate, turning the medium a deep blue. Suspend 1 g ammonium dihydrogen phosphate, 1 g dipotassium hydrogen phosphate, 0.2 g magnesium sulfate, 2 g sodium citrate, 5 g sodium chloride, 15 g agar, and 0.08 g bromothymol blue in a liter of water and heat to boiling. Distribute in tubes and autoclave for 15 minutes at 121 C. Allow to cool to form slants. See also **Koser's citrate medium.**

Sodium Caseinate Agar—A medium used for the counting of bacteria, including those belonging to the order *Actinomycetales* in soil. It is prepared by dissolving 1 g each of sodium caseinate and glucose, 0.2 g each of magnesium sulfate and dipotassium hydrogen phosphate, a trace of ferrous sulfate, and 15 g agar in a liter of water. Adjust the pH to 7.0. Shake to disperse any precipitate before pouring into plates or tubes.

Sodium Chloride Nutrient Broth—Solutions of 5, 10, and 20 per cent are made. To each 1000 ml, add 3 g of beef extract and 5 g peptone; pH 6.8 to 7.0. Used to demonstrate effect of osmotic pressure upon the growth of microorganisms.

Sodium Hippurate Broth—Used in the **hippurate-hydrolysis test.** Add exactly 1 per cent of sodium hippurate to **meat infusion broth.** Put into tubes with graduations or mark the volume with glass marking crayon and sterilize in an autoclave. Inoculate and incubate for 48 hours. Add water up to the mark to replace the moisture lost in the incubation. This is necessary to keep the concentration of the sodium hippurate at 1 per cent. If this is not done, the subsequent concentration of benzoic acid, if formed, will be too great and it may then precipitate and give a false positive test.

Soil Extract-Meat-Egg Medium—Used in the **sporocidal (A.O.A.C.) test** for the propagation of test cultures of clostridia. Add 1.5 g Bacto Egg-Meat Medium dehydrated to 20 × 150-mm test tubes; then add 10 ml garden **soil extract,** plug with cotton, and sterilize at 121 C for 20 minutes. Maintain stock cultures of species of this genus on this medium.

Soil Extract Nutrient Broth—Used in the **sporocidal (A.O.A.C.) test** for the propagation of the test culture of bacilli. Extract 1 pound of garden soil in 1 liter of water, filter several times through S & S No. 588 paper, and dilute to a liter. The pH of this broth should be 5.2 or higher. Add 5 g of Difco beef extract, 5 g of sodium chloride, and 10 g of Armour peptone, boil for 20 minutes, adjust to pH 6.9, filter through paper, dilute to 1 liter, dispense into 20 × 150-mm test tubes, plug with cotton, and sterilize at 121 C for 20 minutes.

Sorbitol Agar—A medium for stock cultures of *Acetobacter.* The components are 20 g sorbitol, 5 g yeast extract, 20 g agar, and a liter of water.

Spray's Method—A procedure for cultivating anaerobic bacteria by use of a modified Petri dish, which consists of a cover and a glass jar with a deep ridge separating the bottom into two sections. Pyrogallic acid is placed in one compartment and sodium hydroxide solution in the other. The culture is inoculated onto agar in the cover. The inoculated agar plate cover is inverted to cap the jar and is sealed with paraffin or a plastic. The oxygen-absorbing solutions are mixed by tilting and the jar is incubated.

Stab Culture—Organisms are inoculated into the butt of a solid medium by stabbing the medium. The growth is anaerobic and is characterized by the terms arborescent, beaded, echinulate, filiform, fusiform, papillate, plumose, rhizoid, and villose or villous in the case of agar media; and crateriform, infundibuliform, napiform, saccate, and stratiform in the case of gelatin media.

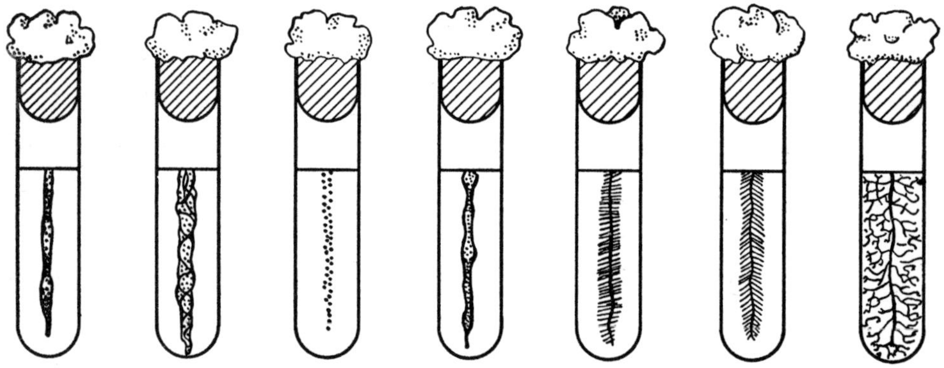

Filiform Echinulate Beaded Papillate Villose Plumose Arborescent

Stab cultures. (After A. H. Bryan and C. G. Bryan, *Bacteriology*, Barnes and Noble, New York, 1953.)

S S Agar—Used for the isolation of *Shigella* and *Salmonella* from stools or materials harboring these organisms. Differentiates organisms fermenting lactose from those not fermenting lactose and inhibits coliform organisms without stopping the growth of gram-negative rods. Generally used in conjunction with **MacConkey's agar.** Suspend and dissolve 10 g lactose, 85 g each of Bacto-bile salts No. 3, sodium citrate, and sodium thiosulfate, 5 g of beef extract, 5 g of Difco proteose peptone, 1 g of ferric citrate, 13.5 g agar, 0.00033 g brilliant green, and 0.025 neutral red in a liter of water, and heat to boiling. Pour 20-ml aliquots into Petri dishes. Allow the medium to solidify in the dishes and dry the surface by partially removing the cover. This medium must not be sterilized. The dehydrated medium is commercially available.

Streak Cultures—Cultures made by applying the organisms with a loop or other instrument to the surface of a medium, usually an agar slant. See page 205.

Streak Plate—A bacterial culture is spread over the surface of an agar plate employing a needle, loop, or bent glass rod. The loop is drawn across the top of the agar by many back and forth streaks. The culture is diluted to a point where many discrete colonies are obtained.

Teague Medium—Used for differentiating *Vibrio comma* colonies, which have large red centers, from *Escherichia coli* colonies, which are pink.

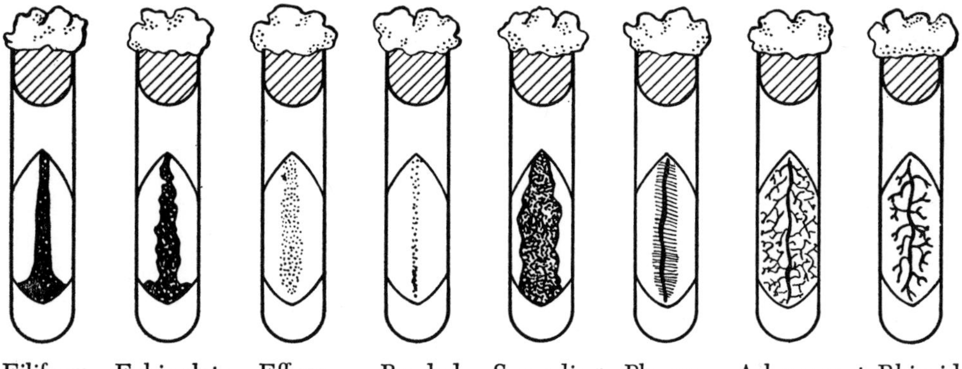

Streak cultures. (After A. H. Bryan and C. G. Bryan, *Bacteriology*, Barnes and Noble, New York, 1953.)

Tellurite Agar Medium—Used for isolating diphtheria organisms. A special agar, such as one made with a pancreatic digest of casein, is used. It is sterilized at 121 C for 15 min, cooled to 50 C and to each 100 ml is added 1 ml of a 1 per cent aqueous potassium tellurite solution and either 5 ml of sterile human serum or 10 ml of sterile citrated or defibrinated blood. *Corynebacterium diphtheriae* produces black, slightly raised colonies with entire or irregular margins. Most other organisms are inhibited.

Tetanus Toxin Broth—Used for toxin production. Lean veal is infused in water overnight. Heat for 1 hour at 45 C and boil for ½ hour. After straining, add 1 per cent Berna peptone, 0.5 per cent sodium chloride, and 1 per cent glucose. Heat until the ingredients are dissolved and adjust pH to 7.2. Sterilize in Arnold sterilizer for 1½ hours on first day and 1 hour on second day.

Tergitol No. 7 Agar Medium—A selective medium for *Escherichia coli* and the coliform group. It is prepared by suspending 15 g agar, 10 g lactose, 5 g peptone, 3 g yeast extract, 0.1 ml Tergitol No. 7, and 0.025 g bromothymol blue in a liter of cold water and boiling to dissolve. It is sterilized by autoclaving at 121 C for 15 minutes.

Tetrathionate Broth—Used for the isolation of salmonella. It is not a favorable medium for *Shigella* or for *Salmonella typhosa*. See **tetrathionate broth, Kauffmann's modification.**

Tetrathionate Broth, Kauffmann's Modification—To each 100 ml broth base add 4 g calcium carbonate and 2 g sodium thiosulfate. Sterilize at 121 C for 20 min. Dissolve 25 g of potassium iodide in a small amount of water and dissolve 20 g iodine in this solution. Dilute to 100 ml. Add 2 ml iodine solution to the cooled broth base. Add 1 ml brilliant green solution (1:1000). Distribute in sterile screw-cap tubes without additional heating. Store at room temperature for not more than 2 weeks.

Thermoacidurans Agar—Used for the culturing of the organism *Bacillus coagulans*, causing flat sour spoilage in canned goods. Suspend 20 g agar, 5 g glucose, 5 g yeast extract, 5 g proteose peptone, and 4 g dipotassium hydrogen phosphate in a liter of water; heat to boiling to dissolve. Distribute in flasks or tubes and autoclave at 121 C for 15 minutes.

Thioglycollate Broth—A medium especially prepared for the cultivation of anaerobic microorganisms. A small amount of agar and thioglycollate salt are added to provide and maintain a low oxygen-reduction potential, as indicated by methylene blue or resazurin. The Brewer modification of this medium is prepared by suspending 10 g thiopeptone, 10 g glucose, 5 g sodium chloride, 2 g dipotassium monohydrogen phosphate, 1 g sodium thioglycollate, and 0.5 g agar, in 750 ml meat infusion. Dissolve by heating. Make up to 1 liter with water and adjust the pH to between 7.4 and 7.6. Add 10 ml of 1:5000 aqueous methylene blue solution. Transfer to tubes, keeping the height of the liquid to 7 cm. Sterilize by autoclaving at 121 C (15 pounds pressure) for 20 minutes. The medium must be stored at room temperature. The color of the reduced medium is amber. A greenish color starting at the top of the medium is indicative of oxidation. If the depth of the green or oxidation color is greater than 1 cm, boil for a few minutes and cool again before use.

Thioglycollate Fluid Medium N. F. X)—Used for determining the sterility of drugs and preparations. Mix 15 g pancreatic digest of casein, 5.5 g glucose, 5.0 g yeast extract, 2.5 g sodium chloride, 0.75 g granulated agar (moisture content less than 15 per cent), and 0.5 g L-cystine in a liter of water and heat on a steam bath until dissolved. Add 0.5 g sodium thioglycollate or 0.3 ml thioglycollic acid to the mixture and adjust the pH with 1 *N* sodium hydroxide solution so that after sterilization it will be 7.1 ± 0.1. If necessary, heat the solution again on a steam bath and filter while hot through a moistened filter paper. Add 1.0 ml of freshly prepared 0.1 per cent sodium resazurin solution, mix completely, distribute in culture tubes, and heat in an autoclave at 121 C for 20 minutes to sterilize. This temperature should be attained in 10 minutes. Cool immediately to 25 C and store at 20 to 30 C, protected from light. If a pink color appears in the upper third portion, reduce the pink by heating in a steam bath.

Tomato Juice Agar—Used for the cultivation of lactobacilli. It consists of 400 ml tomato juice filtered through paper, 10 g peptonized milk, 10 g peptone, 11 g agar, and 600 ml water. Dissolve the milk and peptone in the tomato juice with gentle heating. Adjust the pH to 6.1. Dissolve the agar in water and restore to the original volume. Combine the tomato juice mixture and the hot agar. Filter through absorbent cotton and autoclave at 121 C for 8 minutes.

Triple Sugar Iron Agar—A medium containing glucose, lactose, and sucrose used in the routine examination of stools for identifying gram-negative enteric pathogens. Hydrogen sulfide production can also be determined.

Trypticase Soy Agar—A solid medium made with a pancreatic digest of casein and other nutrients used as a blood agar base and for the cultivation of *Brucella* sp. and other fastidious organisms.

Trypticase Soy Broth—A broth medium made with pancreatic digest of casein and other nutrients which is used for blood culture and for general cultivations of fastidious organisms.

Tryptone Broth—Used to obtain cultures for the indole differentiation test. Add 10 g Bacto-tryptone to a liter of water and heat while stirring until dissolved. Place 5-ml aliquots in tubes and sterilize in an autoclave at 121 C (15 pounds pressure) for 20 minutes.

Tryptose Agar—A medium used for the cultivation and isolation of brucella and other pathogens from milk.

Tryptose Broth—A medium used for the isolation of brucella from blood specimens.

Tuberculin Broth—A medium for tuberculin production. It consists of infused, chopped, lean beef in a liter of water held for 1 hour at 45 C and filtered; 1 per cent peptone and 0.5 per cent sodium chloride are added; pH is adjusted to 7.1. After boiling, the mixture is filtered and 5 per cent glycerol is added. It is sterilized in an autoclave.

Tyrode's Solution—One of thc component parts of a tissue culture for the cultivation of viruses *in vitro*. It is part of the suspending fluid which furnishes mineral nutrients and glucose. Other parts are the live tissue cells and the inoculum. It consists of 8 g sodium chloride, 0.2 g potassium chloride, 0.2 g calcium chloride, 0.1 g magnesium chloride, 0.05 g sodium acid phosphate, 1 g sodium bicarbonate, 1 g glucose, and 1000 ml triple distilled water.

Waksman's Medium—Used in soil microbiological work for the isolation of fungi. A mineral acid is used to avoid utilization of organic acid by the molds. It is prepared by dispersing 15 g of agar and dissolving 10 g glucose, 5 g peptone, 1.0 g monopotassium dihydrogen phosphate, 0.5 g crystallized magnesium sulfate in 1 liter of water. After sterilization and while still in a liquid state, add 0.5 to 0.6 ml *N* sulfuric acid to adjust the pH to between 3.8 and 4.0. Most bacteria will not grow in this medium because it is too acid.

Wilson-Blair Bismuth Sulfite Medium—Used to differentiate the colon–typhoid–dysentery group. *Escherichia coli* is inhibited. *Salmonella typhosa* gives a metallic sheen and is black. *S. paratyphi* colonies are green, dry, and flat. *S. schottmuelleri* reduces sulfite to sulfide in the presence of glucose, giving black colonies.

TABLE 8a. INDICATORS

TABLE 8b. PREPARATION OF STOCK SOLUTIONS OF HYDROGEN-ION INDICATORS

TABLE 8c. METHODS OF EXPRESSING HYDROGEN-ION CONCENTRATIONS

TABLE 8d. McILVAINE'S STANDARD BUFFER SOLUTIONS

TABLE 8e. CLARK'S STANDARD BUFFER SOLUTIONS

Andrade's Solution—An indicator solution containing 0.5 per cent of an aqueous solution of acid fuchsin made alkaline with 1 *N* sodium hydroxide solution to just past the color change. It is used in culture media to detect the production of acid by bacteria. pH 7.2, colorless; acid, pink; alkaline, pale yellow.

Bromochlorophenol Blue, Bromchlorphenol Blue—Dibromodichlorophenolsulfonphthalein has a pH range of 3.2 to 4.8. The acidic color is yellow, and the alkaline color is blue. The pH indicator is prepared by dissolving 0.1 g in 8.6 ml 0.02 *N* sodium hydroxide solution and diluting to 250 ml with water.

Bromocresol Green, Bromcresol Green—Tetabromo-*m*-cresolsulfonphthalein has a pH range of 3.8 to 5.4. The acidic color is yellow and the alkaline color blue. The pH indicator is prepared by dissolving 0.1 g in 7.15 ml of 0.02 *N* sodium hydroxide solution diluted to 250 ml with water.

Bromocresol Purple, Bromcresol Purple—Dibromo-*o*-cresolsulfonphthalein has a pH range of 5.2 to 6.8. The acidic color is yellow, and the alkaline color is purple. The pH indicator is prepared by dissolving 0.1 g in 9.25 ml 0.02 *N* sodium hydroxide solution and diluting to 250 ml with water.

Bromophenol Blue, Bromphenol Blue—Tetrabromophenolsulfonphthalein has a pH range of 3.0 to 4.6. The acidic color is yellow, and the alkaline color is blue. The indicator solution is prepared by dissolving 0.1 g in 7.45 ml 0.02 *N* sodium hydroxide solution and diluting to 250 ml with water.

Bromophenol Red, Bromphenol Red—Dibromophenolsulfonphthalein has a pH range of 5.4 to 7.0. The acidic color is yellow, and the alkaline color is red. The pH indicator is prepared by dissolving 0.1 g in 9.75 ml of 0.02 *N* sodium hydroxide solution and diluting to 250 ml with water.

Bromothymol Blue, Bromthymol Blue—Dibromothymolsulfonphthalein has a pH range of 6.0 to 7.6. The acidic color is yellow and the alkaline color is blue. The pH indicator is prepared by dissolving 0.1 g in 8 ml of 0.02 *N* sodium hydroxide solution and diluting to 250 ml with water.

Chlorophenol Red, Chlorphenol Red—Dichlorophenolsulfonphthalein has a pH range of 5.0 to 6.7. The acidic color is yellow and the alkaline color is red. The pH indicator is prepared by dissolving 0.1 g in 11.8 ml of 0.02 *N* sodium hydroxide solution and diluting to 250 ml with water.

Congo Red—An indicator with a pH range of 3.0 to 5.2. The acidic color is blue and the alkaline color is red. The indicator solution is prepared by dissolving the dye in water to form a 0.1 per cent solution.

***o*-Cresolphthalein**—An indicator with a pH range of 8.2 to 9.8. It is colorless in acid solution and is red in alkaline solution. The indicator solution is prepared by dissolving sufficient dye in ethyl alcohol to give a 0.04 per cent solution.

Cresol Red—*o*-Cresolsulfonphthalein has a pH range of 7.2 to 8.8. The acidic color is yellow and the alkaline color is red. The pH indicator solution is prepared by dissolving 0.1 g in 13.1 ml 0.02 *N* sodium hydroxide solution and diluting to 250 ml with water. Cresol red also has a very acid pH range of 0.2 to 1.8. In this range the acid color is red and the alkaline color is yellow.

Cresolsulfonphthalein—See **cresol red.**

Dibromocresolsulfonphthalein—see **bromocresol purple.**

Dibromothymolsulfonphthalein—See **bromothymol blue.**

Litmus—An indicator derived from various species of lichens, principally *Lecanora subfusea* var. *variolosa.* Consists mainly of azolitmin and erythrolitmin. The commercial indicator has a pH range of 4.5 to 8.3. The acid color is red and the alkaline color is blue. The indicator solution may be prepared by dissolving 1 g in 100 ml of water. Usually used as litmus paper, or as an indicator in milk to show acid or alkaline reduction by microorganisms.

Metacresol Purple—*m*-Cresolsulfonphthalein is an indicator with two principal ranges, one in the very acid range and the other in the slightly alkaline range. The pH range in the very acid region is 1.2 to 2.8, with the more acidic color being red and the less acidic color being yellow. The pH range in the slightly alkaline region is 7.4 to 9.0, the acidic color being yellow and the alkaline color purple. To prepare the indicator solution, dissolve 0.1 g in 13.1 ml 0.02 *N* sodium hydroxide solution and dilute to 250 ml with water.

Methyl Orange—Sodium 4′-dimethylaminoazobenzene-4-sulfonate has a pH range of 3.1 to 4.4. The acidic color is orange-red, and the alkaline color is yellow.

Methyl Red—4′-Dimethylaminoazobenzene-2-carboxylic acid has a pH range of 4.4 to 6.2. The acidic color is red, and the alkaline color is yellow. The pH indicator is prepared by dissolving 0.1 g in 300 ml ethyl alcohol and diluting to 500 ml with water.

Neutral Red—2-Methyl-3-amino-6-dimethylaminophenazine, dark-green powder, soluble in water and alcohol, forming a red solution. It has a pH range of 6.8 to 8.0. The acidic color is red and the neutral color yellow. The pH indicator solution is prepared by dissolving 0.1 g in 70 ml alcohol and diluting with water to 100 ml. A 1 per cent aqueous solution (50 to 60 per cent dye content) is used as a **stain.**

Phenolphthalein—An indicator with a pH range of 8.3 to 10.0. Colorless in the acidic range, the alkaline color is red. To prepare the indicator solution, add 1.0 g phenolphthalein to 100 ml 95 per cent alcohol.

Phenol Red—Phenolsulfonphthalein has a pH range of 6.8 to 8.4. The acidic color is yellow, and the alkaline color is red. To prepare the indicator solution, dissolve 0.1 g in 14.1 ml of 0.02 *N* sodium hydroxide solution and dilute to 250 ml with water.

Phenolsulfonphthalein—See **phenol red.**

Poirrer's Blue—The sodium or potassium salt of triphenylrosanilinesulfonate. Dark-blue powder, soluble in water and alcohol. Used as a stain and indicator, with a pH range 11.0 (blue) to 13.0 (violet-red). See **lactophenol-cotton blue solution.**

Resazurin—$C_{12}H_7NO_4$; dark-red crystals with a greenish luster; insoluble in water, soluble in dilute alkali solution (0.1 g in 20 ml 0.1 *N* sodium hydroxide solution diluted to 500 ml for the indicator solution), sparingly soluble in alcohol. Acidic color orange, basic color dark violet; pH range 3.8 to 6.5.

Tetrabromo-*m*-cresolsulfonphthalein—See **bromocresol green.**

Tetrabromophenolsulfonphthalein—See **bromophenol blue.**

Thymol Blue—Thymolsulfonphthalein. An indicator with two principal ranges. The pH range on the acid side is 1.2 to 2.8, the acidic color being red, and the alkaline color yellow. The pH range on the alkaline side is 8.0 to 9.6, the acidic color being yellow and the alkaline color blue. The indicator solution is prepared by dissolving 0.1 g in 10.75 ml 0.02 *N* sodium hydroxide solution and diluting to 250 ml with water.

Thymolsulfonphthalein—See **thymol blue.**

TABLE 8b. PREPARATION OF STOCK SOLUTIONS OF HYDROGEN-ION INDICATORS

Indicator, common name	Indicator, chemical name	Weight, g	0.05 *N* NaOH, ml	Water, ml	Concentration for use, %	Range, pH
Bromphenol blue	Tetrabromophenolsulfonphthalein	0.1	3.0	22.0	0.04	3.0–4.6 Y–B[a]
Bromcresol green	Tetrabromocresolsulfonphthalein	0.1	2.9	22.1	0.04	4.0–5.8 Y–B
Bromcresol purple	Dibromocresolsulfonphthalein	0.1	3.7	21.3	0.04	5.2–6.8 Y–P
Bromthymol blue	Dibromothymolsulfonphthalein	0.1	3.2	21.8	0.04	6.0–7.6 Y–B
Phenol red	Phenolsulfonphthalein	0.1	5.7	19.3	0.02	6.8–8.4 Y–R
Cresol red	Cresolsulfonphthalein	0.1	5.3	19.7	0.02	7.2–8.8 Y–R
Thymol blue	Thymolsulfonphthalein	0.1	4.3	21.7	0.04	8.0–9.6 Y–B

[a] Y = yellow, B = blue, P = purple, R = red.

TABLE 8c. METHODS OF EXPRESSING HYDROGEN-ION CONCENTRATIONS

Reaction	Fraction of normality[a]	Hydrogen ions per liter, g	Logarithms of H-ion concentrations	pH
Acid	*N*/1	1.0	0.00	0.0
Acid	*N*/10	0.1	$\bar{1}.00$	1.0
Acid	*N*/100	0.01	$\bar{2}.00$	2.0
Acid	*N*/1,000	0.001	$\bar{3}.00$	3.0
Acid	*N*/10,000	0.000,1	$\bar{4}.00$	4.0
Acid	*N*/100,000	0.000,01	$\bar{5}.00$	5.0
Acid	*N*/1,000,000	0.000,001	$\bar{6}.00$	6.0
Neutral	Pure water	0.000,000,1	$\bar{7}.00$	7.0
Alkaline	*N*/1,000,000	0.000,000,01	$\bar{8}.00$	8.0
Alkaline	*N*/100,000	0.000,000,001	$\bar{9}.00$	9.0
Alkaline	*N*/10,000	0.000,000,000,1	$\overline{10}.00$	10.0
Alkaline	*N*/1,000	0.000,000,000,01	$\overline{11}.00$	11.0
Alkaline	*N*/100	0.000,000,000,001	$\overline{12}.00$	12.0
Alkaline	*N*/10	0.000,000,000,000,1	$\overline{13}.00$	13.0
Alkaline	*N*/1	0.000,000,000,000,01	$\overline{14}.00$	14.0

[a] With respect to hydrogen or hydroxyl ions.

TABLE 8d. McILVAINE'S STANDARD BUFFER SOLUTIONS

pH	0.1 *M* Citric acid, ml	0.2 *M* Na_2HPO_4, ml	pH	0.1 *M* Citric acid, ml	0.2 *M* Na_2HPO_4, ml
2.2	196.0	4.0	5.2	92.8	107.2
2.4	187.6	12.4	5.4	88.5	111.5
2.6	178.2	21.8	5.6	84.0	116.0
2.8	168.3	31.7	5.8	79.1	120.9
3.0	158.9	41.1	6.0	73.7	126.3
3.2	150.6	49.4	6.2	67.8	132.2
3.4	143.0	57.0	6.4	61.5	138.5
3.6	135.6	64.4	6.6	54.5	145.5
3.8	129.0	71.0	6.8	45.5	154.5
4.0	122.9	77.0	7.0	35.3	164.7
4.2	117.2	82.8	7.2	26.1	173.9
4.4	111.8	88.2	7.4	18.3	181.7
4.6	106.5	93.5	7.6	12.7	187.3
4.8	101.4	98.6	7.8	8.5	191.5
5.0	97.0	103.0	8.0	5.5	194.5

TABLE 8e. CLARK'S STANDARD BUFFER SOLUTIONS[a,b]

(Add the volumes noted in columns 2, 3, and 4 to a 200-ml volumetric flask and dilute to volume with water at 20 C.)

Hydrochloric acid and potassium chloride mixtures

pH	5 *M* HCl, ml	5 *M* KCl, ml	pH	5 *M* HCl, ml	5 *M* KCl, ml
1.2	64.5	50.0	1.8	16.6	50.0
1.4	41.5	50.0	2.0	10.6	50.0
1.6	26.3	50.0	2.2	6.7	50.0

Hydrochloric acid and potassium hydrogen phthalate mixtures

pH	5 *M* HCl, ml	5 *M* $KHC_8H_4O_4$, ml	pH	5 *M* HCl, ml	5 *M* $KHC_8H_4O_4$, ml
2.2	46.70	50.0	3.2	14.70	50.0
2.4	39.50	50.0	3.4	9.90	50.0
2.6	32.95	50.0	3.6	5.97	50.0
2.8	26.42	50.0	3.8	2.63	50.0
3.0	20.32	50.0			

Potassium hydrogen phthalate and sodium hydroxide mixtures

pH	5 *M* $KHC_8H_4O_4$, ml	5 *M* NaOH, ml	pH	5 *M* $KHC_8H_4O_4$, ml	5 *M* NaOH, ml
4.0	50.0	0.40	5.2	50.0	29.95
4.2	50.0	3.70	5.4	50.0	35.45
4.4	50.0	7.50	5.6	50.0	39.85
4.6	50.0	12.15	5.8	50.0	43.00
4.8	50.0	17.70	6.0	50.0	45.54
5.0	50.0	23.85	6.2	50.0	47.00

Monopotassium dihydrogen phosphate and sodium hydroxide mixtures

pH	5 *M* KH_2PO_4, ml	5 *M* NaOH, ml	pH	5 *M* KH_2PO_4, ml	5 *M* NaOH, ml
5.8	50.0	3.72	7.0	50.0	29.63
6.0	50.0	5.70	7.2	50.0	35.00
6.2	50.0	8.60	7.4	50.0	39.50
6.4	50.0	12.60	7.6	50.0	42.80
6.6	50.0	17.80	7.8	50.0	45.20
6.8	50.0	23.65	8.0	50.0	46.80

[a] After W. M. Clark, *The Determination of Hydrogen-Ions*. 3rd. Ed., Williams & Wilkins, Baltimore, 1928.
[b] These values are about 0.03 to 0.04 pH unit too low.

TABLE 8e. CLARK'S STANDARD BUFFER SOLUTIONS[a,b] (*Continued*)

Boric acid, potassium chloride, and sodium hydroxide mixtures

pH	5 *M* H_3BO_3, ml	5 *M* KCl, ml	5 *M* NaOH, ml	pH	5 *M* H_3BO_3, ml	5 *M* KCl, ml	5 *M* NaOH, ml
7.8	50.0	50.0	2.61	9.0	50.0	50.0	21.30
8.0	50.0	50.0	3.97	9.2	50.0	50.0	26.70
8.2	50.0	50.0	5.90	9.4	50.0	50.0	32.00
8.4	50.0	50.0	8.50	9.6	50.0	50.0	36.85
8.6	50.0	50.0	12.00	9.8	50.0	50.0	40.80
8.8	50.0	50.0	16.30	10.0	50.0	50.0	43.90

TABLE 9. MICROBIOLOGICAL REAGENTS AND TESTS

Acetylmethylcarbinol Test—See **Voges-Proskauer test.**

Acid Alcohol—A solution consisting of 3.0 ml of hydrochloric acid (sp. gr. 1.19), and sufficient 95 per cent alcohol to make 100 ml. Used in the acid-fast staining technique for organisms, such as *Mycobacterium tuberculosis.*

Acrolein Test for *Clostridium Perfringens*—The organism, *C. perfringens,* has the ability of converting glycerol to acrolein. Inoculate about 0.1 ml of culture or a small piece of infected tissue, or equivalent specimen, into a tube of bromocresol purple broth base, consisting of 10 g of Bacto proteose peptone No. 3, 1 g beef extract, 5 g sodium chloride, and 0.015 g bromocresol purple in a liter of water to which has been added 3 per cent of glycerol and 0.15 per cent of agar. Incubate at 37 C and examine each hour to note the change of indicator color to yellow. This generally occurs in 4 to 6 hours. Centrifuge the culture and transfer 1 ml of the supernatant to a test tube. Add 1 ml of Schiff reagent and mix. Shake occasionally over a period of 20 minutes. The production of a purple color is indicative of the formation of acrolein from the glycerol.

Ammonia Test—Incubate an inoculum in a medium containing peptone or protein at 37 C for 5 days. Remove the culture from the incubator and heat. Wet a piece of filter paper with **Nessler's reagent** and hold it over the vapors from the culture. The filter paper turns red, brown, or black, depending upon the amount of ammonia present. See also **Thomas method.**

Available Chlorine Germicidal Equivalent Concentration Method (A.O.A.C.)—A test applicable to water miscible disinfectants and useful for determining the available chlorine germicidal equivalent concentrations in products offered for use as germicidal rinses for previously cleaned nonporous surfaces, especially where speed of action and capacity are essential considerations.

Apparatus. The apparatus used is the same as that described for the **phenol coefficient method (A.O.A.C.) *Salmonella typhosa* variation.**

Reagents. Phenol Solution. The phenol used is the same as that detailed in the **phenol coefficient method (A.O.A.C.) *Salmonella typhosa* variation.**

Sterile Buffer Solution—pH 8.5. Add 88 ml of a solution containing 11.61 g dipotassium hydrogen phosphate, K_2HPO_4, in 1 liter of water to 12 ml of a solution containing 9.08 g potassium dihydrogen phosphate, KH_2PO_4, in 1 liter of water and sterilize at 121 C for 20 minutes in cotton plugged Erlenmeyer flasks.

Standard Sodium Hypochlorite Stock Solution. Prepare a 5 per cent sodium hypochlorite stock solution and store in a tightly closed bottle in a refrigerator. Determine the exact available chlorine concentration at frequent intervals by titration with arsenious oxide or other standard method.

Culture Media. The culture media used are the same as those described for the **phenol coefficient method (A.O.A.C.) *Salmonella typhosa* variation.**

Test Organisms. Use *Salmonella typhosa* A.T.C.C. No. 6539 or *Staphylococcus aureus* A.T.C.C. No. 6538, or both.

Procedure. Determine the resistance of the test culture to phenol as detailed in the **phenol coefficient method (A.O.A.C.) *Salmonella typhosa* variation,** and use cultures with the resistance specified. Prepare in sterile glass-stoppered cylinders solutions of sodium hypochlorite containing 200, 100, and 50 ppm available chlorine in the sterile buffer solution. Transfer 10 ml of each solution to 25 × 150-mm bacteriological test tubes, place tubes in a 20 C water bath, and allow them to come to temperature.

Starting with the tube containing 200 ppm available chlorine, add 0.05 ml of test culture prepared as in the phenol coefficient method, shake, and return to the water bath. After 1 minute, transfer to a tube of appropriate subculture medium, using a flamed 4-mm loop. At 1.5 minutes add another 0.05 ml culture to the 200 ppm chlorine solution, shake, and return to the bath. After an additional 1-minute interval (2.5 minutes in the test), make a second subculture in the same manner, and in 30 seconds, or at 3 minutes time in the test, add another 0.05 ml of culture, shaking, and returning to the water bath. After another 1-minute interval (4.0 minutes in the test), make another transfer to a tube subculture medium. Repeat this series of manipulations to give a total of ten added increments. This will require a total time for each solution of 14.5 minutes and the addition of 0.5 ml of total culture with subculture at standard 1-minute intervals after the addition of culture aliquots. At the conclusion of the test, shake all the subculture tubes and incubate for 48 hours at 37 C.

Repeat this series of manipulations with solutions containing 100 and 50 ppm of available chlorine. Prepare a solution of the unknown germicide, at the concentration recommended for use or selected for study, in sterile distilled water in a glass-stoppered graduate. Transfer 10 ml to a 25 × 150-mm bacteriological test tube, place in the water bath, and allow to come to temperature. Repeat the test procedure with this solution.

To be considered equivalent in disinfecting activity to 200 ppm of available chlorine, the unknown germicide must show the absence of growth in as many consecutive tubes of subculture tube series as the 200 ppm available chlorine standard. Determine in the same manner the activity equivalent to 100 and 50 pm of available chlorine.

Example:

Germicide	Concentration, ppm available Cl	Subculture series									
		1	2	3	4	5	6	7	8	9	10
NaOCl control	200	−	−	−	−	−	+	+	+	+	+
	100	−	−	−	+	+	+	+	+	+	+
	50	−	−	+	+	+	+	+	+	+	+
Unknown	25	−	−	−	−	−	+	+	+	+	+
	20	−	−	−	−	+	+	+	+	+	+
	10	−	+	+	+	+	+	+	+	+	+

− = no growth. + = growth.

From the result in the table, a 25 ppm solution of the unknown germicide could be considered equivalent to a 200 ppm solution of available chlorine, and 20 ppm solution equivalent to 100 ppm of available chlorine, but 10 ppm solution of the unknown germicide would not be considered equivalent in germicidal activity to 50 ppm of available chlorine.

Draw conclusions relative to germicidal equivalent concentrations only when the resistance of the test culture to the sodium hypochlorite control is such that at least 1 negative increment is obtained at 50 ppm concentration and 1 positive increment is obtained at the 200 ppm level.

Brilliant Green—A triphenylmethane dye, $C_{27}H_{34}N_2O_2S$, golden glistening crystals, soluble in water or alcohol and producing a green color. It is used to inhibit the growth of gram-positive organisms and permits the unrestricted development of the coliform group.

Bromocresol Purple Milk Reactions—The microbiological reactions of bromocresol purple milk are analogous to those of *litmus milk* and therefore have the same use, except that bromocresol purple is not reduced and therefore cannot be used for reduction reactions.

Bromothymol Blue Test—A test for mastitis in cows. Bromothymol blue indicator, 0.1 g in 8 ml of 0.02 *N* sodium hydroxide solution diluted to 250 ml with water, is added to 3 ml of freshly drawn milk: normal milk is greenish-yellow; a light green indicates slightly infected milk; green-blue to blue indicates highly infected milk.

Brucella Ring Test—A quick method for determining if cows are infected with brucellosis. Place 2 ml of milk and 2 drops of a specially prepared hematoxylin-stained suspension of *B. abortus*. Mix the contents of the tube and incubate at 37 C for 1 hour. If antibodies for *B. abortus* are present, the specially prepared suspension is agglutinated. There is a blue-violet color on the top of the milk layer in positive reactions.

Camp Test—Blood agar plate is streaked down the center with a beta toxin producing strain (*Staphylococcus aureus*). Each of the suspected streptococci are streaked at right angles to first streaks. Incubate at 37 C overnight. A clear zone between the streaks of staphylococci and streptococci is positive for *S. agalactiae* which is associated with bovine mastitis.

Capsular Swelling Test—A test for the diagnosis of an infection with *Haemophilus influenzae*. Diagnostic typing serum is mixed with an equal quantity of pathologic fluid on a hollow ground slide and is covered with a cover slip. Swelling of the capsule is a positive reaction.

Carbohydrate Fermentation Tests—Fermentation tests are used to identify microorganisms. The media for such tests are prepared by adding 0.5 per cent of the carbohydrate in question to a sugar-free medium, such as tryptose broth. Acid-base indicators, such as bromocresol purple or phenol red, are used to detect the formation of acid or, on occasion, alkali. Durham and Smith fermentation tubes are commonly used for the detection of gas. The carbohydrates more commonly used to differentiate microorganisms are glucose (dextrose), maltose, sucrose (saccharose), lactose, xylose, arabinose, rhamnose, starch, inulin, dextrin, and glycogen. Polyhydric alcohols used for analogous tests are glycerol (glycerin), sorbitol (sorbite), mannitol (mannite), dulcitol (dulcite), and inositol (inosite). Still other differentiating substances are the glycosides esculin and salicin.

Catalase Test—Place a drop of 25 to 30 per cent hydrogen peroxide on a clean glass slide and emulsify a test colony or a small amount of growth in it. Bubbling is catalase positive. Micrococci, staphylococci, and diphtheroids produce catalase, thus liberating oxygen from hydrogen peroxide causing the bubbling in the catalase test. Members of the tribe *Streptococceae* do not cause bubbling.

Cholera Red Reaction—*Vibrio comma* reduces nitrates to nitrites and concomitantly produces indole. When nitrites and indole are produced in a peptone medium, the addition of a few drops of concentrated sulfuric acid gives a cherry-red color. This test is not strictly specific for the cholera vibrio.

Citrate Utilization—Inoculate the surface of **Simmons citrate agar** lightly and, in addition, inoculate a tube containing nutrient agar. Incubate both tubes and examine daily. A positive test is indicated by growth, usually accompanied by a change in the color of the indicator to blue. If no growth occurs in the specimen tube, examine the control tube of nutrient agar for viability of the organism. The specimen tube must be inoculated lightly to minimize the transfer of nutrients along with the inoculum.

Cleaning Solution—A solution for cleaning glassware. Pour 1 liter of concentrated commercial sulfuric acid into 35 ml of a saturated aqueous solution of technical grade sodium dichromate. *Adhere strictly to the instruction of pouring the sulfuric acid into the water.*

Coagulase Test—A test used to determine the virulence of the *Staphylococcus aureus* group. Active coagulase-producing strains, when added to small amounts of diluted plasma (1 part plasma + 4 parts normal saline) and incubated at 37 C, cause clot formation within 2 to 3 hours. Food poisoning strains of staphylococci are generally coagulase positive.

Procedure. Add 0.5 to 1 ml of a 24-hour broth culture to 0.5 ml of citrated human blood plasma or to an equivalent solution of commercial dehydrated plasma. Place the test tube in a water bath at 37 C and read the tube at frequent intervals over a 3-hour period. Look at the tube again at the end of 6 or 8 hours, and, if necessary, place it in an incubator overnight. Observe it again at the end of 12 to 18 hours. The formation of a clot shows coagulase is present.

As an alternative procedure, transfer a typical opaque, golden-orange or white colony from the original plate in which the isolation was made to an agar slant and incubate for 12 hours or somewhat longer. Transfer 1 loopful to 0.5 to 1 ml of plasma and proceed with the method as detailed.

In a variation suggested by Levine, run the test on undiluted plasma and on plasma diluted with 2 volumes of physiological salt solution.

Slide Procedure. Arrange two slides side by side and put a drop of water on each with the aid of a 0.04-ml loop. Select a suspected colony from the original plate and make a homogeneous suspension on one slide with a minimum of spreading. Make a thin smear of the bacteria on the other slide for identification by staining. Mix a large loopful of fresh citrated human plasma on the first slide with the suspension of organisms. The production of clumping within 10 seconds, as viewed under the microscope, shows that a coagulase-positive strain of staphylococci is present.

Dimethyl-alpha-Naphthylamine Solution—A solution used with sulfanilic acid solution to test for the reduction of nitrates. Bacteria being investigated are incubated in broth containing 0.01 per cent sodium nitrate. After 48 hours or less, a drop of sulfanilic acid and a drop of dimethyl-alpha-naphthylamine solutions are added. A brown or red color is a positive test for the presence of nitrites. The solution consists of 100 ml glacial acetic acid, 250 ml water, and 2.1 ml dimethyl-alpha-naphthylamine.

***p*-Dimethylaminobenzaldehyde-trichloroacetic Acid Test**—See **Jacobs' indole test.**

Ehrlich-Bohme Indole Test—*Reagent.* Dissolve 2 g of *p*-dimethylaminobenzaldehyde in 190 ml of 95 per cent ethyl alcohol and add 20 ml of hydrochloric acid.

Procedure. Incubate a **tryptone broth** at 37 C for 4 or 5 days. Transfer 5 ml of the culture to a test tube. Run 1 ml of the reagent down the side of the tube. Run 1 ml of a 1 per cent aqueous solution of potassium persulfate down the side of the tube also. A red color forming after a few minutes is indicative of indole.

Ehrlich's Indole Reagent—Dissolve 4 g *p*-dimethylaminobenzaldehyde in a mixture of 80 ml concentrated hydrochloric acid and 380 ml 95 per cent ethyl alcohol.

Eijkman Test—A test for the presence of *Escherichia coli.* Buffered lactose broth tubes are inoculated with the suspected organisms and incubated at 45.5 C. *Escherichia coli* can produce gas at this temperature.

Feulgen Reaction—A reaction to test for the presence of desoxyribonucleic acid (DNA) found in nuclear materials. On hydrolysis of DNA, the aldehyde groups of the desoxyribose portions are left free. These impart a violet color to the reduced (decolorized) fuchsin in Schiff's reagent. The reaction is not wholly specific for nuclear material, since the cytoplasm membrane of many bacteria show that it and some feulgen positive bodies may be formed by coagulation resulting from hydrolysis.

Fibrinolysis Test—A test to demonstrate the production of streptokinase by beta-hemolytic streptococci. Dilute 0.2 ml of oxalated human plasma, prepared by adding 0.02 g of potassium oxalate to 10 ml of blood and centrifuging with 0.8 ml of physiological saline solution. Add 0.5 ml of an 18 to 24 hour, turbid, broth culture of the specimen streptococcus. Mix immediately, add 0.25 ml of a 0.25 per cent aqueous solution of calcium chloride, mix again, and place in a water bath at 37 C. A solid coagulum should form in 10 minutes. Examine the tube frequently to note liquefaction.

Formaldehyde Test for Biologics—A modification of the phenylhydrazine-ferricyanide method, sometimes termed the Schryver method, can be used for the estimation of formaldehyde in toxoids. A standard curve can be made for such determinations with a given photoelectric instrument so that it is not necessary to prepare new standards for each set of determinations.

Reagents. Potassium Ferricyanide Solution. Prepare a 5 per cent solution of potassium ferricyanide by dissolving 5 g of $K_3Fe(CN)_6$, analytical reagent, in water and make up to 100 ml of solution in a volumetric flask. This solution must be prepared fresh daily.

Phenylhydrazine Reagent. Dissolve 1.38 g of phenylhydrazine hydrochloride, C_6H_5-$NHNH_2 \cdot HCl$, in water and make up to 100 ml of solution in a volumetric flask. This solution must be prepared daily.

Standard Formaldehyde Solution. Transfer 8.2 ml of 37 per cent formalin solution to a liter volumetric flask and dilute to 1 liter with water. This solution contains approximately 3 mg/ml. The exact concentration should be estimated by the Ripper bisulfite method. The potassium sulfite solution for standardization should be prepared from potassium metabisulfite which should be standardized against standard iodine solution, standardized in turn against a primary potassium dichromate standard solution.

Procedure. Transfer 2 ml of each of the toxoid samples with the aid of pipettes to 10-ml volumetric flasks and make to volume with water. Mix thoroughly. Set up a series of half-ounce or 15-ml glass-stoppered vials, tubes, or bottles. Transfer a 1- or 2-ml aliquot of the diluted sample to each of these glass-stoppered vessels. Add 4 or 3 ml of water to bring the volume to 5 ml. Mix. Add 1 ml of 5 per cent potassium ferricyanide solution, restopper, and shake. Add 4 ml of concentrated hydrochloric acid with the aid of a burette or with a pipette equipped with a safety pipetter, restopper, and shake. Add 2 ml of 1.38 per cent phenylhydrazine hydrochloride solution, and shake thoroughly. Allow to stand for 15 minutes. Transfer the solution to the colorimeter tube and back to the reaction vessel several times to free the solution of all gas bubbles. Finally transfer to the colorimeter tube and read the magenta color produced in a Klett-Summerson colorimeter with the No. 54 green filter.

Procedure for Standard Curve. In order to make allowance for the coloring matter normally present in the media used for the production of the toxoid and in the crude bacterial filtrate, some crude bacterial toxin solution before conversion to toxoid should be added to known formaldehyde concentrations.

Dilute 1 ml of crude bacterial toxin solution to 10 ml with water in a volumetric flask. Transfer 2 ml of this diluted toxin solution to a series of 15-ml glass-stoppered bottles. Add 1, 2, or 3 ml of formaldehyde solution containing known concentrations of formaldehyde so that a series of formaldehyde concentrations at 10 to 15 microgram intervals covering the range from 10 to 120 micrograms is obtained. Proceed with the method as detailed.

Fungicidal (A.O.A.C.) Test *Trichophyton interdigitale* Variation—This test is applicable for water-miscible type fungicides used to disinfect inanimate objects.

The highest dilution which kills the spores within 10 minutes is commonly considered as the highest dilution that could be expected to disinfect inanimate surfaces contaminated with pathogenic fungi.

Culture Medium. Carry the fungus on agar slants containing glucose 2 per cent, Difco Neopeptone 1 per cent, agar 2 per cent, adjusted to pH between 6.1 and 6.3. Use the same culture medium in preparing cultures for obtaining conidial suspensions, and use a fluid medium of same nutrient composition but without agar to test the viability of conidia after exposure to the fungicide.

Test Organism. Use as test fungus a typical strain of *Trichophyton interdigitale* isolated from a case of dermatophytosis of the foot. Strain No. 640, A.T.C.C., is suitable. The strain must sporulate freely on artificial media, the presence of abundant conidia being manifested by a powdery appearance on the surface of a 10-day culture, particularly at the top of the agar slant. Confirm by microscopic examination. The conidia-bearing mycelium should peel easily from the surface of the glucose agar. Conidia of required resistance survive 10 minutes of exposure at 20 C to a phenol dilution of 1:60, but not to one of 1:45.

Care of Test Organism. Store the stock culture of fungus on glucose-agar slants at 2 to 5 C. At intervals not exceeding 3 months, transfer it to fresh agar slants, incubate 10 days at 25 to 30 C, and then place in storage at 2 to 5 C until the next transfer period. Do not use a culture that has been kept at or above room temperature for more than 10 days as a source of inoculum for culture purposes. Cultures may be kept at room temperature for the preservation of the strain and for the inoculation of cultures if transferred at intervals not exceeding 10 days.

Preparation of Conidial Suspension. Prepare Petri dish cultures by plating the inoculum at the center of the agar plate and by incubating the culture at 25 to 30 C for 10 but not more than 15 days. Remove the mycelial mats from the surface of five agar plate cultures by means of a sterile spatula or heavy flattened wire. Transfer to a heat sterilized glass tissue grinder (A. H. Thomas Company, size B) and macerate with 25 ml of sterile physiological sodium chloride solution (0.85 per cent NaCl); or to a heat sterilized Erlenmeyer flask containing 25 ml sterile saline with glass beads and agitate thoroughly.

Filter the suspension through sterile absorbent cotton to remove the hyphal elements. Estimate the density of the conidial suspension by counting in a hemacytometer and store at 2 to 10 C as the stock spore suspension (125 to 155 million conidia per ml) for periods up to 4 weeks for use in preparing the test suspensions of conidia. Standardize the test conidial suspensions as needed by diluting stock spore suspension with physiological salt solution so that it contains 5 million conidia per ml.

Procedure. Prepare dilutions of the fungicide. The test procedures are analogous to those used in the **phenol coefficient test.** Place 5-ml portions of each fungicide solution and of the phenol control solutions in 25 × 150-mm culture test tubes, arrange in order of ascending dilutions, and place the tubes in a 20 C water bath until the temperature of the bath is reached.

With a graduated pipette, place 0.5 ml of spore suspension in the first tube of fungicidal solution, shake, and immediately replace the tube in the water bath; 30 seconds later add 0.5 ml of the conidial suspension to a second tube. Repeat these manipulations at 30-second intervals for each fungicidal dilution.

If more convenient, run the test at 20-second intervals. After 5-, 10-, and 15-minute periods of exposure to the fungicide, remove a sample from each conidia-fungicide mixture with the 4-mm loop and place in 10 ml of the glucose broth.

To eliminate the risk of faulty results owing to the possibility of fungistatic action, make subtransfers from the initial glucose broth subculture tubes to fresh tubes of glucose broth, using the 4-mm loop prior to incubation, or make initial subcultures in glucose broth containing either 0.05 per cent sodium thioglycollate, 1.5 per cent iso-octylphenoxypolyethoxyethanol, or a mixture of 0.07 per cent lecithin (Azolectin) and 0.5 per cent "Tween 80" (sorbitan monooleate), whichever gives the lowest result. Incubate the inoculated tubes at 25 to 30 C. Read final results after 10 days; an indicative reading may be made in 4 days.

Gelatin Liquefaction—Used to demonstrate the presence of proteolytic enzymes, more specifically, the enzyme gelatinase. Inoculate nutrient gelatin by repeated stabbing with a straight needle bearing the culture under study and incubate along with an uninoculated tube at 35 C. Examine daily for several days or longer for liquefaction and the type of liquefaction by holding the specimen tube and the control tube in an ice bath. Replace both tubes in the indicator if liquefaction is not observed. The test can also be carried out at 20 to 22 C and liquefaction may be observed directly, but the reaction is much slower than that at higher incubation temperatures.

Gibbs' Reagent—2,6-Dibromoquinonechloroimide; 2,6-dibromo-1,4-benzoquinone-4-chloroimide, $O:C_6H_2Br_2:NCl$. Used as a reagent for the detection and estimation of phenol, particularly in the phosphatase test used to evaluate the efficiency of pasteurization.

Grieg Test—A test which is of diagnostic value for the detection of the *Vibrio comma* organism. A 3 per cent suspension of goat erythrocytes is mixed with an equal volume of a 24-hour broth culture of the organism and is read after 2 to 4 hours of incubation. The organism should be nonhemolytic.

Griess-Ilosvay Reagents—Sulfanilic acid and alpha-naphthylamine. See **nitrate reduction test.**

Hippurate-Hydrolysis Test—A test for *Streptococcus agalactiae*, a beta-hemolytic *Streptococcus* causing bovine mastitis. Dissolve 12 g ferric chloride, $FeCl_3 \cdot 6H_2O$, in 10 ml 2 per cent hydrochloric acid. Transfer 0.8 ml culture in sodium hippurate broth to a small test tube and add 0.2 ml of the reagent. Mix and observe after 10 to 15 minutes. A permanent precipitate of benzoic acid formed by the hydrolysis of the hippurate is a positive reaction.

Hydrogen Sulfide Production Tests—The production of hydrogen sulfide by bacteria can be demonstrated by use of **Kliegler's iron agar** or **triple sugar iron agar.** Such bacteria reduce sulfur-bearing compounds of the medium, such as peptones or sodium thiosulfate, with the formation of hydrogen sulfide which precipitates ferric sulfide, turning the medium brown or black. Hydrogen sulfide production may also be demonstrated by use of filter paper strips impregnated with lead acetate and suspended over the culture medium. The production of a black stain is positive.

IMViC Test—A series of tests employed to differentiate *Escherichia coli* from *Aerobacter aerogenes.* I stands for indole test; M for for methyl red test; V for Voges-Proskauer test; i for euphony; and C for growth in citrate medium.

Indole Test—Certain bacteria, for example, *Escherichia coli,* produce indole during their metabolism. This can be used as a differential test. Shake the culture to be tested with 1 ml of xylol or ether, allow the layers to separate, add a few ml of **Ehrlich's, Kovac's,** or **Jacobs'** indole reagent carefully so that it forms a layer between the medium and the xylol or ether. A pink coloration is positive for indole. The solvent extracts the indole, making the test more sensitive and more specific.

Jacobs' Indole Test—The following can detect directly 1 microgram of indole in 10 ml of test solution or 1 part of indole in 10 million of solution; or, by an extraction modification, it can detect 1 microgram in 100 ml of test solution or 1 part per 100,-000,000.

Reagents. (A) Dissolve 10 g of trichloroacetic acid in 30 ml of chloroform. Add 2 g of *p*-dimethylaminobenzaldehyde. Transfer to a separatory funnel and saturate by shaking with concentrated hydrochloric acid. This reagent is stable for at least 2 months. (B) Dissolve 10 g of trichloroacetic acid in 30 ml of chloroform. Add 2 g of *p*-dimethylaminobenzaldehyde. Add 0.5 ml of acetic anhydride and 2 drops of concentrated sulfuric acid. This reagent is stable for at least 2 days. It is more sensitive than the reagent (A) above.

Detection. Transfer 10 ml of the culture or 10 ml of the sample solution to a separatory funnel. Add 2 ml of chloroform. Shake vigorously and allow to stand for 5 minutes. Swirl to make sure the chloroform layer collects at the bottom. Filter through a filter wetted with chloroform into a small test tube or insert a pledget of cotton into the stem of the separatory funnel and draw off the chloroform layer directly into a test tube. Add 2 drops of either reagent listed above and hold in warm water (50 C) for 0.5 minute. A pink, to rose or red, color is positive for indole. A straw color or light yellow is negative for indole.

Instead of the chloroform extractant, 2 ml of a mixture of equal volumes of chloroform and carbon tetrachloride may be used.

Determination. Shake out twice with chloroform or with the mixed solvent. Filter into a colorimeter tube or a 10-ml volumetric flask as directed above. Make up to volume with the mixed solvent or chloroform and compare against standards treated the same way.

Notes. Only for very low concentrations of indole is the chloroform extraction necessary. In most instances, especially in cultures incubated for 24 hours, the reagents may be added directly to the culture to be tested. The color forms at the interface or is extracted by mild shaking and is found in the bottom chloroform layer.

The addition of 5 ml of acetic anhydride

to reagent (A) does not seem to alter its properties, but if acetic acid is used instead of hydrochloric acid, it does not give the reaction. Dilution with half its volume of carbon tetrachloride reduces its sensitivity. Reagent (B) without acetic anhydride will work only if freshly prepared. It deteriorates rapidly.

With low concentrations of indole of the order of 1 to 0.1 microgram per ml of chloroform, the pink color fades out rather rapidly with reagent (A). With higher concentrations, the color does not fade out even on standing 24 hours. The color formed with reagent (B) does not fade even after standing for hours. When carbon tetrachloride is used as part of the solvent mixture, the color comes up fast but fades out rapidly. It lasts longest with reagent (B) but is weak in intensity.

The reagent is affected by water; consequently when it is shaken with a culture or with aqueous solutions it loses in sensitivity. For greatest sensitivity it is necessary to use the extraction method as detailed above.

Jacobs' Method for Alum in Toxoids—This method is based on the solution of the alum-precipitated biological in a dilute acid-citrate solution, the buffering of the mixture with a tartrate buffer, the neutralization of the test mixture with barium hydroxide, sequestration of the aluminum by use of potassium fluoride with consequent liberation of 3 moles of alkali hydroxide for every mole of aluminum.

$$Al^{+++} + 3OH^- \rightarrow Al(OH)_3$$
$$Al(OH)_3 + 6KF \rightarrow AlF_3 \cdot 3KF + 3KOH$$

and finally estimation of the liberated alkali acidimetrically.

Reagents. Potassium Fluoride, 30 Per Cent Solution. Dissolve 300 g of reagent grade potassium fluoride in water and make up to 1 liter with water. Store in a wax-lined bottle.

Potassium Sodium Tartrate, 30 Per Cent Solution. Dissolve 300 g of reagent grade Rochelle salt in water and make up to 1 liter with water.

Barium Hydroxide, Saturated Solution. Heat 60 g of barium hydroxide, $BaOH \cdot 6H_2O$, or 30 g of BaOH in 1 liter of water to boiling, allow to cool, and filter into a stock bottle.

Hydrochloric Acid, 0.3 *N*. Prepare an approximately 0.3 *N* hydrochloric acid solution in the conventional manner but standardize it in terms of aluminum wire as described below.

Weigh out accurately as closely as possible 26.95 g of pure aluminum wire and dissolve in 200 ml of 1 *N* carbonate-free sodium hydroxide solution. Make the solution just acid with hydrochloric acid (1:1) and boil gently to expel carbon dioxide. Dilute to 1 liter. Standardize aliquots according to the procedure detailed in the method.

Hydrochloric Acid, 0.03 *N*. Prepare a 0.03 *N* hydrochloric acid solution from the 0.3 *N* hydrochloric acid in the conventional manner. Standardize against the standard alum solution or in a manner similar to that given above.

Standard Alum Solution. Weigh out accurately 4.74 g of reagent grade potassium aluminum sulfate, $KAl(SO_4)_2 \cdot 12H_2O$, minimum assay 99.5 per cent, dissolve in water, and dilute with water to make 1 liter. Each milliliter of this solution contains 4.74 mg of alum.

Sodium Citrate, 0.1 Per Cent Solution. Dissolve 1 g of reagent grade sodium citrate in about 500 ml of water, add 8 ml of concentrated hydrochloric acid, mix thoroughly, and make up to 1 liter with water.

Preparation of Sample. Samples customarily vary in volume from 25 to 100 ml. Take an aliquot, after shaking the sample to distribute the precipitate as evenly as possible, and transfer to a glass-stoppered flask. Add an equal volume of the 1 per cent acid-citrate solution. Allow the mixture to stand after shaking until it clears up and becomes brilliant. About 15 minutes is generally required for this. The clear solution is now ready for analysis.

Samples to which citrate solution has already been added are ready to be tested, if they are in complete solution.

Procedure. Transfer 20 ml of the prepared solution of alum-precipitated toxoid in acid-sodium citrate solution to a 125-ml Erlenmeyer flask. Add 3 drops of phenolphthalein indicator solution and 20 ml of 30 per cent potassium sodium tartrate solution. Mix gently and neutralize with saturated barium hydroxide solution to a definite pink end point. Add 20 ml of 30 per cent potassium fluoride solution and mix. Allow the test solution to stand for 5 minutes. Titrate with the standardized 0.03 *N* hydrochloric acid until the pink coloration is discharged and remains discharged for 30 seconds.

To calculate the milligrams of alum per milliliter, multiply the milliliters of 0.03 *N* hydrochloric acid used by 4.74 or the equivalent factor and divide by the volume of toxoid taken from the analysis (in this instance 10 ml of toxoid in 20 ml of the prepared test solution).

Jacobs' Microkjeldahl Method for Biologics—In this method, which is a modification of the Pregl-Parnas-Wagner method, protein and other forms of organic nitrogen are converted to ammonia and fixed as ammonium sulfate by digestion with sulfuric acid. Potassium sulfate is used to raise the temperature of the digestion mixture, and copper sulfate is used as the catalyst. The ammonia formed is liberated by the addition of sodium hydroxide solution, is stream-distilled, trapped in standard hydrochloric acid solution, and the excess hydrochloric acid is estimated titrimetrically with standard sodium hydroxide solution, or the ammonia is trapped in boric acid solution and the amount is determined by direct titration with standard hydrochloric acid.

The apparatus is that of Parnas and Wagner, or the modification of this apparatus by Shepard and Jacobs in which a steam escape is included in the steam generator.

Procedure. Dilute an aliquot portion of the material being analyzed, if necessary, to a known volume in a volumetric flask, so that the amount of nitrogen will be of the order of 0.5 mg/ml. Transfer 1 ml of this solution to a microkjeldahl digestion flask. With the aid of a burette or similar device, add 1 ml of concentrated sulfuric acid and 1 ml of a 4 per cent copper sulfate solution, prepared by dissolving 4 g of $CuSO_4 \cdot 5H_2O$ in water and diluting to 100 ml. Add 1 g of potassium sulfate, mix, and digest on a digestion oven. Raise the heat slowly, boil vigorously, and after the material has been digested, as evidenced by a clear, straw yellow or light green color, reduce and cut off the heat. This process generally takes about 20 minutes. If the mixture does not clear in this time, reduce the heat, carefully add 2 to 3 drops of 30 per cent hydrogen peroxide solution, and then continue heating for 5 to 10 minutes. Allow to cool, add 4 ml of water, and stir to dissolve the salts.

Add 7.0 ml of 0.01 *N* hydrochloric acid, accurately measured, to a 25-ml flask and add a trace of methyl red indicator solution. Allow the water in the steam generator to boil gently, remove the clamp from the line leading from the steam generator to the vapor vessel, and open the pinch clamp or stopcock at the bottom of the steam vessel so that the steam can escape. Transfer the digest from the microkjeldahl digestion flask to the distillation tube through the small funnel. Wash out the microkjeldahl digestion flask with two 2-ml portions of distilled water and add these washings to the distillation tube. Place the receiving flask under the condenser so that the tip of the silver tube condenser is below the standard acid. With the aid of a pipette, add 7 ml of 30 per cent sodium hydroxide solution to the mixture in the distillation tube through the small funnel.

Close the stopcocks or pinch clamps of the small funnel, the vapor vessel, and the steam escape, if one is used, thus compelling the steam to pass through the distillation tube. Distill for exactly 3 minutes. Lower the receiving flask so that the tip of the condenser is about 1 cm above the surface of the distillate. Continue the distillation for another minute. Rinse the tip of the condenser tube with a few drops of water. Add another trace of methyl red indicator solution, if this is necessary. Titrate with standard 0.01 *N* sodium hydroxide solution. One milliliter of standard hydrochloric acid (0.01 *N*) is equivalent of 0.14 mg of nitrogen. Run a blank and subtract the blank from the volume of standard hydrochloric acid used.

Instead of using a known volume of standard hydrochloric acid, trap the ammonia being distilled in 10 ml of *cold* 2 per cent boric acid solution. Proceed with th the method as detailed, but titrate the boric acid solution directly with 0.01 *N* hydrochloric acid. Run a blank and subtract this from the volume of standard hydrochloric acid used.

Procedure with Single Reagent. The method, as detailed above, and the washing procedure and apparatus of Shepard and Jacobs are used, with the exception that 9 ml of the prepared digestion reagent is used in place of the 1 ml of sulfuric acid and the weighed amount of potassium sulfate and copper sulfate.

Because of the increase in volume of the material being digested, attributable to the volume of reagent added, it is necessary to heat the mixture cautiously to prevent excessive frothing while the water is being driven off. Small sections of melting-point tubes or glass beads may be used to avoid bumping and decrease frothing, but care should be exercised not to permit them to get into the distillation tube.

To prepare the single reagent, dissolve 6 g of recrystallized copper sulfate, $CuSO_4 \cdot 5H_2O$, and 105 g of potassium sulfate, K_2SO_4, in 600 ml of water by bringing the mixture to boiling. Cool approximately to room temperature and cautiously add 150 ml of concentrated sulfuric acid. Cool again to room temperature, transfer to a graduated cylinder, and make up to a total volume of 900 ml.

Kolmer Saline Solution—Dissolve 8.5 g of dry, reagent grade sodium chloride and 0.1 g magnesium sulfate in water and dilute to 1 liter.

Kovac's Reagent—A reagent used to test for the presence of indole. It consists of a mixture of 75 ml *n*-amyl alcohol, 25 ml concentrated hydrochloric acid, and 5 g *p*-dimethylaminobenzaldehyde.

Krumwiede-Valentine Method—A method to determine the type of pneumococcus present in sputum. It consists of layering the supernatant of centrifuged sputum with type sera in test tubes. Tubes are placed in a water bath for several minutes at 50 to 55 C. A contact ring indicates the type of pneumococcus present.

Lauryl Sulfate Test—A solubility test for pneumococci with lauryl sulfate sodium. The pneumococci are completely dissolved in a few minutes.

Litmus Milk Reactions—The microbiological reactions of litmus milk are useful for the differentiation of microorganisms, for the results may indicate (1) lactose fermentation, (2) reduction of the litmus indicator, (3) coagulation of the milk protein, and (4) digestion of the casein. Acidity attributable to lactose fermentation or alkalinity is shown respectively by the red or blue color of the indicator; reduction is shown by its decolorization; coagulation is indicated by clotting of the milk, that is, curd formation, and may be due to the formation of acid, producing a firm curd that does not shrink, or to the action of a rennet-type enzyme which produces a soft contraction clot not accompanied by marked acidity; digestion of the casein, shown by partial or complete clearing of the milk, may or may not be preceded by coagulation.

Stormy fermentation is descriptive of the reaction in milk produced by an organism, such as *Clostridium perfringens*, characterized by rapid coagulation followed by active gas production which tears up the clot. Some strains of *C. perfringens* do this slowly.

Mercuric Chloride—$HgCl_2$, mercury bichloride, corrosive sublimate. A disinfectant whose activity is deemed to be due to the coagulation of the cell protoplasm. Contains 73.9 per cent mercury.

Mercuric Chloride Solution—A reagent consisting of 0.1 per cent mercuric chloride in water.

Methylene Blue Reduction Milk Test—A test for determining the quality of milk, by determining the reducing activity of the bacteria. The greater the number of bacteric present, the greater the rate of oxygen consumption by respiration, and consequently the greater the rate of methylene blue decolorization. There are 4 grades of milk on this basis. I. Not decolorized in 8 hours = excellent. II. Decolorized is less than 8 but not less than 6 hours = good. III. Decolorized in less than 6 but not less than 2 hours = fair. IV. Decolorized in less than 2 hours = poor. Place 1 ml methylene blue solution in a regular test tube and add 10 ml of milk to be tested. Place loosely stoppered tubes in a 35.5 C water bath and bring to temperature within 10 minutes. Slowly invert tubes 3 times and replace in water bath. Observe tubes for decoloration after 30 minutes and at hourly intervals thereafter.

Methyl Red Test—A test used to differentiate *Escherichia coli* from *Aerobacter aerogenes.* Incubate an inoculum in buffered glucose-peptone broth at 37 C for 3 to 5 days. To 5 ml culture, add 5 drops methyl red solution. A red color is positive for *E. coli,* whereas a yellow color is indicative of *A. aerogenes.*

Nadi Reagent—A mixture of solutions of dimethyl-*p*-phenylenediamine and alphanaphthol. The reagent is changed to indophenol blue when indophenoloxidase is present.

Nessler's Reagent, Microbiological Modification—A reagent for the detection of ammonia. Dissolve 85 g sodium hydroxide in 800 ml water. Add 68 g Nessler's salt to 100 ml water. Mix both solutions and add sufficient water to make 1 liter. Filter paper turning red after being dipped into the reagent and exposed to the vapor of a heated culture is a positive test.

Neutral Red (Dubos and Middlebrook) Cytochemical Test—A procedure for determining the virulence of mycobacteria. Transfer a loop of culture from a solid medium or 1 ml from a liquid medium to a 15-ml conical centrifuge tube, centrifuge, and wash twice with 5 ml of 50 per cent methyl alcohol. Suspend the bacteria in 5 ml of an aqueous solution of 5 per cent sodium chloride and 1 per cent of sodium barbiturate or other equivalent alkaline buffer solution. Add 0.2 ml of 0.05 per cent aqueous neutral red indicator solution. Allow to stand for 1 hour at room temperature. Virulent strains bind the dye and stain from light pink to deep red. Avirulent strains remain colorless. The color of the suspending buffer solution remains yellow to amber.

Nitrate Reduction Test—Certain species of bacteria reduce nitrate to nitrite. Reagent solution 1 is prepared by dissolving 8 g sulfanilic acid in 1 liter 5 *N* acetic acid. Solution 2 is prepared by dissolving 5 g dimethyl-alpha-naphthylamine in 1 liter of 5 *N* acetic acid. To the test culture (1 to 5 days) add 0.1 ml of solution 1 and swirl. Add solution 2 drop by drop. The formation of a pink to red color is positive; no color change is negative. A test check for the presence of residual nitrate by addition of zinc is recommended because some organisms use both nitrite and nitrate.

Nitrate Reduction Test (Jacobs' Modification)—The common reagents used for nitrate reduction test are the Griess-Ilosvay reagents. The following reagents are better. Prepare powders weighing 100 mg containing 4 mg sulfanilamide, 1 mg *N*-(1-naphthyl)-ethylenediamine dihydrochloride, and 95 mg tartaric acid from a master batch containing 1000 times these amounts. Dissolve a powder in 10 ml of water and add the reagent drop by drop to the test culture. A pink to rose is a positive test. The powder lasts for a year. Similar proportions of sulfanilamide dissolved in acetic acid and *N*-(1-naphthyl)-ethylenediamine dihydrochloride to those detailed in the **nitrate reduction test** can be used.

Nitroso-Indole Reaction or Test—See **cholera red reaction.**

Oxford Cup Method—A method for testing the sensitivity of microorganisms to chemotherapeutic agents.

Procedure. Spread a broth culture of the test organism over the surface of an agar plate and allow to dry for 1 hour in an incubator. Place short cylinders cut from glass tubing on the agar and fill each cylinder with a test dilution of the chemotherapeutic substance or material. Incubate the plate for 12 to 16 hours at 37 C. A circular zone surrounding the cylinder where the bacteria did not grow shows that the organism is sensitive to the chemotherapeutic agent.

Oxidase Test—A diagnostic test for *Neisseria,* used to select colonies for isolation and identification of gonococcus and meningococcus infections. Plate suspicious material on chocolate agar. Flood plate with 1 per cent aqueous solution of dimethyl or tetramethyl-*p*-phenylenediamine hydrochloride and pour off. Positive colonies will turn pink, then purple to black. The test is not specific, since other oxidase-producing organisms will also give a positive test. The organisms are not killed by the test and may be subcultured.

Phenol Coefficient (A.O.A.C. Method) *Salmonella typhosa* Variation—A test designed to evaluate the efficacy of a specimen disinfectant against a standard phenol. The Association of Official Agricultural Chemists variation of the phenol coefficient test is applicable to the testing of disinfectants miscible with water that act against bacteria in a manner somewhat comparable to phenol and that do not exert bacteriostatic effects that cannot be overcome by one of the three subculture media specified in the method.

Apparatus. Water Bath. An insulated, relatively deep water bath with cover having at least 10 well-spaced holes which admit medication tubes (plug test tubes) but not their lips, and capable of maintaining a temperature of 20 C or 37 C for the length of the test.

Racks. Any convenient style of rack may be used. Blocks of wood (the size depending somewhat on the incubator used) with deep holes are satisfactory. The holes should be well spaced to ensure rapid manipulation of tubes. It is also convenient to have them large enough to admit medication tubes while dilutions are made.

Glassware. Sterilize all glassware 2 hours in hot air oven at 180 C. Place pipettes in closed metal containers before sterilizing.

Transfer Loop. Make a 4-mm internal diameter, single loop at one end of 2 to 3 inches of platinum or platinum alloy wire No. 23 B & S gauge. Place the other end in a suitable holder, such as a glass or aluminum rod. Bend the loop at a 30 degree angle with the stem.

Culture Media and Cultures. Nutrient Broth. Boil 10 g of Armour peptone (using the quality specially prepared for testing disinfectants), 5 g of Difco beef extract, and 5 g sodium chloride in 1 liter of water for 20 minutes, dilute to volume with water, and adjust the pH to 6.8, using bromothymol blue indicator to gave a dark green color. Filter through paper, place 10-ml aliquots in 20 × 150-mm bacteriological test tubes, plug with cotton, and sterilize at 121 C for 20 minutes. This broth is used for daily transfers of test cultures.

Nutrient Agar. Disperse 1.5 per cent Bacto agar in nutrient broth and adjust to pH 7.2 to 7.4 (blue-green color with bromothymol blue), tube, plug with cotton, sterilize, and slant.

Subculture Media. Use (1), (2) or (3), whichever gives lowest result.

(1) Nutrient broth prepared as described.

(2) Fluid thioglycollate medium U.S.P. XV.

(3) "Letheen broth": dissolve 0.7 g lecithin (Azolectin) and 5.0 g sorbitan monooleate ("Tween 80") in 400 ml of hot water and boil until clear; add 600 ml of a solution of 10.0 g Armour peptone, 5.0 g of Difco beef extract, and 5 g sodium chloride in water, and boil 10 minutes; adjust with *N* sodium hydroxide solution and/or *N* hydrochloric acid to pH 7.0 ± 0.2 and filter through coarse paper; tube in 10-ml quantities in 20 × 150-mm bacteriological test tubes, plug with cotton, and sterilize at 121 C for 20 minutes.

Medium (2) will usually give lowest results with oxidizing products and products formulated with toxic compounds containing certain heavy metals like mercury.

Medium (3) will usually give lowest results with products containing cationic surfaces active materials like quaternary ammonium compounds.

Test Organism. Use Hopkins strain 26 of *Salmonella typhosa* (Zopf) Weldin, F.D.A., A.T.C.C. No. 6539. Maintain the stock culture on agar slants by monthly transfers. Incubate each new stock transfer 2 days at 37 C; then store at room temperature. Inoculate a tube of nutrient broth from the stock culture and make at least 4 consecutive daily transfers (not more than 30) in nutrient broth incubating at 37 C, before using the culture for testing (if only one daily transfer has been missed it is not necessary to repeat the 4 consecutive transfers). Use 22- to 26-hour cultures of the organism grown in nutrient broth at 37 C in the test. Shake the culture and allow to settle for 15 minutes before using.

Reagent Standard Phenol. Use U.S.P. XV phenol having a congealing point of 40 C or higher. Prepare an accurate 5 per cent stock solution. Keep in well-stoppered amber bottles in a cool place, protected from light. Standardize with 0.1 *N* potassium- or sodium bromide-bromate solution. Make dilutions of 1 in 90 and 1 in 100 for the test with S. *typhosa* directly into the medication tubes.

Test Disinfectant or Surface-Active Agent. Prepare a 1 per cent aqueous solution, or other convenient dilution of the material under test, in a 100-ml glass-stoppered cylinder graduated in 1-ml divisions and subsequently make the final dilutions, from the 1 per cent stock dilution, directly into medication tubes and remove all excess over 5 ml. The range of dilutions should cover the killing limits of disinfectant in 5 to 15 minutes and should at same time be sufficiently close for accuracy.

Procedure. Place these tubes, containing 5 ml each of the final dilutions of disinfectant and of phenol, into the water bath at 20 C and allow to stand for 5 minutes. Add 0.5 ml of the test culture to each of dilutions at time intervals corresponding to intervals at which the transfers are to be made. For instance, by the time ten tubes have been seeded at 30-second intervals, 4.5 minutes will have elapsed, and a 30-second interval intervenes before the transference to the subcultures is started. Add the culture from a graduated pipette of sufficient capacity to seed all of the tubes in any one set.

As a precautionary measure, loosely plug the pipette with cotton at mouth end before sterilizing it. The temperature of the culture should be approximately that of the water bath before it is added.

Hold the medication tubes in a slanting position after removal from bath during inoculation, insert the pipette to just above the surface of the disinfectant test solution and run in the culture without allowing the pipette tip to touch the disinfectant.

After adding the culture, shake the tubes gently but thoroughly to ensure an even distribution of bacteria, and replace in the water bath; 5 minutes after seeding the first medication tube, transfer 1 loopful of the mixture of culture and diluted disinfectant from the medication tube to a corresponding subculture tube.

To facilitate the transfer of uniform drops of medication mixture, hold the tube at a 60 degree angle, and withdraw the loop so that the plane of the loop is parallel with the surface of the liquid. After 30 seconds, transfer a loopful from second medication tube to second subculture tube and continue this process for each successive dilution; 5 minutes after making the first transfer begin the second set of transfers for the 10-minute period, and finally repeat for the 15-minute period.

Gently shake the medication tubes before taking each interval loop subsample for transfer to the subculture medium. Before each transfer, heat the loop to redness in a flame and flame the mouth of every tube. Sterilize the loop immediately after each transfer (before replugging tubes) to allow time for cooling.

Use care in transferring and seeding to prevent the pipette or needle from touching the sides or mouth of the medication tube, and make sure that no cotton threads adhere to inner sides or mouths of the tubes.

Incubate the subcultures 48 hours at 37 C and read the results. Thoroughly shake the individual subculture tubes before incubation. A macroscopic examination is usually adequate. Occasionally a 3-day incubation period, an agar streak, macroscopic examination, or agglutination with antityphoid serum may be necessary to determine feeble growth or suspected contamination.

Calculation. Express the results in terms of phenol coefficient number, or the highest dilution killing the test organism in 10 minutes but not in 5 minutes, whichever most accurately reflects the germicidal value of disinfectant. The "phenol coefficient" is the number obtained by dividing the numerical value of the greatest dilution (denominator of fraction expressing dilution) of disinfectant capable of killing S. *typhosa* in 10 minutes but not in 5 minutes by the greatest dilution of phenol showing the same results.

Example:

Disinfectant (*X*)	*5 min*	*10 min*	*15 min*
1-300	0	0	0
1-325	+	0	0
1-350	+	0	0
1-375	+	+	0
1-400	+	+	+
Phenol			
1-90	+	0	0
1-100	+	+	+

Phenol coefficient would be $\frac{350}{90} = 3.89$.

The test is satisfactory only when the phenol control gives one of the following readings:

Phenol	*5 min*	*10 min*	*15 min*
1-90	+ or 0	+ or 0	0
1-100	+	+	+ or 0

If none of the dilutions of disinfectant shows growth in 5 minutes and killing in 10 minutes, estimate the hypothetical dilution only when any 3 consecutive dilutions show the following results: first, no growth in 5 minutes; second, growth in 5 and 10 minutes but not in 15 minutes; and third, growth in 5, 10, and 15 minutes.

Example:

Disinfectant (X)	*5 min*	*10 min*	*15 min*
1-300	0	0	0
1-350	+	+	+
1-400	+	+	+
Phenol			
1-90	0	0	0
1-100	+	+	0

Phenol coefficient would be $\frac{325}{95} = 3.42$.

To avoid giving the impression of fictitious accuracy, calculate the phenol coefficient to nearest tenth (0.1). Thus, in the examples cited above, the phenol coefficient would be reported as 3.9 and 3.4, instead of 3.89 and 3.42.

It is to be noted that the commonly accepted criterion that disinfectants for general use be at a dilution equivalent in germicidal efficiency to 5 per cent phenol against S. *typhosa* through the use of the calculation of multiplying 20 × S. *typhosa* coefficient to determine the number of parts of water in which 1 part of the germicide should be dissolved or dispersed is subject to confirmation by the **use-dilution method.** Where this criterion is found invalid, the highest dilution that will kill in the **use-dilution method** should be used as the index to the higher dilution for employment in practical disinfection work.

Phenol Coefficient (A.O.A.C. Method) *Staphylococcus aureus* Variation—Perform the test as directed in the **phenol coefficient (A.O.A.C. Method) *Salmonella typhosa* variation,** but change the phenol dilutions and the test organisms. Use a temperature of 20 C unless a different temperature is specified. Use a culture of *Staphylococcus aureus* F.D.A. 209, A.T.C.C. No. 6538 (formerly known as *Micrococcus pyogenes* var. *aureus*), having at least a resistance to phenol at 20 C indicated by following:

Phenol	*5 min*	*10 min*	*15 min*
1-60	+	0	0
1-70	+	+	+

and at 37 C must be as follows:

Phenol	*5 min*	*10 min*	*15 min*
1-80	+	0	0
1-90	+	+	+ or 0

Phenol Solution—A solution consisting of 50.0 g crystalline phenol and water. Melt the crystals for weighing (use caution in handling) and add sufficient water to the phenol to make 1000 ml of solution. This is considered a 5 per cent solution.

Phosphatase Pasteurization Test, Rapid Method—Mix 0.5 ml milk with 10 ml sodium veronal-disodium phenylphosphate buffer solution and incubate at 37 C for 10 minutes. Add 4 drops of 2,6-dibromoquinonechloroimide solution (100 mg in 25 ml absolute alcohol) and, after 5 minutes for color development in the mixture, shake out with 3 ml of a solvent, such as isobutyl alcohol, *n*-butyl alcohol, or amyl alcohol. A blue color is developed in improperly pasteurized milk.

Potassium Tellurite Solution—K_2TeO_3. Soluble in water forming an alkaline solution. A 0.01 per cent solution inhibits most gram-negative bacteria but permits the growth of streptococci and other gram-positive bacteria. In 0.03 per cent solution, most streptococci are inhibited, but staphylococci and corynebacteria are still able to grow. Thus, tellurite can be used for the isolation of *Corynebacterium diphtheriae.*

Reductase Test—A test to determine the quality of milk employing the dye methylene blue thiocyanate. One ml dye solution (1:300,000) is added to 10 ml milk and incubated. Observation of the disappearance of the blue color gives the standard quality of milk. Reading times are 30 minutes, 1 hour, and later. See **resazurin reduction test** and **methylene blue reduction milk test.**

Resazurin Reduction Test—A reduction test used to determine the quality of milk employing the dye resazurin. Resazurin permits readings of degrees of reduction in contrast to methylene blue which changes from blue to colorless.

Schaudinn's Solution—A solution used for fixing fecal smears. It consists of a saturated solution of mercuric chloride, 35 ml of 95 per cent alcohol, and 5 ml of glacial acetic acid.

Schiff Reagent—A reagent used in Endo's medium for the detection of aldehyde groups. Also used in Feulgen reaction test. It consists of 1 g basic fuchsin and 200 ml water. After filtering, add 20 ml *N* hydrochloric acid and 2 g anhydrous sodium bisulfite. Stopper and let stand 24 hours in the dark.

Sporicidal (A.O.A.C.) Test—This test is applicable to germicides to determine the presence or absence of sporicidal activity and the potential effectiveness in disinfecting against specified spore forming bacteria.

Apparatus. Water Bath and Racks. Use the water bath and racks specified in the **phenol coefficient test.**

Glassware. Pyrex lipped test tubes 25 × 150 mm; 100-ml stoppered cylinders graduated in 1-ml divisions; 15 × 110-mm Petri dishes containing mats of two sheets of filter paper. Sterilize all glassware for 2 hours in an air oven at 180 C.

Transfer Loop and Hook. Use the transfer loop and needle described in the **use-dilution (A.O.A.C.) test.**

Suture Loop Carrier. Prepare standard loops from a spool of size 3 surgical silk suture by wrapping the silk around an ordinary pencil three times, slipping the coil so formed off the end of pencil, and holding it firmly with thumb and index finger while passing another piece of suture through coil, then knotting and tying it securely. Shear off the end of the coil and knot the suture to within 1/16 inch. This should provide an overall length of about 2.5 inches of suture in a 2-loop coil that can be conveniently handled in ordinary aseptic transfer manipulations.

Culture Media. Soil Extract Nutrient Broth. Extract 1 pound of garden soil in 1 liter of water, filter several times through S & S No. 588 paper, and dilute to a liter. The pH of this broth should be 5.2 or higher. Add 5 g of Difco beef extract, 5 g of sodium chloride, and 10 g of Armour peptone, boil for 20 minutes, adjust to pH 6.9, filter through paper, dilute to 1 liter, dispense into 20 × 150-mm test tubes, plug with cotton, and sterilize at 121 C for 20 minutes. Use this broth for propagation of the test culture of bacilli.

Nutrient Agar. Prepare as directed in the **phenol coefficient test.** Use slants of this medium for maintaining the stock culture of bacilli.

Modified Fluid Thioglycollate Medium U.S.P. XV. Prepare as directed in the section on culture media and add 20 ml *N* sodium hydroxide solution to each liter prior to dispensing for sterilization. Use this medium for subculturing spores exposed to constant boiling hydrochloric acid. For spores exposed to unknown germicides, use fluid thioglycollate medium U.S.P. XV.

Soil Extract–Meat–Egg Medium. Add 1.5 g Bacto Egg-Meat Medium dehydrated to 20 × 150-mm test tubes, then add 10 ml garden soil extract, plug with cotton, and sterilize at 121 C for 20 minutes. Use this medium for the propagation of test cultures of clostridia and maintain stock cultures of species of this genus.

Test Organisms. Any species of clostridia or bacilli will be adequate. Strains of *Bacillus subtilis* and *Clostridium sporogenes* may be employed in routine evaluations, but the method is applicable for use with strains of *B. anthracis, C. tetani,* or other species.

Reagent. Constant Boiling Hydrochloric Acid. Use for determining the resistance of the dried spores. The exact hydrochloric acid concentration may vary slightly, depending on the atmospheric pressure. At 780 mm the concentration will be 20.17 per cent; at 130 mm it will be 20.29 per cent.

Procedure. Grow all bacilli in soil extract nutrient broth and all clostridia in soil extract–meat–egg medium. Inoculate the tubes, using one loop of the stock culture, and incubate for 72 hours at 37 C. Place the supply of suture loop carriers in Petri dishes matted with filter paper and sterilize at 121 C for 20 minutes. Use new loops for each test.

Place five sterile loops in each 72-hour culture, shake vigorously, and allow to stand for 15 minutes. Withdraw the loops, place in sterile matted Petri dishes, and allow to dry for 22 to 26 hours at room temperature. Make all suture loop transfers with the 2- to 3-inch nichrome wire hook, flamed in the conventional manner between transfers.

Transfer 10 ml of constant boiling hydrochloric acid into a sterile cotton plugged 25 × 150-mm lipped test tube. Place the tube in a 20 C constant temperature water bath and allow to come to temperature. Transfer rapidly four dried, contaminated loop suture carriers to the acid tube. Transfer the remaining dried, contaminated suture loop to the tube of the thioglycollate subculture medium, as a viability control.

After 5, 10, 20, and 30 minutes, withdraw the individual loops from the acid and transfer to individual tubes of thioglycollate subculture medium. Rotate each tube vigorously for 20 seconds, and incubate for 1 week at 37 C. Reliable readings can usually, but not always, be made after 48 hours of incubation.

If it appears that pH of subculture medium has been reduced by carried-over acid to a level below that which will permit the growth of the test organism, transfer the loops to fresh tubes of medium and reincubate for second 7-day period. The test spores should resist the hydrochloric acid for at least 5 minutes and many will resist the acid for the full 30-minute period and longer.

If this test shows that resistant dried spores are present (vegetative cells will not show measurable resistance against constant boiling hydrochloric acid), use duplicate lots of dried, contaminated suture loops in lots of five, drained and dried at same time and held at room temperature for 7 days for tests on the germicide to be investigated for sporicidal activity. Spores dried and held under these conditions will retain their resistance for this period of time or longer.

Place 10 ml of disinfectant at the dilution recommended for use or under investigation in a 25 × 150-mm lipped test tube. Place the tube in the 20 C water bath and allow to come to temperature.

Select a set of five dried, contaminated suture loops shown to be carrying resistant spores of the culture for use in tests on each dilution of the disinfectant. Transfer one suture loop immediately to a tube of thioglycollate subculture medium as the viability control. Then transfer the remaining four loops to the dilution of disinfectant in the water bath. Remove the individual loops at four selected time intervals, for example, 10 minutes, 30 minutes, 1 hour, and 2 hours, transferring them to individual tubes of thioglycollate subculture medium. Agitate all the tubes thoroughly and incubate for 1 week at 37 C.

If no growth occurs, and if there is reason to suspect that the lack of growth may be due to bacteriostasis, transfer each loop to a fresh tube of medium and incubate at 37 C for second period of 7 days. Report results as + (growth) or − (no growth) values.

Dilutions of unknown germicides found to be effective against specific spores in this test may be expected to be effective in disinfecting against the same spores in actual use, that is, if an adequate contact period can be provided.

Streptokinase Test—See **fibrinolysis test.**

Tartrate Utilization—Inoculate **Jordan's tartrate agar** by stabbing. Incubate for a number of days, and examine daily. An acid reaction of the phenol red indicator is a positive reaction.

Thomas Method—A test for the production of ammonia by microorganisms. Incubate an inoculum in peptone medium at 37 C for 5 days. Transfer 0.2 ml of the culture to a tube and dilute with water to 8 ml. Add 1 ml of 4 per cent aqueous phenol solution and 1 ml of sodium hypochlorite solution containing 1 per cent of available chlorine. If ammonia is present, a blue color is obtained. In amber-colored test solutions, a greenish-blue or green color is positive.

Trimethylamine Oxide—$(CH_3)_3NO$, crystals containing 2 moles of water, becoming anhydrous at 96 C and melting at 237 C. Soluble in water and methyl alcohol. Used as a reagent for the differentiation of *Shigella* species, some of which reduce it.

Triphenyltetrazolium Chloride—A reagent used to color enterococci colonies. A 1 per cent aqueous solution of 2,3,5-triphenyltetrazolium chloride is prepared and sterilized at 121 C for 15 minutes. Sufficient is added aseptically to sodium azide **tryptone broth** to give a final concentration of 0.01 per cent.

Trommdorf's Reagent—A reagent for determining the presence of nitrites. Add slowly a boiling mixture of 20 g zinc chloride in 100 ml water to a mixture of 4 g starch water. Stir constantly until the solution is nearly clear. Dilute with water and add 2 g zinc iodide. Dilute to 1 liter and filter.

Urea Solution—A solution which can be used to test for the production of urease by microorganisms. It consists of 20 g urea, 5 g beef extract, 1 g dipotassium phosphate, 0.1 g sodium chloride, 0.3 g magnesium sulfate, 0.1 g calcium chloride, 0.01 g ferric chloride, and 1000 ml tap water. Sterilize by filtration, as urea is destroyed by heat.

Urease Test (Rapid Modification)—Used to screen gram-negative rods showing possible *Salmonella* or *Shigella* reactions in double or triple sugar agar tubes. Inoculate heavily 0.5-ml aliquots of urease rapid test medium and place the tubes along with an uninoculated control into a water bath at 35 to 36 C. The urea of the medium is rapidly hydrolyzed by *Proteus* organisms with the formation of ammonia.

Urease Test (24-Hour Modification)—The objective of this test is the same as the preceding test. Generally commercial media are used. These media are buffered more strongly than the rapid test medium. Incubate overnight before discarding as negative. In addition to *Proteus* species, some paracolon microorganisms produce ammonia by hydrolysis of urea, but they do this more slowly.

Use-Dilution Method (A.O.A.C.) ***Salmonella choleraesuis*** **Variation**—A method designed for the testing of water miscible disinfectants in order to confirm the validity of the **phenol coefficient** and to give a measure of the safe dilution which is to be recommended for use on objects and surfaces where prior cleansing cannot be depended upon to remove interfering organic matter or reduce the bacterial contamination to a sufficiently low level.

Apparatus. The water bath, racks, glassware, and transfer loop are the same as those used in the **phenol coefficient test.** The following additional apparatus is used.

Transfer Loops and Needles. Make a 3-mm right angle bend at the end of 2 to 3 inches of No. 18 B & S gauge nichrome wire. Place the other end in a suitable holder, such as glass or aluminum rod.

Carriers. Use polished stainless steel cylinders (penicillin cups) with outside diameters of 8 ± 0.1 mm. These are obtainable from Erickson Screw Machine Products Co., 25 Lafayette St., Brooklyn, N. Y.

Glassware. Straight-side Pyrex test tubes, 20 × 150 mm; 15 × 110 mm Petri dishes; 100 ml, 300 ml, and liter Erlenmeyer flasks. Sterilize the Petri dishes in closed metal containers. Have available about six sterile Petri dishes matted with a layer of S & S No. 597, 9-cm filter paper.

Culture Media. Use the culture media detailed in the **phenol coefficient test.**

Test Organism. Use *Salmonella choleraesuis* A.T.C.C. 10708. Maintain the stock culture on nutrient agar slants by monthly transfers. Incubate each new stock transfer 2 days at 37 C; then store at room temperature. Inoculate a tube of nutrient broth with the stock culture and incubate at 37 C. Make three consecutive 24-hour transfers; then inoculate tubes of nutrient broth (two for each 10 carriers to be tested), using one loop of inoculum wit heach tube; incubate at 37 C for 44 to 48 hours.

Reagents. Phenol. Prepare a phenol solution as directed in the **phenol coefficient test.**

Sterile Distilled Water. Prepare a stock supply of water in liter flasks, plug with cotton, sterilize at 121 C for 20 minutes, and use to prepare the dilutions of the test materials.

Asparagine Solution. Make a stock supply of 0.1 per cent asparagine solution in water in an Erlenmeyer flask of convenient size, plug with cotton, and sterilize at 121 C for 20 minutes. Use this reagent to cover the metal carriers for sterilization and storage.

Sodium Hydroxide Solution. Approximately normal or 4 per cent. This is used for cleaning the metal carriers prior to use.

Procedure. Soak the ring carriers overnight in *N* sodium hydroxide solution, rinse with tap water until the rinse water is neutral to phenolphthalein indicator solution, and rinse twice with sterile distilled water. Place the cleaned ring carriers in multiples of ten into cotton plugged Erlenmeyer flasks or into 25 × 150-mm cotton plugged Pyrex test tubes. Cover with 0.1 per cent asparagine solution, sterilize at 121 C for 20 minutes, cool, and hold at room temperature.

Transfer 20 sterile ring carriers, using the flamed nichrome wire hook, into 20 ml of 44- to 48-hour nutrient broth test culture in a sterile 25 × 150-mm medication tube. After a 15-minute contact period, remove the cylinders, using the flamed nichrome wire hook, and place them on end in a vertical position in a sterile Petri dish with a filter paper mat. Place in an incubator at

37 C and allow to dry for not less than 10 minutes and not more than 60 minutes. Hold the broth culture for the determination of its resistance to the phenol coefficient method.

Make 1-90 and 1-100 dilutions of the phenol from the 5 per cent stock solution directly into medication tubes. Place the tube for each dilution in the water bath and allow to come to temperature. Make a stock solution of the germicide to be tested in a sterile glass-stoppered cylinder. From this solution make the 10-ml dilutions to be tested, depending upon the phenol coefficient found and/or claimed against *Salmonella typhosa* at 20 C, directly into each of ten 25 × 150-mm medication tubes, and then place the ten tubes into the water bath at 20 C and allow to come to temperature. Determine the dilution to be tested by multiplying the phenol coefficient number found and/or claimed by 20 to determine the number of volumes of water in which one part of the germicide is to be incorporated.

Add 0.5 ml of the test culture suspension to the 1-90 dilution of the phenol control; after a 30-second interval, add 0.5 ml to the 1-100 dilution of the control, using sterile cotton plugged pipettes. After adding the culture, shake the tubes gently but thoroughly to distribute the bacteria uniformly and replace in the bath. Five minutes after seeding the first tube, transfer 1 loopful of the mixture of culture and diluted phenol from medication tube to a corresponding subculture tube. At end of a 30-second interval, transfer a loopful from second medication tube; 5 minutes after making first set of transfers begin a second set of transfers for the 10-minute period; and finally repeat for the 15-minute period. Use the technique of loop sampling, flaming the loop and mouths of tubes, and shaking the medication and subculture tubes as detailed in the **phenol coefficient method.**

Incubate the cultures for 48 hours at 37 C and read the results. Resistance in 44- to 48-hour culture of *Salmonella choleraesuis* should fall within the range specified for the 24-hour culture of *Salmonella typhosa* in the phenol coefficient method.

Add 1 contaminated dried cylinder carrier at 1-minute intervals to each of the 10 tubes of the use-dilution of the germicide to be tested. By the time the 10 tubes have been seeded, 9 minutes will have elapsed, plus a 1-minute interval before the transfer of the first carrier in series to the individual tube of subculture broth. This interval is constant for each tube with a prescribed exposure period of 10 minutes. The 1-minute interval between transfers allows adequate time for flaming and cooling the nichrome wire hook and making the transfer in the manner detailed so as to drain all excess medicant from carrier. Flame the lips of medication and subculture tubes in the conventional manner.

Immediately after placing the carrier in a medication tube, swirl the tube three times before placing it back into the bath. Agitate the subculture tubes thoroughly, incubate 48 hours at 37 C, and report the results as + (growth) or − (no growth) values.

If there is reason to suspect that lack of growth at the conclusion of the incubation period may be due to the bacteriostatic action of medicant adsorbed on the carrier which has not been neutralized by subculture medium employed, transfer each ring to a new tube of sterile medium and reincubate for an additional period of 48 hours at 37 C.

Results showing no growth on all 10 carriers will confirm the phenol coefficient number found. Results showing growth on any of the 10 carriers indicate the phenol coefficient number to be an unsafe guide to the dilution recommended for use. In latter case, repeat test, using less diluting water for the germicide under study. The maximum dilution of the germicide which kills the test organism on the 10 carriers in a 10-minute interval represents the maximum safe use-dilution.

Use-Dilution Method (A.O.A.C.) *Staphylococcus aureus* Variation—Perform the method as detailed for the **use-dilution method (A.O.A.C.) *Salmonella choleraesuis* variation** but change the phenol dilutions and test organism. Use a culture of *Staphylococcus aureus* F.D.A. 209, A.T.C.C. No. 6538 having at least the resistance specified for 24-hour culture at 20 C in the **phenol coefficient method.**

Voges-Proskauer Test—A test to differentiate *Escherichia coli* from *Aerobacter aerogenes.* Add 5 ml 10 per cent hydroxide solution to 10 ml of a glucose-peptone broth culture incubated for 4 days at 37 C. The production of a pink color is indicative of *A. aerogenes. E. coli* produces no color. The color is the result of a reaction of biacetyl (diacetyl), which is formed by the oxidation of the acetylmethylcarbinol produced by the *A. aerogenes* and air, with a constituent of the peptone ingredient. The test can also be carried out in a number of modifications, as, for instance, by adding 1 ml of a 10 per cent potassium hydroxide solution to a glucose phosphate broth culture incubated at 30 C for 5 days, or according to another variation incubated at 30 C for 2 days. Sodium chloride may be substituted for the phosphate.

Winogradsky Test—A test for determining the fertility of a soil which depends on adding mannitol or starch to the soil and inoculating it with *Azotobacter.* The appearance of colonies after a few days of incubation is indicative that good crops may be produced.

TABLE 10. STAINS AND STAINING TECHNIQUES

The dyes mentioned in this section and elsewhere in this text should be those certified by the Biological Stain Commission

Aceto-Carmine—An excess of carmine is boiled in 45 per cent acetic acid. Filter to obtain a clear solution.

Albert's Stain—See **Laybourn's stain.**

Anthony's Capsule Stain—A staining solution consisting of 1.0 g of crystal violet (85 per cent dye content) and 100 ml water. Prepare smear and air-dry. Stain for 2 minutes with **crystal violet solution.** Wash with 20 per cent copper sulfate solution. Blot dry.

Auramine O Stain—Dissolve 0.1 g auramine O in 10 ml 95 per cent alcohol. Dissolve 3 ml liquefied phenol in 97 ml water. Add the auramine O solution and mix. See **fluorescent dye method.**

Azur II—A mixture of equal quantities of methylene blue and methylene azur. Also known as azur blue II, methylene azur II and Azur II "Giemsa." A deep-green powder soluble in water with a deep-blue color; soluble in alcohol. Used in **Giemsa's stain.**

Azur II–Eosin—A mixture of methylene blue-eosin and methylene azur. Deep-green powder soluble in alcohol and slightly soluble in water. Used in **Giemsa's stain.**

Benians' Congo Red Stain—Dissolve 2 g of Congo red, 80 per cent dye content, in 100 ml of water.

Benians' Method—Put a drop of **Benians' Congo red stain** on a slide. Stir the culture into the drop and spread out into a thick film. Allow to dry and wash with 1 per cent hydrochloric acid. Dry by blotting or air dry. The cells appear unstained against a blue background.

Bismark Brown—A basic azo dye that is a mixture of benzene-*m*-diazo-*bis*-*m*-phenylenediamine hydrochloride ($C_{18}H_{18}N_8 \cdot 2HCl$) and some triaminoazobenzene and other dye bases. It is a dark-brown color that dissolves in hot water. It is used as a contrasting color to methyl violet.

Blood Stain—See **Wright's stain** and **Giemsa's stain.**

Burdon Stain—A stain to demonstrate fat particles in microorganisms. After fixing a smear, flood entire slide with Sudan Black B (0.3 per cent dry dye in 70 per cent alcohol) about 10 minutes. Blot dry, clear in xylol, and counterstain with 0.1 per cent aqueous safranin for 10 seconds. Fat appears as dark, blue-black masses.

Burri's India Ink Method—A stain for spirochetes or bacteria. The organisms are white against a dark field.

Capsule Stains—See **Hiss method, India-ink capsule stain, Gin's method for capsules, Welch's method,** and **Wadsworth's staining method.**

Carbol-Crystal Violet Stain—A stain consisting of 0.4 g **crystal violet** (gentian violet) in 10 ml 95 per cent alcohol. Add 100 ml of a 1 per cent solution of phenol and mix. An alternative stain is prepared by dissolving 2 g of crystal violet (gentian violet) in 10 ml of 95 per cent alcohol by grinding and subsequently mixing with 100 ml of 1 per cent phenol solution.

Carbol-Erythrosin—A staining solution for the examination of *Rhizobium* consisting of 1.0 g erythrosin and 100 ml of a 5 per cent aqueous solution of phenol.

Carbol-Fuchsin Stain—Mix 10 ml of a 10 per cent alcoholic solution of basic **fuchsin** and 100 ml of a 5 per cent aqueous solution of phenol.

Carbol-Fuchsin (Ziehl's)—A solution consisting of 0.3 g basic **fuchsin** (90 per cent dye content) and 10 ml ethyl alcohol. To this, add 5.0 g phenol in 95 ml water.

Carbol-Rose Bengal—See **rose bengal solution.**

Casares-Gill Method—A technique used for flagella staining. The mordant stock solution consists of 10 g tannic acid, 18 g aluminum chloride, $Al_2Cl_6 \cdot 12H_2O$, 10 g zinc chloride, and 1.5 g rosaniline hydrochloride or basic fuchsin dissolved in 40 ml of 60 per cent alcohol. Dilute 1 part of the stock solution with 2 parts of water. Prepare a smear of the flagellated bacteria. Apply the filtered, diluted, mordant solution to the slide, allow to act for 1 to 2 minutes, and wash with water. Flood the slide with **carbol fuchsin stain** and allow to act for 5 minutes. Wash with water and dry by blotting. Flagella appear red.

Centrosome Stain—Aceto-orcein or **aceto-carmine** will stain the centrosome provided that the protein matter in the cytoplasm is not too abundant.

Chrysoidine—A basic azo dye, chrysoidine yellow 2,4-diaminoazobenzene hydrochloride, $C_6H_5N{:}NC_6H_3(NH_2)NH_2 \cdot HCl$. It is a reddish-brown powder soluble in water yielding a brown solution. It is also soluble in alcohol.

Churchman's Method—A method for staining capsules. Prepare a film and dry in air. Flood the film with **Wright's stain** permitting it to remain until almost dry. A pink color will replace the original blue in 3 to 5 minutes. Wash rapidly with water or with a buffer pH 6.4 to 6.5. Do not blot; dry under a fan. The capsule stains a purplish-pink often surrounded by a capsule membrane with a deeper purplish-pink peripheral zone; the body of the organism stains blue.

Crystal Violet—Methylrosaniline chloride; actually a mixture of hexa-, penta-, and tetramethylpararosaniline chlorides; the major component being the hexa derivative. Dark-green granules with a metallic luster. The aqueous solutions are a vivid purple; 1 g is soluble in 40 ml water and 10 ml alcohol.

Crystal Violet Solution—A solution consisting of 2 g of crystal violet, 90 per cent dye content, in 20 ml of 95 per cent alcohol to which is added 80 ml of water.

Crystal Violet Solution (1:1000)—A solution consisting of 1 g crystal violet (90 per cent dye content) and 1 liter water.

Dead Cell Stain—A stain consisting of methylene blue diluted 1:10,000 at pH 5.5. The dead cells in a culture examined microscopically are stained dark blue. This stain is used particularly in the examination of yeast cells.

Differential Stain—A stain used to differentiate between organisms, such as **Gram's stain** in differentiating between gram-positive and gram-negative bacteria.

Diphtheria Stain—See **Laybourn's stain.**

Dorner's Method—A technique used for spore staining. Prepare a heavy suspension of organisms in 2 to 3 drops of water in a small test tube. Add an equal volume of freshly filtered carbol fuchsin. Place tube in boiling water for 10 minutes or more. On a slide mix a loopful of stained preparation with one loopful of **Dorner's nigrosin solution.** Smear thinly and dry rapidly. Spores are red and cell bodies are almost colorless against the dark background of the nigrosin color.

Dorner's Nigrosin Solution—A solution used for the negative staining technique. The solution consists of 10 g nigrosin and 100 ml water. The solution is boiled for 30 minutes and 0.5 ml formalin is added. The solution is then filtered and stored.

Dorner's Stain—See **Dorner's nigrosin solution.**

Ehrlich's Gentian Violet Stain—Solution 1 consists of 1.2 g of **crystal violet** (gentian violet, 90 per cent dye content), dissolved in 12 ml of 95 per cent alcohol. Solution 2 comprises 2 ml of aniline and 98 ml of water. Mix thoroughly, allow solution 2 to stand for a few minutes, and filter. Mix solutions 1 and 2.

Eosin, Eosine—Sodium dibromodinitrofluorescein, $C_{20}H_6O_9N_2Br_2Na_2$. A reddish powder readily soluble in water with a green fluorescence. It is soluble in alcohol. Used as a stain and as an inhibitor of the growth of some microorganisms.

Fat Stains—Fat globules in yeast and other microorganisms can be stained by (1) **Sudan III stain,** (2) **Flemming's solution,** (3) dimethylaminoazobenzene solution, and (4) a weak alkaline solution of dimethyl-*p*-phenylenediamine plus alpha- or beta-naphthol. The colors produced are for (1) red, (2) brown to black, (3) yellow, and (4) blue.

Feulgen Staining—Fix slide in 95 per cent alcohol for 48 hours. Moisten with chloroform for 30 seconds. Dry. Soak with *N* hydrochloric acid for 15 minutes at 60 C. Immerse in **Schiff's reagent** in dark for 2 to 6 hours. Wash in 1 per cent bisulfite solution, rinse with water. Dry. Counterstain with weak green dye solution. Examine.

Flemming's Solution—A stain used for staining fat globules in yeasts. It consists of 15 parts of a 1 per cent solution of osmic acid, I part of glacial acetic acid, and 4 parts of a 2 per cent aqueous solution of chromic acid. The fat globules are stained brown to black.

Fluorescent Antibody Staining—A general method for the specific identification of viable and nonviable microorganisms by use of fluorescein-labeled antiglobulin. Variations of this method have been developed for bacteria, as for instance, *Treponema pallidum, Pseudomonas pseudomallei,* streptococci, leptospira; for protozoa, as for example *Endamoeba histolytica;* and for rickettsia and viruses. As representative of such methods, the specific method for *Treponema pallidum* (see **Fluorescent Antibody Staining Method for Syphilis**) is detailed.

Generally, a gamma globulin preparation is made from selected antiserum by precipitation by ammonium sulfate or by methyl alcohol in the cold. A solution of the purified globulin is prepared by dissolving it in 0.5 *M* carbonate-bicarbonate buffer at pH 9 and it is labeled by adding fluorescein isothiocyanate in the cold. The mixture is stirred for a period of 4 to 18 hours to permit the conjugation to go to completion and the mixture is then dialyzed against phosphate buffered saline solution to free the labeled globulin of any fluorescence. The conjugated globulin can then be stored under refrigeration for subsequent use.

Both direct and indirect procedures have been developed for using labeled antibody. In direct use, a specific labeled antibody is required for each antigen such as a microorganism.

The indirect procedure has two stages. In the first, the specific antigen and the antibody are permitted to react. The excess of the antibody is removed, and a labeled anti-antibody is applied. For instance, a slide preparation containing staphylococci is treated with rabbit antistaphylococcus serum and the excess serum is removed. Subsequently, when labeled antirabbit serum or globulin is applied, the staphylococci are stained. This labeled antirabbit conjugate may be used with other similar antigen-rabbit antiserum preparations.

Fluorescent Antibody Staining Method for Syphilis—*Reagents.* Antigen. *Treponema pallidum,* Nichols strain, extracted from rabbit testicular tissue, in basal medium as used in the *Treponema pallidum* immobilization test. This suspension should contain approximately 50 organisms per microscopic field when counted using a 450× magnification with a dry objective. Store in a refrigerator without preservative.

Labeled Globulin. Fluorescein labeled antihuman globulin of proved reactivity. This reagent is commercially available. It may also be prepared as detailed in the section on **fluorescent antibody staining** with fluorescein isothiocyanate.

Dilute Conjugated Fluorescein. Dilute fluorescein labeled antihuman globulin in phosphate buffered saline containing 2 per cent Tween-80 in the range of 1:5 to 1:320. The dilution to be selected for a particular lot of fluorescein labeled antihuman globulin is optimum when the maximum fluorescence is obtained with strongly reactive serums and a large excess of antihuman globulin is not used.

Phosphate Buffered Saline, pH 7.2. Use Bacto Hemagglutination Buffer No. 0512 or equivalent phosphate buffered saline solution.

Mounting Medium. One part of buffered saline plus 9 parts of glycerol.

Preparation of Serums. Heat clear serums of diluted serums in a 56 C water bath for 30 minutes. Allow to cool to room temperature before testing. If the serums have been heated on a previous day, reheat them for 10 minutes at 56 C. Prepare serum dilutions 1:5 by adding 0.1 ml serum to 0.4 ml buffered saline.

Preliminary Test of Antigen. Compare each new lot of antigen with an antigen of known reactivity before using it in the regular test procedure. A satisfactory antigen should not stain directly or nonspecifically with diluted fluorescein conjugate of known quality. Established reaction patterns for control serums showing "reactive," "weakly reactive," and "nonreactive" results with an accepted antigen should be reproduced with the new antigen.

Procedure. Cut two circles approximately 1 cm in diameter with a diamond stylus on grease-free slides. Smear approximately 0.01 ml of antigen within each circle with a capillary pipette and allow to dry in air. Immerse the slides in acetone for 10 minutes, remove, and dry in air. Cover each antigen smear with approximately 0.03 ml of a 1:5 dilution of the test serum. Test each serum in duplicate on a single slide. Prevent evaporation of serum dilutions on the smears by covering the slides with Petri dish tops or bottoms containing moistened filter paper. Rotate the slides at 100 rpm for 30 minutes in an incubator at 37 C. Rinse the slides with buffered saline solution and soak in two changes of buffered saline for a total of 10 minutes. Blot slides gently with filter paper.

Place approximately 0.03 ml of diluted fluorescein conjugate reagent, previously diluted to the appropriate titer, on each smear. Spread the conjugate with a glass rod in a circular pattern so that the smears are completely covered. Prevent evaporation with the Petri dish covers as detailed. Rotate the slides, warm for 30 minutes at 37 C, and blot as mentioned. Place a very small drop of mounting medium on each smear and apply a cover glass. Examine the slides immediately or preserve them for later examination by placing them in a refrigerator at 6 to 10 C.

Controls. Run the following controls in duplicate for each test. (1) A 1:5 dilution of serum demonstrating moderate to strong reactivity. (2) A 1:5 dilution of serum of weak reactivity. (3) A 1:5 dilution of serum having no reaction. (4) An antigen smear treated only with fluorescein labeled antihuman globulin to serve as the nonspecific staining control.

Reading the Results. Study the smears microscopically, using ultraviolet light and a high power dry objective; the total magnification should be approximately 450×. Check the nonreactive smears with visible illumination to verify the presence of treponemes. Record separately the reactivity of each of the two smears of each serum. Reread the two smears so that four readings are obtained for each serum. Three of these four readings should agree and this result is used for the report. Retest if there is greater disagreement.

Report the results as follows:

Reading	*Report*
4+, Very strongly fluorescent	Reactive
3+, Strongly fluorescent	Reactive
2+, Moderately fluorescent	Reactive
1+, Weakly fluorescent	Weakly reactive
− to ±, Vaguely visible	Nonreactive

Fluorescent Dye Method—A procedure for the identification of acid-fast organisms. Flood a heat-fixed smear with **auramine O stain** for 3 minutes. Wash in water and decolorize for 2 minutes. Drain. (The decolorizing solution is made of 100 ml 70 per cent alcohol, 0.5 ml concentrated hydrochloric acid, and 0.1 g sodium chloride.) Stain again and decolorize for 4 minutes. Wash and dry. Examine with a fluorescence microscope.

Fontana-Tribondeau Method—A method to stain spirochetes. Solution 1 consists of 1 ml acetic acid (glacial), 10 ml 40 per cent formalin, and 100 ml water. Solution 2 consists of 5 g tannic acid and 100 ml 1 per cent phenol. Prepared slide is covered with solution 1 for 1 minute and washed. It is then covered with solution 2 and heated until fluid steams. After washing it is covered with 5 per cent ammoniacal silver nitrate solution. Heat until fluid steams. Wash and dry. Spirochetes are stained dark brown or black.

Fuchsin, Basic—A mixture of the triphenylmethane dyes, **rosaniline** and **pararosaniline** hydrochlorides. Lustrous, green crystals which dissolve in water with a red color. They are also soluble in alcohol.

Fuchsin, Carbol—See **carbol-fuchsin stain.**

Fuchsin Stain—Dissolve 3 g basic fuchsin (90 per cent dye content, certified) in 100 ml 95 per cent alcohol. Allow the solution to stand for 24 hours, mixing at intervals. Dilute 19 ml of this stock solution with 90 ml water for use as the stain or counterstain.

Giemsa's Stain—A stain used for blood smears. Dissolve 3 g azur II-eosin, 0.8 g azur II, 250 ml glycerol, and 250 ml methyl alcohol acetone-free by warming to 60 C. Allow to stand 24 hours and filter. Follow the technique for **Wright's stain.**

Gin's Method for Capsules—India ink or nigrosin (diluted with an equal amount of water) is mixed with a loopful of bacterial suspension at one end of slide. The mixture is spread across a slide with a second slide. Air-dry and stain with carbol fuchsin or gentian violet for a few minutes. Wash, dry, and examine. Bacteria will be stained and capsules unstained with margins outlined by the ink.

Gram's Stain—A stain used for the differentiation of bacteria. It is the most useful of the special differential bacterial stains. It is used routinely as the initial step in examination of cultures and specimens. With its aid, microorganisms are classed as gram positive, gram negative, or gram variable. Gram-positive organisms, at times, become gram negative as a result of aging, autolysis, acidity of the medium, or temperature of incubation. This staining technique was developed by Christian Gram, a Danish scholar, in 1884.

Reagents (*Hucker Modification*). Solution A consists of 2 g crystal violet (90 per cent dye content) and 20 ml ethyl alcohol (95 per cent). Solution B consists of 0.8 g ammonium oxalate and 80 ml water. Mix solutions A and B. Gram's iodine solution is composed of 1 g iodine, 2 g potassium iodide, and 300 ml water. The composition of safranin counterstain is 10 ml safranin (2.5 per cent solution in 95 per cent alcohol) and 100 ml water.

Procedure. A fixed smear is stained for 1 minute with ammonium oxalate **crystal violet solution.** After washing in tap water, flood slide with Gram's iodine solution for about 1 minute. Wash and blot dry. Decolorize with 95 per cent alcohol for 30 seconds, gently agitating the slide. Dry and counterstain with safranin for 10 to 30 seconds. Wash, dry, and examine.

Hansen's Spore Stain—Prepare a smear of the material to be stained. Dry, fix, and stain with hot **carbol fuchsin** for 5 minutes. Decolorize with 5 per cent acetic acid until a light pink color is observed. Wash in water. Stain with **Loeffler's methylene blue** for 3 minutes. Wash in water and dry. Spores stain red.

Hiss Method—A staining technique for bacteria capsules. Mix the exudate or culture into a drop of serum on a slide and smear. Air-dry and fix. Cover the smear with 1 per cent aqueous **crystal violet solution.** Steam gently over a flame for 0.5 to 1 minute. Wash off the stain with a 20 per cent aqueous solution of copper sulfate. Blot dry and examine. The bacteria capsule will take on a pale-blue color, while the cell will appear a darker blue.

Hucker Stain—See **Gram stain (Hucker modification) reagents.**

India-Ink Capsule Stain—Emulsify a minute amount of material relatively free from bacteria in a small loop of salt solution, water, or broth on a slide. Add a small loop of India ink and cover with a cover slip spreading the fluid to a very thin film. Examine with an oil-immersion objective, reducing the light, until the bacterial bodies are distinctly in focus. The bacterial bodies are not stained and the capsules appear as halos around the bacteria against a dark background. See **nigrosin solution.**

Indirect Stain—A stain or ink which will color the background but not the organisms so that it can be observed by contrast. See **nigrosin solution.**

Intravital Staining—The staining of bacteria in wet preparations, such as hanging drop. **Methylene blue** solution or cresyl blue is introduced into the drop of culture before sealing with a cover slip.

Jenner's Stain—A polychrome stain prepared by mixing 0.5 per cent eosin in methyl alcohol with 0.5 per cent methylene blue in methyl alcohol in the ratio of 5:4, or by dissolving the precipitate formed by mixing a 1.25 per cent aqueous solution of eosin with an equal volume of 1 per cent aqueous solution of methylene blue in methyl alcohol. Used for staining borrelias.

Johnson's Iron-Alum Hematoxylin Stain—A method for making mounts of intestinal protozoa, especially for staining *Balantidium coli.* Fix thin films on slides or cover glasses in **Schaudinn's solution** plus 5 to 10 per cent acetic acid at 37 to 45 C for 10 minutes; in 95 per cent alcohol plus iodine (wine color) for 5 minutes; in 70 per cent alcohol for 5 minutes. Rinse in tap water for 3 minutes, and in 4 per cent iron-alum solution for 15 minutes. Stain in 0.5 per cent aqueous hematoxylin made from 10 ml 5 per cent solution in 95 per cent alcohol, plus 90 ml water for 10 minutes. Decolorize in 0.25 per cent iron-alum solution, flagellates 6 to 10 minutes, amoeba 12 minutes. Wash in running water for 3 to 30 minutes; dehydrate in alcohol; clear in xylol; and mount. The nuclear structures are defined.

Kinyoun's Carbol-Fuchsin—Rosaniline hydrochloride 4 g (basic fuchsin), 8 ml phenol, 20 ml 95 per cent alcohol, and 100 ml water. A stain recommended for the examination of *Mycobacterium tuberculosis.* It requires no heat. See **Ziehl-Neelsen stain.**

Kulp's Staining Modification—A modification of **Loeffler's staining** procedure for **flagella.**

Lactophenol-Cotton Blue Solution—A mounting fluid prepared by dissolving a mixture of 20 ml melted phenol, 20 ml lactic acid, 40 ml glycerol, and 20 ml water by heating to 70 C. After solution, add 0.05 g cotton blue or Poirrier's blue. Place a drop of this solution on a slide and tease apart a small amount of a fungus in it. Place a thin cover slip over the preparation and examine under the microscope.

Laybourn's Stain—With this stain the granules of diphtheria bacilli stain an intense black, the bars dark green, and the intervening portions light green. Fix the smears by heat. Flood with Laybourn's stain reagent solution 1 for 3 to 5 minutes (1 minute with methyl green). Drain without washing. Flood with solution 2 for 1 minute, wash, **blot dry**, and examine.

Reagents. Dissolve 0.15 g toluidine blue O and 0.2 g malachite green in 1 ml glacial acetic acid, 2 ml 95 per cent alcohol, and 100 ml water. Allow the mixture to stand for 24 hours and filter. This is reagent solution 1. Reagent solution 2 is prepared by dissolving 2 g iodine and 3 g potassium iodide in a small amount of water and diluting to 300 ml.

Leifson Method—A method for staining flagella. Solution A consists of 1.5 per cent sodium chloride in water; solution B consists of 3 per cent tannic acid in water; solution C consists of 0.9 g pararosaniline acetate and 0.3 g pararosaniline hydrochloride in 100 ml alcohol. Mix solutions A, B, and C in equal proportions. To a fixed smear (do not use heat) that has been incubated for 10 to 15 minutes, add 1 ml of the stain. Leave at room temperature for 8 to 15 minutes. Rinse gently with tap water. Counterstain with 1 per cent aqueous methylene blue solution.

Ljubinsky's Stain Method—This is a stain used to show the granules in *Corynebacterium diphtheriae.* The granules appear dark blue or black, with the rest of the cell reddish or yellowish. Stain the heat-fixed smear with Ljubinsky's reagent solution A for 1 minute; wash with water; stain with solution B for 30 seconds; wash with water, blot dry or dry in air, and examine.

Reagents. Solution A consists of 2.5 g methyl violet 2 B or crystal violet dissolved in 50 ml glacial acetic acid and 950 ml water. Solution B consists of 5.6 g chrysoidin dissolved in 1 liter water, or of 0.1 g Bismark brown Y in 100 ml water.

Loeffler's Alkaline Methylene Blue Stain Reagent—Add 100 ml dilute potassium hydroxide solution (0.01 per cent by weight) to 30 ml ethyl alcohol containing 0.3 g methylene blue (90 per cent dye content).

Loeffler's Methylene Blue Stain—A stain used for the differentiation of the metachromatic granules, which stain intensely, from the cytoplasm of the cell. Commonly used for the examination of throat cultures and smears for diphtheria bacilli. The dye develops polychrome properties on treatment with alkali or on aging. Constituents of the polychrome dye have a marked affinity for the granules. These stain purple while the body of the cell stains blue.

Reagents. Dissolve 0.3 g certified methylene blue in 30.0 ml 95 per cent ethyl alcohol and add 100 ml water.

Procedure. Cover the smear, prepared in the customary manner, with the dye solution and allow to stain for 1 minute. Wash with water, blot dry, and examine.

Lugol's Iodine Solution (Gram's Modification)—A mordant used in the **Gram stain** consisting of 1.0 g iodine, 2.0 g potassium iodide, and 300 ml water. Dissolve the iodine in a small volume of potassium iodide solution and then add the remainder of the water. It is best to prepare a fresh solution every 2 weeks. Iodine will also reveal the presence of glycogen in yeast cells.

Machiavello's Stain—Dissolve 0.25 g basic fuchsin in 100 ml phosphate buffer of pH 7.4. Prepare a smear. Filter the stain over the smear and leave for 4 minutes. Drain, wash with 0.5 per cent citric acid, and then with water. Stain with 1 per cent aqueous methylene blue. Both intra- and extracellular rickettsiae stain red; the cellular material stains blue. The method is used for culture smears and not for tissue sections.

Malachite Green—A triphenylmethane dye used in **Laybourn's stain** for **diphtheria** bacilli and for staining spores with safranin as the counterstain.

Malachite Green Solution—A 5 per cent aqueous malachite green solution is used in Conklin's modification of the **Wirtz method** of spore staining. Used also as a counterstain. A 5 per cent solution consists of 5.0 g malachite green and 100 ml water. In Bartholomew and Mittwer's "cold" method of spore staining, a 7.6 per cent aqueous malachite green solution is employed.

Meissner's Iodine Solution—A reagent for the examination of *Azotobacter* consisting of 7.0 g iodine, 20.0 g potassium iodide, and 100 ml water.

Methyl Blue—Brilliant cotton blue, sodium triphenyl-*p*-rosanilinesulfonate. See **Poirrier's blue** (Table 8a).

Methylene Blue—Methylthionine chloride, $C_{16}H_{18}ClN_3S \cdot 3H_2O$, 2,8-tetramethyldiaminothiazonium chloride, a thiazine dye, commonly used as a microbiological stain and also as an indicator in media, such as eosin-methylene blue agar. Dark-green crystals with a bronze luster; 1 g is soluble in about 25 ml water and about 65 ml alcohol.

Methylene Blue Solution—(1) A dilute alcoholic solution used as a stain consisting of 0.3 g methylene blue (90 per cent dye content), 30 ml 95 per cent alcohol, and 100 ml water. (2) Add 1 methylene blue thiocyanate tablet, certified by the Biological Stain Commission and having a dye content per tablet of approximately 8.8 mg, to 200 ml autoclaved or boiled water. Store in a light-resistant, stoppered flask in a cool dark place. Prepare fresh solutions weekly for the reduction milk test.

Moeller's Method—A procedure for staining spores. See **spore stain.**

Negative Staining—A procedure in which a suspension of bacteria is mixed with a material or substance, such as India ink or **nigrosin.** The bacteria are white or colorless against a dark background. The bacterial cell is not penetrated by the dye, but a part of the cell may be covered if the ink or nigrosin is too thick.

Neisser Stain—A method for the staining of metachromatic granules. Solution 1 is prepared by mixing 20 ml 95 per cent alcohol with 1 g methylene blue. To this, 50 ml acetic acid (glacial) and 930 ml water are added. Solution 2 consists of 1 g crystal violet, 10 ml 95 per cent alcohol, and 300 ml water. Solution 3 is made by dissolving 1 or 2 g chrysoidin in 300 ml water. The prepared slide is stained for 10 seconds using a mixture of 2 parts of solution 1 to 1 part of solution 2. Wash. Stain with solution 3. Wash and blot dry. Examine. Bacilli appear brown or show a dark-blue, round body at both ends.

Neutral Stain—A solution consisting of acid and basic dyes containing two colored ions in the molecule. Neutral stains are selective stains.

Newman-Lampert Stain—A bacterial stain for milk. Place 40 ml tetrachloroethane in a flask, add 54 ml 95 per cent ethyl alcohol, and heat to 70 C. Add the solvent to 1.0-1.2 g certified methylene blue chloride, shake until the dye is dissolved, and add 6 ml glacial acetic acid slowly to the dye solution. Filter. With the aid of this stain, the milk can be fixed on the slide, the fat is removed, and the bacteria are stained for microscopic observation.

Procedure. Transfer 0.01 ml milk to the slide with the aid of a pipette or with the aid of a calibrated loop. Spread over 1 sq cm. Dry more than 5 minutes to avoid cracks. Place the slide in the staining jar. Remove immediately and allow to dry. Wash to remove excess stain. Dry in air and examine.

Newman's Stain—A stain used on milk smears in order that bacteria can be counted. It consists of 2 g methylene blue, 60 ml 95 per cent ethyl alcohol, 40 ml xylene, and 6 ml glacial acetic acid. The dye should be dissolved in warm alcohol and filtered. The stain should be applied for about 1 minute before washing in water.

Nicolle's Carbol—Crystal Violet Stain—See **carbol-crystal violet stain.**

Nigrosin Solution—A solution consisting of 10 g of water-soluble nigrosin, a black dye made by heating aniline and aniline hydrochloride with nitrobenzene and a metal, and 100 ml water. After placing in a boiling water bath for 0.5 hour, add 0.5 ml of a formalin preservative and filter 3 times. Nigrosin solution is used chiefly for negative staining.

Nile Blue A—Aminonaphthodiethylaminophenoxazine sulfate. Stains fatty acids blue. A 0.5 or 2 per cent alcoholic solution is used as a stain. Its pH range is from 10 to 11, with the color in the lower range blue and the color in the higher range pink.

Osmic Acid—A preparation used for demonstrating fat in microorganisms. It consists of 0.1 g osmic acid and 100 ml water. The solution should be kept in a dark stoppered bottle and care should be exercised in using it, because of dangerous fumes. Fat globules are stained dark brown or black.

Pappenheim's Method—A procedure for staining acid-fast bacteria in order to differentiate *Mycobacterium tuberculosis,* which stains red, from *M. lacticola* (*M. smegmatis*), which is decolorized. Heat-fix a smear and stain for 2 minutes with carbol fuchsin. Pour off dye without washing and cover with **Pappenheim's stain,** draining the latter off slowly. Repeat 4 or 5 times. The methylene blue is a counterstain.

Pappenheim's Stain—Dissolve 1 g rosolic acid (corallin) in 100 ml absolute alcohol and saturate with methylene blue. Add 20 ml glycerol.

Pararosaniline—A triphenylmethane dye which is one of the components of basic **fuchsin.** Brownish-red crystals, soluble in alcohol and slightly soluble in water.

Polychrome Stains—Stains which are used for the staining of exudates and pus in which bacteria are observed in relation to cellular elements. **Wright's stain, Jenner's stain,** and **Giesma's stain** are examples.

Relief Staining—A method for staining bacteria and spirochetes. Mix a small quantity of culture with a drop of 2 per cent aqueous Congo red solution. Allow to dry. Wash with 1 per cent hydrochloric acid in absolute alcohol. Examine with an oil immersion lens after blotting dry. Background is blue. Organisms are not stained.

Rosaniline—A triphenylmethane dye which is one of the components of basic **fuchsin.** Brownish-red crystals, soluble in alcohol and slightly soluble in water.

Rose Bengal Solution—A counterstain consisting of 1.0 g rose bengal (80 per cent dye content), 0.01 g calcium chloride, and 100.0 ml 5 per cent aqueous phenol solution.

***p*-Rosolic Acid**—Also known as corallin and aurin. Used in **Pappenheim's stain.** Red crystals with a metallic luster. Very soluble in alcohol yielding a yellow solution and almost insoluble in water.

Safranin Solution—A stain consisting of 2.5 g safranin and 100 ml 95 per cent alcohol. This is the concentrated alcoholic solution. For stain or counterstain, use 10 ml of the above with 90 ml water.

Selective Stain—A stain used for specific parts of an organism, such as the capsule, flagella, etc.

Spore Stain—See **malachite green solution, Dorner's method,** and **Wirtz's method.**

Stoltenberg's Stain—A solution consisting of 1 g malachite green, 0.2 g toluidine blue O, 0.04 g hematoxylin, 12 ml glacial acetic acid, 12 ml 95 per cent ethyl alcohol, and 400 ml water. The solution is used to stain metachromatic granules. Flood heat-fixed smear with stain for 3 minutes. Wash with water and dry. Metachromatic granules stain red, the cell green.

Sudan III, Sudan G—$C_6H_5N{:}NC_6H_4N{:}$-$NC_{10}H_6OH$, tetrazobenzene-β-naphthol, Oil Red, Oil Scarlet. An oil-soluble dye which occurs as a reddish-brown powder that is insoluble in water and is soluble in many organic solvents and oils.

Sudan III Stain—A preparation used for demonstrating fat in microorganisms. It consists of 0.1 g **Sudan III** and 1000 ml of a 50:50 glycerol, alcohol solution. Fat globules are stained red.

Thionine, Thionin—3,7-Diaminophenothiazonium chloride; Lauth's violet. Black-green crystals; soluble in hot water forming a blue, then violet, solution. A 0.5 per cent solution, 85 to 95 per cent dye content, is used as a nuclear stain. It is also used for counting bacteria in milk and for the differentiation of brucella because in 1:200,000 concentration, *Brucella abortus* fails to grow.

Toluidine Blue O—3-Amino-7-dimethylamino-2-methyl-phenazathionium chloride, $C_{15}H_{16}ClN_3S$, is a green crystalline powder with a bronze luster; about 5.5 g is soluble in 100 ml water at room temperature, but only slightly soluble in alcohol with a blue-violet color. A 0.3 to 1 per cent aqueous solution (80 per cent dye content) is used as a stain. See also **Stoltenberg's stain.**

Van Ermengen's Method—A method for staining flagella. Solution A consists of 60 ml 20 per cent tannic acid solution, 30 ml osmic acid solution, and 4 to 5 drops of glacial acetic acid. Solution B consists of 5 g gallic acid, 3 g tannic acid, 10 g fused potassium acetate dissolved in 350 ml water. Place the prepared slide in solution A for 1 hour at room temperature or for 5 minutes at 100 C. Wash in water and with alcohol. Cover with 0.25 per cent silver nitrate solution for 3 seconds. Cover with solution B for a few minutes. Use silver nitrate again until preparation is black. Wash with water, blot, and examine.

Van Gieson's Stain for Negri Bodies (Williams' Modification)—A smear of brain tissue is prepared on a slide. Fix slide for 10 seconds with neutral methyl alcohol (0.1 per cent picric acid is added). Blot dry and flood slide with a solution consisting of 0.5 ml saturated alcoholic solution basic fuchsin, 10.0 ml saturated alcoholic solution methylene blue, and 30 ml water. Heat to steaming and wash in water. Dry and examine.

Vital Staining—Staining cells in the living state or staining microorganisms without prior fixation. Knaysi claims that at neutral or moderately acid pH the living protoplasm does not stain, and staining of the protoplasm even to a slight degree is an evidence of death. Most common so-called vital stains are **neutral red** (Table 8a), **methylene blue, nile blue,** and cresyl red.

Wadsworth's Staining Method—A method for staining capsules. Prepare slide. Fix in formalin (40 per cent) for 2 to 5 minutes. Wash. Flood with gentian violet for 2 minutes. Add **Gram's iodine reagent** for 2 minutes. Decolorize with 95 per cent alcohol. Flood with fuchsin (dilute aqueous solution). Wash and dry.

Welch's Method—A procedure used to stain capsules. Prepare a slide. Cover with glacial acetic acid and pour off after a few seconds. Cover with aniline water-gentian violet mixture, usually 3 or 4 times, until the acid is removed and leave on for 3 minutes. Wash in 2 per cent sodium chloride solution. Examine. The capsules will appear a pale violet.

Wirtz's Method—A staining procedure for the examination of bacterial spores. Bartholomew and Mittwer's modification is as follows: Fix the smear by passing through the flame 20 times. Stain 10 minutes with 7.6 per cent aqueous malachite green without heat. Rinse with water for about 10 seconds. Stain 15 seconds with 0.25 per cent aqueous safranin. Rinse and blot dry. The spore stains green and the cell red. This modification has the advantage that the stain is not heated.

Wright's Stain—A polychrome stain made by heating in an Arnold sterilizer at 100 C for 60 minutes 0.9 g methylene blue and 100 ml 0.5 per cent aqueous sodium carbonate solution. Cool and filter. Add 1 g eosin Y and 500 ml water. Mix and filter to obtain precipitate. Dissolve 0.1 g of precipitate in 60 ml neutral, acetone-free methyl alcohol, allow to stand for 36 hours, and filter. Used for pus and sediments to study bacteria in relation to cellular elements.

Wright's Stain Method—Prepare slide and apply **Wright's stain** for 1 minute. Dilute with water and allow to stand for about 10 minutes. Wash in water. Dry and examine.

Ziehl-Neelsen Method—A staining technique for mycobacteria. Cover preparation with carbol fuchsin and steam over a Bunsen flame 5 minutes; do not boil; add additional stain to prevent drying. Wash with water, decolorize with acid alcohol, and stain with methylene blue for 10 to 30 seconds. Wash with water, blot dry, and examine. The acid-fast bacteria appear red against a blue background. Other bacteria also appear blue.

Ziehl's Carbol-Fuchsin Stain—See **carbol-fuchsin.**

TABLE 11a. TEMPERATURE CONVERSION TABLE

TABLE 11b. SATURATED STEAM TEMPERATURES

TABLE 12a. MOST PROBABLE NUMBERS USING VARIOUS NUMBERS OF TUBES WITH NOT MORE THAN 3 DILUTIONS

TABLE 12b. MOST PROBABLE NUMBERS USING 5 TUBES

TABLE 12c. MOST PROBABLE NUMBERS USING 3 TUBES

TABLE 11a. TEMPERATURE CONVERSION TABLE

The numbers in boldface type refer to temperatures, either in degrees centigrade or Fahrenheit. For conversion of a temperature from Fahrenheit degrees to centigrade degrees, the equivalent temperature is given in the left column; for conversion of a temperature from degrees centigrade to degrees Fahrenheit, the equivalent temperature will be found in the column on the right.

C		F	C		F	C		F
−73.3	**−100**	−148	−7.22	**19**	66.2	8.89	**48**	118.4
−67.8	**−90**	−130	−6.67	**20**	68.0	9.44	**49**	120.2
−62.2	**−80**	−112	−6.11	**21**	69.8	10.0	**50**	122.0
−56.7	**−70**	−94	−5.56	**22**	71.6	10.6	**51**	123.8
−51.1	**−60**	−76	−5.00	**23**	73.4	11.1	**52**	125.6
−45.6	**−50**	−58	−4.44	**24**	75.2	11.7	**53**	127.4
−40.0	**−40**	−40	−3.89	**25**	77.0	12.2	**54**	129.2
−34.4	**−30**	−22	−3.33	**26**	78.8	12.8	**55**	131.0
−28.9	**−20**	−4	−2.78	**27**	80.6	13.3	**56**	132.8
−23.3	**−10**	14	−2.22	**28**	82.4	13.9	**57**	134.6
−17.8	**0**	32	−1.67	**29**	84.2	14.4	**58**	136.4
−17.2	**1**	33.8	−1.11	**30**	86.0	15.0	**59**	138.2
−16.7	**2**	35.6	−0.56	**31**	87.8	15.6	**60**	140.0
−16.1	**3**	37.4	0	**32**	89.6	16.1	**61**	141.8
−15.6	**4**	39.2	0.56	**33**	91.4	16.7	**62**	143.6
−15.0	**5**	41.0	1.11	**34**	93.2	17.2	**63**	145.4
−14.4	**6**	42.8	1.67	**35**	95.0	17.8	**64**	147.2
−13.9	**7**	44.6	2.22	**36**	96.8	18.3	**65**	149.0
−13.3	**8**	46.4	2.78	**37**	98.6	18.9	**66**	150.8
−12.8	**9**	48.2	3.33	**38**	100.4	19.4	**67**	152.6
−12.2	**10**	50.0	3.89	**39**	102.2	20.0	**68**	154.4
−11.7	**11**	51.8	4.44	**40**	104.0	20.6	**69**	156.2
−11.1	**12**	53.6	5.00	**41**	105.8	21.1	**70**	158.0
−10.6	**13**	55.4	5.56	**42**	107.6	21.7	**71**	159.8
−10.0	**14**	57.2	6.11	**43**	109.4	22.2	**72**	161.6
−9.44	**15**	59.0	6.67	**44**	111.2	22.8	**73**	163.4
−8.89	**16**	60.8	7.22	**45**	113.0	23.3	**74**	165.2
−8.33	**17**	62.6	7.78	**46**	114.8	23.9	**75**	167.0
−7.78	**18**	64.4	8.33	**47**	116.6	24.4	**76**	168.8

TABLE 11a. TEMPERATURE CONVERSION TABLE (*Continued*)

C		F	C		F	C		F
25.0	**77**	170.6	116	**240**	464	327	**620**	1148
25.6	**78**	172.4	121	**250**	482	332	**630**	1166
26.1	**79**	174.2	127	**260**	500	338	**640**	1184
26.7	**80**	176.0	132	**270**	518	343	**650**	1202
27.2	**81**	177.8	138	**280**	536	349	**660**	1220
27.8	**82**	179.6	143	**290**	554	354	**670**	1238
28.3	**83**	181.4	149	**300**	572	360	**680**	1256
28.9	**84**	183.2	154	**310**	590	366	**690**	1274
29.4	**85**	185.0	160	**320**	608	371	**700**	1292
30.0	**86**	186.8	166	**330**	626	377	**710**	1310
30.6	**87**	188.6	171	**340**	644	382	**720**	1328
31.1	**88**	190.4	177	**350**	662	388	**730**	1346
31.7	**89**	192.2	182	**360**	680	393	**740**	1364
32.2	**90**	194.0	188	**370**	698	399	**750**	1382
32.8	**91**	195.8	193	**380**	716	404	**760**	1400
33.3	**92**	197.6	199	**390**	734	410	**770**	1418
33.9	**93**	199.4	204	**400**	752	416	**780**	1436
34.4	**94**	201.2	210	**410**	770	421	**790**	1454
35.0	**95**	203.0	216	**420**	788	427	**800**	1472
35.6	**96**	204.8	221	**430**	806	432	**810**	1490
36.1	**97**	206.6	227	**440**	824	438	**820**	1508
36.7	**98**	208.4	232	**450**	842	443	**830**	1526
37.2	**99**	210.2	238	**460**	860	449	**840**	1544
37.8	**100**	212.0	243	**470**	878	454	**850**	1562
43	**110**	230	249	**480**	896	460	**860**	1580
49	**120**	248	254	**490**	914	466	**870**	1598
54	**130**	266	260	**500**	932	471	**880**	1616
60	**140**	284	266	**510**	950	477	**890**	1634
66	**150**	302	271	**520**	968	482	**900**	1652
71	**160**	320	277	**530**	986	488	**910**	1670
77	**170**	338	282	**540**	1004	493	**920**	1688
82	**180**	356	288	**550**	1022	499	**930**	1706
88	**190**	374	293	**560**	1040	504	**940**	1724
93	**200**	392	299	**570**	1058	510	**950**	1742
99	**210**	410	304	**580**	1076	516	**960**	1760
100	**212**	413	310	**590**	1094	521	**970**	1778
104	**220**	428	316	**600**	1112	527	**980**	1796
110	**230**	446	321	**610**	1130	532	**990**	1814
						538	**1000**	1832

TABLE 11b. SATURATED STEAM TEMPERATURES

Gauge pressure lbs/sq. in.	*Temperature C*	*Temperature F*
0	100.0	212.0
1	101.9	215.4
2	103.6	218.5
3	105.3	221.5
4	106.9	224.4
5	108.4	227.1
6	109.8	229.6
7	111.3	232.3
8	112.6	234.7
9	113.9	237.0
10	115.2	239.4
11	116.4	241.5
12	117.6	243.7
13	118.8	245.8
14	119.9	247.8
15	121.0	249.8
16	122.0	251.6
17	123.0	253.4
18	124.1	255.4
19	125.0	257.0
20	126.0	258.8
21	126.9	260.4
22	127.8	262.0
23	128.7	263.7
24	129.6	265.3
25	130.4	266.7
26	131.3	268.3
27	132.1	269.8
28	132.9	271.2
29	133.7	272.7
30	134.5	274.1

TABLE 12a. MOST PROBABLE NUMBERS (MPN) PER 100 MILLILITERS OF SAMPLE USING VARIOUS NUMBERS OF TUBES WITH NOT MORE THAN 3 DILUTIONS[a]

Number of Positive Tubes in Dilutions			Combinations of Portions Planted in Ml			Number of Positive Tubes in Dilutions			Combinations of Portions Planted in Ml				
Low	Middle	High	2-10 2-1 2-0.1	1-10 5-1 1-0.1	1-50 5-10 1-1	Low	Middle	High	5-10	5-10 1-1	5-10 1-1 1-0.1	5-100 1-50 1-10	5-100 5-10
0	0	1	4.5	6.7	1	0	0	1			2	0.18	
0	0	2	9			0	1	0		2	2	0.19	0.18
0	1	0	4.6	6.8	1	0	2	0					0.37
0	1	1	9.2	14	2.1	0	3	0					0.56
0	1	2	14			0	4	0					0.75
0	2	0	9.4	14	2.2	0	1	1			4	0.38	
0	2	1	14	21	3.3	1	0	0	2.2	2.2	2.2	0.20	0.20
0	2	2	19			1	0	1			4.4	0.40	
0	3	0		22	3.5	1	1	0		4.4	4.4	0.42	0.41
0	3	1		30	4.7	1	2	0					0.62
0	4	0		31	5	1	3	0					0.84
0	4	1		39	6.4	1	4	0					1.1
0	5	0		40	6.8	1	1	1			6.7	0.63	
0	5	1		49	8.3	2	0	0	5.1	5	5	0.44	0.45
1	0	0	6	11	1.4	2	0	1			7.5	0.68	
1	0	1	12	24	2.9	2	1	0		7.6	7.6	0.71	0.69
1	0	2	19			2	2	0					0.94
1	1	0	13	26	3.1	2	3	0					1.2
1	1	1	20	45	4.9	2	4	0					1.5
1	1	2	28			2	1	1			10	0.97	
1	2	0	21	51	5.5	3	0	0	9.2	8.9	8.8	0.77	0.79
1	2	1	29	76	7.9	3	0	1			12	1.1	
1	2	2	37			3	1	0		12	12	1.1	1.1
1	3	0		89	9	3	2	0					1.4
1	3	1		120	12	3	3	0					1.8
1	4	0		150	15	3	4	0					2.1
1	4	1		210	21	3	1	1			16	1.5	
1	5	0		390	39	4	0	0	16	15	15	1.3	1.3
2	0	0	23			4	0	1			20	1.7	
2	0	1	50			4	1	0		21	21	1.8	1.7
2	0	2	95			4	2	0					2.2
2	1	0	62			4	3	0					2.8
2	1	1	130			4	4	0					3.5
2	1	2	210			4	1	1			27	2.4	
2	2	0	240			5	0	0		39	38	2.2	2.4
2	2	1	700			5	0	1			96	3.1	
						5	1	0			240	4.7	3.5
						5	2	0					5.4
						5	3	0					9.2
						5	4	0					16

[a] From "Most Probable Numbers for Evaluation of Coli-Aerogenes Tests by Fermentation Tube Method," *Reprint No. 1621*, *Public Health Repts. 49*, 393 (1934, revised 1940); and *Public Health Repts. 40*, 693 (1925) *Reprint No. 1029* p. 14.

TABLE 12b. MOST PROBABLE NUMBERS (MPN) PER 100 MILLILITERS OF SAMPLE

Using 5 Tubes
With 10, 1, and 0.1 ml Volumes

Pos[a]			MPN	Pos[a]			MPN	Pos[a]			MPN	Pos[a]			MPN	Pos[a]			MPN	Pos[a]			MPN
10	1	0.1		10	1	0.1		10	1	0.1		10	1	0.1		10	1	0.1		10	1	0.1	
0	0	0	0	1	0	0	2	2	0	0	4.5	3	0	0	7.8	4	0	0	13	5	0	0	23
0	0	1	1.8	1	0	1	4	2	0	1	6.8	3	0	1	11	4	0	1	17	5	0	1	31
0	0	2	3.6	1	0	2	6	2	0	2	9.1	3	0	2	13	4	0	2	21	5	0	2	43
0	0	3	5.4	1	0	3	8	2	0	3	12	3	0	3	16	4	0	3	25	5	0	3	58
0	0	4	7.2	1	0	4	10	2	0	4	14	3	0	4	20	4	0	4	30	5	0	4	76
0	0	5	9	1	0	5	12	2	0	5	16	3	0	5	23	4	0	5	36	5	0	5	95
0	1	0	1.8	1	1	0	4	2	1	0	6.8	3	1	0	11	4	1	0	17	5	1	0	33
0	1	1	3.6	1	1	1	6.1	2	1	1	9.2	3	1	1	14	4	1	1	21	5	1	1	46
0	1	2	5.5	1	1	2	8.1	2	1	2	12	3	1	2	17	4	1	2	26	5	1	2	64
0	1	3	7.3	1	1	3	10	2	1	3	14	3	1	3	20	4	1	3	31	5	1	3	84
0	1	4	9.1	1	1	4	12	2	1	4	17	3	1	4	23	4	1	4	36	5	1	4	110
0	1	5	11	1	1	5	14	2	1	5	19	3	1	5	27	4	1	5	42	5	1	5	130
0	2	0	3.7	1	2	0	6.1	2	2	0	9.3	3	2	0	14	4	2	0	22	5	2	0	49
0	2	1	5.5	1	2	1	8.2	2	2	1	12	3	2	1	17	4	2	1	26	5	2	1	70
0	2	2	7.4	1	2	2	10	2	2	2	14	3	2	2	20	4	2	2	32	5	2	2	95
0	2	3	9.2	1	2	3	12	2	2	3	17	3	2	3	24	4	2	3	38	5	2	3	120
0	2	4	11	1	2	4	15	2	2	4	19	3	2	4	27	4	2	4	44	5	2	4	150
0	2	5	13	1	2	5	17	2	2	5	22	3	2	5	31	4	2	5	50	5	2	5	180
0	3	0	5.6	1	3	0	8.3	2	3	0	12	3	3	0	17	4	3	0	27	5	3	0	79
0	3	1	7.4	1	3	1	10	2	3	1	14	3	3	1	21	4	3	1	33	5	3	1	110
0	3	2	9.3	1	3	2	13	2	3	2	17	3	3	2	24	4	3	2	39	5	3	2	140
0	3	3	11	1	3	3	15	2	3	3	20	3	3	3	28	4	3	3	45	5	3	3	180
0	3	4	13	1	3	4	17	2	3	4	22	3	3	4	31	4	3	4	52	5	3	4	210
0	3	5	15	1	3	5	19	2	3	5	25	3	3	5	35	4	3	5	59	5	3	5	250
0	4	0	7.5	1	4	0	11	2	4	0	15	3	4	0	21	4	4	0	34	5	4	0	130
0	4	1	9.4	1	4	1	13	2	4	1	17	3	4	1	24	4	4	1	40	5	4	1	170
0	4	2	11	1	4	2	15	2	4	2	20	3	4	2	28	4	4	2	47	5	4	2	220
0	4	3	13	1	4	3	17	2	4	3	23	3	4	3	32	4	4	3	54	5	4	3	280
0	4	4	15	1	4	4	19	2	4	4	25	3	4	4	36	4	4	4	62	5	4	4	350
0	4	5	17	1	4	5	22	2	4	5	28	3	4	5	40	4	4	5	69	5	4	5	430
0	5	0	9.4	1	5	0	13	2	5	0	17	3	5	0	25	4	5	0	41	5	5	0	240
0	5	1	11	1	5	1	15	2	5	1	20	3	5	1	29	4	5	1	48	5	5	1	350
0	5	2	13	1	5	2	17	2	5	2	23	3	5	2	32	4	5	2	56	5	5	2	540
0	5	3	15	1	5	3	19	2	5	3	26	3	5	3	37	4	5	3	64	5	5	3	920
0	5	4	17	1	5	4	22	2	5	4	29	3	5	4	41	4	5	4	72	5	5	4	1600
0	5	5	19	1	5	5	24	2	5	5	32	3	5	5	45	4	5	5	81	5	5	5	2400+

[a] Number of positive tubes with each of 3 volumes used.

TABLE 12c. MOST PROBABLE NUMBERS (MPN) PER 100 MILLILITERS OF SAMPLE
Using 3 Tubes
With 10, 1, and 0.1 ml Volumes

No. of Positive Tubes in Dilutions			MPN per 100 ml	No. of Positive Tubes in Dilutions			MPN per 100 ml
10 ml	1 ml	0.1 ml		10 ml	1 ml	0.1 ml	
0	0	0		2	0	0	9.1
0	0	1	3	2	0	1	14
0	0	2	6	2	0	2	20
0	0	3	9	2	0	3	26
0	1	0	3	2	1	0	15
0	1	1	6.1	2	1	1	20
0	1	2	9.2	2	1	2	27
0	1	3	12	2	1	3	34
0	2	0	6.2	2	2	0	21
0	2	1	9.3	2	2	1	28
0	2	2	12	2	2	2	35
0	2	3	16	2	2	3	42
0	3	0	9.4	2	3	0	29
0	3	1	13	2	3	1	36
0	3	2	16	2	3	2	44
0	3	3	19	2	3	3	53
1	0	0	3.6	3	0	0	23
1	0	1	7.2	3	0	1	39
1	0	2	11	3	0	2	64
1	0	3	15	3	0	3	95
1	1	0	7.3	3	1	0	43
1	1	1	11	3	1	1	75
1	1	2	15	3	1	2	120
1	1	3	19	3	1	3	160
1	2	0	11	3	2	0	93
1	2	1	15	3	2	1	150
1	2	2	20	3	2	2	210
1	2	3	24	3	2	3	290
1	3	0	16	3	3	0	240
1	3	1	20	3	3	1	460
1	3	2	24	3	3	2	1100
1	3	3	29				

TABLE 13. *SHIGELLA* SEROTYPES

TABLE 14. KAUFFMANN-WHITE SCHEMA OF *SALMONELLA* SEROTYPES

TABLE 13. *SHIGELLA* SEROTYPES[a]

	Shigella Commission 1950	Shigella Commission 1953	Ewing 1949	Ewing	Kauffmann and Ferguson 1947	Boyd 1938	Boyd 1940 1946	Weil and others 1944	English (older)	German	Other
Group A *S. dysenteriae*	1	1	I								*Bacterium shigae* *Shiga-Kruse*
	2	2	II							I	*S. ambigua*, *S. schmitzii*, *B. ambiguus*
	3	3	III								Q771, type 8524, *S. arabinotarda*
	4	4	IV								Q1167 *S. arabinotarda B*
	5	5	V								Q1030
	6	6	VI								Q454
	7	7	VII								Q902
		8									Serotype 599-52
Group B *S. flexneri*				Abbreviated Formula							
	1a	1a	I	I:4	1b	V	I	I	V	BC	Flexner
	1b	1b	I	I:4, 6	1a			I, III	VZ	A	
	2a	2a	II	II:4	2a	W	II	II	W	D	Strong, Hiss-Russell
	2b	2b	II	II:7, 8, 9	2b			II, VII	WX	DX	
	3	3	III	III:6, 7	3		III	III	Z	H	
	4a	4a	IV	IV:4	4a	103	IV	IV		F	Lentz Y2
	4b	4b	IV	IV:6	4b	103Z	IV	III, IV		J	
	4									F	*S. saigonensis*, *S. rio*
	5	5	V		5	P.119	V	V(V, VII)		G	
	6	6	VI		6	88	VI	VI		L	*S. newcastle*, Newcastle and Manchester bacilli
	X	X	X	—:7, 8, 9				VII	X		
	Y	Y	Y	—:4				VIII	Y	Y	Hiss-Russell
Group C *S. boydii*	1	1	I			170		IX			
	2	2	II			P.288		X			
	3	3	III			D.1		XI			
	4	4	IV			P.274		XIV		R	
	5	5	V			P.143		XIII			
	6	6	VI			D.19		XII			
	7	7	VII							N	Lavington, type T, *S. etousae*
		8									Serotype 112
		9								P	Serotype 1296/7
		10									Serotype 430
		11									Serotype 34
Group D *S. sonnei*			*S. sonnei*								Sonne-Duval, Sonne III, *S. ceylonensis-A*

[a] After Edwards and Ewing, *Identification of Enterobacteriaceae*, Burgess, Minneapolis, 1955.

TABLE 14. KAUFFMANN-WHITE SCHEMA OF *SALMONELLA* SEROTYPES[a]

Group	No.	Serotype	Somatic antigens	Flagellar antigens	
				Phase 1	Phase 2
A	1	*Salmonella paratyphi*	I, II, XII	a	—
B	2	*Salmonella kisangani*	I, IV, V, XII	a	1, 2
	3	*Salmonella hessarek*	IV, XII	a	1, 5
	4	*Salmonella fulica*	IV, V, XII	a	1, 5
	5	*Salmonella arechavaleta*	IV, V, XII	a	1, 7
	6	*Salmonella bispebjerg*	I, IV, XII	a	e, n, x
	7	*Salmonella abortivoequina*	IV, XII	—	e, n, x
	8	*Salmonella tinda*	I, IV, XII, XXVII	a	e, n, z_{15}
	9	*Salmonella schottmuelleri*	I, IV, V, XII	b	1, 2
	10	*Salmonella limete*	I, IV, XII, XXVII	b	1, 5
	11	*Salmonella schleissheim*	IV, XII, XXVII	b, z_{12}	—
	12	*Salmonella abony*	I, IV, V, XII	b	e, n, x
	13	*Salmonella abortusbovis*	I, IV, XII, XXVII	b	e, n, x
	14	*Salmonella wagenia*	I, IV, XII, XXVII	b	e, n, z_{15}
	15	*Salmonella wien*	IV, XII	b	1, w
	16	*Salmonella abortusovis*	IV, XII	c	1, 6
	17	*Salmonella altendorf*	IV, XII	c	1, 7
	18	*Salmonella bury*	IV, XII, XXVII	c	z_6
	19	*Salmonella stanley*	IV, V, XII	d	1, 2
	20	*Salmonella cairo*	I, IV, XII, XXVII	d	1, 2
	21	*Salmonella schwarzengrund*	I, IV, XII, XXVII	d	1, 7
	22	*Salmonella sarajane*	IV, XII, XXVII	d	e, n, x
	23	*Salmonella duisburg*	IV, XII	d	e, n, z_{15}
	24	*Salmonella salinatis*	IV, XII	d, e, h	d, e, n, z_{15}
	25	*Salmonella saintpaul*	I, IV, V, XII	e, h	1, 2
	26	*Salmonella reading*	IV, XII	e, h	1, 5
	27	*Salmonella kaposvar*	IV, V, XII	e, (h)	1, 5
	28	*Salmonella kaapstad*	IV, XII	e, h	1, 7
	29	*Salmonella chester*	IV, V, XII	e, h	e, n, x
	30	*Salmonella sandiego*	IV, V, XII	e, h	e, n, z_{15}
	31	*Salmonella derby*	I, IV, XII	f, g	—
	32	*Salmonella essen*	IV, XII	g, m	—
	33	*Salmonella hato*	IV, V, XII	g, m, s	—
	34	*Salmonella california*	IV, XII	g, m, t	—
	35	*Salmonella kingston*	I, IV, XII, XXVII	g, s, t	—
	36	*Salmonella budapest*	I, IV, XII	g, t	—
	37	*Salmonella typhimurium*	I, IV, V, XII	i	1, 2
	38	*Salmonella sp.*	I, IV, XII, XXVII	i	1, w
	39	*Salmonella texas*	IV, V, XXI	k	e, n, z_{15}
	39a	*Salmonella azteca*	IV, V, XII	l, v	1, 5
	40	*Salmonella bredeney*	I, IV, XII, XXVII	l, v	1, 7
	41	*Salmonella kimuenza*	I, IV, XII, XXVII	l, v	e, n, x
	42	*Salmonella brandenburg*	IV, XII	l, v	e, n, z_{15}
	43	*Salmonella banana*	IV, V, XII	m, t	—
	44	*Salmonella heidelberg*	IV, V, XII	r	1, 2
	45	*Salmonella coeln*	IV, V, XII	y	1, 2
	46	*Salmonella ball*	I, IV, XII	y	e, n, x

[a] After Edwards and Ewing, *Identification of Enterobacteriaceae*. Burgess, Minneapolis, 1955.

TABLE 14. KAUFFMANN-WHITE SCHEMA OF *SALMONELLA* SEROTYPES (*Continued*)

Group	No.	Serotype	Somatic antigens	Flagellar antigens	
				Phase 1	Phase 2
B	47	*Salmonella kiambu*	IV, XII	z	1, 5
	48	*Salmonella indiana*	IV, XII	z	1, 7
	49	*Salmonella stanleyville*	IV, V, XII	z_4, z_{23}	1, 2
	50	*Salmonella haifa*	I, IV, V, XII	z_{10}	1, 2
	51	*Salmonella ituri*	I, IV, XII	z_{10}	1, 5
	52	*Salmonella brancaster*	I, IV, XII	z_{29}	—
C_1	53	*Salmonella sanjuan*	VI, VII	a	1, 5
	54	*Salmonella austin*	VI, VII	a	1, 7
	55	*Salmonella oslo*	VI, VII	a	e, n, x
	56	*Salmonella denver*	VI, VII	a	e, n, z_{15}
	57	*Salmonella brazzaville*	VI, VII	b	1, 2
	58	*Salmonella edinburg*	VI, VII	b	1, 5
	59	*Salmonella georgia*	VI, VII	b	e, n, z_{15}
	60	*Salmonella leopoldville*	VI, VII	b	z_6
	61	*Salmonella choleraesuis*	VI, VII	c	1, 5
	62	*Salmonella hirschfeldii*	VI, VII, Vi	c	1, 5
	63	*Salmonella typhisuis*	VI, VII	c	1, 5
	64	*Salmonella decatur*	VI, VII	c	1, 5
	65	*Salmonella birkenhead*	VI, VII	c	1, 6
	66	*Salmonella sp.*	VI, VII	c	e, n, z_{15}
	67	*Salmonella mission*	VI, VII	d	1, 5
	68	*Salmonella amersfoort*	VI, VII	d	e, n, x
	69	*Salmonella livingston*	VI, VII	d	1, w
	70	*Salmonella lomita*	VI, VII	e, h	1, 5
	71	*Salmonella norwich*	VI, VII	e, h	1, 6
	72	*Salmonella braenderup*	VI, VII	e, h	e, n, z_{15}
	73	*Salmonella montevideo*	VI, VII	g, m, s	—
	74	*Salmonella menston*	VI, VII	g, s, t	—
	75	*Salmonella garoli*	VI, VII	i	1, 6
	76	*Salmonella thompson*	VI, VII	k	1, 5
	77	*Salmonella daytona*	VI, VII	k	1, 6
	78	*Salmonella singapore*	VI, VII	k	e, n, x
	78a	*Salmonella escanaba*	VI, VII	k	e, n, z_{15}
	79	*Salmonella concord*	VI, VII	l, v	1, 2
	80	*Salmonella irumu*	VI, VII	l, v	1, 5
	81	*Salmonella bonn*	VI, VII	l, v	e, n, x
	82	*Salmonella potsdam*	VI, VII	l, v	e, n, z_{15}
	83	*Salmonella colorado*	VI, VII	l, w	1, 5
	84	*Salmonella jerusalem*	VI, VII	l, w	z_{10}
	85	*Salmonella nessziona*	VI, VII	l, z_{13}	1, 5
	86	*Salmonella makiso*	VI, VII	l, z_{28}	z_6
	87	*Salmonella oranienburg*	VI, VII	m, t	—
	88	*Salmonella virchow*	VI, VII	r	1, 2
	89	*Salmonella infantis*	VI, VII	r	1, 5
	90	*Salmonella colindale*	VI, VII	r	1, 7
	91	*Salmonella papuana*	VI, VII	r	e, n, z_{15}
	92	*Salmonella richmond*	VI, VII	y	1, 2
	93	*Salmonella bareilly*	VI, VII	y	1, 5

TABLE 14. KAUFFMANN-WHITE SCHEMA OF *SALMONELLA* SEROTYPES (*Continued*)

Group	No.	Serotype	Somatic antigens	Flagellar antigens	
				Phase 1	Phase 2
C_1	94	*Salmonella hartford*	VI, VII	y	e, n, x
	95	*Salmonella mikawashima*	VI, VII	y	e, n, z_{15}
	96	*Salmonella aeququatoria*	VI, VII	z_4, z_{23}	e, n, z_{15}
	97	*Salmonella kralendyk*	VI, VII	z_4, z_{24}	—
	98	*Salmonella eschweiler*	VI, VII	z_{10}	1, 6
	99	*Salmonella mbandaka*	VI, VII	z_{10}	e, n, z_{15}
	100	*Salmonella tennessee*	VI, VII	z_{29}	—
	101	*Salmonella lille*	VI, VII	z_{38}	—
C_2	102	*Salmonella curacao*	VI, VIII	a	1, 6
	103	*Salmonella narashino*	VI, VIII	a	e, n, x
	104	*Salmonella nagoya*	VI, VIII	b	1, 5
	105	*Salmonella gatuni*	VI, VIII	b	e, n, x
	106	*Salmonella shipley*	VI, VIII	b	e, n, z_{15}
	107	*Salmonella banalia*	VI, VIII	b	z_6
	108	*Salmonella utah*	VI, VIII	c	1, 5
	109	*Salmonella bronx*	VI, VIII	c	1, 6
	110	*Salmonella belem*	VI, VIII	c	e, n, x
	111	*Salmonella quiniela*	VI, VIII	c	e, n, z_{15}
	112	*Salmonella muenchen*	VI, VIII	d	1, 2
	113	*Salmonella manhattan*	VI, VIII	d	1, 5
	114	*Salmonella newport*	VI, VIII	e, h	1, 2
	115	*Salmonella kottbus*	VI, VIII	e, h	1, 5
	116	*Salmonella lindenburg*	VI, VIII	i	1, 2
	117	*Salmonella takoradi*	VI, VIII	i	1, 5
	118	*Salmonella bonariensis*	VI, VIII	i	e, n, x
	119	*Salmonella litchfield*	VI, VIII	l, v	1, 2
	120	*Salmonella manchester*	VI, VIII	l, v	1, 7
	120a	*Salmonella holcomb*	VI, VIII	l, v	e, n, x
	121	*Salmonella fayed*	VI, VIII	l, w	1, 2
	121a	*Salmonella baragwanath*	VI, VIII	m, t	1, 5
	121b	*Salmonella germiston*	VI, VIII	m, t	e, n, x
	122	*Salmonella bovismorbificans*	VI, VIII	r	1, 5
	123	*Salmonella hidalgo*	VI, VIII	r	e, n, z_{15}
	124	*Salmonella tananarive*	VI, VIII	y	1, 5
	125	*Salmonella praha*	VI, VIII	y	e, n, z_{15}
	126	*Salmonella sp.*	VI, VIII	z_4, z_{23}	—
	127	*Salmonella duesseldorf*	VI, VIII	z_4, z_{24}	—
	128	*Salmonella tallahassee*	VI, VIII	z_4, z_{32}	—
	129	*Salmonella hadar*	VI, VIII	z_{10}	e, n, x
	130	*Salmonella glostrup*	VI, VIII	z_{10}	e, n, z_{15}
	131	*Salmonella sanga*	(VIII)	b	1, 7
	132	*Salmonella virginia*	(VIII)	d	—
	133	*Salmonella emek*	(VIII), XX	g, m, s	—
	134	*Salmonella kentucky*	(VIII), XX	i	z_6
	135	*Salmonella amherstiana*	(VIII)	l, (v)	1, 6
	136	*Salmonella hindmarsh*	(VIII)	r	1, 5
	137	*Salmonella corvallis*	(VIII), XX	z_4, z_{23}	—
	138	*Salmonella albany*	(VIII), XX	z_4, z_{24}	—

TABLE 14. KAUFFMANN-WHITE SCHEMA OF *SALMONELLA* SEROTYPES (*Continued*)

Group	No.	Serotype	Somatic antigens	Flagellar antigens	
				Phase 1	Phase 2
D	139	*Salmonella miami*	I, IX, XII	a	1, 5
	140	*Salmonella sendai*	I, IX, XII	a	1, 5
	141	*Salmonella saarbruecken*	I, IX, XII	a	1, 7
	142	*Salmonella lomalinda*	IX, XII	a	e. n. x
	143	*Salmonella durban*	IX, XII	a	e, n, z_{15}
	144	*Salmonella onarimon*	I, IX, XII	b	1, 2
	145	*Salmonella alabama*	IX, XII	c	e, n, z_{15}
	146	*Salmonella typhosa*	IX, XII, Vi	d	—
	147	*Salmonella ndolo*	IX, XII	d	1, 5
	148	*Salmonella strasbourg*	IX . . .	d	1, 7
	149	*Salmonella zega*	IX, XII	d	z_6
	150	*Salmonella jaffna*	IX, XII	d	z_{35}
	151	*Salmonella eastbourne*	I, IX, XII	e, h	1, 5
	152	*Salmonella israel*	IX, XII	e, h	e, n, z_{15}
	153	*Salmonella berta*	IX, XII	f, g, t	—
	154	*Salmonella enteritidis*	I, IX, XII	g, m	—
	155	*Salmonella blegdam*	IX, XII	g, m, q	—
	156	*Salmonella pensacola*	IX, XII	g, m, t	—
	157	*Salmonella dublin*	I, IX, XII	g, p	—
	158	*Salmonella rostock*	I, IX, XII	g, p, u	—
	159	*Salmonella moscow*	IX, XII	g, q	—
	160	*Salmonella neasden*	IX, XII	g, s, t	e, n, x
	161	*Salmonella seremban*	IX, XII	i	1, 5
	162	*Salmonella marylebone*	IX, XII	k	1, 2
	163	*Salmonella claibornei*	I, IX, XII	k	1, 5
	164	*Salmonella mendoza*	IX, XII	l, v	1, 2
	165	*Salmonella panama*	I, IX, XII	l, v	1, 5
	166	*Salmonella kapemba*	IX, XII	l, v	1, 7
	167	*Salmonella goettingen*	IX, XII	l, v	e, n, z_{15}
	168	*Salmonella daressalaam*	I, IX, XII	l, w	e, n
	169	*Salmonella napoli*	I, IX, XII	l, z_{13}	e, n, x
	170	*Salmonella javiana*	I, IX, XII	l, z_{28}	1, 5
	171	*Salmonella shoreditch*	IX, XII	r	e, n, z_{15}
	172	*Salmonella haarlem*	IX . . .	z	e, n, x
	173	*Salmonella wangata*	IX, XII	z_4, z_{22}	—
	174	*Salmonella portland*	IX, XII	z_{10}	1, 5
	175	*Salmonella canastel*	IX, XII	z_{29}	1, 5
	176	*Salmonella sp.*	IX, XII	z_{35}	z_6
	177	*Salmonella fresno*	IX, XII	z_{38}	—
	178	*Salmonella gallinarum*	I, IX, XII	—	—
	179	*Salmonella pullorum*	IX, XII	—	—
E_1	180	*Salmonella oxford*	III, X	a	1, 7
	181	*Salmonella butantan*	III, X	b	1, 5
	182	*Salmonella shangani*	III, X	d	1, 5
	183	*Salmonella vejle*	III, X	e, h	1, 2
	184	*Salmonella muenster*	III, X	e, h	1, 5
	185	*Salmonellaanatum*	III, X	e, h	1, 6

TABLE 14. KAUFFMANN-WHITE SCHEMA OF *SALMONELLA* SEROTYPES (*Continued*)

Group	No.	Serotype	Somatic antigens	Flagellar antigens	
				Phase 1	Phase 2
E_1	186	*Salmonella nyborg*	III, X	e, h	1, 7
	187	*Salmonella newlands*	III, X	e, h	e, n, x
	188	*Salmonella meleagridis*	III, X	e, h	1, w
	189	*Salmonella westhampton*	III, X	g, s, t	—
	190	*Salmonella zanzibar*	III, X	k	1, 5
	190a	*Salmonella newrochelle*	III, X	k	1, w
	191	*Salmonella nchanga*	III, X	l, v	1, 2
	192	*Salmonella london*	III, X	l, v	1, 6
	193	*Salmonella give*	III, X	l, v	1, 7
	194	*Salmonella clerkenwell*	III, X	l, w	z
	195	*Salmonella uganda*	III, X	l, z_{12}	1, 5
	195a	*Salmonella rutgers*	III, X	l, z_{40}	1, 7
	196	*Salmonella elizabethville*	III, X	r	1, 7
	197	*Salmonella simi*	III, X	r	e, n, z_{15}
	198	*Salmonella weltevreden*	III, X	r	z_6
	199	*Salmonella amager*	III, X	y	1, 2
	200	*Salmonella orion*	III, X	y	1, 5
	201	*Salmonella bolton*	III, X	y	e, n, z_{15}
	202	*Salmonella stockholm*	III, X	y	z_6
	202a	*Salmonella alexander*	III, X	z	1, 5
	203	*Salmonella lexington*	III, X	z_1	1, 5
	204	*Salmonella coquilhatville*	III, X	z_1	1, 7
	205	*Salmonella cairina*	III, X	z_{35}	z_6
	206	*Salmonella macallen*	III, X	z_{36}	—
E_2	207	*Salmonella goerlitz*	III, XV	e, h	1, 2
	208	*Salmonella newington*	III, XV	e, h	1, 6
	209	*Salmonella selandia*	III, XV	e, h	1, 7
	210	*Salmonella cambridge*	III, XV	e, h	1, w
	211	*Salmonella newbrunswick*	III, XV	l, v	1, 7
	212	*Salmonella kinshasa*	III, XV	l, z_{13}	1, 5
	213	*Salmonella tuebingen*	III, XV	y	1, 2
	214	*Salmonella binza*	III, XV	y	1, 5
	215	*Salmonella manila*	III, XV	z_{10}	1, 5
	215a	*Salmonella hamilton*	III, XV	z_{27}	
E_3	216	*Salmonella minneapolis*	(III), (XV), XXXIV	e, h	1, 6
	217	*Salmonella canoga*	(III), (XV), XXXIV	g, s, t	—
	218	*Salmonella thomasville*	(III), (XV), XXXIV	y	1, 5
	219	*Salmonella illinois*	(III), (XV), XXXIV	z_{10}	1, 5
	220	*Salmonella harrisonburg*	(III), (XV), XXXIV	z_{10}	1, 6
E_4	221	*Salmonella chittagong*	(I), III, X, (XIX)	b	z_{35}
	222	*Salmonella niloese*	I, III, XIX	d	z_6
	223	*Salmonella senftenberg*	I, III, XIX	g, s, t	—
	224	*Salmonella taksony*	I, III, XIX	i	z_6
	225	*Salmonella krefeld*	I, III, XIX	l, w	y
	226	*Salmonella schoeneberg*	I, III, XIX	z	e, n, z_{15}
	227	*Salmonella simsbury*	I, III, XIX	z_{27}	—
F	228	*Salmonella marseille*	XI	a	1, 5
	229	*Salmonella luciana*	XI	a	e, n, z_{15}

TABLE 14. KAUFFMANN-WHITE SCHEMA OF *SALMONELLA* SEROTYPES (*Continued*)

Group	No.	Serotype	Somatic antigens	Flagellar antigens	
				Phase 1	Phase 2
F	230	*Salmonella pharr*	XI	b	e, n, z_{15}
	231	*Salmonella chandans*	XI	d	e, n, x
	231a	*Salmonella montgomery*	XI	d, a	d, e, n, z_{15}
	232	*Salmonella chingola*	XI	e, h	1, 2
	233	*Salmonella aberdeen*	XI	i	1, 2
	234	*Salmonella veneziana*	XI	i	e, n, x
	235	*Salmonella pretoria*	XI	k	1, 2
	236	*Salmonella abaetetube*	XI	k	1, 5
	237	*Salmonella maracaibo*	XI	l, v	1, 5
	238	*Salmonella senegal*	XI	r	1, 5
	239	*Salmonella rubislaw*	XI	r	e, n, x
	240	*Salmonella solt*	XI	y	1, 5
	241	*Salmonella sp.*	XI	z_{10}	1, 2
	242	*Salmonella telhashomer*	XI	z_{10}	e, n, x
G	243	*Salmonella atlanta*	XIII, XXIII	b	—
	244	*Salmonella ibadan*	XIII, XXII	b	1, 5
	245	*Salmonella mississippi*	I, XIII, XXIII	b	1, 5
	246	*Salmonella mishmarhaemek*	I, XIII, XXIII	d	1, 5
	247	*Salmonella friedenau*	XIII, XXII	d	1, 6
	248	*Salmonella grumpensis*	XIII, XXIII	d	1, 7
	249	*Salmonella telelkebir*	XIII, XXIII	d	e, n, z_{15}
	250	*Salmonella wichita*	I, XIII, XXIII	d	z_{37}
	251	*Salmonella habana*	I, XIII, XXIII	f, g	—
	252	*Salmonella sp.*	XIII, XXIII	g, s, (t)	—
	253	*Salmonella borbeck*	XIII, XXII	l, v	1, 6
	254	*Salmonella worthington*	I, XIII, XXIII	l, w	z
	255	*Salmonella worcester*	I, XIII, XXIII	m, t	e, n, x
	256	*Salmonella nachshonim*	I, XIII, XXIII	z	1, 5
	257	*Salmonella poona*	XIII, XXII	z	1, 6
	258	*Salmonella bristol*	XIII, XXII	z	1, 7
	259	*Salmonella delplata*	I, XIII, XXIII	z_4, z_{23}	—
	260	*Salmonella cubana*	I, XIII, XXIII	z_{29}	—
	261	*Salmonella clifton*	XIII, XXII	z_{29}	1, 5
H	262	*Salmonella heves*	VI, XIV, XXIV	d	1, 5
	263	*Salmonella florida*	(I), VI, XIV, XXV	d	1, 7
	264	*Salmonella albuquerque*	VI, XIV, XXIV	d	z_6
	265	*Salmonella onderstepoort*	(I), VI, XIV, XXV	e, h	1, 5
	266	*Salmonella caracas*	(I), VI, XIV, XXV	g, m, s	—
	267	*Salmonella boecker*	VI, XIV	l, v	1, 7
	268	*Salmonella horsham*	(I), VI, XIV, XXV	l, v	e, n, x
	269	*Salmonella madelia*	(I), VI, XIV, XXV	y	1, 7
	270	*Salmonella carrau*	VI, XIV, XXIV	y	1, 7
	271	*Salmonella homosassa*	(I), VI, XIV, XXV	z	1, 5
	272	*Salmonella sundsvall*	(I), VI, XIV, XXV	z	e, n, x
	273	*Salmonella siegburg*	VI, XIV, XVIII	z_4, z_{23}	—
	274	*Salmonella uzaramo*	(I), VI, XIV, XXV	z_4, z_{24}	—
I	275	*Salmonella brazil*	XVI	a	1, 5
	276	*Salmonella hull*	XVI	b	1, 2

TABLE 14. KAUFFMANN-WHITE SCHEMA OF *SALMONELLA* SEROTYPES (*Continued*)

Group	No.	Serotype	Somatic antigens	Flagellar antigens	
				Phase 1	Phase 2
I	277	*Salmonella hvittingfoss*	XVI	b	e, n, x
	278	*Salmonella vancouver*	XVI	c	1, 5
	279	*Salmonella gaminara*	XVI	d	1, 7
	280	*Salmonella nottingham*	XVI	d	e, n, z_{15}
	281	*Salmonella weston*	XVI	e, h	z_6
	282	*Salmonella szentes*	XVI	k	1, 2
	283	*Salmonella orientalis*	XVI	k	e, n, z_{15}
	284	*Salmonella shanghai*	XVI	l, v	1, 6
	285	*Salmonella salford*	XVI	l, v	e, n, x
	286	*Salmonella rowbarton*	XVI	m, t	—
	287	*Salmonella lisboa*	XVI	z_{10}	1, 6
	288	*Salmonella jacksonville*	XVI	z_{29}	—
Further groups	289	*Salmonella kirkee*	XVII	b	1, 2
	290	*Salmonella bleadon*	XVII	(f), g, t	—
	291	*Salmonella matadi*	XVII	k	e, n, x
	292	*Salmonella morotai*	XVII	l, v	1, 2
	293	*Salmonella michigan*	XVII	l, v	1, 5
	294	*Salmonella carmel*	XVII	l, v	e, n, x
	295	*Salmonella usumbura*	XVIII	d	1, 7
	296	*Salmonella memphis*	XVIII	k	1, 5
	297	*Salmonella cerro*	XVIII	z_4, z_{23}	—
	298	*Salmonella blukwa*	XVIII	z_4, z_{24}	—
	299	*Salmonella minnesota*	XXI	b	e, n, x
	299a	*Salmonella gwaai*	XXI	z_4	z_{24}
	300	*Salmonella seattle*	XXVIII	a	e, n, x
	301	*Salmonella langford*	XXVIII	b	e, n, z_{15}
	302	*Salmonella kaltenhausen*	XXVIII	b	z_6
	303	*Salmonella mundonobo*	XXVIII	d	1, 7
	304	*Salmonella taunton*	XXVIII	k	e, n, x
	305	*Salmonella sp.*	XXVIII	l, v	e, n, z_{15}
	306	*Salmonella chicago*	XXVIII	r	1, 5
	307	*Salmonella kibusi*	XXVIII	r	e, n, x
	308	*Salmonella pomona*	XXVIII	y	1, 7
	309	*Salmonella telaviv*	XXVIII	y	e, n, z_{15}
	310	*Salmonella ezra*	XXVIII	z	1, 7
	311	*Salmonella urbana*	XXX	b	e, n, x
	312	*Salmonella godesburg*	XXX	g, m	—
	313	*Salmonella landau*	XXX	i	1, 2
	314	*Salmonella morehead*	XXX	i	1, 5
	315	*Salmonella donna*	XXX	l, v	1, 5
	316	*Salmonella matopeni*	XXX	y	1, 2
	317	*Salmonella bodjonegoro*	XXX	z_4, z_{24}	—
	318	*Salmonella adelaide*	XXXV	f, g	—
	319	*Salmonella gambia*	XXXV	i	e, n, z_{15}
	320	*Salmonella monschaui*	XXXV	m, t	—
	321	*Salmonella alachua*	XXXV	z_4, z_{23}	—
	322	*Salmonella kasenyi*	XXXVIII	e, h	1, 5
	323	*Salmonella korovi*	XXXVIII	g, m, s	—

TABLE 14. KAUFFMANN-WHITE SCHEMA OF *SALMONELLA* SEROTYPES (*Continued*)

Group	No.	Serotype	Somatic antigens	Flagellar antigens	
				Phase 1	Phase 2
Further groups	324	*Salmonella mgulani*	XXXVIII	i	1, 2
	325	*Salmonella inverness*	XXXVIII	k	1, 6
	326	*Salmonella lindi*	XXXVIII	r	1, 5
	327	*Salmonella emmastad*	XXXVIII	r	1, 6
	328	*Salmonella freetown*	XXXVIII	y	1, 5
	329	*Salmonella colombo*	XXXVIII	y	1, 6
	330	*Salmonella champaign*	XXXIX	k	1, 5
	331	*Salmonella riogrande*	XL	b	1, 5
	332	*Salmonella johannesburg*	I, XL	b	e, n, x
	333	*Salmonella duval*	I, XL	b	e, n, z_{15}
	334	*Salmonella allandale*	I, XL	k	1, 6
	335	*Salmonella waycross*	XLI	z_4, z_{23}	—
	336	*Salmonella uphill*	XLII	b	e, n, x
	336a	*Salmonella rand*	XLII	z	e, n, z_{15}, z_{16}
	337	*Salmonella weslaco*	XLII	z_{36}	—
	338	*Salmonella berkley*	XLIII	a	1, 5
	339	*Salmonella milwaukee*	XLIII	f, g	—
	340	*Salmonella ahuza*	XLIII	k	1, 5
	341	*Salmonella kingabwa*	XLIII	y	1, 5
	342	*Salmonella niarembe*	XLIV	a	1, w
	343	*Salmonella deversoir*	XLV	c	e, n, x
	344	*Salmonella windhoek*	XLV	g, t	1, 5
	345	*Salmonella bulawayo*	XLIX	z	1, 5
	346	*Salmonella greenside*	L	z	e, n

TABLE 15. PHENOL COEFFICIENTS

TABLE 15. PHENOL COEFFICIENTS [a]

Substance	Against *Salmonella typhosa*		Against *Staphylococcus aureus*	
	37 C	20 C	37 C	20 C
Acetophenone	4.2			
N-(Acylcolaminoformylmethyl)-pyridinium chloride	200	111	200	150
	343	222	571	500
Alkylbenzyldimethylammonium chlorides	271-429	176-317	293-407	150-362
		233[b]		323[b]
		158[c]		181[c]
Almond oil	4.5			
m-Amoxyphenol	38		36	
o-Amoxyphenol	22		23	
o-sec-Amoxyphenol	18		20	
p-Amoxyphenol	29		30	
p-sec-Amoxyphenol	19		26	
Amyl alcohol	0.8		0.6	
2-Amyl-4-bromophenol	62		571	
2-*sec*-Amyl-4-bromophenol	33		150	
4-*tert*-Amyl-2-bromophenol	33		150	
2-*sec*-Amyl-4-chloro-3,5-dimethylphenol	15.6 (approx.)		750	
2-Amyl-4-chlorophenol	156		500	
2-*sec*-Amyl-4-chlorophenol	47		312	
4-Amyl-2-chlorophenol	80		286	
4-*tert*-Amyl-2-chlorophenol	32		125	
3-Amyl-2-cresol	250[d]			
3-Amyl-4-cresol	250[d]			
4-Amyl-3-cresol	280[d]			
Amyl *p*-hydroxyphenyl sulfide	14.5		24.5	
4-Amylphenol	53		125	
	104		20	
4-*tert*-Amylphenol	30		94	
4-Amylresorcinol	33		30	
	47			
Amyl salicylate	4			
Anethole	11			
Anisaldehyde	7			
Aniseed oil	3.5			
Anthranilic acid	2			
Azochloramid	543		236	

[a] These data have been selected from the literature covering the period from 1919 to 1959. They represent values obtained by variations of a method originally known as the Hygienic Laboratory (U.S. Public Health Service) method, modified by Reddish, standardized as the FDA (U.S. Food and Drug Administration) method by Ruehle and Brewer, and superseded by the A.O.A.C. (*Methods of Analysis*, Association of Official Agricultural Chemists) method. Because of these variations and individual variations in technique, "phenol coefficients" are not to be taken as absolute values. It must also be understood that the values given for mercurials, quaternary ammonium compounds, and compounds yielding available chlorine must be interpreted with caution.

[b] Quaternary inactivating medium used.

[c] By use-dilution method.

[d] Rideal-Walker method.

TABLE 15. PHENOL COEFFICIENTS (*Continued*)

Substance	Against *Salmonella typhosa*		Against *Staphylococcus aureus*	
	37 C	20 C	37 C	20 C
Backhousia citriodora oil	16			
Benzaldehyde	9			
Benzyl acetate	2			
Benzyl alcohol	5			
2-Benzyl-4-chlorophenol	71		200	
2-Benzyl-4-chloro-3-methylphenol	18.3		375	
2-Benzyl-4-chloro-3,5-dimethylphenol			750	
o-Benzyloxyphenol	19		15	
p-Benzyloxyphenol	21		14	
Benzylphloroglucinol	8 (approx.)			
4-Benzylresorcinol	18	18.3	14	11.3
Bergamot oil	4			
Bithionol. See **2,2′-thiobis(4,6-dichlorophenol).**				
Borneol	10			
Bornyl acetate	6			
Bothagrass oil	1.5			
4-(4-Bromobenzyl)resorcinol		55		51
5-Bromo-4-benzylresorcinol		37		45
4-Bromo-2-butylphenol	156		313	
4-Bromo-2-cyclohexylphenol	23		429	
4-Bromo-2-ethylphenol	31		25	
2-Bromo-4-hexylphenol	20		625	
4-Bromo-2-hexylphenol			1250	
2-Bromo-4-hydroxydiphenyl	150		63	
4-Bromo-2,4-dihydroxydiphenylmethane	55		51	
5-Bromo-2,4-dihydroxydiphenylmethane	37		45	
2-Bromo-3,3-dimethoxy-4-propylphenol			357	
3-Bromo-4-hydroxydiphenylmethane	19		170	
5-Bromo-4-hydroxydiphenylmethane	26		295	
4-Bromo-2-methylphenol	12.5		11.3	
	31.3		25	
2-Bromophenol	3.8		3.7	
	3.3		3.1	
4-Bromophenol	5.4		4.6	
	6		5	
2-Bromo-4-phenylphenol	140-160			
2-Bromo-4-phenylphenol, sodium salt	128-147			
4-Bromo-2-propylphenol	62		62	
m-Butoxyphenol	20		18	
o-Butoxyphenol	9.8		10	
p-Butoxyphenol	14		9.3	
Butyl alcohol	0.3		0.2	
2-*sec*-Butyl-4-chloro-3,5-dimethylphenol	29		563	
6-*sec*-Butyl-4-chloro-3-methylphenol	50		500	
2-Butyl-4-chlorophenol	141		257	
4-Butyl-2-chlorophenol	86		94	
4-Butyl-*m*-cresol	100[d]			
3-Butyl-*o*-cresol	60[d]			

TABLE 15. PHENOL COEFFICIENTS (*Continued*)

Substance	Against *Salmonella typhosa*		Against *Staphylococcus aureus*	
	37 C	20 C	37 C	20 C
3-Butyl-*p*-cresol	95[d]			
4-Butylphenol	47		44	
	70		21	
4-Butylresorcinol	22		10	
	15			
Camphor	6.2			
Capraldehyde	7			
Caprylaldehyde	16			
Caraway oil	5.4			
Cardamom oil	10			
Cassia oil	1.4[d]			
	6		5.7	
Ceepryn chloride. See **cetylpyridinium chloride.**				
Cetab. See **cetyltrimethylammonium bromide.**				
Cetramide. See **cetyltrimethylammonium bromide.**				
Cetylpyridinium chloride	228	133[b]	337	350
		95[c]		230[b]
				128[c]
Cetyltrimethylammonium bromide	150		650	300
			1000	500
4-(4-Chlorobenzyl)resorcinol	63		40	
5-Chloro-4-benzylresorcinol	48		36	
4-Chloro-2-cyclohexylphenol	26		438	
4-Chloro-2-diethylmethyl-3,5-dimethylphenol	<13		1143	
4-Chloro-6-diethylmethyl-3-methyl-phenol	23		625	
4-Chloro-2,4-dihydroxydiphenylmethane	63		40	
5-Chloro-2,4-dihydroxydiphenylmethane	48		37	
4-Chloro-3,5-dimethylphenol	30		26	
4-Chloro-2-ethyl-3,5-dimethylphenol	46		106	
4-Chloro-2-ethyl-6-isopropyl-3-methylphenol	57		200	
4-Chloro-6-ethyl-3-methylphenol	64		50	
2-Chloro-4-ethylphenol	17.2		15.7	
4-Chloro-2-ethylphenol	29		34	
2-Chloro-4-heptylphenol	16.7		375	
4-Chloro-2-heptylphenol	20 (approx.)		1500	
2-Chloro-4-hexylphenol	23		500	
4-Chloro-2-hexylphenol	23 (approx.)		1250	
2-Chloro-4-hydroxydiphenyl	120			
3-Chloro-4-hydroxydiphenylmethane	36		125	
5-Chloro-4-hydroxydiphenylmethane	74		215	
4-Chloro-2-isopropyl-3,5-dimethylphenol	81		313	
4-Chloro-6-isopropyl-3-methylphenol	107		150	
4-Chloro-3-methyl-6-*sec*-octylphenol	21 (approx.)		>89	
4-Chloro-3-methyl-2-phenethylphenol			375	

TABLE 15. PHENOL COEFFICIENTS (*Continued*)

Substance	Against *Salmonella typhosa*		Against *Staphylococcus aureus*	
	37 C	20 C	37 C	20 C
2-Chloro-4-methylphenol	6.3		7.5	
4-Chloro-2-methylphenol	12.5		12.5	
4-Chloro-3-methylphenol	10.7		11.3	
4-Chloro-3-methyl-6-propylphenol	133		200	
4-Chloro-2-octylphenol			1750	
4-Chloro-2-phenethylphenol	100		375	
2-Chlorophenol	2.5		2.9	
	3.6		3.8	
4-Chlorophenol	4.3		4.3	
	3.9		4.0	
2-Chloro-4-phenylphenol	130			
2-Chloro-4-phenylphenol, sodium salt	73-80			
2-Chloro-4-propylphenol	40		32	
4-Chloro-2-propylphenol	93		93	
Cineol	3.5			
Cinnamaldehyde	8.8-17			
Cinnamic acid	2.5[d]			
Cinnamon leaf oil	7.5[d]			
Cinnamyl alcohol	5			
Citral	18.8-19.5			
Citronella oil	5.5			
Citronellic acid	1[d]			
Citronellol	8.6-14			
Clove oil	5.5-8.5			
Coconut alkylresorcinols	100			
Coumarin	3.2-4			
Creosote, synthetic	1.4		0.7	
Creosote, wood	3.9		3.8	
	3.6			
p-Cresol	2.0-2.3		2.3	
Cresol	2.5[d]			
Cresol Compound N. F.		2.3		1.6
Cresylic disinfectants		3.5-5.5		2.4-3.0
CTAB. See **cetyltrimethylammonium bromide.**				
Cymene	8			
D.C.M.X. See **2,4-dichloro-3,5-dimethylxylenol.**				
Decyl alcohol	5			
2,4-Dibromophenol	19		22	
4,6-Dibromoresorcinol	4.0		4.5	
2,4-Dichloro-3,5-dimethylxylenol	250		160	
Dichlorophene. See **2,2′-methylenebis(4-chlorophenol).**				
2,4-Dichlorophenol	13.3		12.7	
4,6-Dichlororesorcinol	3.2		3.9	
4,6-Diethylresorcinol	10			

TABLE 15. PHENOL COEFFICIENTS (*Continued*)

Substance	Against *Salmonella typhosa* 37 C	Against *Salmonella typhosa* 20 C	Against *Staphylococcus aureus* 37 C	Against *Staphylococcus aureus* 20 C
2,4-Dihydroxydiphenylmethane. See **4-benzylresorcinol.**				
2,4-Dimethylphenol. See **2,4-xylenol.**				
2,5-Dimethylphenol. See **2,5-xylenol.**				
2,6-Dimethylphenol. See **2,6-xylenol.**				
3,4-Dimethylphenol. See **3,4-xylenol.**				
4,6-Dipropylresorcinol	18			
Doryphora sassafras oil	13			
Emulsept. See ***N*-(acylcolaminoformylmethyl)pyridinium chloride.**				
m-Ethoxyphenol	3.6		3.0	
o-Ethoxyphenol	1.8		1.6	
p-Ethoxyphenol	1.5		1.5	
Ethyl alcohol	0.04		0.04	
3-Ethyl-*p*-cresol	12.5[d]			
4-Ethyl-*m*-cresol	12.5[d]			
Ethyl decab. See **ethyldimethyloleylammonium bromide.**				
Ethyldimethyloleylammonium bromide	228	133	262	250
Ethylmercuric chloride	88		233	
4-Ethylphenol	6.3-7.5		6.3-10	
Ethylresorcinol	1.6			
Eucalyptus australiana oil	5			
Eucalyptus citriodor oil	8			
Eucalyptus cneorifolia oil	7.5			
Eucalyptus dives oil	8			
Eucalyptus oil	1.6[d]			
Eucalyptus radiata oil	10			
Eugenol	14.4		9.7	
Fennel oil	13.0			
G-4. See **2,2′-methylenebis(4-chlorophenol).**				
G-5, See **2,2′-methylenebis(4,6-dichlorophenol).**				
G-5-S. See **2,2′-thiobis(4,6-dichlorophenol).**				
G-11. See **2,2′-methylenebis(3,4,6-trichlorophenol).**				
G-11-S. See **2,2′-thiobis(3,4,6-trichlorophenol).**				
Geraniol	11.5-21			
Geranium oil	6.5			
Geranyl acetate	0			
Guaiacol, natural	1.6		1.7	
Guaiacol, synthetic	1.1		1.1	
Heliotropin. See **piperonal.**				
4-Heptenylpyrogallol			120	

TABLE 15. PHENOL COEFFICIENTS (*Continued*)

Substance	Against *Salmonella typhosa*		Against *Staphylococcus aureus*	
	37 C	20 C	37 C	20 C
Heptyl alcohol	6.8			
4-Heptyl-*m*-cresol	30[d]			
m-Heptyloxyphenol	21		330	
o-Heptyloxyphenol	9.7		37	
p-Heptyloxyphenol	17		200	
4-Heptylphenol	16.7		625	
	20		21	
4-Heptylpyrogallol			50	
4-Heptylresorcinol	30		280	
3,3′,5,5′,6,6′-Hexachloro-2,2′-dihydroxydiphenylmethane. See **2,2′-methylenebis(3,4,6-trichlorophenol).**				
Hexachlorophene. See **2,2′-methylenebis(3,4,6-trichlorophenol).**				
4-Hexenylresorcinol		40	150	
Hexyl alcohol	2.3			
4-Hexyl-*m*-cresol	275[d]			
3-Hexyl-*o*-cresol	180[d]			
3-Hexyl-*p*-cresol	175[d]			
m-Hexyloxyphenol	46		125	
o-Hexyloxyphenol	17		28	
p-Hexyloxyphenol	18		100	
2-Hexylphenol	15		26	
4-Hexylphenol	33		313	
	90			
Hexylphloroglucinol	8			
4-Hexylresorcinol	33		67	
	45-56		98	
Hyamine 1622. See ***p*-tert-octylphenoxyethoxyethyldimethylbenzylammonium chloride.**				
Hydrochloric acid	3-7			
Hydrochloric acid (1%); mercuric chloride (1:1000) solution			257	
Hydrocinnamaldehyde	7			
Hydrocinnamylphloroglucinol	8 (approx.)			
4-Hydrocinnamylresorcinol	89			
Hydrogen sulfide	0		2.3	
Hydroquinone	>12		0.4	
Hydroquinone monoethers. See corresponding *p*-alkoxyphenol, e.g., for hydroquinone monomethyl ether, see ***p*-methoxyphenol.**				
Hydroquinone monohydrocinnamyl ether	10		13	
m-Hydroxybenzoic acid	2.6		2.1	
Hydroxycitronellol	5.3			
2-Hydroxydiphenyl	33			
m-Hydroxydiphenyl oxide	40			
o-Hydroxydiphenyl oxide	17			

TABLE 15. PHENOL COEFFICIENTS (*Continued*)

Substance	Against *Salmonella typhosa*		Against *Staphylococcus aureus*	
	37 C	20 C	37 C	20 C
p-Hydroxydiphenyl oxide	41			
m-Hydroxydiphenyl sulfide	68			
o-Hydroxydiphenyl sulfide	33			
p-Hydroxydiphenyl sulfide	115			
p-Hydroxyphenylphenyl sulfide	16.8		23	
Iodine		170-233		e
2% dilute alcohol solution		4.1-5.2		e
2% U.S.P. solution		3.2-4.1		e
2% isotonic solution		4.4-5.5		e
3% dilute alcohol solution		5.5-7.5		e
3% solution (diluted with alcohol from old 7% U.S.P. tincture of iodine)		5.3-6.1		e
Tincture, U.S.P. (old, 7%)	18		22-32	
Isoamylresorcinol	46			
Isobutylresorcinol	12.8			
Isoeugenol	10.2			
Isohexylresorcinol	105			
Isomenthol	20			
Isopropyl alcohol	0.6		0.5	
Isosafrole	12			
Kachigrass oil	3.6			
Lauryl aldehyde	1			
Lavender oil	1.6[d]			
	4.4			
Lemon oil	0.4[d]			
	3.8			
Lemongrass oil	17			
Leptospermum citratum oil	15			
Limonene	1			
Linalool	7			
	13			
Linalyl acetate	3.5			
	5.3			
"Listerine"	0.02		0.01	
"Lysol"	1.9		3.5	
Menthol	20		5.1	
Menthone	10			
Merbromin	2.7		5.3	1.7
Solution	0.7		0.1	
Mercuric chloride	775		166	
Solution, 1:1000		100	186	143
Mercurochrome. See **Merbromin.**				
Merthiolate. See **Thimerosal.**				

[e] Activity approximately the same against *Staphylococcus aureus.*

TABLE 15. PHENOL COEFFICIENTS (*Continued*)

Substance	Against *Salmonella typhosa*		Against *Staphylococcus aureus*	
	37 C	20 C	37 C	20 C
Metaphen. See **Nitromersol.**				
m-Methoxyphenol	1.3		1.2	
4-Methylresorcinol			1.5	
Methyl alcohol	0.026		0.03	
Methyl anthranilate	6.5			
Methyl benzoate	3.0			
Methyl eugenyl ether	13.5			
4-Methylphenol. See ***p*-cresol.**				
Methyl salicylate	5.5			
2,2′-Methylenebis(4-chlorophenol)	25-50		15-40	
2,2′-Methylenebis(4,6-dichlorophenol)	5-15		15-40	
2,2′-Methylenebis(3,4,6-trichlorophenol)	5-15		15-40	
β-Naphthol			11.4	
Neroli oil	5.5			
Nitromersol	1792		2250	
Solution	30		12.5	
m-Nitrophenol	3 (approx.)			
Nonyl alcohol	13			
m-Nonyloxyphenol	3.4		650	
4-Nonylresorcinol	0		980	
9-Octadecenyldimethylethylammonium bromide. See **ethyldimethyloleylammonium bromide.**				
Octyl alcohol	21		0.6	
m-Octyloxyphenol	2		580	
p-Octyloxyphenol			360	
p-*tert*-Octylphenoxyethoxyethyldimethylbenzylammonium chloride	257	200 167[b] 115[c]	300	323 230[b] 214[c]
4-Octylresorcinol	400		680	
Onyx BTC. See **alkylbenzyldimethylammonium chlorides.**				
Onyxide. See **ethyldimethyloleylammonium bromide.**				
Orange oil, sweet	2.2			
Orris otto	3.5			
"O-syl" (saponated formula containing 2-phenylphenol)		5.6	4.0	3.3
Orcinol	0.53			
Patchouli oil	3.5			
Pelargonaldehyde	22			

TABLE 15. PHENOL COEFFICIENTS (*Continued*)

Substance	Against *Salmonella typhosa*		Against *Staphylococcus aureus*	
	37 C	20 C	37 C	20 C
"Petroleum acids"				
Distillation fraction C				
200-203	4.3			
212-215	5.9			
224-227	11.6			
236-239	18.8			
248-251	15.3			
260-263	16.5			
Pettigrain oil	3.5			
Phellandral	9.3			
Phellandrene	1			
Phemerol. See ***p*-tert-octylphenoxyethoxyethyldimethylbenzylammonium chlorides.**				
m-Phenethoxyphenol	35		39	
o-Phenethoxyphenol	22		21	
p-Phenethoxyphenol	25		29	
Phenethyl alcohol	9			
Phenethylphloroglucinol	8 (approx.)			
4-Phenethylresorcinol	41		21	
Phenol	1	1	1	1
β-Phenoxyethyldimethyldodecylammonium bromide		433		521
m-Phenoxyphenol	40		37	
o-Phenoxyphenol	17		11	
p-Phenoxyphenol	41		28	
Phenylethyl alcohol. See **phenethyl alcohol.**				
Phenylmercuric nitrate	250[d]	625	300	
2-Phenylphenol. See **"O-syl."**				
4-Phenylpropylresorcinol. See **hydrocinnamylresorcinol.**				
5-Phenylresorcinol			12	
Phloroglucinol	0.35			
Pine oil disinfectants			0	
Rosin soap type				
60% pine oil	5-9			
	2-3			
Hygienic Laboratory formulation	3.5-4.5			
Sulfonated oil type	8-9			
Pinene	1			
Piperitone	8			
Piperonal	2.8			
m-Propoxyphenol	6.9		5.4	
o-Propoxyphenol	4.1		3.8	
p-Propoxyphenol	5.4		4.1	
Propyl alcohol	0.1		0.08	
4-Propyl-*m*-cresol	34[d]			
4-Propylphenol	20		16.3	
4-Propylresorcinol	4.8		3.7	
Pyrochatechol	0.9		0.6	

TABLE 15. PHENOL COEFFICIENTS (*Continued*)

Substance	Against *Salmonella typhosa*		Against *Staphylococcus aureus*	
	37 C	20 C	37 C	20 C
Pyrochatechol monoethers. See corresponding *o*-alkoxyphenol, e.g., for pyrochatechol monomethyl ether, see ***o*-methoxyphenol.**				
Pyrochatechol monohydrocinnamyl ether	15		19	
Pyrogallol	0.8			
Quartol. See **ethyldimethyloleylammonium bromide.**				
Resorcinol	0.4		0.4	
Resorcinol monoethers. See corresponding alkoxyphenol, e.g., for resorcinol monomethyl ether, see ***m*-methoxyphenol.**				
Resorcinol 4-chlorobenzyl ether	61		38	
Resorcinol monobenzyl ether	21		16	
Resorcinol monohydrocinnamyl ether	34		89	
Resorcinol monophenylpropyl ether. See **resorcinol monohydrocinnamyl ether.**				
Roccal. See **alkylbenzyldimethylammonium chlorides.**				
Rose otto	7			
Rosemary oil	5.2			
Safrole	10.8			
Salicylic acid			0.087	
Sandalwood oil	1.2			
Santalum album oil	1.5			
"Santophen"				
Percentage of chlorophenylphenol in solutions of 40% coconut oil soap:				
1%	0.6		0	
2%	2.8		1.0	
3%	4.7		5.0	
4%	6.5		8.0	
Silver citrate	24		5.5	
Silver lactate	3.7		1.0	
Silver nitrate	6.7		0.7	
Silver protein, mild	0.4		0.11	
Silver protein, strong	0.9		0.14	
Sulfur, colloidal	2.9		3.6	
Tar-oil disinfectants		2.8-11.1		0.4-2.0
Tetrachlorophene. See **2,2′-methylene-bis(4,6-dichlorophenol).**				
Terpineol	7.5			
Thimerosal	600	40-50	62.5	40-50
2,2′-Thiobis(4,6-dichlorophenol)	5-15		15-40	
2,2′-Thiobis(3,4,6-trichlorophenol)			15-40	
Thyme oil	12.2			

TABLE 15. PHENOL COEFFICIENTS (*Continued*)

Substance	Against *Salmonella typhosa*		Against *Staphylococcus aureus*	
	37 C	20 C	37 C	20 C
Thymol	25		27	
2,4,6-Tribromoresorcinol	6.4		6.4	
2,4,5-Trichlorophenol	40 (pH 6)			
2,4,5-Trichlorophenol	1 (pH 10)			
2,4,6-Trichlorophenol	23		25	
2,4,6-Trichlororesorcinol	5.0		4.3	
Tridecyl aldehyde	3			
Triethylphloroglucinol	2.5			
Undecylenaldehyde	6			
Vanillin	3.5 5.4			
Verbena oil	9.2			
Wintergreen oil	4.5			
2,4-Xylenol	5.0	5.0	4.4	4.2
2,5-Xylenol	5.0	5.0	4.4	4.2
2,6-Xylenol	3.8	5.0	4.4	4.2
3,4-Xylenol	5.0	5.0	3.8	4.2
Zephiran. See **alkylbenzyldimethylammonium chlorides.**				
Zephirol. See **alkylbenzyldimethylammonium chlorides.**				

TABLE 16. SOME BACTERIAL DISEASES OF HUMAN BEINGS AND ANIMALS

TABLE 17a. SOME VIRAL DISEASES OF HUMAN BEINGS

TABLE 17b. ARBO (ARTHROPOD-BORNE ANIMAL) VIRUSES

TABLE 18. SOME RICKETTSIAL PARASITES OF HUMAN BEINGS AND ANIMALS

TABLE 16. SOME BACTERIAL DISEASES OF HUMAN BEINGS AND ANIMALS

Disease	Microorganism	Host	Mode of Transmission
Actinobacillosis. See **wooden tongue**			
Actinomycosis. See **lumpy jaw.**			
Anthrax	*Bacillus anthracis*	Sheep, cattle, swine, and other animals	Soil-borne; contaminated feed, water; infected carcasses
		Man	Contact with infected animal materials, such as carcasses and hides; soil
Bacterial influenza	*Haemophilus influenzae*	Man	Probably droplet infection
Bacteroidosis	*Spherophorus necrophorus*	Man and animals necrotic lesions	Feces-borne; unsanitary conditions
Black leg	*Clostridium chauvoei*	Cattle and other animals	Soil-borne; infected wounds
Botulism	*Clostridium parabotulinum, C. botulinum*	Man	Ingestion of spoiled food containing toxin
Brucellosis	*Brucella abortus*	Cattle, man	Ingestion of contaminated milk
	Brucella melitensis	Goat, sheep, man	Ingestion of contaminated milk
	Brucella suis	Swine, man	Contact
Bubonic plague. See **plague.**			
Chanchroid	*Haemophilus ducreyi*	Man	Sexual contact
Chicken cholera	*Pasteurella multocida*	Fowl	Infected feed, water; contact
Cholera	*Vibrio comma*	Man	Contaminated water, food; feces-borne
Conjunctivitis	*Haemophilus aegyptius*	Man	Contact
	Moraxella lacunata	Man	Not known
Diphtheria	*Corynebacterium diphtheriae*	Man	Contact
Dysentery, bacillary	*Shigella flexneri* and other *Shigella* sp.	Man	Contaminated water, food; feces-borne; fly-borne
	Vibrio jejuni	Cattle	Contaminated water, feed, manure-borne
Epidemic cerebrospinal meningitis	*Neisseria meningitidis*	Man	Respiratory tract of carrier
Erysipelas	*Erysipelothrix insidiosa*	Swine, sheep, birds	Contaminated feed, water, soil; feces-borne
Erysipeloid	*Erysipelothrix insidiosa*	Man	Contact; wound infection
Foal pneumonia	*Corynebacterium equi*	Horse, swine, cattle	Possibly *in utero*
Food poisoning. See **botulism, gastroenteritis.**			
Fowl typhoid	*Salmonella gallinarum*	Birds	Feces-borne

TABLE 16. SOME BACTERIAL DISEASES OF HUMAN BEINGS AND ANIMALS (*Continued*)

Disease	Microorganism	Host	Mode of Transmission
Fusospirochetal disease	*Borrelia vincentii, B. buccalis, Fusobacterium fusiforme* associated with vibrios and cocci	Man	Patient's mouth
Gas gangrene	*Clostridium perfringens*	Man	Wound infection; soil-borne
Gaseous lymphadenitis	*Corynebacterium pseudotuberculosis*	Sheep; horses, cattle	Contaminated feed and water
Gastroenteritis	*Staphylococcus aureus Salmonella enteritidis*	Man; rodents	Spoiled food containing toxin; and bacteria; faces-borne
Genitourinary infections	*Escherichia coli*	Man; animals	Feces-borne; from normal flora of intestinal tract
Glanders	*Actinobacillus mallei*	Horse; man	Contaminated feed, water; contact
Gonorrhea	*Neisseria gonorrhoeae*	Man	Sexual contact
Hansen's disease. See **leprosy.**			
Haverhill fever	*Streptobacillus moniliformis*	Man	Ingestion of contaminated milk
Hemorrhagic septicemia	*Pasteurella multocida*	Domestic animals, birds; man	Contaminated water, feed; contact; bites
Icterohemoglobinuria	*Clostridium haemolyticum*	Cattle; sheep	Contaminated feed and water; soil-borne
Infectious coryza	*Haemophilus gallinarum*	Chickens	Contact
Infectious keratitis	*Moraxella bovis*	Cattle	Contact
Infectious necrotic hepatitis	*Clostridium novyi* Type B	Sheep	Soil-borne
Johne's disease	*Mycobacterium paratuberculosis*	Cattle, sheep	Contact; contaminated feed and water; feces-borne
Lamb dysentery	*Clostridium perfringens*	Sheep	Wound infection; soil-borne
Leprosy	*Mycobacterium leprae*	Man	Not known
Leptospirosis. See **Weil's disease, Stuttgart's disease, swineherd's disease.**			
Listerosis	*Listeria monocytogenes*	Man, birds, domestic animals	Not known
Lobar pneumonia	*Diplococcus pneumoniae*	Man	Contact

TABLE 16. SOME BACTERIAL DISEASES OF HUMAN BEINGS AND ANIMALS (*Continued*)

Disease	Microorganism	Host	Mode of Transmission
Lumpy jaw	*Actinomyces bovis*	Cattle, horse, swine, man	Not known
Malignant edema	*Clostridium speticum*	Horse, cattle, sheep, man	Manure- and soil-borne; wound infection
Malta fever. See **brucellosis.**			
Mastitis	*Streptococcus agalactiae, S. dysgalactiae*	Cattle	Contaminated milking equipment and utensils
Melioidosis	*Pseudomonas pseudomallei*	Rodents, man	Bite of rat flea or mosquito
Meningoencephalitis. See **listerosis.**			
Meningitis. See **epidemic cerebrospinal meningitis;** also **lobar pneumonia**			
Moore's infectious leukemia. See **fowl typhoid.**			
Paratyphoid fever	*Salmonella paratyphi, S. hirschfeldii*	Man	Feces-borne
Plague	*Pasteurella pestis*	Man, rodents	Rodent flea bite; droplet infection
Pneumonia	*Klebsiella pneumoniae*	Man, horse, cattle	Contact
Pneumonic plague. See **plague.**			
Prepucial infection	*Haemophilus haemoglobinophilus*	Dog	Sexual contact
Pseudoglanders	*Corynebacterium pseudotuberculosis*	Horse	Contact
Pseudotuberculosis	*Corynebacterium pseudotuberculosis*	Cattle	Contact
Puerperal fever	Hemolytic streptococci	Man	Contact
Pullorum disease. See **fowl typhoid.**			
Purulent meningitis	*Haemophilus influenzae*	Man, principally children	Contact
Pyelonephritis	*Corynebacterium renale*	Cattle, swine; sheep horses; dogs	Not known
Pyocyanosis	*Pseudomonas aeruginosa*	Man	Probably contact; droplet infection
Rat-bite fever	*Spirillum minus Streptobacillus moniliformis*	Man, rodents	Rat bite
Relapsing fever, epidemic, European	*Borrelia recurrentis*	Man	Louse
Rheumatic fever	Pyogenic streptococci	Man	Contact
Salmonellosis. See also **paratyphoid fever** and **typhoid fever.**	*Salmonella* species	Man	Contaminated water and food

TABLE 16. SOME BACTERIAL DISEASES OF HUMAN BEINGS AND ANIMALS (*Continued*)

Disease	Microorganism	Host	Mode of Transmission
Scarlet fever	*Streptococcus pyogenes*	Man	Droplet infection; contaminated milk
Shigellosis. See also **dysentery.**	*Shigella* species	Man	Feces-borne
Soft chancre. See **chancroid.**			
Spirochetosis	*Borellia theileri*	Cattle	Tick vector
Spontaneous polyarthritis	*Streptobacillus moniliformis*	Mice, rodents	
Strangles	*Streptococcus equi*	Horse	Contaminated feed, water; contact
Stuttgart's disease	*Leptospira* serotype *canicola*	Dog	Contact; contaminated water
Subacute endocarditis	Viridans or enterococcus streptococci; *Staphylococcus aureus*	Man	Contact
Suppurative polyarthritis	*Streptococcus dysgalactiae*	Sheep, particularly lambs	
Swineherd's disease	*Leptospira* serotype *pomona*	Swine, cattle, man	Contact; contaminated water
Syphilis	*Treponema pallidum*	Man	Sexual contact
Trench mouth. See **fusospirochetal disease.**			
Tuberculosis	*Mycobacterium tuberculosis* var. *hominis*	Man	Contact
	Mycobacterium tuberculosis var. *bovis*	Cattle, man	Contact; contaminated milk
Tularemia	*Pasteurella tularensis*	Man, rodents	Contact with infected carcasses; insect vector
Typhoid fever	*Salmonella typhosa*	Man	Contaminated water and food; feces-borne
Undulant fever. See **brucellosis.**			
Ulcerative lymphangitis	*Corynebacterium pseudotuberculosis*	Horse	Contact; wound infection
Vincent's angina. See **fusospirochetal disease.**			
Weil's disease	*Leptospira icterohaemorrhagiae*	Man, domestic animals, rodents	Contact; contaminated water
Whooping cough	*Bordetella pertussis*	Man	Droplet infection; contact
Wooden tongue	*Actinobacillus lignieresii*	Cattle, swine	Not known

TABLE 17a. SOME VIRAL DISEASES OF HUMAN BEINGS

Disease	Virus	Mode of transmission	Incubation period, days	Selective action	Immunity conferred	Inclusion bodies	Size, mμ	Prophylaxis
Adenovirus group			5-7				90	
Acute respiratory disease (ARD)		Probably contact; via respiratory tract		Respiratory tract (principally military personnel)	Relatively solid			Vaccine available for types 3, 4, and 7
Pharyngitis and pharyngoconjunctival fever		Person to person; via respiratory tract		Throat, eyes (mainly children)	Specific neutralizing antibody produced			None
Epidemic keratoconjunctivitis (EKC)		Not known		Eyes (industrial workers)	Possibly of short duration			None
B virus	*Scelus beta*	Bite of monkey		Nervous system	After attack		125	
Chickenpox	*Briareus varicellae*	Contact, droplet infection	14-21	Dermotropic, skin and mucous membranes	One attack	Cytoplasmic and intranuclear	210-243	Convalescent serum
Cold, common	*Tarpeia premens*	Contact, droplet infection	1-5	Respiratory tract	For short period	None	50-70	Vaccine available for some strains
Cowpox	*Borreliota variolae* var. *bovis*	Contact, vaccination	3	Dermotropic	Variable duration	Cytoplasmic		Vaccination
Coxsackie		Contact, droplet infection feces	2-4		Antibodies formed		25-30	None
Group A Herpangina				Throat				
Group B								
Pleurodynia				Pleuritic pains				
Summer grippe				Fever				
Aseptic meningitis				Stiff neck and back				
ECHO viruses		By fecal contamination		Aseptic meningitis			10-15	None
Encephalitis		Contact, insects		Neurotropic	One attack	None		None
Australian X	*Erro incognitus*							
Equine	*Erro equinus*						25-40	
Far east. See **spring-summer.**								
Japanese B	*Erro japonicus*						10-30	
Russian. See **spring-summer.**								
St. Louis	*Erro scelestus*						20-30	
Spring-summer	*Erro silvestris*						15-25	
West Nile	*Erro nili*						20-30	
Equine infectious anemia	*Trifur equorum*	Contact, ingestion of milk, flies		Blood, also dermotropic			10-60	
Enteric cytopathogenic human orphan. See **ECHO viruses.**								
German measles		Contact droplet infection	10-21	Dermotropic, skin and mucous membranes	One attack	None	800	None
Hemorrhagic fever		Arthropod vector	14-21	Vascular system				None

TABLE 17a. SOME VIRAL DISEASES OF HUMAN BEINGS (*Continued*)

Disease	Virus	Mode of transmission	Incubation period, days	Selective action	Immunity conferred	Inclusion bodies	Size, mμ	Prophylaxis
Hepatitis								
Infectious (Hepatitis virus A)		Contact with human beings, blood transfusions	15-40	Liver, gastro-intestinal tract	Poorly defined			Normal immune gamma globulin
Serum (Hepatitis virus B)		Parenteral inoculation	60-160	Liver, gastro-intestinal tract	Possibly inherent or acquired			Adequate sterilization of instrument; storage of blood for 6 months
Herpes simplex	*Scelus recurrens*	Contact. also initiation as by fever, light rays	1-2	Dermotropic	None	Intranuclear	100-150	None
Herpes zoster	*Briareus varicellae*	Contact	12-15	Dermotropic, neurotropic	One attack	Cytoplasmic and intranuclear	210-250	None
Hydrophobia. See **rabies.**								
Infantile paralysis. See **poliomyelitis.**								
Influenza	*Tarpeia alpha, T. beta*	Contact, droplet infection	3-8	Respiratory tract	For short period	None	80-120	Vaccine for some strains available
Louping ill	*Erro scoticus*	Tick bite, contact		Central nervous system	Probably one attack		15-20	
Lymphocytic choriomeningitis	*Legio erebea*	Probably contact and insects	1.5-3	Central nervous system, blood	One attack	None	40-60	Serum from recovered patients neutralizes virus
Measles	*Briareus morbillorum*	Contact, droplet infection	10-14	Dermotropic, skin and membranes respiratory tract	One attack	Probably cytoplasmic		Vaccine in developmental stage; gamma globulin
Molluscum contagiosum	*Molitor hominis*	Contact	14-50	Dermotropic	Not known	Cytoplasmic	195-250	None
Mumps	*Rabula inflans*	Contact, droplet infection	5-21	Salivary glands, gonads	One attack	Cytoplasmic	90-135	Convalescent serum
Parotitis. See **mumps.**								
Poliomyelitis, anterior	*Legio debilitans*	Contact, gastro-intestinal tract or respiratory tract	7-14	Central nervous system	One attack	None	28	Killed and attenuated live virus vaccines
Primary atypical pneumonia		Direct contact with infected persons	7-21 12-14 (average)	Respiratory tract	Not known; second attacks occur			None
Pseudolymphocytic choriomeningitis	*Legio simulans*	Probably contact		Central nervous system	Probably one attack		150-220	None
Rabies	*Formido inexorabilis*	Rabid animal bite	Variable 27-70 or longer	Central nervous system	Vaccination gives short period	Cytoplasmic Negri bodies	160-250	Cautery of wound; series of vaccine injections of attenuated virus

TABLE 17a. SOME VIRAL DISEASES OF HUMAN BEINGS (*Continued*)

Disease	Virus	Mode of transmission	Incubation period, days	Selective action	Immunity conferred	Inclusion bodies	Size, $m\mu$	Prophylaxis
Rift valley fever	*Charon vallis*	Possibly mosquitos; not by contact	5-6	Liver, blood, vicerotropic	4-5 years		23-35	Neurotropic strain immunizes lambs
Rubella. See **German measles.**								
Rubeola. See **measles.**								
Shingles. See **herpes zoster.**								
Smallpox	*Borreliota variolae* var. *hominis*	Contact	6-15	Dermotropic	One attack	Guarnieri cytoplasmic bodies and Paschen intranuclear bodies	245-300	Vaccination with vaccinia virus
Swineherd's disease	*Legio suariorum*	Contact pig feces		Central nervous system, eyes	One attack			
Vaccinia. See **cowpox.**								
Varicella. See **chickenpox.**								
Variola. See **smallpox.**								
Verruca. See **warts.**								
Warts	*Molitor verrucae*	Contact	30-60 experimental	Dermotropic	Possibly local area	Intranuclear		None
Yellow fever	*Charon evagatus*	Mosquito bite, not by contact	4-13	Vicerotropic, liver	One attack	Intranuclear	12-19	Vaccine available

TABLE 17b. ARBO (ARTHROPOD-BORNE ANIMAL) VIRUSES [a]

Group	Virus	Abbreviation	Isolation in Nature from			Antibodies in man	Human disease in most severe form	Vector, suspected vector or isolations from	Isolation of virus reported from
			Man	Other vertebrates	Arthropods				
A	Chikungunya		+		+	+	Dengue-like	Mosquito	East Africa, South Africa
	Eastern Equine Encephalomyelitis	EEE	+	+	+	+	Encephalitis	Mosquito	Brazil, Canada, Cuba, Dominican Republic, Eastern United States, Mexico, Panama, Philippines
	Mayaro		+			+	Systemic		Bolivia, Brazil, Trinidad
	Middelburg				+	+		Mosquito	South Africa
	Semliki Forest				+	+		Mosquito	East Africa, West Africa
	Sindbis			+	+	+		Mosquito	Egypt, India, South Africa
	Venezuelan Equine Encephalomyelitis	VEE	+	+	+	+	Encephalitis; influenza-like	Mosquito	Brazil, Colombia, Equador, Trinidad, Venezuela
	Western Equine Encephalomyelitis	WEE	+	+	+	+	Encephalitis	Mosquito	Argentina, Canada, Mexico, United States
B	Bat Salivary Gland Virus			+					California, Texas
	Dengue Type 1		+			+	Fever. Rash, lymphadenopathy, muscle and joint pains	Mosquito	Hawaii, India, Japan, Malaya, New Guinea
	Dengue Type 2		+			+	As Dengue Type 1	Mosquito	India, New Guinea, Trinidad, Uganda
	Ilheus		+		+	+		Mosquito	Brazil, Guatemala, Honduras, Trinidad
	Japanese B	JBE	+	+	+	+	Encephalitis	Mosquito	East Asian Mainland, Guam, India, Japan, Malaya, Ryukyus
	Murray Valley	MVE	+			+	Encephalitis	Mosquito	Australia, New Guinea
	Ntaya				+	+		Mosquito	Uganda
	Spondweni				+	+		Mosquito	South Africa
	St. Louis	SLE	+	+	+	+	Encephalitis	Mosquito	United States, Trinidad
	Uganda S				+	+		Mosquito	Tanganyika, Uganda
	Wesselsbron		+	+	+	+	Influenza-like	Mosquito	South Africa
	West Nile	WN	+	+	+	+	Dengue-like	Mosquito	Egypt, India, Israel, Uganda
	Yellow Fever	YF	+	+	+	+	Hepatitis	Mosquito	Equatorial Africa and America
	Zika		+	+	+	+	Systemic	Mosquito	Nigeria, Uganda
	Diphasic Meningoencephalitis, Diphasic Milk Fever		+	+	+	+	Diphasic Fever, meningeal signs	Tick	Northwestern USSR
	Kyasanur Forest Disease	KFD	+	+	+	+	Hemorrhagic fever	Tick	India
	Louping-Ill		+	+	+	+	Encephalitis	Tick	Great Britain, Czechoslovakia, USSR (see **Russian Spring-Summer Virus**)
	Omsk Hemorrhagic Fever		+		+	+	Hemorrhagic fever	Tick	USSR (Siberia, Great Barabin Steppes)
	Russian Spring-Summer Encephalitis	RSSE	+		+	+	Encephalitis	Tick	Austria, Czechoslovakia, Hungary, Malaya, Poland, USSR, Yugoslavia
C	Apeu			+				Mosquito	Brazil (Para)
	Marituba		+	+	+	+	Systemic	Mosquito	Brazil (Para)
	Oriboca		+	+		+	Systemic	Mosquito	Brazil (Para)

[a] After J. Casals and W. C. Reeves in T. M. Rivers and F. L. Horsfall, eds., *Viral and Rickettsial Infections of Man,* 3rd ed., J. B. Lippincott Co., Philadelphia, 1959.

TABLE 17b. ARBO (ARTHROPOD-BORNE ANIMAL) VIRUSES (*Continued*)

Group	Virus	Abbreviation	Isolation in Nature from: Man	Isolation in Nature from: Other vertebrates	Isolation in Nature from: Arthropods	Antibodies in man	Human disease in most severe form	Vector, suspected vector or isolations from	Isolations of virus reported from
Ungrouped	Anopheles A				+			Mosquito	Colombia
	Anopheles B				+			Mosquito	Colombia
	Bunyamwera		+		+	+		Mosquito	South Africa, Uganda
	Bwamba		+			+	Systemic		Uganda
	California Encephalitis Virus				+	+	Encephalitis	Mosquito	Western United States
	Pongola				+	+		Mosquito	South Africa
	Rift Valley Fever		+	+	+	+	Systemic	Mosquito	Kenya, South Africa, Uganda
	Simbu				+	+		Mosquito	South Africa
	Turlock			+	+			Mosquito	Western United States
	Wyeomyia				+			Mosquito	Colombia
	Colorado Tick Fever		+		+	+	Systemic	Tick	Western United States
	Crimean Hemorrhagic Fever		+		+	+	Hemorrhagic Fever	Tick	USSR (Crimea)
	Sandfly Fever—Naples Strain		+				Systemic	Phlebotomus	Southern Italy
	Sandfly Fever—Sicilian Strain		+			+	Systemic	Phlebotomus	Egypt, Sicily

TABLE 18. SOME RICKETTSIAL PARASITES OF HUMAN BEINGS AND ANIMALS

Disease	Microorganism	Mode of transmission	Host	Size, μ	Tissue affected	Immunity	Prophylaxis and treatment
African tick fever. See **boutoneuse fever.**							
Anaplasmosis							
Benign	*Anaplasma centrale*		Cattle	0.4-0.95 0.65 (avg)	Blood cells	No natural	
Malignant	*A. marginale*	Possibly arthropod vector	Cattle	0.3-0.8 0.5-0.6 (avg)	Blood cells	No natural	
Ovine	*A. ovis*		Sheep, goats	0.4-0.8 0.5 (avg)	Blood cells	No natural	
Boutoneuse fever	*Rickettsia conorii*	Dog tick to man	Man, dogs	0.3-0.4 × 1.0-1.75			No vaccine
Conjunctivitis							
Inclusion (swimming pool)	*Chlamydia oculogenitalis*	Contact vaginal canal; contaminated water	Man, baboon, monkeys		Conjunctiva: lower urogenital tract		Antibiotics and sulfonamides
Infectious kerato-	*Ricolesia bovis*		Cattle		Conjunctiva and cornea		
	R. caprae		Goats		Conjunctiva and cornea		
	R. lestoguardii		Swine		Conjunctiva and cornea		
Roup, ocular	*R. conjunctivae*		Fowl	0.2 × 2	Conjunctiva and cornea		
Encephalomyelitis, bovine	*Miyagawanella pecoris*		Cattle	0.375	Brain, peritoneum	Antibodies produced	Antibiotics (Aureomycin and tetracycline)
Heartwater	*Cowdria ruminantium*	Tick to host	Sheep, goats, cattle	0.2-0.5	Hydropericardium	Incomplete	
Lymphogranuloma venereum	*Miyagawanella lymphogranulomatosis*	Sexual contact	Man	0.2-0.35	Genitalia, lymph and nervous systems	Poor	Antibiotics (tetracycline, chloroamphenicol); sulfonamides
Murine typhus. See **typhus, endemic.**							
Ophthalmia	*Colesiota conjunctivae*		Sheep	0.2-2	Conjunctiva and cornea		
Ornithosis	*Miyagawanella ornithosis*	Inhalation, ingestion, contact	Man, birds	*ca.* 0.2	Respiratory tract, blood and nervous systems	Poor in man	Antibiotics; not susceptible to sulfonamides
Parrot fever. See **psittacosis.**							
Psittacosis	*M. psittaci*	Inhalation, contact	Man, psittacine birds	*ca.* 0.2	Respiratory tract		Sulfonamides especially sulfadiazine; tetracyclines
Pneumonitis							
Feline	*M. felis*		Cats	*ca.* 0.2	Respiratory tract		Antibiotics like *ornithosis*
Louisiana	*M. louisianae*		Man	*ca.* 0.2	Respiratory tract, blood		Antibiotics
Mouse	*M. bronchopneumoniae*	Contact	Mice and other rodents		Respiratory tract		Sulfonamides and antibiotics

TABLE 18. SOME RICKETTSIAL PARASITES OF HUMAN BEINGS AND ANIMALS (*Continued*)

Disease	Microorganism	Mode of transmission	Host	Size, μ	Tissue affected	Immunity	Prophylaxis and treatment
Pneumonitis							
Viral	*Miyagawanella illinii*	Contact	Man		Respiratory tract		
	M. pneumoniae	Contact	Man		Respiratory tract		Antibiotics
Q fever	*Coxiella burnetii*	Host to tick to host; inhalation of dried material; contact: contaminated milk	Man, domestic animals, rodents	Rods 0.25 × 0.4-0.5; Bipolar 0.25 × 1; Diplobacilli 0.25 × 1.5	Respiratory tract	Solid in guinea pigs	Tetracyclines and chloramphenicol; vaccine available
Rickettsialpox	*Rickettsia akari*	Mite bite	Man	0.6 × 0.9-1.4	Skin	Produced	Tetracyclines
Rickettsiosis							
Bovine	*Ehrlichia bovis*	Tick to host	Cattle	Colonies 1 × 6-11	Circulating monocytes		
Canine	*E. canis*	Tick to host	Dogs	0.2-0.3			
Ovine	*E. ovina*	Probably tick to host	Sheep	Colonies or plaques 2-8			
Rocky mountain spotted fever	*Rickettsia rickettsii*	Tick bite	Man, rodents	0.6 × 1.2	Skin, vascular endothelium	Prolonged	Antisera; vaccine
Scrub typhus. See **tsutsugamushi fever.**							
Trachoma	*Chlamydia trachomatis*	Contact	Man, primates	0.2-0.35; plaques 10	Cornea and conjunctiva		Sulfonamides and antibiotics
Trench fever	*Rickettsia quintana*	Louse feces into broken skin	Body louse, man	0.2-0.4	Skin, spleen, eyes	Partial	
Tsutsugamushi fever	*R. tsutsugamushi*	Mite bite	Man, rodents	0.3-0.5 × 0.8-2	Skin, lymph system	Produced; less complete than typhus	Chloroamphenicol and tetracyclines
Typhus							
Endemic	*R. typhi*	Flea feces into skin	Man	0.35-0.6 × 0.7-1.3; 0.45 × 1.0 (avg)	Skin, nervous system, respiratory tract	Prolonged	*p*-Aminobenzoic acid and antibiotics like chloroamphenicol and chlorotetracycline
Epidemic	*R. prowazekii*	Man to louse to man; louse feces	Man	0.5-0.7 × 0.5-2; 0.5 × 1.1 (avg)	Skin, respiratory tract, nervous system	Prolonged but not always permanent	Hyperimmune antisera; attenuated living strain vaccine

TABLE 19a. DIFFERENTIATION OF *BRUCELLA*

TABLE 19b. DIFFERENTIATION OF CLOSTRIDIA

TABLE 19c. DIFFERENTIATION OF THE COLON-AEROGENES GROUPS

TABLE 19d. DIFFERENTIATION OF DIPHTHERIA AND DIPHTHEROID ORGANISMS

TABLE 19e. COLONY AND GROWTH CHARACTERISTICS OF GRAM-NEGATIVE INTESTINAL BACILLI ON DIFFERENTIAL MEDIA

TABLE 19f. DIFFERENTIATION OF *NEISSERIA*

TABLE 19g. REACTIONS OF *SALMONELLA* AND *SHIGELLA*

TABLE 19h. DIFFERENTIATION OF STAPHYLOCOCCI FROM MICROCOCCI

TABLE 19i. DIFFERENTIATION OF STREPTOCOCCI FROM PNEUMOCOCCI

TABLE 19a. DIFFERENTIATION OF *BRUCELLA*

Brucella	Increased atmospheric carbon dioxide required for primary isolation	Duration of hydrogen sulfide formation (days)	Growth on media containing	
			Thionine	Basic fuchsin
abortus	+	2	−	+
melitensis	−	±1	+	+
suis	−	4	+	−

TABLE 19b. DIFFERENTIATION OF CLOSTRIDIA

Clostridium	Hemo-lysis	Aero-bic growth	Egg yolk agar re-action	Gela-tin	In-dole	Glu-cose	Mal-tose	Lac-tose	Su-crose	Sali-cin	Litmus milk	Spores	Patho-genicity
aerofetidum	−	−	−	+	−	+	+	+	−	+	A, C, G	O, E	−
bifermentans	+	−	+	+	+	+	+	−	−	−	C, D	O, E	(+)
botulinum	+	−	+	+	−	+	+	−	−	−	A	O, E	+
butyricum	−	−	−	−	−	+	+	+	+	+	A, C, G	O, E	−
capitovale	(+)	−	−	+	(+)	+	−	−	−	−	A, (C)	O, T	−
carnis	+	+	−	−	−	+	+	+	+	+	G	O, E	+
difficile	(+)	−	−	−	−	+	−	−	−	+	−	O, E	+
fallax	+	−	?	−	−	+	+	+	+	+	A, C, G	O, E	(+)
hastiforme	−	−	?	+	−	−	−	−	−	−	C, D	O, E	−
histolyticum	+	+	−	+	−	−	−	−	−	−	D	O, E	+
lentoputrescens	+	−	?	+	−	−	−	−	−	−	C, D	S, T	−
multifermentans	+	−	−	−	−	+	+	+	+	+	A, C, G	O, E	−
novyi	+	−	+	+	−	+	+	−	−	−	A	O, E	+
parabotulinum	(+)	−	+	+	−	+	+	−	−	(+)	(A), C, D	O, E	+
perfringens													
Type A	+	−	+	+	−	+	+	+	+	−	A, C, G	O, E	+
septicum	+	−	−	+	−	+	+	+	−	+	C, G	O, E	+
sphenoides	+	−	−	−	(+)	+	+	+	(+)	+	A, C	S, E-T	−
sporogenes	+	−	+	+	−	+	+	−	−	−	C, D	O, E	−
tetani	+	−	−	+	+	−	−	−	−	−	C	S, T	+
tetanomorphum	+	−	−	−	(+)	+	+	−	−	−	−	S, T	−
tertium	+	+	−	−	−	+	+	+	+	+	A, C, G	O, T	−

Reactions in parentheses are variable.
A—Acid, C—Clot, G—Gas, D—Digested, O—Oval, S—Spherical, T—Terminal, E—Eccentric (subterminal to near-central).

TABLE 19c. DIFFERENTIATION OF THE COLON-AEROGENES GROUPS

Species	Methyl-red test	Voges-Proskauer reaction	Indole production	Citrate utilization	Gelatin liquefaction	Hydrogen sulfide formation
Escherichia coli	+	−	+	−	−	−
Escherichia freundii	+	(−)	(+)	+	−	+
Aerobacter aerogenes	−	+	(−)	+	−	(−)
Aerobacter cloacae	−	+	−	+	+	(−)
Klebsiella pneumoniae	(+)	(−)	−	(+)	−	−

The reactions enclosed in parentheses are the usual ones: exceptions have been reported.

TABLE 19d. DIFFERENTIATION OF DIPHTHERIA AND DIPHTHEROID ORGANISMS

Corynebacterium	Fermentation Tests		Hemolysis	Oxygen requirements	Virulence for guinea pigs or chicks
	Glucose	Sucrose			
acnes	+	− or +	?	Microaerophilic	−
diphtheriae	+	− (few +)	+ or −	Aerobic and facultative	+
pseudodiphtheriticum	−	−	−	Aerobic and facultative	−
pyogenes	+	− or +	+	Aerobic and facultative	+
typhi	+	−	?	Anaerobic	−
ulcerans	+	− or +	?	Aerobic and facultative	+
xerosis	+	+	−	Aerobic and facultative	−

TABLE 19e. COLONY AND GROWTH CHARACTERISTICS OF GRAM-NEGATIVE INTESTINAL BACILLI ON DIFFERENTIAL MEDIA

Species	Eosin-methylene blue agar plate	Desoxycholate-citrate agar and SS (Salmonella-Shigella) agar plates	Kligler's Iron Agar (with phenol red indicator, alkaline is red; acid, yellowish)[a]		Hydrogen sulfide formation
			Slant	Butt	
	Coli-aerogenes group ferment lactose and grow into large, opaque colonies; also absorb dye to give color to colony. Nonlactose-fermenting pathogenic species develop as small, colorless, translucent colonies	Lactose-fermenting organisms either are completely inhibited or produce reddish colonies. Nonlactose-fermenting organisms grow into small, clear, colorless, translucent colonies	The small amount of acid produced from glucose (0.1%) is diffused, leaving alkaline slant. The larger amount of acid from lactose (1%) gives acid slant	Organisms producing acid from either glucose or lactose give acid butt, with or without gas (bubbles in medium)	
Escherichia	Large colonies with large, dark (almost black) centers, and with greenish metallic sheen	Inhibited; if any growth, it is pink and opaque, opacity spreading to surrounding medium	Acid	Marked acid and gas	+ and −
Aerobacter and *Klebsiella*	Large pinkish mucoid colonies with small, dark-brown or black centers; rarely show metallic sheen	Same as *Escherichia*	Acid, returning to neutral or alkaline after several days	Marked acid and gas	−
Salmonella	Translucent, colorless, or pinkish colonies, later may have bluish tint	Large translucent colonies, domed, shiny, smooth, and colorless	Alkaline	Acid and gas (moderate). *S. typhosa* and *S. gallinarum* are anaerogenic	+ (few −)
Shigella	Small, translucent, colorless colonies	Same as *Salmonella* colonies, except smaller. After 24 hours, colonies of *S. sonnei* may be red	Alkaline, *S. sonnei* may produce acid after several days	Acid	−
Proteus	Translucent, colorless, spreading colonies	Same as *Salmonella*, spreading inhibited	Alkaline	Acid and gas	+ and −
Paracolons	Same as *Salmonella*	Same as *Salmonella*. After 24 hours, may be red	Alkaline. May produce acid after several days	Acid and gas or acid only	+ and −
Pseudomonas	Same as *Shigella*	Same as *Shigella*	Alkaline; usually purplish	Unchanged or acid	−
Alcaligenes	Same as *Shigella*	Same as *Shigella*	Alkaline	Unchanged	−

[a] Triple sugar iron agar gives the same reactions except that many paracolons will produce an acid slant because of sucrose fermentation.

TABLE 19f. DIFFERENTIATION OF *NEISSERIA*

Neisseria	Fermentation Tests				22 C growth	Agglutination with meningococci sera	Special colony feature
	Glucose	Maltose	Fructose	Sucrose			
catarrhalis	—	—	—	—	+	—	Large, grayish-white
flava	A	A	A	—	—	—	Yellow
flavescens	—	—	—	—	?	—	Golden yellow
gonorrhoeae	A	—	—	—	—	—	Small, round, convex
meningitidis	A	A	—	—	—	+	Small, round, bluish-gray
perflava	A	A	A	A	+	—	Greenish-yellow, adherent to medium
sicca	A	A	A	A	+	—	Large, wrinkled, impossible to emulsify
subflava	A	A	—	—	±	—	Greenish-yellow, adherent to medium

A = acid formed.

TABLE 19g. REACTIONS OF *SALMONELLA* AND *SHIGELLA*

Substrate or test	*Salmonella*	*Shigella*
Glucose	Acid and gas[a]	Acid[b]
Lactose	—	Variable[c]
Sucrose	—	Variable[c]
Mannitol	+ (usually)	
Salicin	—	—
Adonitol	—	—
Sorbitol	+ (usually)	Variable
Urease	—	—
Citrate	Variable	—
Methyl red	+	+
Voges-Proskauer	—	—
Indole	—	Variable
Hydrogen sulfide	+ (usually)[d]	—[e]
Motility	+[f]	—
Gelatin	— (usually)	—
Nitrate	+	+

[a] *S. typhosa* and *S. gallinarum* are anaerogenic. Rare anaerogenic strains of other types.

[b] Certain biochemical variants of *Shigella flexneri* 6 (Newcastle, Manchester) produce gas from fermentable substances.

[c] When acid is produced, the reaction is delayed for several days.

[d] *S. paratyphi* A and rare strains of *S. typhosa* and other types do not produce hydrogen sulfide.

[e] The sensitive paper tests may show some hydrogen sulfide production by some strains.

[f] All motile rods may have nonmotile variants. *Salmonella gallinarum* is nonmotile.

TABLE 19h. DIFFERENTIATION OF STAPHYLOCOCCI FROM MICROCOCCI

Species	Size	Grouping	Pigment	Blood agar colonies	Gelatin[a] liquefaction	Mannitol[a] fermentation
Staphylococcus aureus	Cells relatively small	Irregular grape-like clusters	Ivory to golden yellow. White variants often seen. Formerly white varieties were known as *S. albus* and lemon-yellow-colored varieties as *S. citreus*	Surface colonies usually hemolytic; deep colonies nonhemolytic. White and yellow varieties usually nonhemolytic	+; white and yellow usually slow	A (usually)
Micrococcus (species)	Cells often larger than those of *Staphylococcus*	Many have no definite arrangement in groups; others are arranged symmetrically in groups of 4 or 8	White, yellow, or rarely pink; varies with species or strains	Usually nonhemolytic	−	−

[a] The listed reactions are the usual ones; there are some exceptions.
+ = Positive reaction.
− = Negative reaction.
A = Acid formed.

TABLE 19i. DIFFERENTIATION OF STREPTOCOCCI FROM PNEUMOCOCCI

Species	Appearance of deep colonies in blood agar[a]	Morphology in liquid media	Capsule	Fermentation Tests				Bile solubility
				Lactose	Salicin	Mannitol	Inulin	
Streptococcus pyogenes	Beta	Usually long chains	±	+	+	−	−	−
Streptococcus salivarius	Alpha	Usually short chains	−	+	−	−	−	−
Streptococcus faecalis[b]	Gamma or alpha	Pairs and short chains	−	+	+	+	−	−
Anaerobic streptococci	Gamma or beta (rare)							
Diplococcus pneumoniae	Alpha	Lance-shaped diplococci or short chains	+[c]	+	−	−	+	+

[a] The three principal types of appearance of deep colonies in blood-agar plates are as follows:

Alpha discoloration and hemolysis—In the immediate vicinity of the deep colony some red cells remain intact and are frequently discolored greenish (viridans type) or brownish. In the fully developed alpha zone the intact cells are, in turn, surrounded by a zone of more or less complete hemolysis. The hemolysis is intensified by refrigeration of the plate culture.

Beta hemolysis—The deep colony is immediately surrounded by a perfectly clear zone in which no intact red cells remain.

Gamma appearance—There is neither discoloration nor hemolysis surrounding the deep colony. It may happen that, after 24 hours incubation, a culture may present the gamma appearance; after 48 hours the colonies may be surrounded by slight greenish discoloration; after refrigeration of the plate overnight, typical zones of alpha hemolysis may develop. This trend of events is rather characteristic of *S. faecalis.*

[b] Enterococci have the Lancefield group D polysaccharide.

[c] A quellung reaction of the pneumococcus capsules occurs with specific antiserum and formerly was used as a rapid method of recognizing a pneumococcus.

TABLE 20a. TOXINS

TABLE 20b. ANTITOXINS AND ANTISERA

TABLE 20c. TOXOIDS AND VACCINES

TABLE 20a. TOXINS[a]

Toxin	Production	Test animal	Unit of potency	Use
Botulinus	Meat infusion media	Mouse, guinea pig		
Diphtheria	Veal broth	250-g guinea pig	One M.L.D.[b] is the smallest amount that will kill a 250-g guinea pig on the 4th day. One L+ dose is the smallest amount which, when injected with N.I.H.[c] standard unit of antitoxin, will cause death of a 250-g guinea pig on the 4th day	Schick test. Standardization of diphtheria antitoxin. Immunization of horses. Production of toxin-antitoxin. Production of toxoid, purified toxoid, and polyvalent vaccines
Erysipelas streptococcus	Special bouillon	Man	One S.T.D.[d] is the smallest amount that will cause an erythema at least 1 cm in diameter when injected intradermally in a susceptible person	Standardization of erysipelas streptococcus antitoxin. Immunization of horses
Meningococcus	Special liquid media	Man	One S.T.D. is the smallest amount that will cause an erythema at least 1 cm in diameter when injected intradermally in a susceptible person	Standardization of meningococcus antitoxin. Immunization of horses. Skin test for susceptibility
Perfringens (*C. perfringens*)	Special bouillon	Pigeon	One test dose is the smallest amount that will kill a 350-g pigeon in 24 hours in the presence of one standard unit of perfringens antitoxin	Standardization of perfringens (*C. perfringens*) antitoxin. Immunization of horses
Puerperal septicemia streptococcus	Special bouillon	Man	One S.T.D. is the smallest amount that will cause an erythema at least 1 cm in diameter when injected intradermally in a susceptible person	Standardization of puerperal septicemia antistreptococcic serum (antitoxin). Immunization of horses
Scarlet fever	1. Veal bouillon for skin testing and human immunization 2. Special broth for immunizing horses	Man	One S.T.D. is the smallest amount that will cause an erythema at least 1 cm in diameter in 48 hours when injected intradermally in a susceptible person	Dick test. Active immunization of susceptibles. Standardization of scarlet fever antitoxin. Immunization of horses
Tetanus	2% glucose broth	250-g guinea pig	One M.L.D. is the smallest amount that will kill a 250-g guinea pig on the 4th day in the presence of $\frac{1}{4}$ unit of N.I.H. standard antitoxin	Standardization of tetanus antitoxin. Immunization of horses. Tetanus toxoid, purified toxoid, and polyvalent vaccines

[a] After Parke, Davis & Company and A. H. Bryan and G. G. Bryan, *Bacteriology, Principles and Practice*, 5th ed., Barnes & Noble, New York, 1953.
[b] Minimum lethal dose.
[c] National Institutes of Health.
[d] Skin test dose.

TABLE 20b. ANTITOXINS AND ANTISERA[a]

Product	Production	Test animal	Unit of potency
Antianthrax serum	Native antiserum from the horse	*In vitro* test	Potency proved by agglutination tests. Each lot must agglutinate *B. anthracis* in 1:6400 dilution
Antidysenteric serum (polyvalent)	Native antiserum from the horse	1. *In vitro* test 2. Mouse	1. The finished antiserum must agglutinate strains of *Shigella dysenteriae* and *S. flexneri*, and compare favorably with N.I.H.[b] standard antiserum 2. In addition, each lot may be standarized by mouse protection tests as required by the British Ministry of Health
Antimeningococcic serum	Native antiserum from the horse	*In vitro* test	The finished antiserum must agglutinate all four Gordon types of *Neisseria meningitidis* and compare favorably with N.I.H. standard antiserum
Antipneumococcic serum Types I and II (Felton)	Euglobulin fraction of antiserum from the horse	White mouse	One unit is the smallest amount which will protect a white mouse against one million lethal doses of pneumococci
Antistreptococcic serum (polyvalent)	Refined, concentrated antiserum from the horse	*In vitro* test	Potency proved by agglutination tests with various strains of hemolytic and nonhemolytic streptococci
Botulinus antitoxin		Intravenous mouse tests	Polyvalent must protect against *Clostridium parabotulinum* and *C. botulinum* types toxins
Diphtheria antitoxin	Refined, concentrated antiserum from the horse	250-g guinea pig	One unit is the least amount that will protect a 250-g guinea pig from one L+ dose of diphtheria toxin for at least 4 days
Diphtheria antitoxin, despeciated	Enzyme treated, refined, concentrated antiserum from horse	250-g guinea pig	Same as above
Erysipelas streptococcus antitoxin	Refined, concentrated antiserum from the horse	Man	One unit is that amount of antitoxin that will completely neutralize one S.T.D.[c] of erysipelas streptococcus toxin
Meningococcus antitoxin	Native antiserum from the horse	Man	One unit is 10 times the amount that neutralizes one S.T.D. of meningococcus toxin
Perfringens antitoxin	Refined, concentrated antiserum from the horse	Pigeon	One unit is the amount which will protect a 350-g pigeon against one test dose of perfringens toxin for 24 hours
Puerperal septicemia antistreptococcic serum (antitoxin)	Refined, concentrated antiserum from the horse	Man	Standardized by antitoxin content. One unit of puerperal septicemia antistreptococcic serum is that amount which completely neutralizes one S.T.D. of puerperal septicemia Streptococcus toxin
Scarlet fever antitoxin	Refined, concentrated antiserum from the horse	Man	One unit of scarlet fever antitoxin (N.I.H.) is the least amount which completely neutralizes 50 S.T.D.'s of scarlet fever toxin. The original neutralizing unit of the Scarlet Fever Committee is that amount of antitoxin which completely neutralizes one S.T.D. of scarlet fever toxin
Tetanus antitoxin	Refined, concentrated antiserum from the horse	350-g guinea pig	One unit is 10 times the least amount which will protect a 350-g guinea pig from one L+ dose of tetanus toxin for at least 4 days
Tetanus antitoxin, despeciated	Enzyme treated, refined, concentrated antiserum from horse	350-g guinea pig	Same as above

[a] After Parke, Davis & Company and A. H. Bryan and C. G. Bryan, *Bacteriology, Principles and Practice*, 5th ed., Barnes & Noble, New York, 1953.
[b] National Institutes of Health.
[c] Skin test dose.

TABLE 20c. TOXOIDS AND VACCINES [a]

Item	Product	Toxicity	Antigenic value	Contains not more than
Alum pptd. diphtheria toxoid	Sterile suspension of diphtheria toxoid pptd. by alum	See **diphtheria toxoid**	Inject SC four 450-550 g guinea pigs with not more than ½ recommended total human immunizing dose. 3-4 weeks later pooled serum contains not less than 2 units/ml of antitoxin	15 mg alum in one injection dose
Alum pptd. tetanus toxoid	Sterile suspension of tetanus toxoid pptd. by alum	See **tetanus toxoid**	Inject SC four 450-550 g guinea pigs with not more than ½ recommended total human immunizing dose. 5-6 weeks later pooled serum contains not less than 2 units/ml of antitoxin	15 mg alum in one injection dose
Alum pptd. diphtheria and tetanus toxoids	Sterile suspension of a mixt. of alum pptd. diphtheria and tetanus toxoids	See **diphtheria** and **tetanus toxoids**	Must conform to standards for both diphtheria and tetanus toxoids	15 mg alum in one injection dose
Alum pptd. diphtheria and tetanus toxoids and pertussis vaccine	Sterile suspension prepared by treating a mixt. diphtheria and tetanus toxoids and pertussis vaccine with alum combined in such a way as to yield a product contg. the recommended immunizing dose for each component	See **diphtheria** and **tetanus toxoids**	Must conform to standards for both diphtheria and tetanus toxoids	15 mg alum in one injection dose
Alum pptd. pertussis vaccine	Sterile suspension of pertussis vaccine pptd. by alum and resuspended		Potency not less than 4 protective units	15 mg alum in one injection dose
Aluminum hydroxide adsorbed diphtheria toxoid	Sterile suspension of diphtheria toxoid adsorbed on aluminum hydroxide	See alum pptd. diphtheria toxoid		0.85 mg Al in one injection dose
Aluminum hydroxide adsorbed tetanus toxoid	Sterile suspension of tetanus toxoid adsorbed on aluminum hydroxide	See alum pptd. tetanus toxoid		Ditto above
Aluminum hydroxide adsorbed diphtheria and tetanus toxoids	Sterile suspension prepared mixing aluminum hydroxide adsorbed diphtheria and tetanus toxoids	See alum pptd. diphtheria and tetanus toxoids		Ditto above
Aluminum hydroxide adsorbed diphtheria and tetanus toxoids and pertussis vaccine	Sterile mixture of diphtheria and tetanus toxoids and pertussis vaccine adsorbed on aluminum hydroxide	See alum pptd. diphtheria and tetanus toxoids and pertussis vaccine		Ditto above
Cholera vaccine	Sterile suspension in isotonic sodium chloride soln. of equal amounts of Inaba and Ogawa strains of killed *Vibrio comma*		The Inaba strain and the Ogawa strain must have an antigenic value not less than N.I.H. Inaba strain 35-A-3 and Ogawa strain 41, respectively	Must contain 8 billion cholera organisms in each ml
Diphtheria toxoid	Sterile soln. of formaldehyde treated products of *Corynebacterium diphtheriae*	Inject SC four 300-400 g guinea pigs with at least 5 × human immunizing dose but not less than 2 ml: no local or general symptoms of diphtheria poisoning appear in 30 days	Inject SC ten 270-320 g guinea pigs with not more than ⅛ volume total human immunizing dose. Not more than 6 weeks later challenge by injecting each animal with 10 MLD of diphtheria: 80% must survive 10 days	Not more than 0.02% residual free formaldehyde

[a] pptd. = precipitated; SC = subcutaneous; mixt. = mixture; contg. = containing; N.I.H. = National Institutes of Health; MLD = minimum lethal dose.

TABLE 20c. TOXOIDS AND VACCINES (*Continued*)

Item	Product	Toxicity	Antigenic value	Contains not more than
Diphtheria toxoid, purified	Sterile soln. of diphtheria toxoid purified by pptn. with (1) alcohol in the cold, (2) polyphosphates (Jacobs' method), or (3) trichloroacetic acid and subsequent solution in an appropriate solvent	Same as diphtheria toxoid	Same as diphtheria toxoid	
Pertussis vaccine	Sterile bacterial fraction or suspension in isotonic NaCl soln. of killed *Bordetella pertussis* (formerly *Hemophilus pertussis*) strain of high antigenic potency		Potency not less than 4 protective units per individual immunizing dose	
Plague vaccine	Sterile suspension in isotonic NaCl soln. of killed *Pasteurella pestis*			Not less than 2 billion plague bacilli in each ml
Poliovirus vaccine				
Sabin type	Attenuated live strains of poliovirus; administered orally			
Salk type	Mixture of Brunhilda, Lansing, and Leon types of poliovirus grown in monkey kidney tissue and killed by treatment with formaldehyde; administered by injection	Must pass N.I.H. tests to prove that all poliovirus has been killed		
Rabies vaccine	Suspension of attenuated or killed, fixed rabies virus obtained from brain tissue of rabbits infected with fixed rabies virus			
Smallpox vaccine	Aqueous suspension of living vaccina virus (cowpox) in the visicular tissue obtained under aseptic conditions from calves		Remove hair, scarify lightly skin of rabbits, 2250-2750 g. Apply to parallel areas test vaccine and N.I.H. vaccine in doses 1:100, 1:1000, 1:3000, 1:10000, and 1:30000: The lesions produced by test vaccine exceed or equal the control vaccine	Contains 40-60% glycerol
Tetanus toxoid	Sterile soln. of formaldehyde-treated products of *Clostridium tetani*	Inject SC four 300-400 g guinea pigs with 5 × human immunizing dose but not less than 2 ml: no symptoms of tetanus poisoning in 21 days	Inject SC ten 300-400 g guinea pigs with not more than ⅓ total human immunizing dose: Not more than 6 weeks later challenge by injecting SC each animal with 2 ml contg. 10 MLD tetanus toxin; 80% must survive 10 days	Contains not more than 0.02% residual free formaldehyde
Tetanus toxoid, purified	Sterile soln. of tetanus toxoid purified by pptn. with (1) alcohol in the cold, (2) polyphosphates (Jacobs' method), or (3) trichloroacetic acid and subsequent solution in an appropriate solvent	Same as tetanus toxoid	Same as tetanus toxoid	
Typhoid vaccine	Sterile suspension in isotonic NaCl soln. of killed high antigenic strain of *Salmonella typhosa*			Each ml must contain one billion typhoid bacilli

TABLE 20c. TOXOIDS AND VACCINES (*Continued*)

Item	Product	Toxicity	Antigenic value	Contains not more than
Typhoid and paratyphoid vaccine	Sterile suspension in isotonic NaCl soln. of high antigenic strains of killed *Salmonella typhosa* (typhoid), *S. paratyphi* (paratyphoid A), and *S. schottmülleri* (paratyphoid B) using smooth paratyphoid strains			Each ml must contain one billion typhoid bacilli and 250 millions each of the paratyphoid organisms
Typhus vaccine	Sterile suspension of the refined material from an aqueous suspension of yolk sac membrane of eggs in which strains of emidemic typhus rickettsiae were grown and killed by the addition of not more than 1% by volume of formaldehyde soln.			
Yellow fever	Living virus of an attenuated strain of high antigenic activity and safety; cultured by growing virus in living egg embryo; the virus infected chick embryo is pulped, suspended in water, distributed in ampoules, dried by freeze-drying, filled with nitrogen, and sealed; it is rehydrated just before use			Must not contain human serum

TABLE 21. PREPARATION OF TEST DILUTIONS

TABLE 21. PREPARATION OF TEST DILUTIONS

Method 1 Using 90 ml blanks

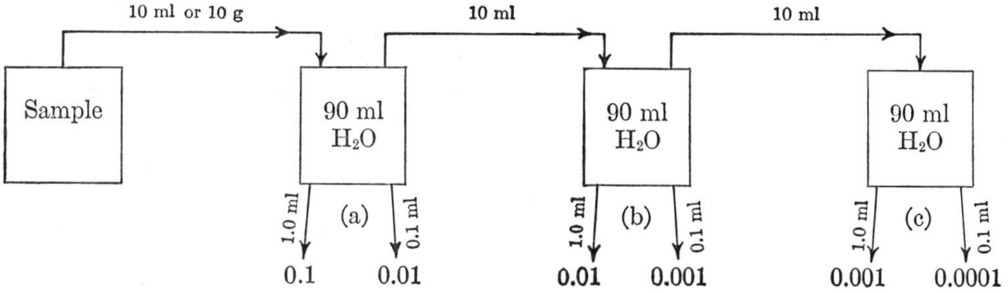

(a) 100 ml contains 10 g or ml product
  10 ml contains 1 g or ml product
  1 ml contains 0.1 g or ml product
  0.1 ml contains 0.01 g or ml product

(b) 10 ml pipetted over from (a) represents or contains 1 g product.
  Therefore 100 ml of (b) contains 1 g or ml product
  10 ml of (b) contains 0.1 g or ml product
  1 ml of (b) contains 0.01 g or ml product
  0.1 ml of (b) contains 0.001 g or ml product

(c) 10 ml pipetted over from (b) represents or contains 0.1 g or ml product.
  Therefore 100 ml of (c) contains 0.1 g or ml product
  10 ml of (c) contains 0.01 g or ml product
  1 ml of (c) contains 0.001 g or ml product
  0.1 ml of (c) contains 0.0001 g or ml product

Method 2 Using 99 ml blanks

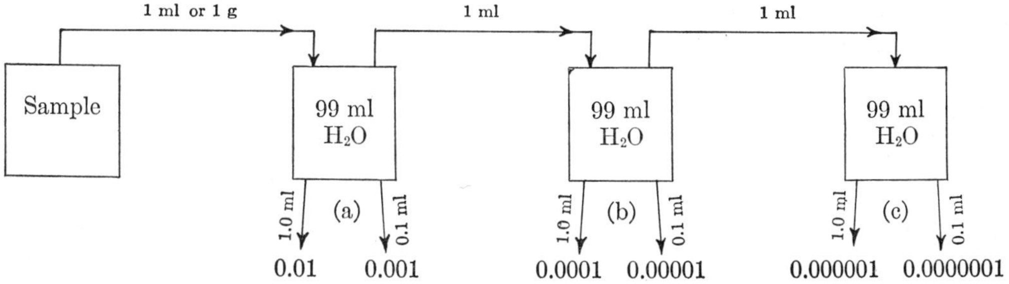

(a) 100 ml contains 1 ml or g product
  10 ml contains 0.1 ml or g product
  1 ml contains 0.01 ml or g product
  0.1 ml contains 0.001 ml or g product

(b) 1 ml pipetted over from (a) contains 0.01 ml/g product.
  Therefore 100 ml (b) contains 0.01 g or ml product
  10 ml (b) contains 0.001 g or ml product
  1 ml (b) contains 0.0001 g or ml product
  0.1 ml (b) contains 0.00001 g or ml product

(c) 1 ml pipetted over from (b) contains 0.0001 g or ml product
  Therefore 100 ml of (c) contains 0.0001 g or ml product
  10 ml of (c) contains 0.00001 g or ml product
  1 ml of (c) contains 0.000001 g or ml product
  0.1 ml of (c) contains 0.0000001 g or ml product

TABLE 21. PREPARATION OF TEST DILUTIONS (*Continued*)

Method 3 Using both 90 ml and 99 ml blanks

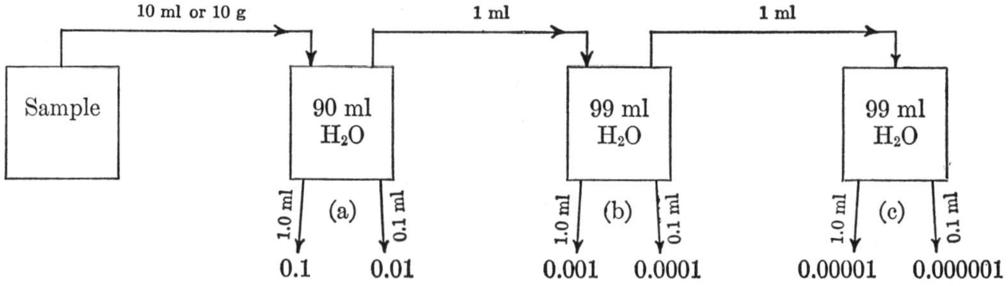

(a) 100 ml contains 10 ml or g product
10 ml contains 1 ml or g product
1 ml contains 0.1 ml or g product
0.1 ml contains 0.01 ml or g product

(b) 1 ml pipetted over from (a) contains 0.1 g or ml product
Therefore 100 ml of (b) contains 1 g or ml product
10 ml of (b) contains 0.01 g or ml product
1 ml of (b) contains 0.001 g or ml product
0.1 ml of (b) contains 0.0001 g or ml product

(c) 1 ml pipetted over from (b) contains 0.001 ml or g product
Therefore 100 ml of (c) contains 0.001 g or ml product
10 ml of (c) contains 0.0001 g or ml product
1 ml of (c) contains 0.00001 g or ml product
0.1 ml of (c) contains 0.000001 g or ml product

Method 4

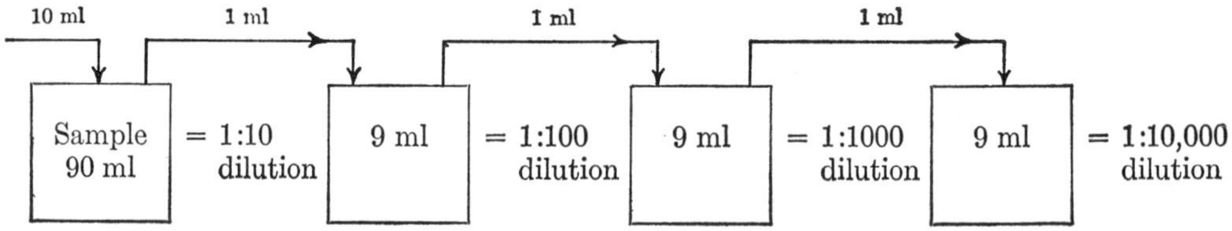